Computer Communications and Networks

Computer Communications and Networks

John R Freer BSc, DMS, CEng, FIEE
Principal Consultant
Software Sciences Limited

Pitman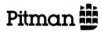

PITMAN PUBLISHING
128 Long Acre, London WC2E 9AN

A Division of Longman Group UK Limited

First published in Great Britain 1988
Reprinted 1989, 1991

British Library Cataloguing in Publication Data
Freer, John R.
   Computer communications and networks.
   1. Computer systems. Communication
networks
   I. Title
   004.6

ISBN 0 273 02789 1

Printed and bound in Singapore

Contents

Preface

Computer communications is one of the most rapidly developing technologies and it is a subject with which everyone in the computer systems profession should be familiar. *Computer communications and networks* is an introduction to communications technology and system design for practising and aspiring computer professionals.

The subject is described from the computer system designer's point of view rather than from the communications engineer's viewpoint. The presentation is suitable for introductory reading as well as for reference. The emphasis is on practical, rather than theoretical, aspects and on technology which will become more important in the future. The majority of the subject matter applies to civil and military communications but some aspects which are unique to military applications have been included where considered significant.

Computer communications is a rapidly changing and highly complex subject. Sufficient practical knowledge of the subject is not usually gained at university or college but is generally developed over a period of several years by trial and error, attending courses, reading reference books and journals; this book attempts to simplify and speed up the process by bringing together a body of information which is otherwise distributed throughout many books and journals. The information is presented in a framework which makes a wider understanding of the subject possible.

Basic knowledge of communications is assumed, a general familiarity with computer systems is anticipated in later chapters, and, where relevant, theory is explained.

Chapters 1 to 4 describe the basic principles and techniques which enable all forms of computer communication. Chapters 5 and 6 describe layered network architectures and interface standards which play an important part in the development of efficient and flexible computer communications. Chapters 7 and 8 describe and compare the more significant, modern local area networks and wide area networks. Network models and performance prediction is introduced, with examples, in Chapter 9. Chapter 10 introduces computing and software aspects and Chapter 11 introduces communications security, an increasingly important requirement in civil and military applications.

Many aspects involved in communications network design and implementation are discussed in Chapter 12. A glossary of computer communications terms is given to assist readers in their understanding of terminology which is used throughout the book and in the industry.

JRF.

Computer Systems series

Consultant Editor: John Freer, Principal Consultant, Software Sciences
Limited

Also by John Freer
Systems Design with Advanced Microprocessors

1 Data communication concepts and alternatives

1.1 Trends in computer communications and networks

The first binary data communication system was demonstrated by Cooke and Wheatstone in 1839. This used six parallel wires to control the position of five needles which pointed to the letters of the alphabet. The first machine to use serial binary data communication was the teleprinter, developed by Emil Baudot in 1874. The Baudot Code uses five bits to represent the letters of the alphabet and a figures shift character, after which code combinations are interpreted as numbers.

Teleprinters transmit data serially in 5-bit characters with an additional start bit to indicate the beginning of each character and stop bits to indicate the end of each character, as shown in Figure 1.1. The potential cost saving by using serial transmission on long-distance lines was enormous; one pair of wires was required in each direction, in place of six. Other advantages of the teleprinter were the rapid keying method and the printed output in a form which anyone could read, which was a vast improvement over the Morse code telegraph systems.

Fig. 1.1 Baudot character format with five data bits, a start bit and stop bits

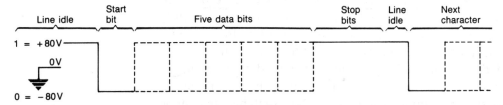

Early computer systems used only local communications to link the central processor to peripherals and terminals. Peripherals typically used parallel, multiwire cables and the terminals, often closely related to teleprinters, used serial interfaces such as the 20 mA current loop. For remote access, teleprinters could be used with, for example, 80-0-80 volt signalling levels transmitting at 50 bit/s.

The techniques and equipment necessary for high-speed data

1

communications were developed in the 1960s. Frequency shift keying modems were capable of transmitting data over dedicated wires at speeds of 1200 bit/s or over the public switched telephone network at 300 bit/s. The introduction of video display units capable of transmitting data at 1200 bit/s and minicomputers capable of transferring data at much higher speeds led to the development of data communications networks and higher-speed data transmission equipment in the late 1960s and 1970s.

Government and corporate data communication networks became popular in the 1970s as organisations realised the advantages offered in efficiency and profitability. The availability of information supplied by computer systems is now crucial in many organisations, particularly information from many locations which must be coordinated both accurately and speedily.

Financial institutions, such as banks, have adopted extensive data communications networks since the mid-1970s because they have realised the increased profitability offered and the need to remain efficient and competitive. The use of local area networks to interconnect computers and terminals within a building or group of buildings has become popular since 1980. The high-capacity low-cost communication offered by local area networks has made distributed computing a reality, and office automation services, such as electronic mail, further improve efficiency. The technology for these recent developments in local communications has grown from advances in VLSI semiconductors and the need for local communications has been created largely by the availability of low-cost microcomputers.

It is now common for users connected to a local area network to communicate with computers or terminals on other local area networks via gateways linked by a wide area network. Long-distance communications employed by wide area networks may use satellite links, or terrestrial links multiplexed on microwave, fibre optic or coaxial bearers. Links which have a low utilisation frequently employ packet switched networks. Analog speech bandwidth channels can support data rates in excess of 9.6 kbit/s using modern modems and digital channels are available with data rates up to 2 Mbit/s. Where data communication is required by mobile users, cellular radio systems connected to the public switched telephone network are available in many areas.

In the future, it is probable that international standards will play a major role in fostering the growth of computer communications. The Open Systems Interconnection (OSI) standards will permit any pair of computers to communicate reliably regardless of the manufacturer. The adoption of the CCITT X.25 and X.75 standards for packet switched communication has already made international packet switched communication a reality.

2

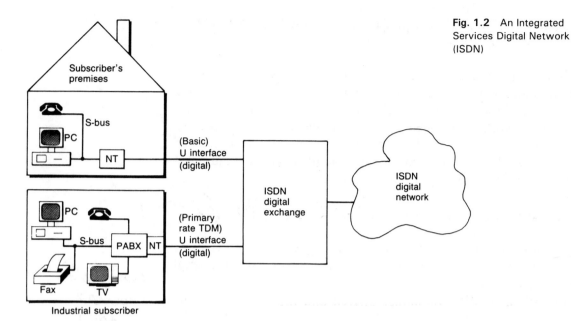

Fig. 1.2 An Integrated Services Digital Network (ISDN)

Subscriber's premises

S-bus

PC

NT

(Basic)
U interface
(digital)

ISDN
digital
exchange

ISDN
digital
network

PC

S-bus

PABX NT

(Primary
rate TDM)
U interface
(digital)

Fax TV

Industrial subscriber

Adoption of the X.400 standard will take electronic mail from being a series of isolated facilities within individual organisations to a network of interconnected public and private networks providing electronic mail services across the world. The Teletex standards (F.200) permit high-speed text communication replacing the present low-speed Telex system for global communication.

Future trends in communications bearers and interfaces will lead to Integrated Services Digital Networks (ISDNs) which will provide an end-to-end digital connection for all voice (digitised), data, telemetry, facsimile and video applications (see Figure 1.2). When implemented, these ISDNs will offer more flexible, lower-cost, higher-capacity data transmission services with a set of new OSI-compatible protocols and interfaces.

1.2 Messages, characters, bit streams, symbols and waveforms

1.2.1 Messages and structured data

The term 'data communication' is used to describe the transmission of computer-related records which have a structured format and are generally unintelligible in the transmitted form, being 80 to 85% numeric. Messages and word processing communications, on the other hand, consist of unformatted text except for the standard placement of names for the source and destination and are generally unintelligible to a computer but intelligible to a human.

Each structured data record type is identified by a transaction code and the data is organised into predefined fields which contain a specified maximum number of characters. Other forms of digital transmission such as digitised voice, facsimile or video do not use structured data records with the exception, in some circumstances, of telemetry which can use fixed data fields and formats. Figure 1.3 shows a message made up of ASCII characters.

1.2.2 Characters, bytes and octets

also 16 bit now

A byte of data consists of eight bits but an octet of data consists of eight bits with the least significant bit transmitted first on a serial link. A character is an alphanumeric or punctuation member from a set of orthogonal figures or a special control figure used by the communications equipment or protocol. Table 1.1 shows the ASCII seven-bit character set which is a national variation of the International Standards Organisation (ISO-646) seven-bit code. Other variations include the CCITT V.3 character set.

Not all serial now

Another commonly used character code is Extended Binary Coded Decimal Interchange Code (EBCDIC) which is used by IBM, this 8-bit code makes 256 characters available whereas the 7-bit codes make 128 characters available. A 7-bit code is frequently accompanied by a parity (check) bit filling an 8-bit frame. The ISO/DIS-6937 standard uses the eighth bit to indicate that the other seven bits are structured data. Another way to extend the character set is to use the escape (ESC) character followed by another character to call up alternative character sets. More than fifty alternative character sets have been registered by the ISO TC/97/SC2 committee, including Greek and Cyrillic alphabets, special symbols and control characters used in typesetting.

1.2.3 Bit streams and symbols

The characters which make up a message, or octets which make up a file transfer, are transmitted, one after the other, as a bit stream where a bit is the fundamental data unit represented as a 1 or 0, mark or space in a digital system. For example, Figure 1.4 shows the bit stream corresponding to the message CAN transmitted in 7-bit ASCII characters. A 1 bit is represented by the mark or current flowing state, which by convention is also the state of the line when idle, with no data being sent. A 0 bit is represented by a space or no current flowing state.

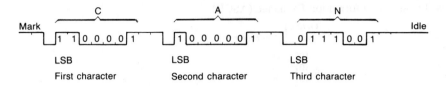

Mark   Idle

| 1 | 1 | 0 | 0 | 0 | 0 | 1 | | 1 | 0 | 0 | 0 | 0 | 0 | 1 | | 0 | 1 | 1 | 1 | 0 | 0 | 1 |

LSB   LSB   LSB

First character   Second character   Third character

C   A   N

Fig. 1.4 The bit stream corresponding to the ASCII characters : CAN

A symbol is a basic transmission element which is used to transmit groups of bits. For example, a quaternary phase shift keying system has four possible values of phase shift (or a set of four symbols). The bit stream is broken into groups of two bits (dibits) and a symbol is allocated to each of the four possible combinations of two bits: 00, 01, 10, 11. Figure 1.5 shows how the message CAN is broken into groups of three bits for transmission as one of eight possible symbols in an 8-ary phase modulated transmission system.

MSB

| C | A | N |

1 0 0   0 0 1   1   1 0   0 0 0   0 1   1   0 0   1 1 1 0   7-bit ASCII

4   1   6   0   3   1   6   8-ary symbols

Fig. 1.5 The message CAN transmitted in 3-bit groups which make up 8 possible symbols for 8-ary transmission

Data rate is measured in bits per second. When groups of K bits are combined to form a transmission symbol which has a transmission duration T, then

$$\text{Data rate} = \frac{K}{T}$$

1.2.4 Waveforms and baud rates

A digital waveform is the voltage or current signal on the transmission medium which represents the digital symbols. A baseband system applies a voltage or current pulse waveform directly to the medium but a modem modulates a sinusoidal carrier in frequency, phase, or amplitude or in both phase and amplitude according to the bits or symbols.

The baud is a unit of signalling speed equal to the number of discrete conditions or symbols per second. The baud rate is the same as the data rate, in bits per second, only if each symbol represents one bit. A baud is the reciprocal of the unit interval which is the shortest pulse duration measured in seconds.

A modem which transmits dibits in a quaternary phase modulated system with a rate of 2400 bit/s transmits 1200 symbols per second and therefore has a baud rate of 1200 baud. A baseband system with no start and stop pulses has a baud rate equal to the bit rate. A five-bit start-stop asynchronous transmission with start and data

Table 1.1 American Standard Code for Information Exchange (ASCII)

Octal code	Character		Octal code	Character	
000	NUL	(Blank)	100	@	
001	SOH	(Start of Header)	101	A	
002	STX	(Start of Text)	102	B	
003	ETX	(End of Text)	103	C	
004	EOT	(End of Transmission)	104	D	
005	ENQ	(Enquiry)	105	E	
006	ACK	(Acknowledge (Positive))	106	F	
007	BEL	(Bell)	107	G	
010	BS	(Backspace)	110	H	
011	HT	(Horizontal Tabulation)	111	I	
012	LF	(Line Feed)	112	J	
013	VT	(Vertical Tabulation)	113	K	
014	FF	(Form Feed)	114	L	
015	CR	(Carriage Return)	115	M	
016	SO	(Shift Out)	116	N	
017	SI	(Shift In)	117	O	
020	DLE	(Data Link Escape)	120	P	
021	DC1	(Device Control 1)	121	Q	
022	DC2	(Device Control 2)	122	R	
023	DC3	(Device Control 3)	123	S	
024	DC4	(Device Control 4—Stop)	124	T	
025	NAK	(Negative Acknowledge)	125	U	
026	SYN	(Synchronization)	126	V	
027	ETB	(End of Text Block)	127	W	
030	CAN	(Cancel)	130	X	
031	EM	(End of Medium)	131	Y	
032	SUB	(Substitute)	132	Z	
033	ESC	(Escape)	133	[	(Opening Bracket)
034	FS	(File Separator)	134	\	(Reverse Slant)
035	GS	(Group Separator)	135	]	(Closing Bracket)
036	RS	(Record Separator)	136	∧	(Circumflex)
037	US	(Unit Separator)	137	—	(Underline)
040	SP	(Space)	140	`	(Opening Single Quote)
041	!		141	a	
042	"		142	b	
043	#		143	c	
044	$		144	d	
045	%		145	e	
046	&		146	f	
047	'	(Closing Single Quote)	147	g	
050	(		150	h	
051	)		151	i	
052	*		152	j	
053	+		153	k	
054	,	(Comma)	154	l	
055	-	(Hyphen)	155	m	
056	.	(Period)	156	n	
057	/		157	o	
060	0		160	p	
061	1		161	q	
062	2		162	r	
063	3		163	s	
064	4		164	t	
065	5		165	u	
066	6		166	v	
067	7		167	w	
070	8		170	x	
071	9		171	y	
072	:		172	z	
073	;		173	{	(Opening Brace)
074	<	(Less Than)	174	|	(Vertical Line)
075	=		175	}	(Closing Brace)
076	>	(Greater Than)	176	~	(Overline (Tilde)
077	?		177	DEL	(Delete/Rubout)

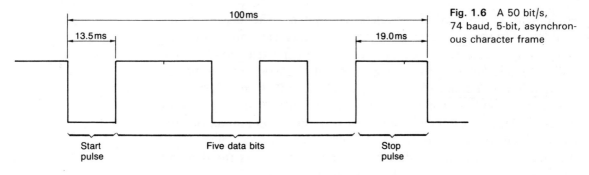

Fig. 1.6 A 50 bit/s, 74 baud, 5-bit, asynchronous character frame

Start pulse — Five data bits — Stop pulse

pulses each of 13.5 ms duration plus a stop pulse of 19 ms giving a character duration of 100 ms (see Figure 1.6) has a signalling speed of

$$\frac{1}{13.5 \times 10^{-3}s} = 74 \text{ bauds}$$

and a bit rate of

$$\frac{5 \text{ bits}}{100 \times 10^{-3}s} = 50 \text{ bit/s}$$

Bit rate is relevant to the computer engineer or user because it defines the speed at which data enters or leaves the computer but baud rate is more significant for the telecommunications engineer because it is more closely related to the range of frequencies or bandwidth of the media measured in Hertz (1 Hz = one cycle/second).

1.3 Digital/analog, serial/parallel, simplex/half-duplex/full-duplex

1.3.1 Digital v. analog

The first telecommunications bearers carried digital information in the form of current which either energised or de-energised a solenoid at the remote end. The speed of these transmissions was extremely low with around 1 bit/s data rates. Later telephone systems had a bandwidth which was wide enough to make the human voice intelligible and national telephone networks now transmit analog signals in the frequency range of 300 Hz to 3.3 kHz.

If digital pulses are transmitted through an analog telephone network, a highly distorted and attenuated version emerges at the far end because the high and low frequency components of the square wave cannot be transmitted by the limited bandwidth of the network. Other problems occur because the direct current component of the square wave does not reach the far end when transformer coupled

7

equipment is employed in the telephone system. The answer to this problem is to use a modem which transmits a carrier tone within the frequency range 300 Hz to 3.4 kHz through the telephone system and to modulate the digital signal on this carrier by amplitude modulation, frequency shift keying or phase shift keying.

Use of the public switched telephone network, or dedicated lines which provide an extended frequency response, was mandatory for early computer communications because the national telecommunications organisations could offer no alternatives. As the demand for higher data rate digital communications developed, many national telecommunications organisations provided all-digital communications lines such as the British Telecom KiloStream and MegaStream services. Many local area networks use baseband digital transmission in twisted pair or coaxial cable.

There are many advantages to be gained by transmitting data in digital form; these include:

a) Correctly designed digital circuits are less susceptible to distortion and interference.

b) Digital signals may be regenerated to extend the length of the link without accumulating additional noise and distortion as would be the case with analog repeaters (see Figure 1.7).

c) The ability to achieve extremely low error rates on digital circuits.

d) Complex functions such as statistical multiplexing and digital switching may be implemented on digital systems at low cost because the signals do not require expensive modems for conversion into digital form before they may be processed.

e) Digital multiplexing is much simpler than frequency division multiplexing on analog lines.

f) Digital circuits and components are less expensive and more reliable than analog ones.

g) Various forms of digital signal can be integrated and transmitted together, e.g. data, digitised voice, digitised television and facsimile.

1.3.2 Serial v. parallel

Within computers it is usual to employ parallel data paths which transmit 8, 16 or 32 bits simultaneously. Parallel data buses are employed to achieve much higher transmission speeds where the cost of additional wires or tracks on circuit boards is not significant. Parallel interfaces allocate dedicated functions to the wires but serial lines must carry data, control and synchronisation information multiplexed in a bit-by-bit form according to a communication protocol.

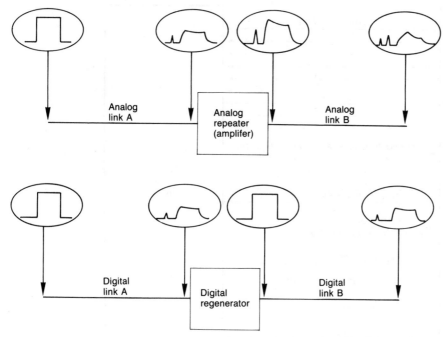

It is common to employ parallel data transfer between computers and high-speed printers or disk drives because the additional cost or size of conductors is not significant and the required data rates can only be achieved using conventional cable if parallel transmission of all bits in the data word is employed. Figure 1.8 shows a typical high-speed printer interface with a separate wire for each bit in the data character and a strobe signal which indicates when the data is valid. Some parallel interfaces include additional control lines for functions such as acknowledgement (data received and ready for more), busy or error.

Serial transmission imposes overheads to serialise the data, add control characters, format the data into frames, and add an appropriate communication protocol. For short distances, parallel transmission may be more cost effective but, as the distance over which data must be transmitted increases, the cost of the additional conductors in a parallel cable compared with a cable for serial transmission becomes more significant. The cost of an interface for a long parallel transmission cable becomes prohibitive over a few hundred metres in length and the variable delays experienced in long cables cause difficulties in ensuring that all bits may be strobed at the same time. The reduction in performance of long parallel transmission systems and the effects of crosstalk in long cables, combined with the cost penalty, make serial transmission preferable for all long-distance data transmission.

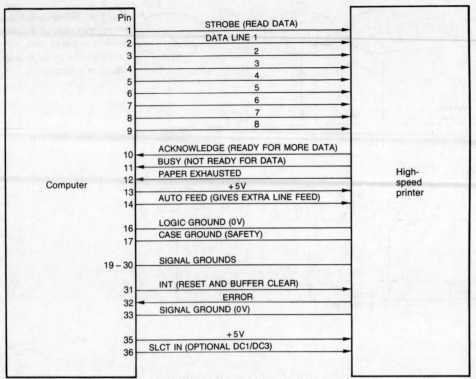

For pins 2 to 9, a TTL high voltage = 1, low = 0.

Data codes with bits 6 and 7 = 0 are non-printing control codes.

Fig. 1.8 A Centronics parallel interface for a high-speed printer

1.3.3 Simplex, half-duplex or full-duplex

Data or message transmission occurs in one of three modes:

1) *Simplex* (transmission in one direction only).
2) *Half-Duplex* (HDX) (transmission in one direction at a time).
3) *Full-Duplex* (FDX) (transmission in both directions simultaneously).

These three modes are illustrated in Figure 1.9.

Full-duplex transmission generally requires a four-wire (two-channel) data link which may cost more than a two-wire link used for simplex or half-duplex transmission. Many synchronous protocols require full-duplex transmission with data being transmitted in one direction while control or error-correcting information is transmitted simultaneously in the other direction.

Simplex transmission is suitable only for devices such as receive-only printers which never transmit information. Few terminals operate in truly full-duplex mode. Many 'dumb' terminals operate in

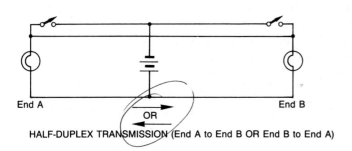

SIMPLEX TRANSMISSION (End A to End B)

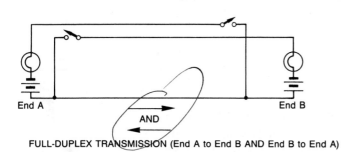

HALF-DUPLEX TRANSMISSION (End A to End B OR End B to End A)

FULL-DUPLEX TRANSMISSION (End A to End B AND End B to End A)

echo-plex mode in which characters from the keyboard are transmitted to the host computer which echoes them back for printing or
display on the screen. This mode permits verification of correct
reception by the host because any corruption of characters will be
evident from the printed or displayed information.

In half-duplex mode, the modems at each end of a link must
switch from transmit to receive after each transmission, under the
control of a request-to-send control signal sent from the data source
to the modem. Some 'dumb' terminals however do not switch the
request-to-send signal and must therefore only be used with full
duplex modems although they never in fact transmit and receive
simultaneously.

1.4 Synchronous / asynchronous

1.4.1 Asynchronous transmission

Serial data links may have synchronous or asynchronous transmission. Synchronous transmission does not require start and stop bits for timing on each character; therefore it is about 20% more efficient than asynchronous transmission but it requires synchronisation of the transmitter and receiver to determine which group of bits constitute a character.

Asynchronous or start-stop transmission is less complex than synchronous because the timing or synchronisation information is part of each character. For this reason it is most often used by inexpensive terminals which transmit single characters. As shown in Figure 1.10, each asynchronous character is accompanied by a start bit which has the opposite polarity (0) to the idle condition of the line (1). The 1 to 0 transition is used to start the internal timers which will

Asynch
— Start bit
per turly

Fig. 1.10 An asynchronous 7-bit character with parity

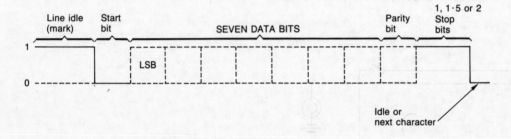

be used to identify the data bits which follow. The stop bit (1) which follows the data and parity bits is the same polarity as the idle condition which the line adopts between characters and it must have a duration of 1, 1.5 or 2 bit periods according to the requirements of the receiving device. Older mechanical teletypes required longer stop pulses to allow the mechanism to coast back to a known position ready for the next start bit but modern electronic asynchronous receivers require only one stop bit to ensure that the next start bit produces a 1 to 0 transition.

Asynchronous transmission does not require precise synchronism between the transmitter and receiver and characters may be sent at random intervals or continuously but the transmitter and receiver must be aware of the transmission speed to ensure that the interval timers are within a few per cent at both ends of the link (unless an autobaud facility is provided to sense the transmission speed).

Modems operating at data rates up to 1800 bit/s generally employ frequency shift keying and are designed for asynchronous operation without any form of synchronisation between transmitting and receiving modems. Modems operating at data rates of 2400 bit/s or above employ more complex forms of modulation involving symbols which transmit several bit combinations simultaneously. These forms of modulation demand synchronisation between the transmitting and receiving modems so circuits which extract clock data from the transmitted signal are incorporated and this requires continuous transmission of data to maintain synchronisation.

Synchronous modems are only suitable for use with synchronous interfaces and the clock signals required by the computers or terminals are produced by the modem, eliminating any need for start and stop bits and improving the efficiency of the data transmission.

Asynchronous transmission is popular for local direct connection of terminals at speeds up to 19.2 kbit/s. These terminals are commonly used for direct keyboard entry rather than transmission from data buffers at high speed. Remote terminals of this type commonly employ asynchronous modems at data rates up to 1.8 kbit/s.

1.4.2 Synchronous transmission

With synchronous operation, data octets are transmitted in a continuous sequence without start and stop pulses. Either the receiver clock is derived by the modem from the transmitted signal or a separate clock signal must accompany the data from the transmitter to the receiver.

The delimiting of each synchronous character in the continuous string of bits is achieved by using a number of synchronisation characters at the beginning of the block and by counting off groups of 8-bit octets after the final sync character. The sync character has a unique code with an irregular bit pattern to minimise the chance that part of the sync character and part of the successive character create another sync character bit pattern. The ASCII sync character is 10010110 (226 octal).

A synchronous receiver starts in search mode, hunting for a sync character in the received bit stream. When a sync character has been identified, the data is shifted into a data register and a character available flag is raised after every eight bits. Many systems are required to detect two sync characters before the data in order to minimise the probability of false synchronisation and it is common to transmit a third sync character to ensure synchronisation if the first sync character is corrupted in transmission. These additional synchronisation characters are overheads which reduce efficiency but they are unlikely to reach the 20% timing overhead imposed in asynchronous transmission.

Figure 1.11 shows the beginning of a synchronous transmission with two sync characters. Synchronous transmission is generally used

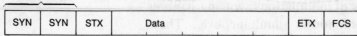

Two sync characters

SYN	SYN	STX	Data		ETX	FCS

Fig. 1.11 SYNC characters preceding a synchronous Bisync transmission

with a computer or intelligent terminal which has internal data storage and can output blocks of characters at the maximum line speed to maintain efficiency of the link.

1.5 Parity / CRC / LRC / EDC / ARQ

1.5.1 Parity

Communications channels are frequently subjected to many forms of interference including:

a) Induced transient voltages from lightning strikes or the switching of heavy electrical currents.
b) Nearby radio transmitters or electronic equipment.
c) Crosstalk from other lines.
d) Birds or helicopters flying through microwave links.
e) Faulty connectors or damage to cables.

Interference may only affect one bit in a block of data but if undetected this may have serious consequences. At high data rates it is much more likely that many bits in a block of data will be corrupted. Error detection and correction information may be added to a character or a block of data to detect corruption in transmission and in some cases the correct information may be determined and substituted at the receiver.

Parity may be applied to each character (vertical parity or vertical redundancy check) or to a complete block of data (horizontal parity or horizontal redundancy check). *Vertical parity* adds a bit to each character. For odd parity the number of ones in the character is calculated and the appropriate parity bit added to make this number odd. For example, 01001100 would have a 0 parity bit added. An even parity bit is added to make the number of ones in the character even (1 in the example). At the receiver the number of ones in the character is counted and the polarity of the parity bit is checked to determine if corruption has taken place. By convention, odd parity is used on synchronous links and even parity on asynchronous links.

Vertical parity will detect a single bit in error but will not detect even numbers of errors per character. With some multiple bit errors, vertical parity is only about 90% efficient. *Horizontal parity* adds a parity byte to the end of the block of data; each bit in the parity byte containing an odd or even parity bit for the equivalent order bits in all the preceding data bytes. Horizontal parity can reach 98% efficiency in detecting multiple bit errors.

1.5.2   Cyclic redundancy checks (CRC)

A cyclic redundancy check is an error-detection scheme in which a 16-bit check code is generated by taking the remainder after dividing a number, consisting of all the serial bits in a block of data, by a predetermined binary number. A CRC may be generated by software, by a shift register feedback circuit or by a CRC chip.

The use of a CRC on synchronous data links has proved extremely efficient and is now considered a standard protocol feature. CCITT recommendation V.41 standardises the use of cyclic redundancy checks but the order in which the 16 CRC bits are transmitted must be defined for the application.

1.5.3   Longitudinal redundancy check (LRC)

A longitudinal redundancy check is an error-detection scheme which forms an exclusive-OR of transmitted characters. The LRC block check character (BCC) is transmitted following the data block and is checked at the receiving end during the reception of the block. Longitudinal redundancy checks have been found to be less efficient than cyclic redundancy checks in detecting errors.

1.5.4   Forward error correction (FEC)

Error detection and correction (EDC) codes such as Hamming codes, Reed-Muller codes or Blocking codes may be added to transmitted data. These codes contain sufficient redundant information to detect several corrupt bits and in most cases to correct one or more bits. This technique of detecting and correcting errors without retransmission is called forward error correction (FEC). The overhead of redundancy required by EDC codes becomes a smaller proportion of the data block size, the larger the block becomes.

Table 1.2 summarises the performance of six common error detection and EDC methods applied to a block of 32 successive bytes of data. The Orchard code is a proprietary method which is capable of at least the same performance as double data repetition and Hamming codes in error detection and correction but requires many fewer redundant data bits per 8-bit byte.

With severe error rates, EDC may break down; in these circumstances it may be better to transmit the data several times and take a

Table 1.2 Comparison of error-detection and EDC methods for a block of 32 bytes

Method	Errors detected	Errors corrected	Redundant bits per byte
Parity	1, usually more	None	1
Repetition	2, usually more	1, usually more	16
Blocking	2, usually more	1	1.3
Hamming	2, usually more	1, usually 2, perhaps more	5
Orchard	Many	2, perhaps more	1
Reed-Muller	Many	3 per byte, perhaps more	17.6

majority vote for each bit in the block. Many EDC codes cannot cope with burst errors which produce several errors in each EDC protected block. To reduce this problem the data from each EDC block may be dispersed by a technique known as *interleaving* in which serial data is written into the rows of a matrix, and serial data for transmission is read from the columns of the matrix (see Figure 1.12). At the receiver the data is de-interleaved by the reverse process before being passed to the EDC system.

Fig. 1.12 Dispersal of burst errors by interleaving

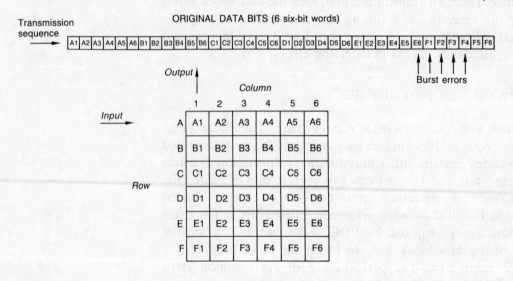

Transmission sequence →

ORIGINAL DATA BITS (6 six-bit words)

A1 A2 A3 A4 A5 A6 B1 B2 B3 B4 B5 B6 C1 C2 C3 C4 C5 C6 D1 D2 D3 D4 D5 D6 E1 E2 E3 E4 E5 E6 F1 F2 F3 F4 F5 F6

Burst errors

Output

Column

	1	2	3	4	5	6
A	A1	A2	A3	A4	A5	A6
B	B1	B2	B3	B4	B5	B6
C	C1	C2	C3	C4	C5	C6
D	D1	D2	D3	D4	D5	D6
E	E1	E2	E3	E4	E5	E6
F	F1	F2	F3	F4	F5	F6

Input →

Row

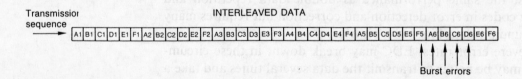

Transmission sequence →

INTERLEAVED DATA

A1 B1 C1 D1 E1 F1 A2 B2 C2 D2 E2 F2 A3 B3 C3 D3 E3 F3 A4 B4 C4 D4 E4 F4 A5 B5 C5 D5 E5 F5 A6 B6 C6 D6 E6 F6

Burst errors

1.5.5 Automatic repeat request (ARQ)

Automatic repeat request is a technique for checking incoming data for errors and automatically requesting a retransmission if an error is detected. A CRC may be used to detect errors in each block of data and, if the CRC calculated by the receiver does not match the transmitted CRC, a retransmission is requested by sending a negative acknowledgement (NAK) message to the transmitter. A satisfactory CRC check on a data block results in an acknowledgement message (ACK). The transmitter must store all blocks of data transmitted until they are acknowledged (see Figure 1.13).

Three basic forms of ARQ systems are commonly employed:

1) Stop-and-wait ARQ which stops transmission at the end of each block of data and waits for an acknowledgement. If a NAK is received, the original block of data is retransmitted and if an ACK is received, the next block of data is transmitted. The major disadvantage of this technique is the idle time after each block transmission but the control protocol is simple.

2) Go-back-*N* ARQ which requires a full duplex channel to receive the ACK or NAK for the previous blocks while later blocks are being transmitted. This technique avoids the idle

Fig. 1.13 Transmission of acknowledgements (ACKs) and negative acknowledgements (NAKs) in three forms of automatic repeat request (ARQ) system

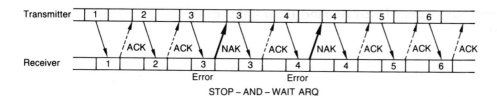

STOP – AND – WAIT ARQ

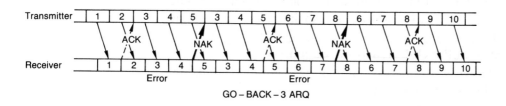

GO – BACK – 3 ARQ

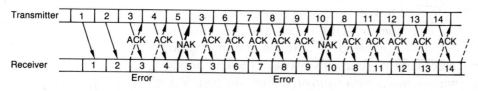

SELECTIVE REPEAT CONTINUOUS ARQ

17

time inherent in stop-and-wait ARQ but a larger data buffer is required to store up to N blocks which may have been transmitted before an acknowledgement is received. A NAK results in the N previous blocks (back to the last block for which an ACK was received) being retransmitted. The SDLC protocol specifies that N can be up to 7 blocks transmitted before an acknowledgement is received.

3) Selective-repeat ARQ permits the transmitter to continue until a NAK is returned. Only the faulty block, which is identified in the NAK, is retransmitted. The processing involved in repeating only selected blocks is more complex than go-back-N ARQ but no redundant blocks are retransmitted. Continuous selective ARQ returns an ACK or NAK for each block but not necessarily immediately upon reception.

ARQ requires much less redundancy to be added to blocks of data than an EDC system and feedback is given to the transmitter which may decide to cease operation if no responses are received. With severe error rates the ARQ system may become saturated by requests for retransmission since a single-bit error in a block results in a retransmission. Under these conditions ARQ may be combined with limited EDC in each block.

1.6 Character / byte-count / bit-oriented data link control protocols

1.6.1 Protocol levels

A protocol is a set of rules which ensure the orderly exchange of information between two or more parties. Because of the proliferation of different data communication protocols it has become difficult to identify the control functions associated with any single one. To ease this situation, protocols may be divided into four or more layers (seven in the OSI model). (See Figure 1.14.)

Protocols which are commonly applied to data links may be considered in a hierarchy of layers:

a) *Level 1, the physical link* defines the electrical and functional interchange which establishes, maintains and disconnects the physical link between the two ends.

b) *Level 2, data link control* (DLC): contains the functions which transfer data reliably over a single communications link and includes control functions between the end nodes.

c) *Level 3, communications path control*: defines the formatting and control procedures for end-to-end connections in a

NETWORK

18

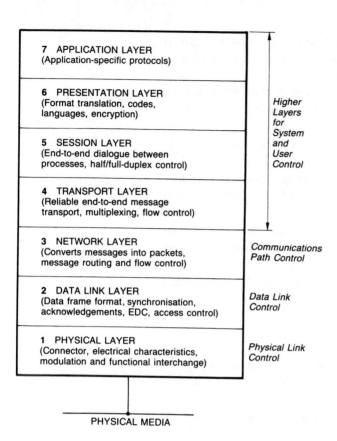

7 APPLICATION LAYER (Application-specific protocols)	
6 PRESENTATION LAYER (Format translation, codes, languages, encryption)	*Higher Layers for System and User Control*
5 SESSION LAYER (End-to-end dialogue between processes, half/full-duplex control)	
4 TRANSPORT LAYER (Reliable end-to-end message transport, multiplexing, flow control)	
3 NETWORK LAYER (Converts messages into packets, message routing and flow control)	*Communications Path Control*
2 DATA LINK LAYER (Data frame format, synchronisation, acknowledgements, EDC, access control)	*Data Link Control*
1 PHYSICAL LAYER (Connector, electrical characteristics, modulation and functional interchange)	*Physical Link Control*

PHYSICAL MEDIA

Fig. 1.14 Protocol layers in the ISO Open Systems Interconnection (OSI) model

network of more than one data link. Functions include message routing and flow control.

d) *Levels 4 and above, system and user control*: identify the characteristics of the information being transferred such as character codes, data format and device control; also co-ordinate the transfer of data between the user's applications programs and the operating system.

Level 1 interface standards include RS-232-C, RS-422 and X.21.

Level 2 data link control protocols include IBM Bisync (character oriented), DEC DDCMP (byte count oriented) and ISO HDLC (bit oriented).

Level 3 protocols include the level 3 X.25 packet switching procedures.

Level 4 and above includes IBM SNA, DEC DNA and layer 4 to 7 ISO OSI standards.

1.6.2 Data link control

Data link control protocols may be classified according to the message-framing technique employed:

a) *Character-oriented protocols* use special characters, such as STX, to indicate the beginning of a data block and ETB to indicate the end of a block.

b) *Byte count protocols* use a header which includes a special identification character and a count indicating the number of bytes in the message.

c) *Bit-oriented protocols* (BOPs) use a special flag character before and after the data block to indicate which bits constitute the data. A common flag character is 01111110 and it is necessary to prevent any sequence of six 1 bits followed by 0 occurring in the data block or this would be interpreted as a flag character. To prevent this accidental transmission of flag characters in the data block, a binary 0 is inserted by the transmitter after any sequence of five 1s. The receiver removes any 0 following a sequence of five 1s in the data block to recover the original bit sequence. This procedure is known as *bit stuffing*.

Bit-oriented protocols are most frequently employed because they are more efficient and reliable. They are also more easily implemented by software because only one frame format is used, field length is not restricted, any character code may be used, and few bit sequences are reserved. Many data link control chips are available to provide bit stuffing, CRC generation and checking plus other control functions for bit-oriented protocols.

1.7 Balanced / unbalanced interfaces

Electrical interfaces may be balanced or unbalanced. Balanced interfaces use a voltage on one line with respect to another line to determine a mark, or logic 1, signal, and the opposite polarity between the two lines to determine a space, or logic 0, signal. An unbalanced signal uses a voltage on the line relative to a reference voltage, usually the signal ground, to determine logic 1 or 0 signals. (See Figure 1.15.)

Balanced interfaces, such as RS-422, have a much greater immunity to errors caused by induced electrical noise than unbalanced interfaces such as RS-232-C and RS-423. An equal voltage should be induced on both conductors of a balanced interface which causes no differential effect; therefore no data corruption should be caused by common mode signals of this type (within the designed common mode voltage range for the circuitry used). A common cause of errors in unbalanced interfaces is associated with differences in the reference voltage at the two ends of the cable. Ground loops

20

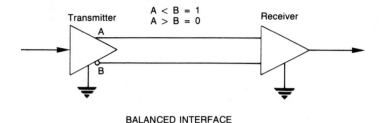

BALANCED INTERFACE

Fig. 1.15 Comparison of balanced and unbalanced interfaces

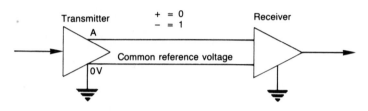

UNBALANCED INTERFACE

can cause the ground reference voltage to vary considerably and buildings may have several volts difference in ground potentials on different floors.

High-speed baseband interfaces are usually balanced because it is possible to operate at higher switching speeds when lower switching voltages are employed. The sensitivity of a receiver may be much greater when balanced interfaces are employed because the noise levels are lower; therefore it is possible to transmit balanced baseband signals over greater distances than unbalanced ones. The symmetrical circuits employed for balanced interfaces reduce the variation in switching speed between positive and negative going edges caused by line capacitance, thus reducing inter-symbol interference and permitting higher-speed operation.

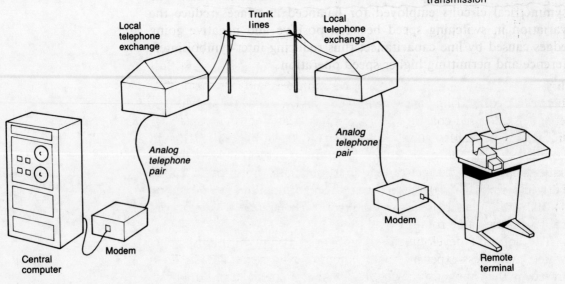

Fig. 2.1 Using the public telephone system for data transmission

2 Communications media

2.1 Introduction

The most basic consideration in data transmission is the media through which the transmission will take place. The recurring cost of the media is frequently the most costly part of long-distance communications but for shorter-distance connections the data communications equipment cost may be dominant. When designing a communications network it is therefore necessary to give much thought to the selection of the combination of data transmission media used and the cost change trends which are always present.

The earliest examples of data transmission associated with computers used the public telephone system which was made up of twisted-pair wires to the local telephone exchange and some form of trunk connection linking the local exchange to an exchange close to the destination (see Figure 2.1). The earlier forms of trunk connection used multicore cable or frequency division multiplexing (FDM) on coaxial cables, but these were often supplemented by microwave links carrying FDM analog transmissions and more recently by time division multiplexed trunks on twisted-pair cables, digital fibre optic links or satellite links.

Transatlantic communication was limited to low-speed telegraph cables and high-frequency radio for voice communications until the first transatlantic submarine telephone cable was laid in 1956. TAT1, between Scotland and Newfoundland, had a capacity of 50 voice channels and used coaxial telephone cable. Later coaxial transatlantic telephone cables have 30 MHz bandwidth but this is small compared with the capacity of fibre optic cables and communications satellite channels. The first undersea fibre optic cable, between the UK and Belgium, became operational in 1986 providing 11 500 voice channels (compared with 23 000 on twelve coaxial cables on the same route).

The constant development of improved communications media which make less-expensive data communications possible is illustrated by the change in the cost of 500 metre coaxial and fibre optic data transmission links between 1983 and 1986 as shown in Figure 2.2. In 1983 fibre optics was the less-expensive option only for data rates above about 25 Mbit/s but in 1986 fibre optics was the less-expensive option for data rates above 10 Mbit/s. Figure 2.3 shows the change in communications media employed for US domestic trunk communications from 1940 onwards.

A current trend is towards an all-digital communications infra-structure and the result will be the provision of integrated services digital networks by the 1990s. Speech will be digitised before transmission and will accompany all other forms of digital transmission through the network. The construction of such a network with low-cost high-speed data transmission available from every telephone outlet will have a considerable impact on the planning of data communication transmission facilities in the future.

2.2 Electrical cable

2.2.1 Twisted-pair cable

As shown in Figure 2.4, twisted-pair cable consists of two insulated conductors which are twisted together to prevent physical separation but, more important, to give a well defined characteristic impedance. Twisting the wires together increases the immunity to electro-magnetic interference by increasing the coupling between the two wires so that interference will affect both more equally. Twisting the wires together also reduces radiation and crosstalk between pairs in a cable because the radiation from current flowing in one wire is almost cancelled out by radiation from current flowing in the return wire of the pair.

A well-defined characteristic impedance is necessary to ensure uniform propagation of high-speed signals down the cable and to permit the equipment connected to have a characteristic impedance which matches the line, therefore transferring the maximum amount of power to the line. A line with a well defined characteristic impedance may be terminated at the ends by a matching value impedance to prevent signals being reflected and causing transmission errors.

Twisted-pair cable is commonly used to connect telephone subscribers to the local exchange, the main reason being the low cost of this form of cable and the defined characteristics. The development of Integrated Services Digital Networks (ISDNs) has made it necessary to transmit baseband digital signals over these twisted-pair cables in place of analog voice signals. Echo cancellation techniques have been developed to transmit two full duplex 64 kbit/s channels

24

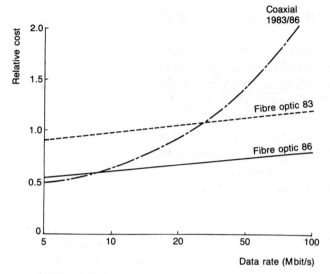

Fig. 2.2 Cost trends for a 500 metre data transmission link comparing coaxial cable with fibre optic cable (including interface equipment)

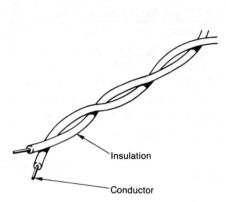

Fig. 2.4 Construction of twisted-pair cable

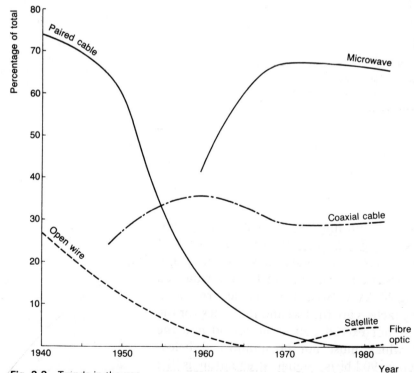

Fig. 2.3 Trends in the use of communications media for US domestic applications

on these twisted-pair cables permitting simultaneous transmission of digitised voice and data.

Unshielded twisted-pair is also used extensively on trunk communications links. Time division multiplexed links operating at 1.544 and 2.048 Mbit/s may be up to 1 mile in length between repeaters but this separation is frequently reduced to achieve less than a one-bit error in a million bits transmitted.

Figure 2.5 shows the attenuation/frequency characteristics for a 24 AWG twisted-pair telephone cable. Loading coils are added to analog voice circuits to make the attenuation constant over the voice frequency range but these must be removed to permit high-speed data transmission.

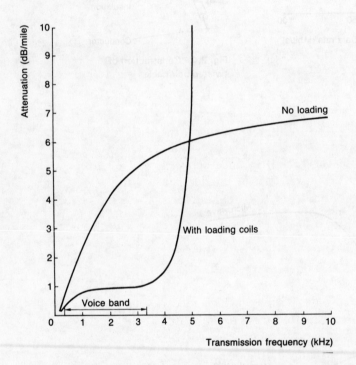

Fig. 2.5 Attenuation/frequency characteristics for a typical 24 AWG twisted-pair cable

Twisted-pair may be used to transmit baseband data at several Mbit/s over distances of 1 km or more but as the speed is increased the maximum length of cable is reduced. Figure 2.6 shows the graph of maximum cable length versus data rate for an RS-422 balanced line driver and receiver using 24 AWG twisted-pair cable terminated in a 100 Ω load. The limiting factors are the rise and fall times for the electrical pulses which must not exceed half a bit period and the attenuation of the signal which must not be diminished below 200 mV peak to peak. Below 90 kbit/s, signal attenuation is the major limiting factor but above 90 kbit/s, rise time requirements are the limiting factor.

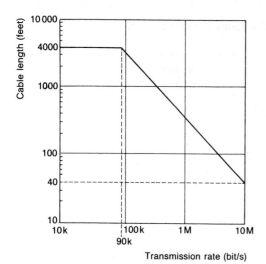

Fig. 2.6 Maximum cable length/data rate for an RS-422 balanced line driver and receiver using 24 AWG twisted pair cable with a 100 Ω load

Several types of twisted-pair cable are available:

a) Low-cost semi-rigid PVC insulated pairs which are most commonly used but have non-uniform impedance and cause excessive reflections. Table 2.1 compares the major characteristics of this type of cable. A typical distance between two successive twists is about six inches which is adequate to balance low-frequency radiation from both conductors. Telephone pair is usually 24 AWG with solid copper wire and PVC insulation.

b) Irradiated PVC and low dielectric insulation, unshielded twisted-pairs which give better electrical characteristics at a slightly higher cost (see Table 2.2).

c) Screened, low dielectric, twisted-pair (Twinax) which meets close electrical tolerance requirements, reduces crosstalk and other interference but is considerably more expensive. Screened twisted-pair gives more than 30 dB noise attenuation compared with non-screened cable and its use is essential to meet the FCC radiation limits with data transmission speeds over 10 Mbit/s.

2.2.2 Screened multicore cable

When several electrical conductors or pairs of wires are required, it is common to incorporate these in a single multicore cable with an overall screen to reduce interference from external sources such as fluorescent lighting or cables carrying switched heavy electrical currents.

27

Table 2.1 Major characteristics of typical low-cost PVC-insulated twisted-pairs

Conductor		Nominal	Impedance	Capacitance
AWG overall	Strands AWG	outside diameter (inches/pair)	(Ω)	(pF/ft)
30	7/38	0.064	115	15
28	7/36	0.070	105	16
26	7/34	0.078	95	18
24	7/32	0.088	85	20
22	7/30	0.102	75	22
20	7/28	0.116	70	25

Table 2.2 Major characteristics of typical low-dielectric-insulation twisted-pairs

Conductor		Nominal	Impedance	Capacitance
AWG overall	Strands AWG	outside diameter (inches/pair)	(Ω)	(pF/ft)
30	7/38	0.068	135	12
28	7/36	0.074	125	13
26	7/34	0.082	110	15
24	7/32	0.092	100	16
22	7/30	0.106	90	18
20	7/28	0.120	80	20

To reduce the crosstalk between cores and permit higher data rates, the design of multicore cables attempts to minimise the inter-core capacitance. Twisted-pairs may be employed to reduce crosstalk by making coupling between conductors in the pair much greater than the coupling to other conductors. Individually screened pairs within a multicore cable provide the best cure for crosstalk but a considerable reduction is achieved by twisting each pair in the cable at a different rate.

Multicore cable is extremely expensive and is not flexible; this makes installation difficult. It is also difficult to trace the source of a break or short associated with one core. A single fault may make it necessary to replace an entire cable. Each conductor in a multicore cable must be identified by a label or colour code. Figure 2.7 shows the construction of a typical large multicore cable.

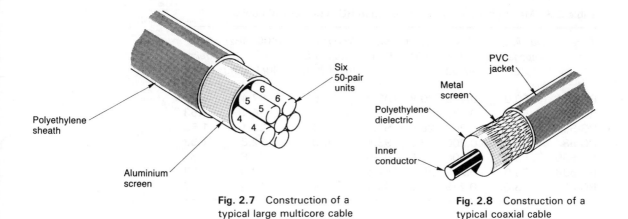

Fig. 2.7 Construction of a typical large multicore cable

Fig. 2.8 Construction of a typical coaxial cable

2.2.3 Coaxial cable

High-frequency electrical current flows in the outer skin of a conductor, making twisted-pair and multicore cables inefficient. This skin effect in metal conductors increases attenuation with the square root of frequency. A coaxial cable surrounds the inner conductor with a dielectric such as polyethylene, and a coaxial tube of solid or braided metal surrounds the dielectric as shown in Figure 2.8.

Coaxial cable is used for high-speed data transmission over distances of several kilometres. Baseband electrical signals may be transmitted down coaxial cable at rates over 10 Mbit/s for about a kilometre but much larger bandwidths and distances may be achieved by using modulated broadband transmission in the coaxial cable. In broadband mode, digital signals are modulated onto a sinusoidal radio frequency carrier with a frequency between 0 and 400 MHz. Many simultaneous digital signals may be carried by using several carrier frequencies separated by a suitable frequency spacing to prevent intermodulation.

Electrical interference is extremely low in coaxial cables if the outer screen has no gaps. The use of carrier frequencies in broadband mode makes the system immune to low-frequency interference caused by fluorescent lights and electrical switching. Baseband transmission, however, may be subject to low-frequency interference passing through the outer screen. A solid, continuous outer screen or double screening may be employed to minimise interference.

Many small coaxial cables are inexpensive because they are made in high volume for domestic television applications but low-loss coaxial cable or broadband cable is much more expensive; it is also larger and less flexible. All coaxial cable has closely toleranced electrical characteristics and is an efficient electrical transmission line.

Table 2.3 Major characteristics of common RG-type coaxial cables

Type	Nominal impedance (Ω)	Max. jacket od (in)	Capacitance pF/ft	pF/m	Nominal attenuation (dB/100 ft)	(400 MHz) (dB/100 m)	Time delay (ns/ft)
RG-174	50.0	0.105	30.8	101.0	17.5	57.4	1.53
RG-58C	50.0	0.199	30.8	101.0	11.0	36.1	1.53
RG-58A	52.0	0.200	28.5	93.5	11.0	36.1	1.53
RG-58	53.5	0.200	28.5	93.5	10.0	32.8	1.53
RG-58B	53.5	0.200	28.5	93.5	10.0	32.8	1.53
RG-59B	75.0	0.246	20.6	67.6	6.7	22.0	1.53
RG-62A	93.0	0.249	13.5	44.3	5.2	17.3	1.20

There are three main classes of coaxial cable:

1) Standard RG-type coax as used for domestic televisions (see Table 2.3). Most RG types are polyethylene-spaced but RG-62 is air-spaced polyethylene. Half-inch diameter coaxial cables such as RG-11 are more suitable than quarter-inch ones for data rates above 30 Mbit/s.

2) Air-spaced-core cables, which have a small diameter, are flame retardant, and have a very low dielectric constant which gives superior electrical properties compared with RG types.

3) Irradiated cellular-polyethylene coaxial cable which is more expensive than air-spaced-core cable but does not produce the small variations in electrical properties which occur when air-spaced-core cable is kinked.

Air-spaced cables have several important properties:

a) Extremely low attenuation, about 14 dB/100 ft at 400 MHz for braided screen versions and 16 to 17 dB for foil screen versions.

b) The propagation velocity is about 80% of the velocity of light compared with about 66% for polyethylene-spaced cables and 69% for teflon-spaced cables.

c) Lower cost than teflon-spaced cables and irradiated cellular-polyethylene-spaced cables.

Coaxial cable is used for trunk FDM links in public analog telephone systems. As shown in Figure 2.9, repeaters are required at about one mile intervals to amplify the signal. Regulating repeaters which compensate for cable changes with temperature are required every seven miles (maximum) and equalising repeaters are required every 38 miles (maximum) to compensate for deviations in other repeaters. All these repeaters are powered from the cable and power feed stations are required at intervals of less than 75 miles.

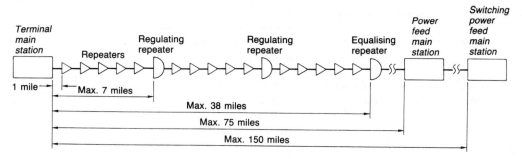

Fig. 2.9 Typical use of repeaters on trunk coaxial cable links

2.3 Fibre optic cable

2.3.1 Fibre optic cable applications

Fibre optic cable is used for many data communication requirements:

a) Local connection of computers to peripherals or control and measuring equipment.

b) Interconnecting local computers and terminals by dedicated fibre optic links, multiplexed fibre optic links, or fibre optic local area networks.

c) Long-distance, high data rate, trunk communications.

In 1954 Van Heel, Hopkins and Kapany published papers showing how a refractive coating on a glass or plastic tube could be used to transmit images. Early applications, developed in the 1950s and 1960s, were for image transmission in devices such as endoscopes but the use of glass fibres in data communication was not possible until low-loss optical fibres were developed in 1968. The first demonstration of data transmission in low-loss cable took place in 1970 at the Corning glass works in the USA. Throughout the 1970s and early 1980s developments reduced the attenuation of optical cable from 20 dB per kilometre to less than 1 dB per kilometre by using high purity silicon.

Fibre optic cable offers many advantages over electrical cables for data transmissions:

a) Higher transmission speed. Light travels down fibre optic cables at over 300 million metres per second whereas electrical signals propagate at 50 to 80% of this speed, depending upon the cable type.

b) Increased transmission capacity. Data rates over 1 Gbit/s may be transmitted down optical fibres but data rates are limited

31

Table 2.4 Comparison of twisted pair, coax., and optical fibre

	Twisted pair	Coaxial cable	Optical fibre Multimode, laser source
Attenuation at:			
10 MHz	Only suitable	20–120 dB/km	4–7 dB/km
100 MHz	for use up to	40–300 dB/km	4–7 dB/km
400 MHz	about 3 MHz	90–700 dB/km	4–7 dB/km
			(8–18 dB/km, LED source)
RF interference	High	Fair	None
Power budget (max.–min.)	60–80 dB	60–80 dB	20–30 dB
Cost	Low	High, stable	High, falling

to about 10 Mbit/s in twisted pairs, 30 Mbit/s for baseband transmissions in coaxial cable and 400 Mbit/s for broadband radio frequency data transmission in coaxial cable.

c) No electromagnetic interference is generated by fibre optic cable and it is not susceptible to electromagnetic interference, lightning strikes or the nuclear electromagnetic pulse (NEMP) which accompanies a nuclear explosion.

d) There are no ground loop, crosstalk or reflection problems as found with electrical transmission lines.

e) Attenuation increases with distance at a lower rate than for electrical cable making longer cable lengths between repeaters possible. (See Table 2.4.)

f) Bit error rates of around one in 10^9 are typical compared with around one in 10^6 for coaxial cables. This increases data throughput by reducing the number of retransmissions or the amount of redundancy required for error detection and correction.

g) There is no risk of short circuits or electrical sparks which removes the need to line conduit with fire-resistant material and makes fibre optic cable suitable for intrinsically safe applications such as in explosive atmospheres.

h) Typically, fibre optic cable is one tenth of the weight of screened copper cable. This is an important consideration in ships and aircraft.

i) Fibre optic cable is generally smaller and more flexible than electrical cable and takes less time to install. The smaller diameter and lower weight of optical fibre cable makes it possible to supply much greater lengths of cable per drum.

j) Fibre optic cable is suitable for use over a wide temperature range.

k) Eavesdropping is more difficult with fibre optic cable because there is no electromagnetic radiation, inductive taps do not work, and it is necessary to penetrate the sheath in order to monitor transmitted data. Tapping is more easily detected with fibre optic cable by using a time domain reflectometer or measuring signal loss.

l) Growth in data capacity may be achieved by adding data channels using different light wavelengths to existing fibre optic cable.

m) Fibre optic cable has a higher resistance to corrosive atmospheres and liquids than electrical cables.

n) Raw materials for manufacturing glass fibres are plentiful and costs are expected to reduce relative to the cost of metal cables.

o) The operational life and mean time between failure of fibre optic cables is superior to electrical cables. This does not necessarily apply to connectors and light sources/detectors.

p) The installation and maintenance costs for long-distance and medium-distance fibre optic links are less than those for electrical cables.

2.3.2 Fibre optic cable variations

IGNORE to P 42

Fibre optic cable cores may be made from glass or plastic (polymer). Plastic fibre is more rugged, it has a smaller bend radius, and connectors may be fitted more easily, without polishing the ends or using epoxy adhesive. Plastic fibre has a larger core diameter which makes connectors less sensitive to alignment errors and introduces less coupling loss. The cable is also less sensitive to production impurities. A cable using a plastic core does not require additional strengthening members such as Kevlar inserts, resulting in a lower cost than cables using glass cores. The disadvantage of plastic cable cores is that they have a much higher attenuation (hundreds of dB/kilometre) compared with glass fibres which limits their use to local data links up to about 50 metres in length.

Glass fibre is now the natural choice for high-speed, long- and medium-distance data links. In these applications it is important to maximise the bandwidth and length of cable between repeaters where regeneration of the signal is required. This makes the attenuation per kilometre and the bandwidth-distance relationship (in MHz-km) critical factors. Figure 2.10 shows the relationship between attenuation and bandwidth-distance for the more common forms of optical fibre.

An optical fibre consists of a glass or plastic core surrounded by a cladding made of a similar material but with a lower refractive index.

The core transmits the light while the change in refractive index between the core and the cladding causes total internal reflection, hence minimising the amount of light leaking from the fibre. Stepped-index fibres have an abrupt change between the refractive index of the core and the cladding (see Figure 2.11) and graded-index fibres have a gradual, parabolic change in refractive index between the centre of the core and the core-cladding boundary (see Figure 2.12).

Light propagates down a fibre in two ways, monomode and multimode. *Monomode* (see Figure 2.13) has only one propagation path along the length of the core giving a high bandwidth. To

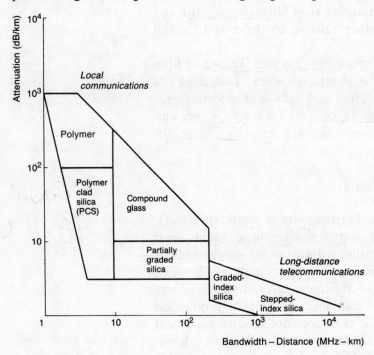

Fig. 2.10 Attenuation/bandwidth-distance relationship for several common forms of optical fibre

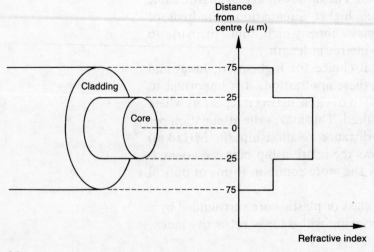

Fig. 2.11 A stepped index optical fibre showing the refractive index profile

minimise the number of reflections from the core edges, the core should be as small as possible. Difficulties in fabricating and joining monomode fibres resulted in multimode fibres being developed (see Figure 2.14). *Multimode* fibres have a larger core diameter and there are many propagation paths, reflecting from the edges of the core.

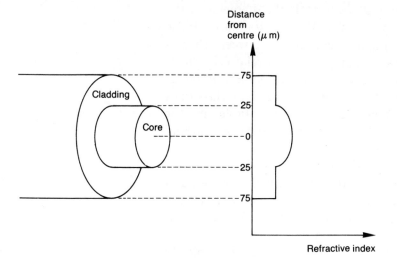

Fig. 2.12 A graded index optical fibre showing the refractive index profile

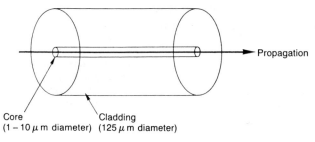

Fig. 2.13 Monomode propagation in a stepped index optical fibre

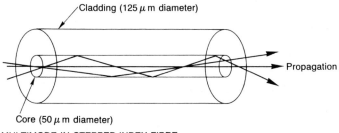

Fig. 2.14 Multimode propagation in stepped and graded index optical fibres

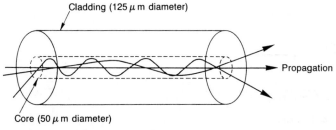

35

This results in pulse dispersion when the elements of a pulse arrive at different times after undergoing different numbers of internal reflections, resulting in reduced data transmission rates.

There are three common forms of fibre construction:

1) *Stepped-index multimode.* The core diameter is typically 50–60 μm but can be up to 200 μm while the diameter of the cladding usually conforms to the 125 μm standard. Pulse dispersion is high, limiting bandwidth to between 10 and 50 MHz-km, and applications are limited to relatively short, low-speed data links or industrial control cables. Polymer stepped-index fibres cost less and weigh less than glass ones and can withstand more flexing but they are suitable only for links up to 50 m in length and frequently have a cladding diameter of 1.0 mm.

2) *Stepped-index monomode.* The core diameter is small, typically 1–10 μm and the cladding diameter usually conforms to the 125 μm standard. Pulse dispersion is low and bandwidths of several GHz-km are possible but high manufacturing and jointing costs have prevented its widespread use.

3) *Graded-index multimode.* The core diameter is typically 50–60 μm and the cladding diameter 125 μm. Light is refracted back from the outer parts of the core preventing

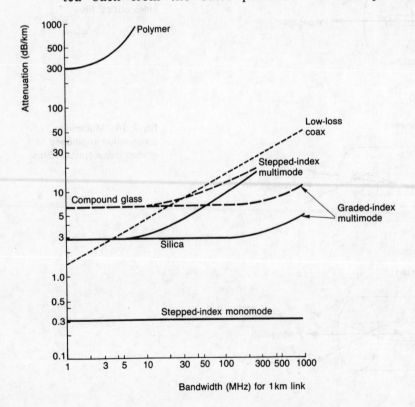

Fig. 2.15 Attenuation/bandwidth characteristics for common forms of optical fibre compared with low-loss coaxial cable

reflections from the core-cladding boundary as would be experienced with stepped index fibres. Although many propagation modes exist, the velocity is higher than in stepped-index multimode fibres which reduces pulse dispersion. The bandwidth can exceed 1 GHz-km and this type of fibre has been used for most of the early long-distance fibre optic data links.

Figure 2.15 compares the bandwidth and attenuation for the common forms of optical fibre with low-loss coaxial cable.

The numerical aperture (NA) of an optical fibre defines a characteristic of the fibre in terms of its acceptance of impinging light. NA may alternatively be expressed as $\sin \theta$ where θ is the maximum acceptance angle for total internal reflection. This light-gathering ability influences the coupling loss between light sources or detectors and fibres or between fibre ends in a connector. The light accepted by a fibre in air has a definitive relationship with the combinations of core and cladding construction of the fibre. Figure 2.16 shows typical numerical apertures for optical fibres of various dimensions and the expected values of attenuation/km and bandwidth-distance.

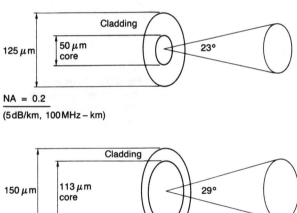

NA = 0.2
(5 dB/km, 100 MHz – km)

Fig. 2.16 Typical values for numerical aperture, attenuation/km and bandwidth-distance for various fibre dimensions

NA = 0.25
(20 dB/km, 25 MHz – km)

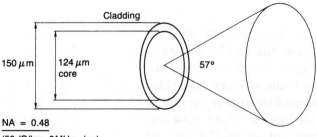

NA = 0.48
(50 dB/km, 8 MHz – km)

2.3.3 Light sources and detectors

The light source must be selected to emit a wavelength of light which experiences the minimum attenuation in the fibre used. Figure 2.17 shows a typical attenuation/wavelength characteristic for polymer fibres and Figure 2.18 shows typical characteristics for a monomode glass fibre. The polymer fibre has its lowest attenuation in the visible region of the spectrum with windows at 0.65 μm and 0.57 μm. Glass fibre has its minimum attenuation windows at about 1.2–1.3 μm and 1.5–1.6 μm.

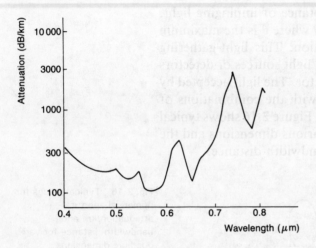

Fig. 2.17 Typical attenuation/wavelength characteristic for polymer fibre

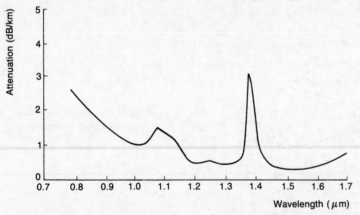

Fig. 2.18 Typical attenuation/wavelength characteristic for monomode glass fibre

The earliest low-cost light sources were based on gallium arsenide phosphide (GaAsP) which is used for light-emitting diodes and emits light at about 0.65 μm. These low-cost light sources are ideal for polymer fibre applications. Gallium aluminium arsenide (GaAlAs) sources are also available; these higher-priced light sources are more suited to glass fibre applications and emit light at about 0.84 μm. GaAsP sources have a typical power output of about 100 μW and

GaAlAs gives about 10 mW output. For this reason GaAsP is used primarily on short links. GaAsP sources have a typical life of greater than 10^6 hours and GaAlAs lasers have a typical life of greater than 20 000 hours.

High-performance systems using the 1.3 μm window in glass fibres frequently use indium phosphide/gallium indium arsenide phosphide (InP/GaInAsP) laser diodes which generate coherent light at 1.3 μm. It is possible to construct fibre optic systems with more than one transmission channel by using two or more different wavelengths of light. (Wavelength multiplexing is discussed in Chapter 3.)

Components are now available to construct long-distance high-speed data links using monomode fibres and 1.3 μm or 1.5 μm InP/GaInAsP laser diodes. The light detectors used for these longer infra-red wavelengths include germanium avalanche photodiodes (APD) but less noisy materials such as InGaAs, InGaAsP and AlGaAsSb are being developed for use in APDs. Alternatively, pin photodiodes may be used as detectors in low-noise low-capacitance amplifier circuits. The light detectors used at shorter wavelengths are silicon pin photodiodes and silicon APDs which are sensitive to wavelengths below about 1 μm.

2.3.4 Optical connectors and couplers

Two of the factors which slowed down the adoption of fibre optics were the lack of inexpensive, easily fitted connectors and a lack of standards for fibres and connectors. The adoption of a 125 μm diameter standard for cladding has assisted the development of connectors for glass fibre. The most common form of connector is the SMA connector (see Figure 2.19) which accepts a single fibre, the end of which must be polished before fitting. Multiway connectors

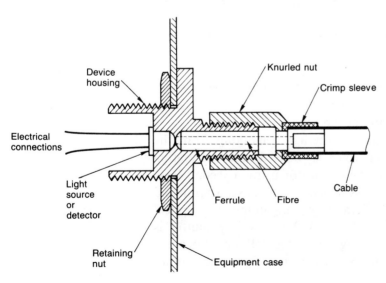

Fig. 2.19 Cross-section of a typical SMA connector

are available from several manufacturers. The US Electronic Industries Association (EIA) is developing fibre optic interface standards. EIA 475-01 is the standard for a straight terminus monomode fibre connector.

Long-distance communications links have many lengths of cable spliced together to avoid the losses associated with optical connectors. Small-diameter monomode fibres are particularly difficult to align. The V-groove splicing method uses a V-groove in a block of metal to hold the two lengths of fibre while epoxy resin is applied. When the resin has set it is removed and given additional protection. The arc fusion method uses an electric arc formed between two electrodes to fuse the fibre ends together and an alternative method uses a precision gas torch to fuse the fibre ends. Losses caused by these splicing methods are generally in the range 0.5 to 2 dB.

Low-cost plastic connectors are available for use with short inter/intra-equipment links; these introduce 2–3 dB loss. The use of plastic fibres or bundles of glass fibres makes careful alignment of fibres unnecessary and makes the cable more flexible. One type of connector with an integral light source and detector may be attached to two plastic cables in 15 seconds. This fitting time is achieved by incorporating cable-cutting blades in the connector.

Losses introduced by butt-jointed fibres are caused by variations in the core diameter, circularity, profile and concentricity, or the cladding dimensions. All these factors are outside the control of connector manufacturers but another set of losses arise because of the connector; these include lateral, angular and coaxial misalignment of the cores and deviation from the desired perpendicular mirror finish on the cable ends. Reflection loss due to a joint is 0.36 dB for glass fibres; this may be eliminated by inserting an index-matching liquid between the ends but dry connections are preferable in connectors.

Several forms of optical fibre connectors are available. The general types are:

a) Precision alignment ferrules which align half the fibre cladding to a reference surface such as a cylinder or wedge. Optical losses are typically in the range 0.5 to 2 dB.

b) Lens connectors which transform light emerging from the fibre into a parallel beam which is focused onto the mating fibre in the other part of the connector using a second lens. This makes the connector less sensitive to axial separation and improves lateral offset tolerance by expanding the optical field. Typical losses are 1 to 2 dB, but a safety shutter is required to prevent eye damage from the collimated beam.

c) Kinematic location connectors which use alignment components which slide over each other and lock into position. One example is the triple ball connector which uses three ball bearings to align the fibre. When pushed together, the ball clusters in each half of the connector slide over one another and mesh together. Typical losses are in the region 0.8 to 1.5 dB.

d) Connectors with integral light sources and detectors which use plastic cable for links up to 30 m at 100 kbit/s.

One of the major difficulties in using fibre optics for local area networks is the high insertion loss of passive tee couplers which are used to connect stations onto a bus cable or optical trunk. Local area networks which use regenerative repeaters at each node in a ring avoid this problem but an alternative approach is to use a star coupler. Each station is connected to a star coupler by a transmit fibre and a receive fibre as shown in Figure 2.20. Light entering from one station is equally divided between all the output cables, making the operation functionally the same as a bus but topologically a star. The star coupler is a passive device constructed by fusing together optical fibre. The division loss for an N-port transmissive star coupler is 10 log N.

Figure 2.21 compares the losses in local area networks based on tee connections or a star coupler. It is obvious that a tee system will be

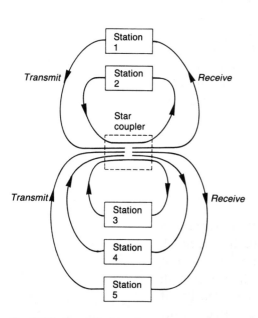

Fig. 2.20 An optical local area network using a passive star coupler

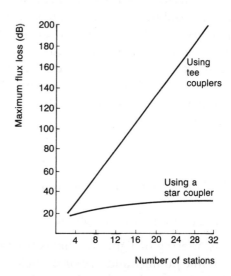

Number of stations

Assumptions: Connector loss = 1 dB
Mixing loss at each tee coupler = 2 dB
Coupling ratio for each tee coupler = 10 dB
Insertion loss for the star coupler = 8 dB

Fig. 2.21 Comparison of losses in local area networks using tee connections and star couplers

41

unable to support more than about eight stations when maintaining a practical margin between source power and detector sensitivity but a star system could support up to 32 stations. (For more information on fibre optic systems, see reference 2.2.)

2.4 Free-space optical links

2.4.1 Suitable applications for free-space optical links

A free-space optical link is basically a fibre optic link with free space substituted for the optical fibre. The optical transmitter produces a narrow beam which is aimed at a sensor which may be located at a distance up to several kilometres with a direct line of sight. Typical applications are between buildings on a university campus where a road prevents cables being installed easily or between buildings in a city where a cable provided by the local telephone company is excessively costly.

Free-space optical communications links are a high bandwidth alternative to local microwave links or electrical cables. Performance of optical links may be impaired by heavy rain or fog but they are immune to electrical interference and do not require a license from the radio licensing authority. Free space optical links provide a means of avoiding the delays which occur when the local telephone company is requested to provide a cable link.

Recent improvements in optical sources and detectors have increased the range and bandwidth of free space optical links while reducing the cost. Free-space links are available for voice channels and data channels up to 45 Mbit/s. Reliable communication is generally possible up to 2 km. For distances over 2 km a microwave link is preferable.

2.4.2 Free-space link technology

There are two major atmospheric effects on free-space optical links:

1) Scattering of light attenuates the optical signal in proportion to the number and size of particles suspended in the air. Small particles such as fog, dust and smoke have an effect which is related to their density and size in relation to the wavelength of the infra-red radiation used. Fog with a high density of particles, 1 to 10 μm in diameter, has the greatest effect on the light beam. Larger smoke particles or rain have a lower density and therefore have less effect.

2) Shimmer (caused by air movement resulting from variations in air temperature) causes differences in air density and hence refractive index along the beam. This scatters some of the light from the beam. The effect of shimmer may be reduced by raising the beam well above any hot surfaces and by using multiple emitters. Light from each emitter is differently affected by shimmer and the beams are averaged at the receiver.

Figure 2.22 shows the atmospheric attenuation rate and attenuation caused by rain and fog over the visible, infra-red, sub-millimetre, millimetre and microwave parts of the spectrum. A fade margin to cope with adverse weather conditions may need to be over 24 dB yet still maintain a good bit error rate. Free-space data links using millimetre waves (30 GHz to 300 GHz) will probably become available by 1990. These links provide similar performance to infra-red links but are less affected by atmospheric attenuation, fog and rain and the antennas are much smaller than those required for micro-wave links.

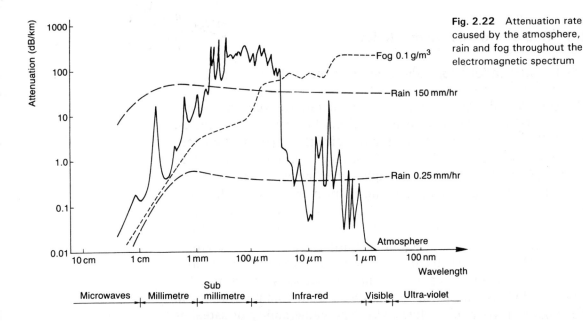

Fig. 2.22 Attenuation rate caused by the atmosphere, rain and fog throughout the electromagnetic spectrum

The major sections of a free-space optical link system are shown in Figure 2.23. For high-speed digital transmission, baseband modulation is generally used. The optical transmitter may be a non-coherent light-emitting diode for short distances but the inability of non-coherent sources to focus their light into narrow beams makes it necessary to use lasers for longer distances. The optical receiver is

43

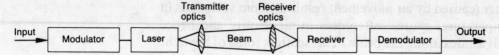

Input → Modulator → Laser → Transmitter optics → Beam → Receiver optics → Receiver → Demodulator → Output

Fig. 2.23 The major components of a free space optical link system

selected to match the transmitter. Silicon photodiodes and GaAlAs lasers form an efficient combination because their optical spectra match. For higher bandwidths, high resistivity pin photodiodes and avalanche photodiodes are used.

In the USA all laser manufacturers must have their products certified for safety. Links using non-coherent light-emitting diodes are generally incapable of producing a highly collimated beam which could be hazardous to someone looking into the beam. Coherent laser light however may be focused by the human eye into small spots which can damage the retina. The American National Standards Institute has established a system for classifying the nature of laser hazards and links must be classified according to the circumstances in which they may present a hazard.

2.5 Radio and microwave links

2.5.1 Applications for radio transmission of data

The earliest radio transmissions were digital, transmitting Morse code and teleprinter signals using relatively low carrier frequencies, up to a few MHz. The transmission of voice then became dominant at high frequencies (HF: 3 to 30 MHz), very high frequencies (VHF: 30 to 300 MHz), and ultra high frequencies (UHF: 300 to 3000 MHz). The radio spectrum and its primary uses are shown in Figure 2.24. Radio teleprinters operating at low transmission speeds have been used on the high-frequency band for many years but it is only recently that higher-speed data transmission has been adopted on the VHF and UHF bands for communication between mobile terminals and static computers or message-processing centres. HF was virtually written off for long-distance data communications in the 1960s in favour of satellite links. The vulnerability of satellites has caused a recent resurgence in the use of HF as a back-up medium, particularly for military purposes.

The earliest common use of radio data links was in the microwave region or super high frequency (SHF: 3 to 30 GHz) band of the radio spectrum. The development of transmitting and receiving techniques for radar operating in the SHF band led to the development of wideband microwave communications links in the 1950s. Line-of-

Fig. 2.24 The radio spectrum and its primary uses

Frequency (Hz)	Wavelength	Classification	Applications
3000 G	100 μm	Infra-red	Data links
		Tremendously High Frequency (THF) (sub-millimetre waves)	
300 G	1 mm	Extremely High Frequency (EHF) (millimetre waves)	Radar. Data links.
30 G	1 cm	Super High Frequency (SHF) (microwaves)	Radar. Microwave communications.
3 G	10 cm	Ultra High Frequency (UHF)	TV Broadcasting. Mobile short range comms.
300 M	1 m	Very High Frequency (VHF)	FM broadcasting. Mobile short-range comms.
30 M	10 m	High Frequency (HF)	Broadcasting and long-distance comms.
3 M	100 m	Medium Frequency (MF)	Broadcasting and medium-distance comms.
300 k	1000 m	Low Frequency (LF)	Broadcasting
30 k	10 km	Very Low Frequency (VLF)	Long-distance telegraphy and navigation.
3 k	100 km	Infra Low Frequency (ILF)	
300	1000 km	Extremely Low Frequencies (ELF)	

sight SHF transmissions do not suffer from many of the propagation and interference problems of lower-frequency bands and the higher-frequency transmission makes it possible to transmit data at many Mbit/s. The earliest microwave systems carried television signals and frequency division multiplexed telephony links but they are now used extensively to carry time division multiplexed data channels. The use of terrestrial microwave links has some advantages over satellite relayed microwave links; these include continuous operation, maintenance provision and a shorter propagation time.

Microwave links require repeaters at regular intervals to relay the signal over high ground and to regenerate weak signals. In some places such as in water or inaccessible regions, it is not practical to install towers and microwave repeaters at regular intervals so troposcatter systems are used. Troposcatter systems use UHF or SHF signals which are beamed at low angles to ensure reflection from the troposphere (about 10 km above the earth's surface). These systems make multi-channel telephony or time division multiplexed data transmission (at rates up to 2 Mbit/s) possible over distances up to about 500 km.

In the early 1970s the armed forces and owners of fleets of vehicles began to require digital communications between mobile units and base stations using the VHF and UHF radio bands. Typical applications are: data links to transmit track information between naval vessels; communications between terminals carried in army vehicles or manpacks and their local command vehicles; and the transmission of messages between terminals in taxis, public utility vehicles, police, ambulance or fire vehicles and a central control station. The use of data communications in place of voice communications makes it possible to store and display messages when the vehicle is unattended or in motion.

Earlier data communications systems for mobile terminals relied on VHF and UHF radio nets using a central station with an outbound frequency and possibly a different common frequency for responses from the mobile units. Contention between many incoming calls is resolved by the central station polling the terminals or by a collision detection and retransmission method.

Cellular radio systems are now available in many areas. These permit the transmission of digital information from handheld terminals or terminals in mobile vehicles to any subscriber on the public telephone system. A network of fixed base stations, each with many radio transmitters and receivers, is used to communicate with mobile users, the closest cell taking over the call and linking it to the desired subscriber on the public telephone network.

Radio telemetry systems operating at VHF and UHF are used to transfer bursts of data from remote logging sites to central data processing facilities. The cost of radio transmission is generally much lower than a network of landlines when many logging sites are located in inaccessible regions where cables are not available.

2.5.2 Propagation and interference problems

HF radio has a narrow channel separation and is notorious for propagation and interference problems; these factors have until recently made high-speed digital communication impractical. Developments in narrow band modulation methods, data encoding methods, error correction techniques and link sounding techniques (to establish the ideal frequency for transmission) have made the HF band a practical data transmission medium where other services are not available.

HF radio waves may travel between the transmitter and receiver by three modes (see Fig 2.25):

1) Sky wave, which is reflected from the ionosphere, about 100 km above the earth and received on the ground at distances up to thousands of kilometres away.

46

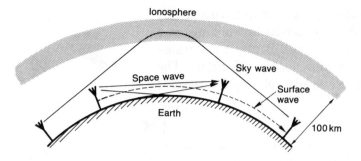

2) Surface wave, which travels directly to the receiver for distances up to about 100 km following the curvature of the earth.

3) Space wave, which travels by a straight path or by a single reflection from the earth's surface.

Sky wave signals are subjected to fading or changes in the amplitude of the received signal caused by changes in the attenuation of the atmosphere. General fading changes the amplitude of all frequency components of the signal equally but selective fading reduces some frequency components more than others. Phase differences between received signals which have followed different transmissions paths create considerable signal distortion and make many forms of modulation unsuitable.

The crowded HF band and long transmission range makes interference between transmitters on nearby frequencies common. To get satisfactory bit error rates on HF radio links it is necessary to use a narrow bandwidth transmission method (usually single sideband) and to filter out all unwanted frequencies at the receiver. The narrow bandwidth reduces the achievable data rate and special modems are used to reduce the effects of selective fading and multipath distortion. Surface and space wave transmission are the only reliable HF modes and it is often necessary to incorporate error detection and correction codes to achieve a practical bit error rate. (For more information see reference 2.1.)

Data transmission on VHF and UHF is not susceptible to ionospheric fading unless sporadic atmospheric reflections occur at times of high sunspot activity but multipath distortion (caused by signals being reflected from buildings, and terrain features) can cause similar problems, especially in mobile operation. Noise from vehicle electrics and other equipment can cause loss of data especially at the low VHF frequencies. To overcome these effects it is necessary to incorporate error detection and correction (EDC) codes with the data and to use interleaving which spreads bursts of errors over several data blocks, giving the EDC a chance to operate efficiently.

47

Reception of VHF radio communications in urban environments presents a number of problems. These are caused by buildings and other obstacles blocking the propagation path between the transmitter and receiver or by irregular terrain causing reflections. The signal strength at the receiver exhibits considerable local variations which in general take three forms:

1) Median path loss over irregular terrain which, in general, follows an inverse fourth power law when plotted against range, particularly when the distances involved are less than 15 km (i.e. when the distance from the base station is doubled, the signal strength is reduced by a factor of 16). Local terrain features can however cause considerable variations from this median value.

2) Slow fading which is caused by large natural terrain features. The variations in signal strength occur over distances which are large compared with the carrier wavelengths. The average values of fading taken over distances of a few tens of wavelengths are often found to follow a log-normal distribution with a standard deviation of 5–10 dB.

3) Superimposed on the slow fading are much more rapid variations, known as fast fading. These variations are caused by multiple reflections from buildings and other obstacles in close proximity to the vehicle. Typically the signal strength can change by as much as 30 dB over a distance of half a wavelength. A Doppler shift in the received frequency has been found to accompany fast amplitude fading.

The design of the receiver, in particular its signal-to-noise ratio and its automatic gain control capability, is important in coping with these fading effects. The human ear is capable of tolerating large amounts of distortion and a wide range of loudness, but the modem used in a digital transmission system must be carefully designed to ensure satisfactory operation in conditions of severe fading and poor signal-to-noise ratio if the system is to avoid a large number of errors and retransmissions.

2.5.3 Mobile radio data transmission

The control of large numbers of mobile units over a single voice radio channel is extremely inefficient because the information takes a long time to transmit, compared with digital transmissions, and the contention for channel access is time consuming. For these reasons, a maximum of about 150 mobile units is generally considered to apply to a voice channel. By employing digital transmission of data, the message time is considerably reduced and the synchronisation of responses from the mobile units may be performed in a manner which reduces contention. A data-only system may accommodate over 500 mobile units while achieving low message delay times.

Further advantages of data transmission over voice transmission include:

a) Transmission time and delay are reduced.
b) Privacy of message content is guaranteed (unless sophisticated monitoring equipment is used).
c) Transmission errors may be virtually eliminated.
d) Radio 'chatter' may be eliminated.
e) Several messages may be stored and displayed without operator involvement.
f) The system can maintain a complete log of messages.
g) Automated dispatching systems become feasible.
h Automatic reception and message transmission reduces the workload on the mobile operator.

A mixed voice and data channel does not offer the advantages of an all-digital system but many digital systems retain the ability for a mobile to request access on an associated voice channel.

The most important figure of merit for a data modem is its bit error rate, BER, under adverse signal-to-noise ratios. This defines the ratio of incorrect bits compared with the number of correct bits received with a specified level of signal-to-noise ratio at its input. Typical levels of BER for VHF mobiles in urban areas are about 1 bit in 1000 received in error prior to the application of error detection and correction techniques.

The type of modulation employed and the data transmission rate considerably influence the achievable BER with a given signal-to-noise ratio at the input.

The traditional type of modulation employed for radio transmissions is frequency shift keying, FSK, in which an audible tone is switched between one frequency which represents a binary 1 and a second frequency which represents a binary 0. The maximum achievable data rate for FSK transmission in an urban radio environment is 600–1200 bit/s.

More recent methods of data modulation have been developed which make possible the transmission of data at up to 4.8 kbit/s using the 3 kHz audio bandwidth of a standard mobile radio transceiver. A synchronous protocol with automatic error correction is commonly used to avoid the need for a retransmission if small numbers of erroneous bits are received from the modem but this may halve the effective data rate of the channel by adding many redundant EDC bits to the data.

To overcome multipath fading, base stations may employ diversity reception, that is two or more receivers located in different places. The signals from mobile units are decoded by each receiver and are sent by land line to the central network controller where the signals without errors are combined. Message errors which are not overcome by the error correcting code and diversity reception cause a negative acknowledgement and are retransmitted.

Cellular mobile telephone systems use up to two thousand 25 kHz full-duplex channels between 860 and 960 MHz to provide communication between mobile telephone users and the nearest base station. Channel frequencies are reused in cells which are not adjacent; this demands short-range UHF communications and therefore makes the size of each cell between 12 and 15 km, reducing to less than 5 km in some urban areas (see Figure 2.26).

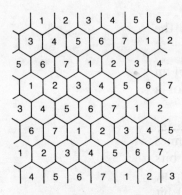

Fig. 2.26 Allocation of channel frequencies in a cellular mobile telephone system

When a subscriber moves from one cell to another, the control and switching system which links all the base stations transfers the call within a nominal 300 ms hand-off period. Automatic routing is provided for calls which are intended for a mobile subscriber, regardless of whereabouts.

Mobile data terminals may be fitted with voice band modems to communicate through the analog cellular mobile telephone systems and the public switched telephone network.

Modems for cellular radio systems may be simple, inexpensive devices, operating at 1.2 or 2.4 kbit/s and plugging into the telephone socket, or they may be more expensive units with encryption and/or an internal data buffer which stores data during the hand-off period. Hand-off from one cell to another occurs when the vehicle moves across the boundary or when one cell transfers calls to another because its capacity is fully utilised. The lost of carrier in such a hand-off may abort the entire transmission.

All modems or terminals for cellular radio need to incorporate some form of error detection and correction to cope with multipath fading, co-channel interference and cross-channel interference. Some cellular radio systems give the users freedom to select any

50

modem which is suitable for use with the local public switched telephone network while other network operators (such as Racal-Vodafone in the UK) determine the error correction protocol. The Vodafone protocol is called CDLC and includes a set of procedures or standards covering each layer of the communications requirement:

a)	Physical (connection) level	V.25 bis.
b)	Physical (channel) level	V.21, V.22, V.23, V.26.
c)	Link set up (supervisory)	ISO HDLC.
d)	Link control (supervisory)	ISO HDLC.
e)	Error detection	CRC-16.
f)	Error correction	FEC block or convolution.
g)	Code independence	ISO HDLC or block.

Other network operators such as Cellnet use the EPAD error correction protocol which allows the subscriber to access the British Telecom MultiStream X.25 network, bypassing the public switched telephone network and providing 1200 bit/s digital transmission with V.22 or V.21/23 modem compatibility.

All-digital cellular systems are being proposed to cope with the predicted saturation of the analog systems by 1990. Three modulation and multiple access schemes have been proposed:

1) Wideband time division multiple access (TDMA).
2) Narrowband time division multiple access.
3) Slow-frequency-hopping code division multiple access (CDMA).

Voice transmission will be achieved by digitising speech at 16 kbit/s; this will be stored in blocks and transmitted in the slots of a TDMA system or by spreading it over a wide bandwidth along with many other CDMA signals to make more channels available.

Radio-based local area networks are used on industrial sites to avoid the problems of cable installation and to provide full freedom for mobile terminals. A typical system may use a single master station and many thousands of individually addressed slave stations, all operating on one carrier frequency. In the UK this type of telemetry system may use one of eight 25 kHz channels in the UHF band. Operation at 1 mW transmitter output makes a typical range of 500 m available but operation at 10 mW output makes 1.5 km range available. Data transmission at 2 kbit/s is typical and interfaces are available for a wide range of industrial controllers, analog and digital interfaces for control and data logging applications.

One of the major problems in mobile radio has been the shortage of available frequency channels in the VHF and UHF bands. In the 1950s the UK made 50 kHz separation VHF channels available; this was reduced to 25 kHz, then to 12.5 kHz, and further reductions are being considered. To operate in bands of less than 12.5 kHz, new forms of modulation are required such as single sideband (SSB) in place of the conventional amplitude and frequency modulation systems. SSB makes possible the transmission of data at 2.4 kbit/s on a 5 kHz separation channel.

2.5.4 Digital troposcatter

Digital troposcatter is used for military communications and in parts of the world where it is not practical to use trunk cables or microwave links. UHF and SHF transmissions may be used. UHF antennas are larger structures than SHF antennas and therefore operation in the 2.4 GHz and 4.4 GHz bands is used by mobile systems. Frequency bands may need to change throughout the day and night to maintain satisfactory performance in changing tropospheric conditions.

Diversity reception is frequently employed to minimise the effect of fading caused by changes in the signal path. Transmitter powers of several kilowatts are typical and operating ranges vary with the type of terrain, climatic conditions, the data transmission rate used, and the elevation of the transmitter and receiver antennae (see Figure 2.27). Bit error rates in the range 1 in 10^3 to 1 in 10^6 are achieved.

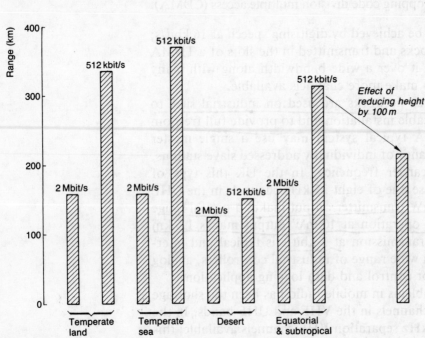

Fig. 2.27 Typical variations in range of troposcatter transmissions caused by climatic conditions, data transmission rate and antenna elevation

A mobile troposcatter system manufactured by Marconi uses analog frequency division multiplexing techniques to transmit up to 300 speech channels or quaternary phase shift keying to transmit a baseband digital signal at bit rates up to 2.048 Mbit/s. The baseband channel may be time division multiplexed to accommodate several digital channels.

2.5.5 Microwave links

Microwave links are extensively used to carry telephone trunks where coaxial or fibre optic cables are not practical. A direct line of sight is required for transmission in the SHF band so it is necessary to locate microwave antennae on high towers or on top of hills to ensure a direct path with the minimum number of intervening repeaters.

The most common microwave communication frequency bands are at 2, 4, 6 and 6.8 GHz. Early transmissions used frequency modulation for analog frequency division multiplexed voice channels but digital transmission is now used in the data networks. A 140 Mbit/s microwave data link may provide 1920 voice channels (the same number as on an analog link) or various combinations of 2 Mbit/s time division multiplexed channels. Highly efficient modulation systems such as reduced bandwidth quaternary phase shift keying are now employed making it possible to double the data rate to 280 Mbit/s.

Microwave links may have bit error rates in the range 1 in 10^5 to 1 in 10^{11} depending upon the signal-to-noise ratio at the receivers on each link. Propagation problems encountered on microwave links include heavy rain which can cause attenuation of up to 10 dB/km and multipath fading which causes distortion of the received signal and an increased error rate; this may be reduced by suitable adaptive equalisers. Short gaps in the received signal may occur when flocks of birds fly through the microwave beam but this is an infrequent occurrence.

2.6 Satellite relay

2.6.1 The evolution of satellite communications

The first use of a satellite to relay communications was in 1960 when the Echo satellite was launched by NASA. Echo was a 100 ft diameter aluminised mylar balloon which acted as a passive reflector for radio signals between 960 and 2390 MHz. The small received signal from a passive reflector was not suitable for commercial applications and apart from project West Ford, conducted in 1963 by the US Air Force, all subsequent communications satellites have used active repeaters. Project West Ford placed 480 million copper dipoles in orbit to act as reflectors for 8.3 GHz radio signals.

Figure 2.28 shows the development of communications satellites. Some of the more notable satellites are briefly described here. The Courier satellite, launched in 1960, was the first active repeater; it carried one voice channel and a digital recorder. Telstar, launched in 1962 by AT&T, was the first satellite to transmit and receive simultaneously. It used transmissions in the C band (5.7–6.4 GHz uplink, 3.4–4.2 GHz downlink) for 600 one-way voice circuits or one television channel. The Syncom satellite, launched in 1963, had two 1.8/7.3 GHz repeaters each with 500 kHz bandwidth. In 1965 the USSR launched the Molniya satellite in a high-altitude elliptical orbit.

Following the passage of the US Communications Satellite Act in 1962 the Intelsat organisation was founded in 1964. This multi-national organisation now has a network of satellites which provide about two thirds of the world's transoceanic communications. The Early Bird satellite, launched in 1965 by Intelsat, began the sequence of Intelsat satellites, summarised in Figure 2.29. Early Bird (Intelsat 1) was placed in a synchronous equatorial orbit and had two 25 MHz bandwidth repeaters at 4/6 GHz. Intelsat II was launched in 1967 to a synchronous equatorial orbit and was the first satellite to have a frequency division multiple access (FDMA) capability. It had one 130 MHz bandwidth repeater at 4/6 GHz. Intelsat III, launched in 1968, had two 225 MHz bandwidth repeaters at 4/6 GHz and Intelsat IV, launched in 1971, had twelve 36 MHz bandwidth repeaters. Intelsat V launched in 1980 was the first to use the higher-frequency Ku band (11 to 14 GHz). Intelsat VI satellites launched from 1987 onwards use narrow independent beams and satellite switched time division multiple access (TDMA) to improve efficiency.

The Anik satellite launched in 1972 was the first domestic satellite; it provided twelve 36 MHz bandwidth repeaters for television and communications throughout Canada. The Westar satellite, launched in 1974 by Western Union, was the first US domestic satellite; it also provided twelve 36 MHz bandwidth repeaters with 5 watts output per repeater.

Throughout the 1970s and 1980s the number of satellites in orbit expanded enormously for military applications, civil communications and domestic purposes. In the late 1980s direct television broadcasting by satellite began in the USA, Europe, Japan and Australia, made possible by high-power satellites which needed only 0.5 to 1 metre diameter receiving dishes. Intelsat traffic has grown by about 25% per annum and includes more than 23 satellites serving over 160 parts of the world. To make more efficient use of satellite

Fig. 2.28 A brief history of communications satellites

	INTELSAT VI
	INMARSAT, WESTAR, MEXICO, CS-3/BS-3 (JAPAN)
1985	BROADCAST SAT (LUXEMBOURG), AUSTRALIA, LEASAT, INTELSAT-VA
	INDONESIA, ARABSAT, TELSTAR-3, SATCOL (COLUMBIA), MUS1, GTE
	TV SAT (GERMANY), TC-1 (FRANCE), SPCC, HCI
	WESTAR TRDS, ECS, CS-2 (JAPAN), ANIK
	COMSTAR, INDIA, SBS, DSCS II + III, SIRO-2, MARECS
1980	SBS, INTELSAT V
	SKYNETS
	FLEET SATCOM, JBS
	ETS-2, SIRO (ITALY), RADUGA (USSR), CS (JAPAN)
	SATCOM, LES 8 + 9, COMSTAR, NATO III, INDONESIA
1975	STATSIONAR (USSR), CTS (CANADIAN), MARISAT, INTELSAT IV A
	SKYNET II, WESTAR, ATS 6, SYMPHONIE
	DSCS II
	ANIK
	NATO II, INTELSAT IV, DSCS II
1970	NATO II, ATS-5
	TACSAT, SKYNET I
	LES 6, INTELSAT III
	DODGE, LES 5, DATS, IDCSP, ATS 1, ATS 3
	CGTS, INTELSAT II
1965	LES 1, INTELSAT I (EARLYBIRD), MOLNIYA 1 + 2, LES 2
	ECHO II, SYNCOM
	TELSTAR, WESTFORD, SYNCOM, RELAY
	TELSTAR, RELAY
1960	ECHO I, COURIER

55

Fig. 2.29 Summary of Intelsat communications satellites

1965	INTELSAT I	Early Bird. 240 voice circuits, C-band, 50 MHz
1966	INTELSAT II	First to use FDMA, 240 voice circuits, C-band, 130 MHz
1968	INTELSAT III	1500 voice circuits, 4 tv channels, C-band, 300 MHz
1971	INTELSAT IV	4000 voice circuits, 2 tv channels, C-band, 500 MHz
1975	INTELSAT IVA	6000 voice circuits, 2 tv channels, C-band, 800 MHz
1980	INTELSAT V	12 000 voice circuits, 2 tv channels, C/Ku-band, 2144 MHz
1985	INTELSAT VA	15 000 voice circuits, 2 tv channels, C/Ku-band, 2250 MHz
1987	INTELSAT VI	TDMA with independent beams, 30 000 voice circuits, 3 tv channels, C/Ku-band, 3300 MHz

transmission power than wide angle beam, frequency division multiple access (FDMA) satellites, it is now possible to use all-digital time division multiple access (TDMA) systems with high-intensity spot-beam antennas to relay data bursts from earth stations to selected receivers at various places on the earth's surface.

All communications satellites now use a geostationary orbit, 22 335 miles above the equator, with a speed coinciding with the earth's rotation to make the satellite appear almost stationary. The angular and frequency resolution capability of groundstations made it necessary to separate satellites operating on the same microwave band by 4° of arc, thus limiting the number of communications satellites over popular parts of the earth (such as the quadrant between North America and Europe which is limited to about 20). To double the number of geostationary satellite positions, in 1984 the US Federal Communications Commission reduced the requirement for orbital separation to 2° of arc. This made it necessary to improve the resolution of groundstations by 1987 in order to prevent signals from neighbouring satellites in the same frequency band being picked up as noise at the earth station.

Satellite communications for maritime and aircraft use was made possible by the Inmarsat satellites. The use of small, mobile, wide beam antennas at the groundstation makes it necessary to use high-power transmitters on the satellite. Further developments in the Inmarsat system are expected to include voice transmission at

4.8 kbit/s, the use of multiple spot beams with on-board processing, and high-gain antennas suitable for use in aircraft.

The development of small inexpensive groundstations and a new generation of Ku band communications satellites has resulted in a number of satellite-based data networks being set up for long-distance communications. Telecommunications service organisations in the USA, such as AT&T and McDonnell Douglas, now make small interactive satellite dishes available for computer users to communicate with a remote central host. The AT&T data network (see Figure 2.30) permits about 50 small groundstations known as Very Small Aperture Terminals (VSATs with dishes less than 5 ft diameter) employed by remote users to communicate with a central hub groundstation (with a larger antenna) where the host computer is situated. The hub station creates data packets for transmission at 56 kbit/s and directs the management of the data network. The smaller VSATs send data to the hub at typical data rates of 2400 bit/s. A header informs the hub whether to process or store the data or to transmit it to any combination of VSATs.

The British Telecom SatStream service provides leased dedicated satellite links to data users at rates between 64 kbit/s and 2 Mbit/s. Shared BT groundstations or small mobile groundstations may be used. The small mobile groundstations may be suitable for organisations with temporary offices or new offices awaiting permanent facilities.

Future developments in communications satellite technology include the planned launch of the Advanced Communication Tech-

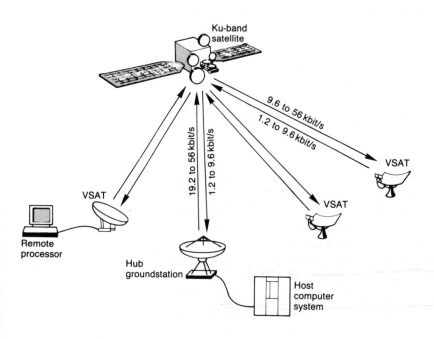

Fig. 2.30 The AT&T data network using a satellite to link very small aperture terminals (VSATs) to a central ground station

nology Satellite (ACTS) about 1990. ACTS will incorporate several new technologies including:

a) An on-board baseband processor (using signal regeneration rather than amplification and frequency translation) for circuit switching (see Figure 2.31). This will allow small ground terminals to use a single hop to communicate with other ground terminals unlike present VSAT terminals which use two hops to communicate via a central hub ground-station.

b) A scanning multibeam antenna providing up to ten times better frequency utilisation than present satellites plus three fixed pencil beams and two scanning, hopping beams with $0.3°$ spots which may dwell for 10 to 100 μs on 120 mile diameter areas before switching in 0.5 μs.

c) An experimental optical laser communications system for high-rate inter-satellite links (up to 4 Gbit/s eventually).

d) High-frequency Ka band (30 GHz uplink and 20 GHz downlink) communications to make more geostationary slots available when all C band and Ku band orbital slots (at $2°$ of arc) are saturated. Ka band suffers from greater atmospheric attenuation than the C and Ku bands, particularly when atmospheric moisture or rain is present, but more bandwidth is available and antennas are smaller.

2.6.2 Practical aspects of satellite communication

Satellite relays may at first sight appear to offer near perfect data communication, with high data rates available over great distances and no distance-related cost increase. There are however many practical aspects which should be considered; these include:

a) Round trip delay is about 0.5 second which creates problems for real-time interactive protocols. Echoplex operation of a terminal is not practical over satellite links and acknowl-edgements must be handled in a manner which does not halt transmission until the ACK is received. A satellite delay compensation unit is available to eliminate the problems caused by delay in many Bisync protocol applications (see Figure 2.32). Propagation delay changes caused by the figure-of-eight movement of a geostationary satellite requires frequent transmission of synchronisation frames.

b) Voice circuits suffer from echo problems which may be eliminated by digital echo cancellers.

c) Satellites have a designed life span of seven to ten years but may suffer malfunctions which cause premature loss of

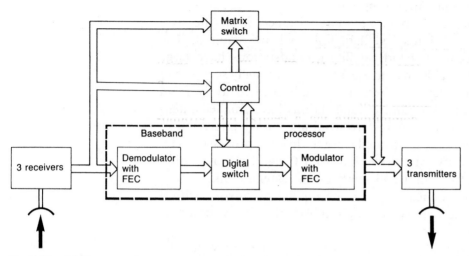

Fig. 2.31 ACTS proposed on-board baseband process-ing for circuit switching

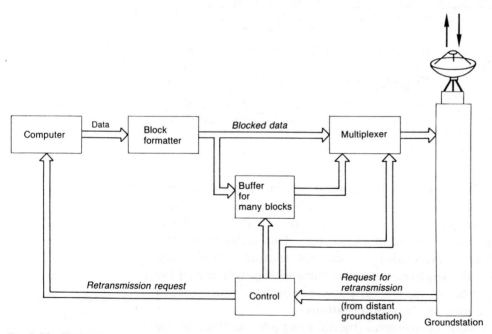

Fig. 2.32 The main functional units in a satellite delay compensation unit

service. It is therefore wise to plan for providing an alternative service in either eventuality.

d) The groundstation may be some distance from the user and expensive high-speed data links will be required. The lower-frequency C-band satellite groundstations have large antennae (about 30 m diameter) and are extremely sensitive to interference; they are therefore usually located away from built-up areas. Ku band groundstations have smaller antennae and are less prone to terrestrial microwave interference, and therefore may be located close to the data processing site. A high-capacity microwave link to a C band groundstation would add to the noise problem on the satellite link.

e) Satellite communications may be tapped by anyone with a receiver in the vicinity of the groundstation. Encryption may be required for privacy.

f) Geostationary satellites undergo periods when they may be unable to function. A solar eclipse occurs when the earth gets between the sun and the satellite; this cuts off the supply of electricity from the solar cells and leads to operation on battery power, often resulting in reduced performance or loss of service. Solar eclipse occurs for 23 days before and after the spring equinox and the autumn equinox. The longest blackout, 72 minutes, occurs on September 21st and March 21st; the duration diminishes as the time from the equinox increases.

Sun transit occurs when the satellite is directly between the sun and the groundstation, causing an increase in thermal noise at the groundstation and a probable loss of signal from the satellite. Sun transit occurs twice a year for five consecutive days during which the signal is lost for about ten minutes.

Geostationary satellites are not in fact stationary with respect to the groundstation. Deviations from an equatorial orbit cause the satellite to move in what appears to be a figure-of-eight pattern of dimensions which are proportional to the inclination of the orbit from the equatorial (typically up to 100 miles per day). This variation in orbit is monitored and corrected by a control station. Stabilisation manoeuvres are also required to prevent the apparent rotation of the satellite once per day (when it is fully stable in orbit) in order to keep the antennae aligned on the groundstations.

Stabilisation may be achieved by spinning the satellite or by three-axis stabilisation using gyroscopes which align the satellite to a spatial reference point. Spin stabilisation is the simpler method but the amount of electricity which may be generated by the solar cells is smaller because they must be located around the drum-shaped body, only half in sunlight at any time. The antennae must also be spun in the opposite direction to maintain alignment with the groundstations.

The frequency of the up-link and down-link may be either C band (4/6 GHz range) or Ku band (11/14 GHz range). C band requires larger antennae and groundstations are susceptible to interference but it has a lower attenuation caused by rain and the amount of the atmosphere in the signal path. Atmospheric attenuation depends upon the slant range and this will be largest for groundstations at the extreme edges of the satellite ground coverage.

The up-link differs from the down-link frequency to permit full duplex operation and it is conventional to use a higher-frequency up-link in the same band as the down-link. More power is therefore available from the groundstation at the higher frequency where more power is required to overcome atmospheric attenuation. Channels with small frequency separation make use of opposite polarisation to minimise interference but direct broadcasting from satellites uses circular polarisation to eliminate the need for polarisation adjustments at the groundstations.

Frequency division multiple access (FDMA) has been used by most communications satellites but time division multiple access (TDMA) is becoming popular because more channels may be accommodated in the same bandwidth, transmitter output power is higher, and there is no intermodulation interference as may be found with FDMA. TDMA however is more complex, expensive and demands critical timing for control. A master groundstation transmits control data through the order wire channel to tell groundstations when to transmit and receive. Data is transmitted in time frames allocated to individual users and no handshake is given. Typical TDMA systems operate at 60 Mbit/s using quadrature phase shift keying over a 36 MHz bandwidth transponder.

3 Modems and multiplexers

3.1 Modulation and keying alternatives

3.1.1 Introduction

Long-distance data communication over analog telephone lines requires a device called a MOdulator-DEModulator or MODEM to convert the digital signals into analog signals with frequencies within the bandwidth of the telephone line. Early data communications depended on dedicated or public switched telephone lines because there were few alternatives.

Telecommunications authorities are now introducing all-digital networks to which the subscriber enters data in digital form through a standard interface, thus making modems unnecessary. There will still be a need for modems to communicate over the analog public switched telephone network for several years before this is replaced by an Integrated Services Digital Network (ISDN). For high-speed dedicated data lines, most telecommunications authorities now provide an all-digital service such as the British Telecom KiloStream and MegaStream.

Where a short transmission path is required for local connections it is possible to use a less-expensive form of limited-distance modem, short-haul modem, line driver or modem eliminator rather than a proper modem. Limited-distance modems or short-haul modems use a form of analog modulation and can operate over standard telephone lines but the longer the line is, the slower the transmission speed must be because sophisticated equalisation techniques required for long-distance operation are not provided.

Line drivers use a baseband transmission technique which avoids the need for modulation of a carrier frequency. A direct current path is required (without amplifiers, loading coils or equalisers) in order to pass the baseband pulses. A form of DC phase encoding is commonly employed to provide simultaneous clock and data transmission and to increase the noise immunity.

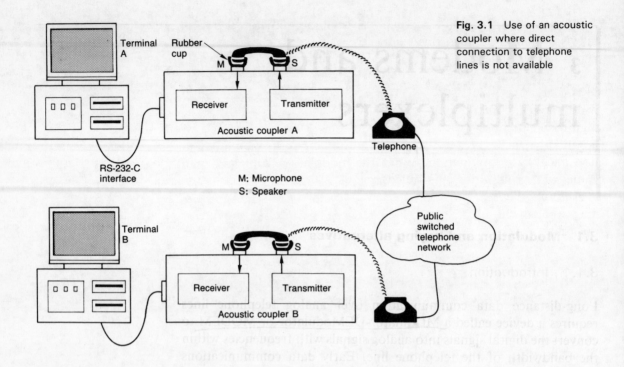

Where no direct connection to the telephone lines is available using equipment approved by the local telecommunications authority, and alternative media are not available, an acoustic coupler is commonly employed (see Figure 3.1). Acoustic couplers have rubber cups which fit over the mouthpiece and earpiece of a telephone handset. The data modulates an audible carrier which is picked up by the telephone mouthpiece and is transmitted by the telephone system to the earpiece of the receiving telephone which is connected to the microphone of a similar acoustic coupler.

Acoustic couplers are only suitable for data rates up to about 1200 bit/s and can suffer from a poor bit error rate which may be in the range 1 to 10^2 to 1 in 10^5 depending on line quality. Early FSK acoustic couplers provided 300 bit/s full-duplex operation (Bell 103 compatible). More recent products such as the Racal-Vadic VA3400 use dibit phase shift keying to provide 1200 bit/s full-duplex operation over the public telephone system.

3.1.2 Amplitude modulation, frequency modulation, phase modulation and quadrature amplitude modulation

Broadcast radio has been using amplitude modulation of a radio frequency carrier (100 kHz to 30 MHz) for audio transmission for many decades. Frequency modulation was adopted for VHF and television sound broadcasting to improve the quality of the received audio signal and to prevent the attenuation of the audio signal when a weak carrier is received.

Modems use a carrier frequency within the transmission bandwidth of voice grade channels, that is between 300 and 3400 Hz. The digital signal modulates the carrier by one or a combination of modulation techniques: amplitude modulation, frequency modulation and phase modulation. When the modulation is digital, with values of 0 and 1 only, it is called *keying*.

Amplitude modulation or *keying*, in which the peak-to-peak magnitude of the carrier is switched between two levels at the rate of the binary signal, is shown in Figure 3.2. Amplitude modulation keying is rarely used alone in modems because it is susceptible to noise and it takes some time to determine signal amplitude but it is often combined with phase modulation in 8-ary transmission systems. Demodulation requires a comparison with the threshold

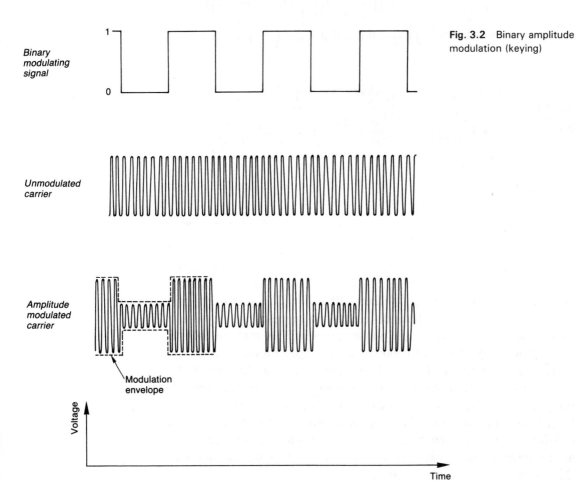

Fig. 3.2 Binary amplitude modulation (keying)

65

amplitude and this is made difficult by carrier attenuation in the transmission media.

Frequency shift keying or *frequency modulation*, in which the frequency of the carrier is varied between two values at the rate of the binary signal (see Figure 3.3), is commonly used in low-speed asynchronous modems, up to about 1.2 kbit/s. The decoding of frequency shift keying (FSK) may be performed simply by detecting the presence of one or other frequency because frequencies are not changed in transmission. This makes FSK suitable for asynchronous transmission where no clock reference is available.

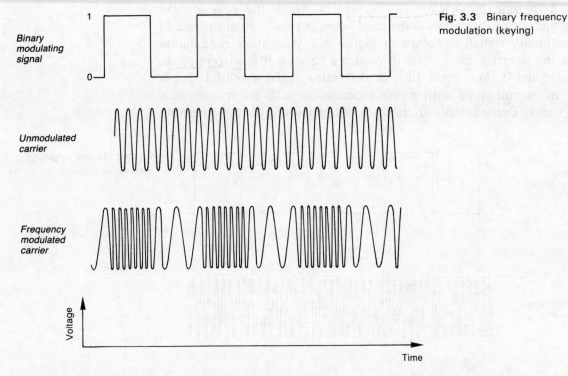

Fig. 3.3 Binary frequency modulation (keying)

Phase modulation or *phase shift keying* (PSK) uses changes in the phase of the carrier with respect to a reference phase, to transmit binary data. Binary phase coherent PSK switches between two carrier signals, with 180° phase difference, to represent binary 0 and 1 as shown in Figure 3.4. *N*-ary phase coherent PSK may be used to switch between *N* phase shift values in high-speed modems.

Binary differential PSK or DPSK uses a phase shift of ± 90° relative to the previous bit to indicate binary 0 or 1 respectively. A four-phase DPSK system transmits dibits using 45° for 00, 135° for 01, 225° for 11, and 315° for 10, as shown in Figure 3.5. Phase modulation requires synchronous data transmission to provide a phase reference and is extensively used by synchronous modems at 1.2, 2.4 and 4.8 kbit/s per second.

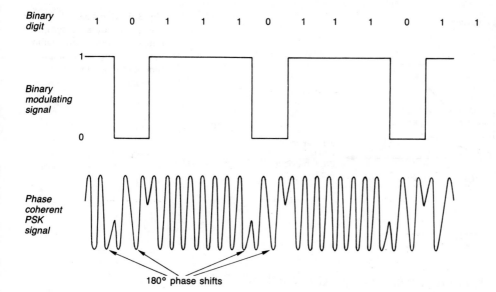

Binary digit 1 0 1 1 1 0 1 1 1 0 1 1

Binary modulating signal

Phase coherent PSK signal

180° phase shifts

Fig. 3.4 Binary phase coherent phase shift keying (PSK)

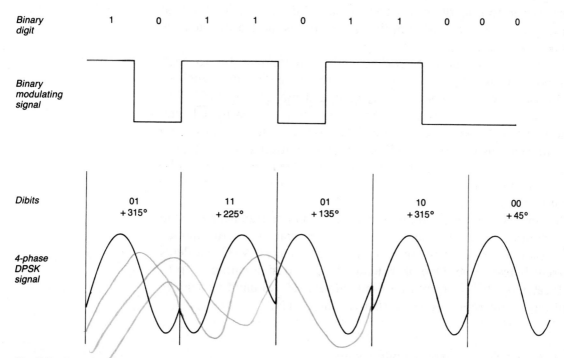

Binary digit 1 0 1 1 0 1 1 0 0 0

Binary modulating signal

Dibits

| 01 | 11 | 01 | 10 | 00 |
| +315° | +225° | +135° | +315° | +45° |

4-phase DPSK signal

Fig. 3.5 Four-phase differential phase shift keying (DPSK)

67

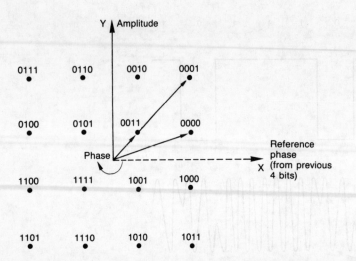

Quadrature amplitude modulation (QAM) combines PSK with amplitude modulation to transmit tribits or 3-bit symbols in high-speed modems operating at 2.4, 4.8 and 9.6 kbit/s. Figure 3.6 shows the symbols which may be transmitted by a 16-symbol phase and amplitude keying system. Quadrature amplitude modulation is used in high-speed modems because phase shift keying is limited by the ability of the receiver to discern the difference between phases which are received too rapidly or are too similar. PSK reaches its practical limits at 4.8 kbit/s and amplitude keying is added to achieve 9.6 kbit/s.

Trellis or convolutional coding adds a redundant bit to each symbol; it is used by the receiver to increase the effective signal-to-noise ratio. V.32 modems use trellis coded modulation (TCM) to increase noise immunity at 9.6 kbit/s on the public switched telephone network. At 9.6 kbit/s the V.32 modem transmits thirty-two five-bit symbols with trellis coding but for operation at 4.8 kbit/s the trellis coding is eliminated by transmitting sixteen four-bit symbols. Trellis coding is also used in the V.33 modem which operates at 14.4 kbit/s over leased lines.

To implement trellis coding, high-performance signal processors are required. The combined use of echo cancellation for full-duplex operation over a two-wire PSTN circuit makes V.32 modems extremely expensive. One proprietary modem design employs up to 512 carriers, each transmitting 6-bit symbols at 7.6 baud to achieve full-duplex operation at 18 kbit/s over the PSTN.

3.1.3 Single sideband transmission

When a carrier of frequency f_c is amplitude-modulated by a

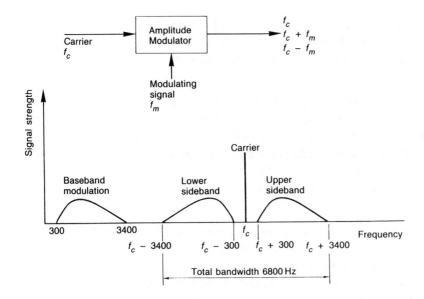

Fig. 3.7 Sidebands produced by amplitude modulating a carrier f_c with a modulating frequency f_m

sinusoidal modulating frequency f_m, the modulated carrier wave contains three frequencies:

1) The original carrier f_c.
2) The sum of the carrier and the modulating frequency $(f_c + f_m)$.
3) The difference between the carrier and the modulating frequency $(f_c - f_m)$ (see Figure 3.7).

The transmitted signal consists of the carrier frequency and two sidebands. The upper sideband of a 300 to 3400 Hz audio channel extends from $(f_c + 300)$ Hz to $(f_c + 3400)$ Hz and the lower sideband is an inverted image of the upper sideband extending from $(f_c - 300)$ Hz to $(f_c - 3400)$ Hz. The total bandwidth of the modulated carrier is $2f_m$ or 6800 Hz for 300 to 3400 Hz modulation.

The total bandwidth required for an amplitude modulated signal is more than is necessary to transmit the modulation because the information is repeated in the second sideband and the carrier transmits no information. Single sideband transmission (SSB) suppresses both the carrier and one sideband to give a bandwidth which is equal to the modulation frequency range. SSB is used for long-distance HF communication and in multichannel frequency division multiplexed trunk links.

3.1.4 Baseband coding

Baseband transmission, without a modulated carrier, is used by line drivers, local serial interfaces and many local area networks. The digital waveform is called a *non-return to zero* (level) or NRZ-L waveform where binary one is represented by one level and binary zero is represented by another level. If the NRZ waveform is directly applied to the transmission medium a number of problems may be encountered:

a) No clock data is available for synchronisation unless a separate clock channel is used; therefore only asynchronous characters with start and stop bits may be transmitted.

b) A direct current path must exist between the transmitter and receiver to transmit any sequence of 1 and 0 bits.

c) Channel noise, which is greatest at low frequencies, cannot be filtered out.

To overcome these problems, data coding techniques are employed. The most popular data coding technique is known as Manchester II. Figure 3.8 shows the Manchester II waveform which corresponds to a binary, non-return to zero (level) sequence. A transition from a high to low voltage in the middle of the bit period designates a binary 1 and a transition from low to high in the middle of the bit period designates a binary 0.

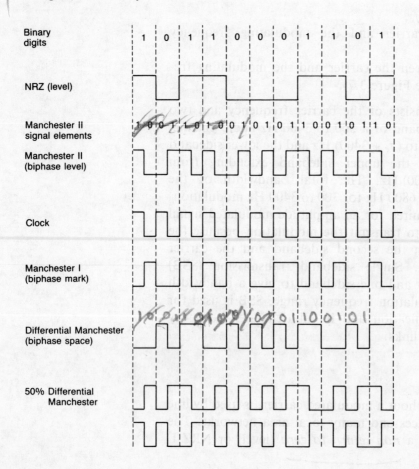

Fig. 3.8 Manchester coding waveforms corresponding to a binary NRZ-L sequence

70

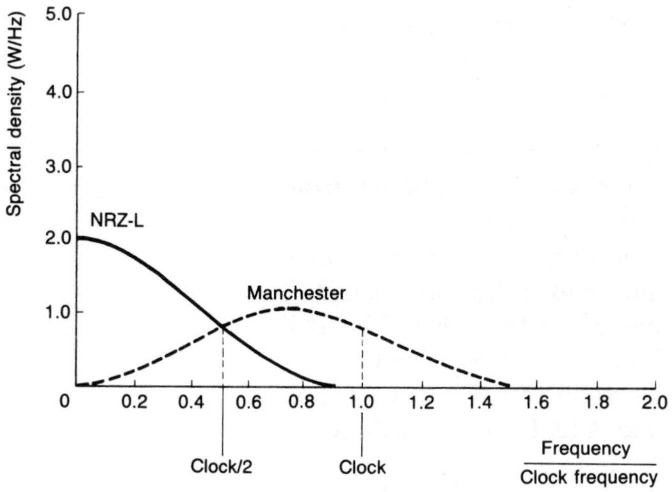

Fig. 3.9 Transmitted power spectrum for NRZ-L and Manchester coded signals

As shown in Figure 3.9, the transmitted power of NRZ-L is in the frequency range from 0 Hz to half of the clock frequency. The transmitted power of Manchester code is from half the clock frequency to the clock frequency. This permits the low-frequency noise in the channel to be filtered out, thus improving the signal-to-noise ratio.

The clock signal required to reconstruct the NRZ data stream corresponding to a synchronous transmission may be obtained from the Manchester data stream because each bit period has at least one transition. This absence of sequences of bit periods without signal level transitions makes it unnecessary to have a direct current transmission path and the communicating devices may be transformer coupled to provide a high degree of isolation from voltages which may be applied to the link or differences in ground potentials at the ends of the link.

The disadvantages of using Manchester encoding are:

a) Encoding and decoding circuitry is required.
b) The channel bandwidth is twice that required for NRZ transmission.

As shown in Figure 3.8, there are several variations of Manchester coding. One, known as differential Manchester, has all the advantages of Manchester II code but unlike Manchester II it is not affected by reversing the polarity of the wires. 50% differential Manchester code has a transition in the middle of each bit period with a second transition at the beginning of a zero-bit period; no second transition occurs at the beginning of a one-bit period. This form of encoding is employed in IEEE 802.5.

71

3.2 Modems

3.2.1 Modem standards

It is essential that modems conform to international standards because modems operating at the same speed, purchased from different manufacturers, must work with each other.

The international standardisation authority is the Consultative Committee on International Telegraphy and Telephony (CCITT) who have drawn up standards for modems since 1964. The Bell standards are widely used in the USA but following the divestiture of Bell, the American Telephone and Telegraph (AT&T) Corporation has reduced powers to set standards and AT&T now contributes to and adopts CCITT standards.

The most popular low-speed full-duplex modem standard was the AT&T 103 with its CCITT counterpart, V.21. Both standards support 300 bit/s transmission but the two standards are incompatible. The problem of incompatibility has been partly overcome for 1200 bit/s modems. The AT&T 212A modem is compatible with the CCITT V.22 modem only if the 212A modem initiates the call. The CCITT V.22 bis standard for 2400 bit/s modems has been adopted by AT&T in the 2224 range but problems arise because fallback to V.22 for 1200 bit/s is called up in V.22 bis and this is not compatible with the AT&T 212A modem. Some 1200 bit/s modems on sale in the USA offer both 212A and V.22 compatibility.

Table 3.1 compares the more popular modem standards adopted by the CCITT and AT&T. Asynchronous modems generally work at

Table 3.1 Comparison of popular CCITT and AT&T modem standards (see p. 73)

KEY	
SYNC	Synchronous
ASYNC	Asynchronous
FDM	Frequency Division Multiplexed
ECT	Echo Cancellation Technique
FSK	Frequency Shift Keying
DPSK	Differential Phase Shift Keying
QAM	Quadrature Amplitude Modulation
bis	Second version of the standard
ter	Third version of the standard
TCM	Trellis-Coded Modulation

In addition to the standards listed in Table 3.1 there are additional CCITT and EIA standards for the interface between the computer or terminal (Data Terminal Equipment, DTE) and the modem (Data Circuit-terminating Equipment, DCE). Most modems use the US Electronic Industries Association (EIA) RS-232-C interface standard or the CCITT equivalent V.24 with V.28 specifying the voltage levels. More recent interface standards are RS-449 and X.21 which permit higher-speed operation than RS-232 and longer cables between the DTE and DCE. Where a parallel interface for an automatic calling unit is required, the RS-366-A interface may be used but it is becoming common to use a serial RS-232-C input.

CCITT recommendation	AT&T equiv.	Data rate (bit/s)	Full/half duplex	Two/four wire	Modulation	Application
V.21	103J/113D	200(V.21) 300 (103) ASYNC	FULL (FDM)	TWO	FSK	Dial-up lines
V.22	212A	1200 SYNC/ ASYNC	FULL (FDM)	TWO	DPSK	Dial-up lines
V.22 bis		2400 SYNC/ ASYNC	FULL (FDM)		QAM	Dial-up lines
V.23	202	1200 or 600 SYNC/ ASYNC	FULL (202), HALF	FOUR TWO	FSK	Dial-up lines
V.26	201B	2400 SYNC	FULL (ECT)	FOUR	DPSK	Leased lines (multipoint V.26)
V.26 bis	201C	2400 or 1200 SYNC	HALF (FULL V.26 ter)	TWO	DPSK	Dial-up lines
V.27	208A	4800 SYNC	FULL HALF	FOUR TWO	DPM	Leased lines (multipoint V.27)
V.27 bis	208A	4800 or 2400 SYNC	FULL HALF	FOUR TWO	DPM	Leased lines multipoint
V.27 ter	208B	4800 or 2400 SYNC	HALF	TWO	DPM	Dial-up lines
V.29	209	9600 SYNC	FULL HALF	FOUR TWO	QAM, 16 point	Leased lines multipoint
V.32		9600 or 4800 SYNC	FULL (ECT)	TWO	TCM, 32 point at 9.6 kbit/s, 16 point at of 4.8 kbit/s	Dial-up lines
V.33		14 400 SYNC	FULL HALF	FOUR TWO	TCM	Leased lines
V.35		48 000 SYNC				60 to 108 kHz group band lines

any data rate up to the specified maximum but synchronous modems work only at specified data rates.

3.2.2 Simplex/half-duplex/full-duplex operation

Simplex operation limits one modem to transmission only and the modem at the other end of the link to reception only. A single pair of wires, known as a two-wire circuit, is adequate because no return data is involved. For half-duplex operation a two-wire circuit is used but only one modem transmits at a time and, each time the transmitting modem switches to receive, a cumbersome and time-consuming line turnaround is required. Line turnaround time can considerably reduce the throughput of a link, particularly when the protocol requires an acknowledgement for each block of data.

To reduce the overhead introduced by line turnarounds for acknowledgements, some modems provide a reverse or secondary channel which takes a small proportion of the channel bandwidth to provide a low data rate full-duplex data path for acknowledgements and control information. Figure 3.10 shows the use of a secondary channel (with a 387 Hz carrier) and a main half-duplex channel (with 1200 and 2200 Hz FSK carriers) in the 202 modem.

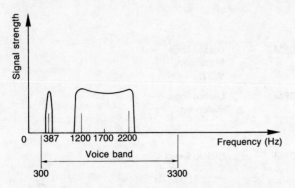

Fig. 3.10 Frequency spectrum for a 202 modem which has a half-duplex main channel and a low data rate secondary channel on a two-wire circuit

Full-duplex operation permits simultaneous transmission of data in both directions using two pairs of wires (a four-wire circuit) or by frequency division multiplexing the bandwidth of a two-wire circuit as shown in Figure 3.11. The 103/113 modems use two FDM sub-channels to give 300 bit/s full-duplex transmission on a two-wire circuit. More advanced modems, such as V.32, use an echo cancellation technique to provide full-duplex operation on a two-wire dial-up circuit.

Echo cancellation uses extensive signal processing to isolate the signal received from a remote modem by subtracting interference caused by the local modem's simultaneous transmission as well as low-power reflections (talker and listener echoes). Echoes are detected from their time delay in relation to the main received signal.

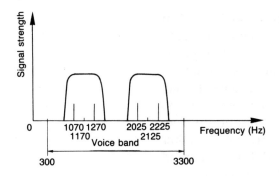

Fig. 3.11 Frequency spectrum for a 103/113 modem which provides full-duplex operation on a two-wire circuit by frequency division multiplexing

The delay is typically between one and 40 ms but this increases to as much as 500 ms for satellite links.

3.2.3 Line conditioning

Analog telephone lines using twisted-pair cable do not have flat characteristics for attenuation and envelope delay over the bandwidth of the channel. Figure 3.12 shows the attenuation and Figure 3.13 shows the envelope delay variation over the audio band for a typical unequalised line. Attenuation and envelope delay distortion increases at frequencies above and below the centre frequency. Inductors and capacitors may be added to lines in order to give a flatter response but lines with this equalisation have higher rental costs.

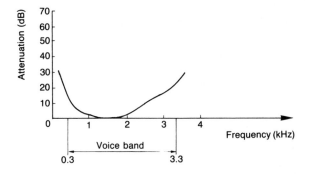

Fig. 3.12 Attenuation changes over the voice band of an unequalised twisted-pair cable

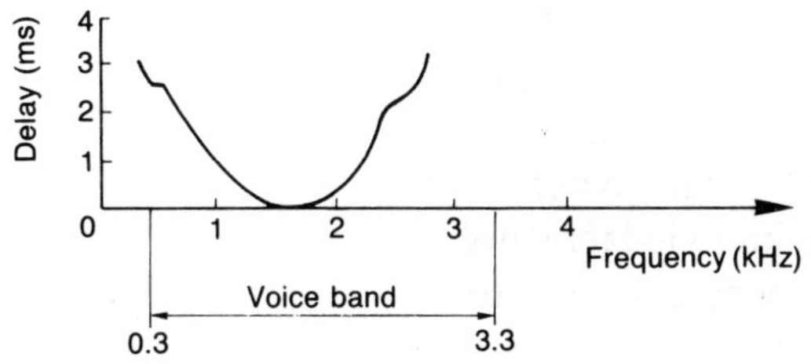

Fig. 3.13 Envelope delay changes over the voice band of an unequalised twisted-pair cable

The public switched telephone network generally suffers from considerable variations in attenuation and envelope delay depending upon the circuits used for a particular call. This is not a problem for voice applications but requires some form of equalisation within the modem at data rates above 2400 bit/s. Fixed-value components may be used within a modem to equalise attenuation and envelope delay. This fixed equalisation or manually adjustable equalisation is adequate for use with relatively slow modems on private lines but automatically adaptive equalisers should be used for high-speed modems or modems on the public switched telephone network.

Automatically adapting equalisers have the advantage of ensuring optimum error rates but they introduce a training time of about 50 ms which occurs before full-duplex operation is possible. This delay becomes a source of inefficiency in polled multipoint systems which have several modems connected to a joined set of lines. Automatic adaptive equalisers sample the line many times per second to determine which parts of the frequency band need enhancement. Modems employing forward compensation perform equalisation before they transmit.

To cancel out the envelope delay variations which cause inter-symbol interference, an automatic equaliser may take the form of an adaptive digital filter. The Mjeller and Spaulding scheme for cyclic equalisation typically achieves equalisation within one or two symbol periods. In this scheme, an equaliser delay line tap is initially set to equal the training period. Once a steady state has been reached using a special training message, the adaptive equalisation is performed by disconnecting the input to the equaliser and cyclically shifting the information contained in the delay line according to a search algorithm until it gives the best match with a local reference store which contains the transmitted training sequence. Once equalisation has been achieved, the equaliser is reconnected to the line and detection takes place using the estimated reference tap position on the delay line.

Limited-distance modems, which transmit baseband data, do not use internal equalisers but they do require a line which has had the loading coils (or other compensation facilities which improve voice transmission) removed. Limited-distance devices do not therefore suffer from training time before full-duplex operation is possible but the line turnaround time (included in the RTS to CTS delay parameter), includes data synchronisation time when synchronous operation is employed. Half-duplex turnaround time, the time required to reverse the direction of transmission and obtain synchronisation, is an important modem parameter when acknowledgements are required and is the counterpart of training time which applies to full-duplex operation.

3.2.4 Calling mode and automatic calling units

Modems may be required to originate or to answer calls on the public switched telephone network. By supporting only the calling or the answer mode, the price of a modem may be reduced but many modems which support both modes and manual or automatic call origination are available at low cost. Central sites which accept calls from remote terminals operate in answer mode while the remote terminals operate in originate mode.

Automatic answering is required for unattended operation on the public switched telephone network. The auto-answer facility performs the equivalent function to picking up the telephone handset to answer the call and closing the hook switch when the call is terminated.

Automatic calling units may be used with a modem which does not have an internal automatic dial facility. Units are available for use with the European dial pulse system or the US touch tone (DTMF) dial system. Some automatic calling units will control more than one modem. The interface to the host computer which generates the number to be called may be either parallel (RS-366-A) or a serial RS-232-C interface which permits remote connection of the automatic calling units through a modem.

3.2.5 Setting up a call

Before two Data Terminal Equipments (DTEs) can communicate, both DTEs must set up a call with the associated modems and the modems must set up the call between themselves using a handshaking procedure. The procedure varies between modems on private lines and those on the public network but there are strong similarities. Figure 3.14 shows the sequence of control signal handshakes for a call on the public switched telephone network using a V.24 interface. Many subsets of the control signals are used for particular applications.

The sequence of operations commences with Date Terminal Ready (DTR) of the call-receiving DTE being raised to inform its modem that it is ready to receive a call. After the number has been dialled the call-receiving modem raises the Ring Indicator (RI). Because DTR is raised, the receiving modem becomes connected to the line and raises Date Set Ready (DSR).

When ready to transmit data, the DTE raises Ready To Send (RTS) which causes the modem to switch its carrier on. When the modem raises Clear To Send (CTS), data may be transmitted. The receiving modem raises Carrier Detect (CD) when the valid carrier is detected on the line and the modem has synchronised to the carrier.

The receiving DTE raises DTR to indicate that it is ready to receive data and the modem responds by raising DSR.

When the transmitting modem raises CTS, the DTE transmits data which causes modulation of the carrier from its modem. When the transmission is complete, the DTE turns RTS off and the modem switches its carrier off and lowers CTS. The receiving modem turns CD off and, if the receiving modem is ready to transmit, it raises RTS which turns on the modem carrier. The modem responds with CTS and the DTE may transmit data. To end the call the transmitting DTE lowers RTS; the modem then turns the carrier off and lowers CTS.

3.2.6 Single-chip modems

More than 70% of modems are used on the public switched telephone network at speeds up to 1200 bit/s. The use of modems on the public switched telephone network will probably continue until the ISDN era but dedicated analog lines are now being replaced by digital links, for which modems are not required. The public switched telephone network offers an ideal means of providing intermittent connections at low cost and many low-cost modems are available based upon single integrated circuits. For higher-speed data transmission on the public switched telephone network, more complex modems such as those based on the V.32 recommendation are available for operation at 9600 bit/s.

Most single-chip modems are designed to meet low-speed, FSK and DPSK modem standards such as V.21, V.22, or V.23. The use of single-chip or single-board modems within the DTE makes a separate modem box and RS-232 interface cable unnecessary. The modem may be accommodated within the computer but it is necessary to get approval from the local telephone company or licensing authority before any new equipment may be connected to the public switched telephone network.

Early single-chip modems were capable of 300 or 600 bit/s operation and were priced relatively high. For this reason, single-board modems were often used but chips are now available at lower prices and for operation at 1200 and 2400 bit/s with 4800 and 9600 bit/s chips in design.

Many single-chip modems require additional chips or modules for filters but others include all the required circuitry except a phone line interface and an RS-232-C level converter chip. Figure 3.15 shows the main elements of the Silicon Systems K212/RCA CD 22212 CMOS chip which interfaces with the DTE by a serial interface or an 8-bit parallel address/data bus.

The CD 22212 complies with the AT&T 103 and 212A modem

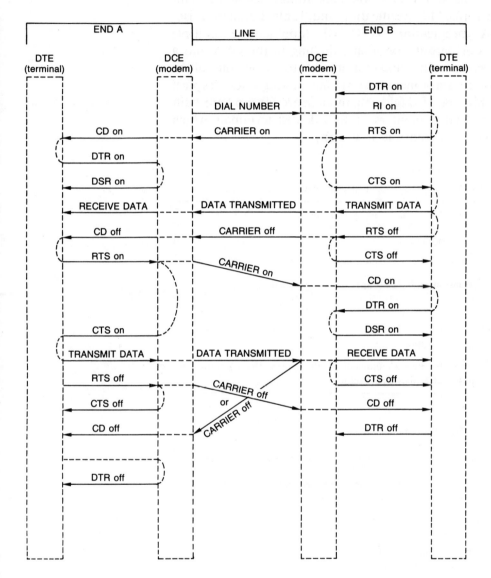

Fig. 3.14 The sequence of
control signal handshakes
for modems with V.24
interfaces on the public
switched telephone network

requirements with a full-duplex 1200 bit/s DPSK main channel and 300 bit/s FSK fallback channel. A later version will be compatible with the CCITT V.22 and V.21 recommendations. Table 3.2 summarises the AT&T 103/113 specification and Table 3.3 summarises the AT&T 212A specification. A DTMF (double-tone multiple frequency) generator permits automatic dialling in the USA and a call-progress detection facility makes it possible to change the calling action in response to dial tones, busy signals or ring back. Typical applications for this type of single-chip modem are for modems built into portable, personal computers or in videotex terminals which receive at 1200 bit/s and transmit at 300 bit/s.

Table 3.2 Summary of AT&T 103/113 modem specification

Data link	*Serial, binary, asynchronous, full-duplex*
Transmission rate	0 to 300 bit/s
Modulation	Frequency shift keying (FSK)
Frequency assignment (for originating and receiving ends)	Transmit at 1070 Hz space, 1270 Hz mark Receive at 2025 Hz space, 2225 Hz mark.
Transmission level	0 to − 12 dBm
Reception level	0 to − 50 dBm, simultaneous with adjacent channel transmitter at as much as 0 dBm

Table 3.3 Summary of AT&T 212A modem specification

Data link	*Serial, binary, asynchronous or synchronous, full-duplex*
Transmission rate	1200 bit/s asynchronous or synchronous; 0 to 300 bit/s asynchronous (fallback)
Modulation	Dibit phase shift keying at 1200 bit/s Frequency shift keying at 300 bit/s
Frequency assignment (for originating and receiving ends)	Transmit at 1200 Hz Receive at 2400 Hz
Phase shift	Dibit 00 = 90° Dibit 01 = 0° Dibit 10 = 180° Dibit 11 = 270°
FSK frequency (for originating and receiving ends)	Transmit at 1070 Hz space, 1270 Hz mark Receive at 2025 Hz space, 2225 Hz mark

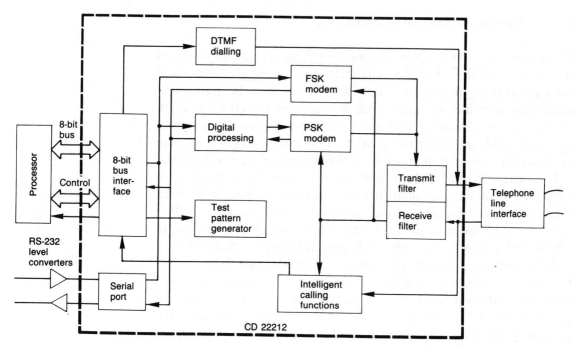

Fig. 3.15 The main elements of a single chip modem

3.3 Multiplexing alternatives

3.3.1 Introduction

Long-distance communications channels and local cable networks are expensive to install or to rent. In order to minimise the cost of communications bearers, various means of sharing a communications channel between several users have been devised; these are known as multiplexing and data concentration techniques.

Multiplexing is a technique for sharing a common channel between several users. Alternative multiplexing techniques include: frequency division multiplexing (FDM), wavelength division multiplexing (WDM, for fibre optics), time division multiplexing (TDM), and code division multiplexing (CDM). CDM includes frequency hopping and spread spectrum techniques for transmitting several digital channels simultaneously over a bandwidth which is greater than the individual channel bandwidths.

A data concentrator is a computer which accepts digital information from several sources and outputs it on lower-speed lines or a smaller number of high-speed lines. Statistical multiplexers may be classed as concentrators.

3.3.2 Frequency division multiplexing

Frequency division multiplexing uses several radio frequency carriers to transmit analog or digital channels down a single broadband coaxial cable or microwave link. The carriers may be frequency, amplitude or phase modulated, using analog or digital data. If an adequate channel spacing is adopted, each channel is independent of the others and, in broadband local area networks, frequencies may be allocated to provide point-to-point links or multi-access channels.

Frequency division multiplexing has been used for long-distance telephone trunk links for many decades and until recently it has been used as the most common means of multiplexing data on satellite links. Long-distance telephony trunks use twelve channel groups in which twelve analog voice channels are amplitude modulated on a series of carriers to occupy a bandwidth of 48 kHz (see Figure 3.16). By using a balanced modulator, the carrier is suppressed. The resulting double sideband signal is passed to a filter which selects the lower sideband for mixing with 11 other channels to produce the frequency spectrum for the group of 12 channels as shown in Figure 3.17.

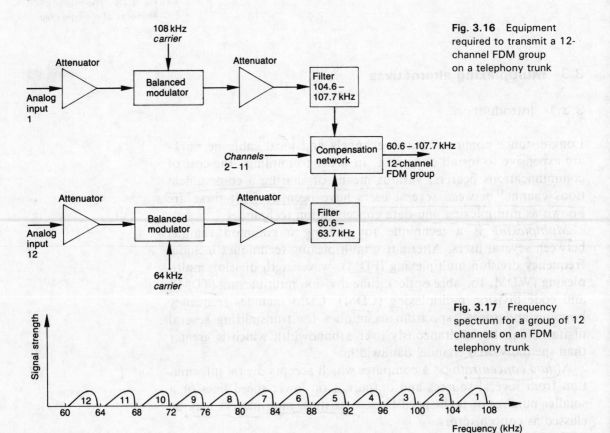

Fig. 3.16 Equipment required to transmit a 12-channel FDM group on a telephony trunk

Fig. 3.17 Frequency spectrum for a group of 12 channels on an FDM telephony trunk

The 12-channel group may be used as a building block to construct 60-channel supergroups; five supergroups may be combined to form a 300-channel mastergroup; and three mastergroups may be combined to form a 3872 kHz bandwidth super-mastergroup; or alternatively 15 supergroups may be combined to form a hypergroup. The receiving end of an FDM link consists of a series of filters and demodulators which extract the groups, then the individual 300-3400 Hz voice channels.

Frequency division multiplexing is used in data-over-voice links to transmit a data channel plus an analog voice channel over one local line from a telephone outlet to the local private exchange. As shown in Figure 3.18 the voice channel may be low-pass filtered and the data modulated on a carrier at around 100 kHz which is within the bandwidth of the local distribution cables. At the local private exchange the data signal is removed by a high-pass filter and demodulator; then, in most applications, the data is directed to a central computer facility located close to the exchange.

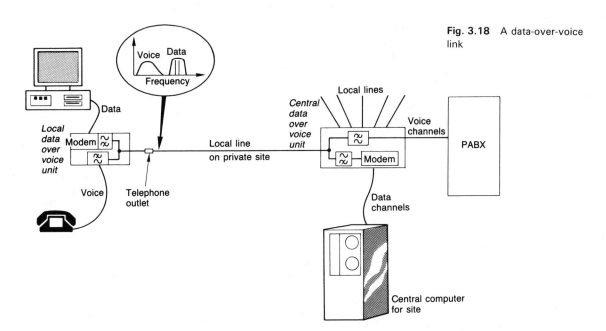

Fig. 3.18 A data-over-voice link

Broadband local area networks employ radio frequency modems to generate the FDM signals. The bandwidth of FDM channels on broadband LANs varies considerably. Low data rate modems typically provide 100 kbit/s full-duplex links with up to 40 channels accommodated per 12 MHz of the frequency spectrum. Some modems operate on a preset frequency and others may be set to the desired frequency by a network controller.

A typical high data rate modem, such as one required by a 10 Mbit/s Ethernet channel, transmits at 54 to 72 MHz and receives at 210.25 to 228.25 MHz when a single-cable system (with a frequency translator at the head end) is used (see Figure 3.19). A dual-cable broadband system using one cable for transmission and a second cable for reception would use the same frequency for transmission and reception, typically 54 to 72 MHz (see Figure 3.20).

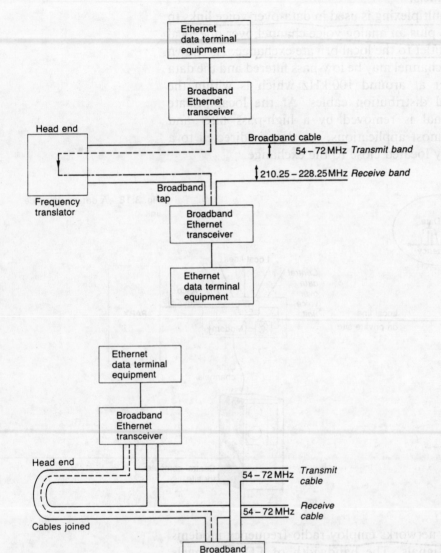

Fig. 3.19 Use of a 10 Mbit/s Ethernet modem on a single-cable broadband system

Fig. 3.20 Use of a 10 Mbit/s Ethernet modem on a dual-cable broadband system

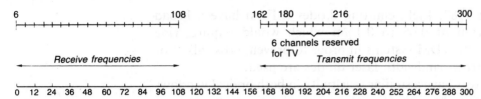

6   108   162 180   216   300

6 channels reserved
for TV

Receive frequencies   Transmit frequencies

0 12 24 36 48 60 72 84 96 108 120 132 144 156 168 180 192 204 216 228 240 252 264 276 288 300

Frequency (MHz)

Fig. 3.21 IEEE 40.1 frequency standard for 6 MHz channels on a broadband cable system

Standard frequency channels have been specified for broadband community antenna television (CATV) or LAN systems. Standard 6 MHz video channels are allocated as shown in Figure 3.21 but modems for data transmission may coexist with video channels. Suitable spaces or guard bands must be provided between channels to prevent intermodulation.

Frequency division multiplexers are available for use on analog voice-grade lines linking distributed terminals. By using the multi-point technique (described in 3.3.4 and 4.3.2) clusters of terminals may share a common frequency sub-channel. Typical sub-channels have a data transmission rate of 50 to 600 bit/s with several sub-channels in a channel (which could alternatively support one 9.6 kbit/s link). The major disadvantages of such frequency division multiplexers are:

a) The inefficient use made of the frequency spectrum compared with time division multiplexers.

b) The limited number of channels available.

c) The relatively large size of frequency division multiplexers which typically employ a card for each frequency channel.

One advantage is that a failure in one channel is unlikely to affect other channels whereas in a TDM unit failure is likely to affect all channels.

3.3.3 Wavelength division multiplexing

Wavelength division multiplexing (WDM) is the fibre optic equivalent of frequency division multiplexing but using light of different wavelengths to transmit several independent channels through one fibre. The bandwidth of an optical fibre in increased by the number of additional channels and the operation of each channel is fully independent.

The development of WDM has been delayed until suitable optical sources became available. Laser diodes in the 0.8 to 0.9 μm optical window have been available for many years but devices operating in the 1.2 to 1.3 μm optical window only recently became available at low cost about 1987. Light-emitting diodes (LEDs) have a broad emission spectrum of 0.05 to 0.1 μm which would require wide channel spacing in WDM systems in order to prevent crosstalk. For this reason, narrow bandwidth laser diodes are used.

Optical detectors have a similar sensitivity in both optical windows but the attenuation characteristics of optical cable limits the range of wavelengths available in the upper window to about 1.21 to 1.35 μm.

An optical multiplexer is used to combine the light from several inputs to one output for transmission and an optical demultiplexer divides received signals into the individual single-wavelength outputs.

Two types of device are available to multiplex and demultiplex WDM signals: those using filters and those using optical gratings. Figure 3.22 shows a multilayer interference filter, which reflects wavelength (a) and lets wavelength (b) pass through to combine both wavelengths in the output fibre. The filter also acts as a demultiplexer to separate wavelengths. Figure 3.23 shows a grating demultiplexer which can separate up to ten wavelengths. The grating demultiplexer has a simple structure but is useful only for systems using laser diodes.

Technology available in 1988 limits the number of wavelengths which may be used in the lower optical window to about 4, and 4 to 6 in the upper window. The limitation is caused by the spectral width and tolerances of laser diodes. Coherent optical systems are being developed using a local oscillator to modulate a laser carrier signal. The coherent detector is highly wavelength selective and may resolve up to 10 000 channels within the two optical windows. Up to 20 dB improvement in receiver sensitivity is achieved by a PSK coherent system compared with a conventional direct detection system.

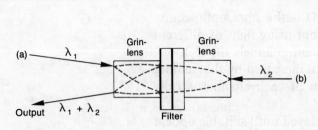

Fig. 3.22 A multilayer interference filter for wavelength division multiplexing

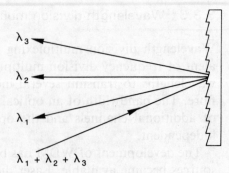

Fig. 3.23 A grating demultiplexer for WDM reception

3.3.4 Time division multiplexing

Time division multiplexing (TDM) slices up the channel data stream into time slots which are assigned to particular users (see Figure 3.24). Nonintelligent time division multiplexers assign time slots to users in a fixed sequence, wasting channel capacity if a user has no data to transmit, but intelligent (statistical) TDM systems use more complex algorithms to allocate time slots to users (see Figure 3.25). Statistical multiplexers assign time slots according to user channel activity and, in some cases, compress the data using coding based upon character frequency.

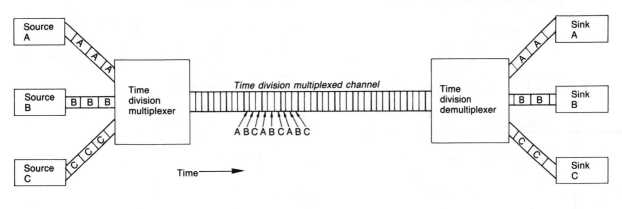

Fig. 3.24 Non-intelligent time division multiplexing

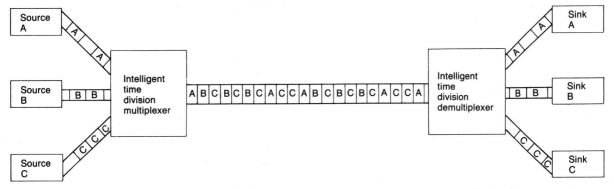

Fig. 3.25 Channel allocation in an intelligent TDM system

TDM is extensively used in telephone networks where voice channels are pulse code modulated into time slots. The analog voice signal is sampled 8000 times per second and the amplitude is represented by an 8-bit word making the data rate of each channel 64 000 bits per second. In Europe, the A-law PCM method is used and on trunk links the voice channels are time division multiplexed in the sequence:

a)	Primary (CEPT)	30 voice channels on	2.048	Mbit/s
b)	Second order	120	on	8.448 Mbit/s
c)	Third order	480	on	34.368 Mbit/s
d)	Fourth order	1920	on	139.264 Mbit/s
e)	Fifth order	7680	on	560.000 Mbit/s

In the USA the μ-law PCM method is used and on trunk links the voice channels are time division multiplexed in the sequence:

a)	Primary (T1)	24 voice channels on	1.544	Mbit/s
b)	Second order (T2)	96	on	6.312 Mbit/s
c)	Third order (T3)	672	on	44.736 Mbit/s
d)	Fourth order (T4)	4032	on	274.176 Mbit/s

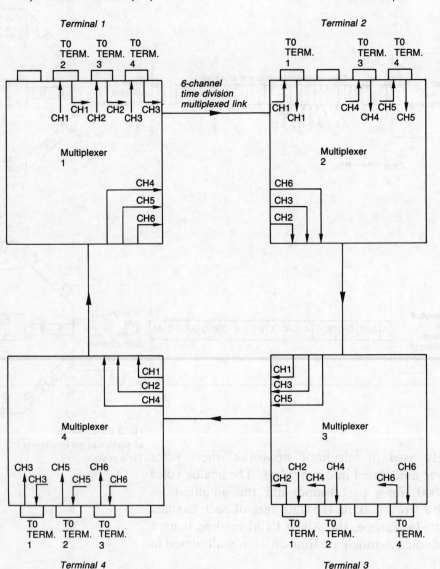

Fig. 3.26 The drop and insert method for wiring TDM channels in a ring of linked multiplexers

The availability of the 1.544 Mbit/s T1 channels to private users in the USA (under the title of the AT&T Account T 1.5 service) has made high data rate, full-duplex data transmission widely available. The equivalent service offered in the UK is the 2.048 Mbit/s BT MegaStream service which uses the CEPT frame format (G.734).

Multiplexers designed for use with T1 or CEPT channels are bit-interleaved or character-interleaved and are mostly designed to accept synchronous data at a variety of data rates from 50 bit/s upwards. Most T1 multiplexers are designed for point-to-point operation but some permit data to be routed to more than one destination by a drop-and-insert system (see Figure 3.26). A T1 TDM transmission frame consists of 192 data bits (arranged as 24 eight-bit words) and one sync bit. One word in each frame is allocated to each of the 24 TDM channels (see Figure 3.27). Many multiplexers subdivide these twenty-four 64 kbit/s channels to give a larger number of lower rate channels. Equipment which requires more than 64 kbit/s can use multiple channels.

The CEPT system uses common channel signalling. Thirty-two 8-bit words make up a CEPT frame with bit 0 used for synchronisation and bit 16 for signalling. Bits 1–15 and 17–31 provide data channels.

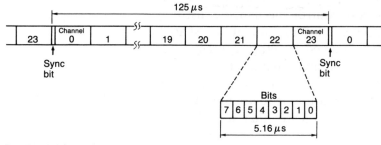

Fig. 3.27 A T1 TDM frame compared with a CEPT frame

T1 FRAME FORMAT

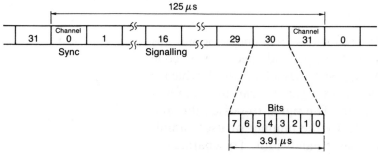

CEPT FRAME FORMAT

Fixed-time-slot TDM accepts data from each user channel in individual bits, bytes or packets by the process of interleaving. The sum of time slots from all of the users makes up a transmission frame. Frame slots (bits, bytes or packets) at the beginning and end of the user time slots in the frame are used for synchronisation of user channels at the input and output (multiplexer and demultiplexer). Frame slots are also used to identify channel loss and to give an indication of link errors.

Bit-interleaved multiplexers detect loss of synchronisation more rapidly than character-interleaved or statistical multiplexers and they provide completely transparent data channels. Only character-interleaved multiplexers are able to improve channel usage for asynchronous data by removing start and stop bits before transmission and replacing them at the demultiplexer.

Time division multiplexers may be used on any type of data transmission system including a packet switched network. Time division multiplexers are available for X.25 packet switched systems; these combine the functions of a packet-interleaved statistical multiplexer for data from several users and a packet assembler/disassembler (PAD) which is required for access to the network.

Local area networks employ a form of time division multiplexing to place data from various users on the network. The mechanisms which determine the order in which users gain access to the communications channel are referred to as access control mechanisms and are described in Chapter 4. Access control mechanisms used by terminals to access a host computer on a multipoint (or shared) communications channel may be classified as either contention or polling. In *contention mode*, each terminal attempts to send data but only the one which reaches the host first can complete its transmission. The other terminals must continue to attempt the data transmission each time the computer indicates that it is free. In *polling mode*, the central computer polls (invites transmission from) each terminal in turn. When a polled terminal has data to send, polling is suspended until the data has been transmitted.

3.3.5 Code division multiplexing

Code division multiplexing (CDM) includes frequency hopping (as employed by tactical military radio) and spread spectrum or code division multiple access (CDMA). CDMA uses a bandwidth which is much larger than that of the modulating signal to transmit data in a media with poor signal-to-noise ratio. The signal-to-noise ratio in a spread spectrum system is degraded by the number of users simultaneously transmitting data in the same bandwidth. To separate the required signal from the apparent noise on the media, a detector is used which correlates the code sequences of an internal pseudo noise sequence generator with the signals from the communications media.

By using the same pseudo noise sequence, the transmitter and receiver can operate in the same bandwidth as those using other sequences, with minimal co-channel interference. A pseudo noise sequence is modulo-2 added to the data signal to spread the bandwidth in proportion to the number of pseudo random bits which are used to modulate each data bit. This is known as *sequence inversion keying modulation*. To obtain synchronisation at the receiver, a locally generated sequence is compared with the incoming signal until the two correlate. The data signal is extracted by the receiver modulo-2 adding the received signal to the same pseudo noise sequence (see Figure 3.28). The transmitted data can only be detected by an authorised recipient in possession of the pseudo noise code sequence in a similar manner to that used in data encryption.

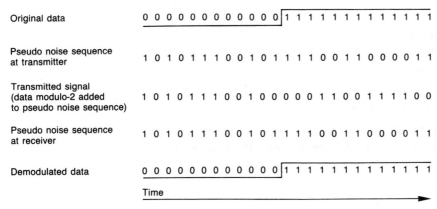

Fig. 3.28 Extraction of data from a received CDMA signal

No commercial systems based on code division multiple access are in use but experimental systems have demonstrated the ability to support up to one hundred 1 Mbit/s channels on a 100 Mbit/s bearer. Similar spread spectrum techniques are used on satellite links to reduce the effects of noise and jamming. Code division multiple access systems can support many modes including point-to-point, broadcast and node group addressing. A major advantage is that they avoid the time delay associated with access to TDM systems.

3.4 Multiplexers and concentrators

3.4.1 Background

The use of FDM for trunk connections in telephone networks became established in the early 1960s and TDM was adopted for similar purposes in the late 1960s. Private data communications on dedicated or dial-up lines used mostly a single channel per line until the 1970s but some frequency division multiplexers were available before then.

The introduction of bit- or character-interleaved time division multiplexers in the early 1970s replaced the inefficient frequency division multiplexers and made the use of multiplexers with modem links popular. To get the optimum amount of asynchronous traffic through a communications channel, statistical time division multiplexers were introduced in the 1980s, based on microprocessor technology. In addition to the multiplexing functions, intelligent statistical multiplexers provide many of the features of earlier minicomputer-based network processors and concentrators, e.g.

a) Error checking
b) Terminal management
c) Line speed selection
d) Protocol selection
e) Protocol conversion
f) Data compression
g) Collection of network statistics
h) Monitoring and line testing
i) Operation with synchronous or asynchronous links.

While modems are being made unnecessary on private lines by the introduction of digital services, multiplexers are still required and many varieties of multiplexer are available including:

a) Bit-interleaved TDM
b) Character-interleaved TDM
c) Statistical TDM with a variety of additional facilities
d) T1 multiplexers for speech and/or data
e) X.25 packet switched system TDM
f) Limited-distance multiplexers
g) Fibre optic multiplexers
h) Switching multiplexers.

T1 multiplexers have become necessary as a result of T1 time division multiplexed links being made available to the private user in 1984. X.25 packet switched systems, made available in the early 1980s, require packet assemblers/disassemblers to connect terminals into the system and X.25 multiplexers provide both statistical multiplexing and PAD functions. Multiplexing is on a packet-interleaving basis.

Limited-distance multiplexers are TDM devices used to connect local terminals to their computer communications controller. The most common type is used with IBM 3270 terminals and replaces expensive coaxial cable from each terminal to the controller. A fibre optic cable or single electrical cable, up to 3 km in length, is used to link two limited-distance multiplexers which provide up to 32 ports for local terminals. An IBM 3274 controller polls each terminal in turn without individual identification; therefore the multiplexer must add the device address to each data packet transmitted and remove the address before passing the packet to the polled device.

Fibre optic multiplexers may use time division multiplexing or wavelength division multiplexing. Bit interleaving is common because more than adequate bit rates are provided by the fibre optic link. Most fibre optic multiplexers are used over limited distances and many use a technique known as *oversampling* to avoid the need for synchronisation bits in the data stream. The use of a synchronous link to transmit asynchronous data in this way is known as *isochronous transmission*.

Switching multiplexers have facilities which permit a single terminal to access several alternative host computers and other terminals (see Figure 3.29). Facilities are included to prevent contention between terminals for a limited number of computer ports. Alternative routing, in the event of a link or computer failure, is available on the more sophisticated units. Typical capacity is over 100 RS-232 ports at 19.2 kbit/s. Switching multiplexers are commonly used in

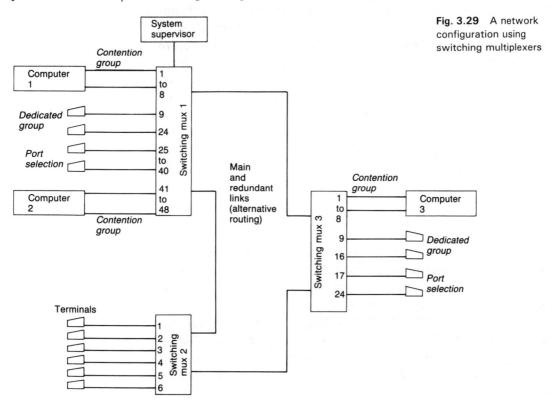

Fig. 3.29 A network configuration using switching multiplexers

distributed networks, and for this reason sophisticated monitoring and control functions are often provided.

3.4.2 Bit- and character-interleaved time division multiplexers

Bit-interleaved multiplexers accept (mostly synchronous) data from the user channels bit-by-bit. Data is transmitted transparently (control characters and all) making it possible to support any form of protocol or encryption. A fixed time slot form of synchronous transmission is commonly employed and unused channels simply transmit mark bits. Bit-interleaved multiplexers do not require large internal data buffers and consequently introduce less delay in transmission. This is a great benefit where echoplex operation is used or where each message must be acknowledged before the next message is transmitted.

Character-interleaved multiplexers take a complete character from a user channel and transmit it in serial form before taking a complete character from the next user channel. A buffer memory is therefore necessary to store characters until they are transmitted in the fixed channel frame slots. The use of this buffer memory introduces transmission delays, making character-interleaved multiplexers unsuitable for use with echoplex terminals.

Character-interleaved multiplexers are most suited to asynchronous applications where a considerable improvement in channel capacity is achieved by removing the start and stop bits before transmission and reinserting them at the demultiplexer. A problem arises when a break signal is employed by the user (this is an extended space symbol used to request disconnection from the host). The automatic insertion of a stop bit by the multiplexer inhibits the break signal. Some multiplexers add a special bit to each character indicating a control character and using a special code for break. This however makes the multiplexer more complex and reduces channel capacity.

3.4.3 Statistical multiplexers

When channel bandwidth is expensive, statistical multiplexers may be used to get the maximum amount of data through a limited bandwidth channel with the minimum delay to data from each channel. This allows more users to share a single line or more commonly permits faster operation by each user. When integrated services digital networks are available, using high-capacity digital channels, it will be less important to optimise line capacity and simple bit-interleaved or character-interleaved multiplexers may be adequate.

Statistical multiplexers are described in more detail because they are currently the most popular form of multiplexer and the use of a statistical multiplexer requires some consideration of the patterns of channel usage and whether the internal data buffer is adequate to cope with unpredictable surges in demand from the connected devices. Bit- and character-interleaved multiplexers do not require such detailed consideration for a particular application because the capacity of each user channel is constant and predictable.

Statistical multiplexers use character-interleaving and suffer from long and variable transmission delays but the microprocessor on which the unit is based is capable of performing many additional functions previously only performed by data concentrators; these include:

a) Transmission of variable-length data blocks according to the activity on individual channels.

b) Checking blocks for errors and requesting retransmission where appropriate.

c) Buffering data waiting for transmission in order to overcome peak loading effects when using a line which is capable of dealing with only the average traffic load.

d) Multipoint configurations of terminals attached to a single computer port may be supported by providing facilities for a master concentrator to poll several remote concentrators as shown in Figure 3.30. The polling may be transparent to the terminals and the host computer.

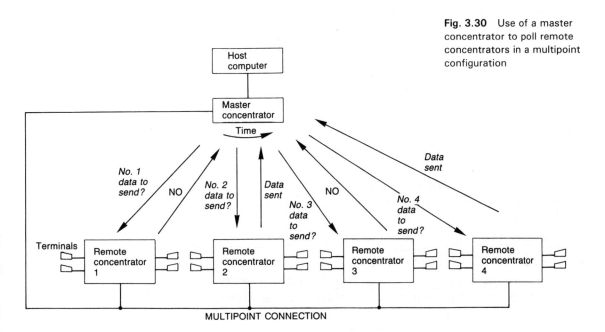

Fig. 3.30 Use of a master concentrator to poll remote concentrators in a multipoint configuration

e) Standard protocols such as X.25 level 2 (LAP-B) may be employed for use in wide area networks with gateways to local area networks.

f) Sophisticated diagnostic facilities may be incorporated.

g) Synchronous and asynchronous users may be mixed and any combination of channel speeds, character code and parity may be supported. Users with different data rates may communicate because data is buffered.

Statistical multiplexers have both transmit and receive buffers to permit storage of data waiting to be transmitted (when the outgoing link operates at a lower rate than the aggregate input rate) and to store received data until the user device is able to accept the data. To prevent loss of data when the buffers are full, flow control is used on the interfaces between the multiplexer and the users.

Two common methods of flow control are:

1) Sending X-on characters to resume data flow and X-off characters to stop data flow.

2) By turning the clear to send (RS-232-C) signal on to resume data flow and off to stop data flow.

The data transmission efficiency of a statistical multiplexer (the ratio of the aggregate slow input rates to the fast output rate, expressed as a percentage) depends on the basic design of the multiplexer, the buffer size and the error rate on the link between the multiplexers. Errors on the line cause retransmissions which slows down the rate at which data is taken from the buffers. Typical data transmission efficiency ratios are:

a) Less than 100% for bit-interleaved multiplexers.

b) A little more than 100% for character-interleaved multiplexers.

c) Up to 1000% for statistical multiplexers.

Figure 3.31 shows the main elements of a typical statistical multiplexer. The basic functions are those of a microcomputer with buffer memories and efficient DMA interfaces to the high-speed line. Communications control chips are commonly employed to implement the framing and error checking aspects of data links and some multiplexers have built-in modems to reduce the overall cost and space required.

Common additional facilities above the basic statistical multiplexer functions include:

a) Downline loading of channel options from a master multiplexer to remote multiplexers without user intervention.

b) Local and remote loopback is often provided to test the

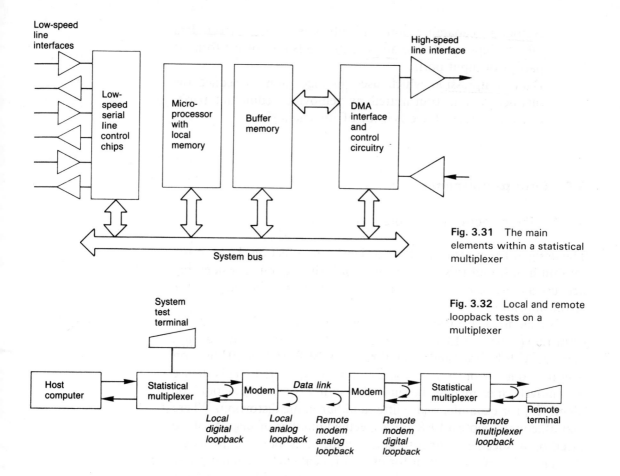

Fig. 3.31 The main elements within a statistical multiplexer

Fig. 3.32 Local and remote loopback tests on a multiplexer

operation of a channel as shown in Figure 3.32. Returned data is checked against transmitted data to detect faults. Self-test facilities are also frequently provided on power-up or at regular intervals.

c) Switching multiplexers include facilities to resolve contention for ports and to connect any terminal or device to any other on the system of local or remote multiplexers.

d) Speed conversion for channels with devices operating at different speeds.

e) Dynamic buffer allocation may be used to share available buffer space between channels and handle greater peak data rates.

f) Alternate routing to make one multiplexer take over the functions of another if any of the interconnecting lines fail.

g) Band splitting which provides two synchronous links between multiplexers. This is used when some input channels contain synchronous data from another multiplexer and avoids remultiplexing.

h) Autobaud capability automatically selects the correct data rate for input ports and autoparity selects the correct form of parity for input ports.

i) Data compression which uses an algorithm to reduce the number of bits transmitted by removing redundant parts, hence increasing the efficiency of the channel.

3.5 Error performance

3.5.1 The effect of line errors

The design of a modem can have a significant effect on the bit error rate on a link and this can influence link throughput considerably because a large proportion of transmission time may be required for retransmissions.

Most modems are stated to have a certain average bit or block error rate (BER or BLER) at a specified bit rate. (Error rates always increase with bit rate and symbol rate.) A BER of 1 in 10^5 has, on average, one error bit in 100 000 bits transmitted. This figure is relatively meaningless because the source of errors should be identified; for example, phase jitter and harmonic distortion. Where manufacturers quote a BER for a specified number-of-degrees phase jitter or a specified signal-to-noise ratio, it is possible to assess the suitability of the modem for use with a channel of similar phase jitter or signal-to-noise ratio but not a channel with both effects combined.

Most modems are unable to cope as well with the quoted sources of error if they are applied simultaneously. If the phase jitter and signal-to-noise ratio of the channel are known, one may be a more significant problem than the other and that performance figure may be given greater weight. If both sources of errors are significant, and figures are not quoted for multiple impairments, laboratory tests or field tests may be the only way to predict operational performance. Field tests may be carried out using network performance monitor facilities, or a bit error rate tester to log the resulting error rates, while the link characteristics are measured with a line test set.

Most AT&T telephone lines in the USA have less than 15° phase jitter and the worst-case noise level (excluding impulse noise) is about − 55 dB while the transmission level is about − 9 dB but this may be reduced to a − 31 dB signal by long-distance transmission. The worst expected signal-to-noise ratio on AT&T lines is therefore 24 dB. The form of modulation used in a modem has a considerable influence on the signal-to-noise ratio (SNR) which may be tolerated

Table 3.4 Typical signal-to-noise ratios for modems

Modem type	Speed (bit/s)	Modulation	Typical SNR for 1 in 10^5 BER (dB)
AT&T 103/V21	To 300	FSK	8
V.22	1200	DPSK (4 phase)	14
V.22 bis	2400	QAM (16 point)	21
V.26 ter	2400	DPSK (4 phase)	17
V.32	4800	QAM (16 point)	over 16
V.32	9600	QAM (32 point)	over 19

before the BER falls below 1 in 10^5. Typical figures are shown in Table 3.4.

From Table 3.4 it is apparent that the margin between the worst expected signal-to-noise ratio and the signal-to-noise margin which may be tolerated by the higher-speed QAM modems is quite small and when combined with phase jitter it is not unlikely that the BER will be degraded.

The occurrence of bursts of impulse noise on a channel causes additional errors which are not included in the modem manufacturer's figures relating to random background noise. Impulse noise may be caused by switching equipment on the public telephone network, atmospheric disturbances, crosstalk (caused by coupling between channels) or line dropout (short loss of signal strength). Errors at the beginning of a message may be caused by delays in equaliser adjustment when the line turns around during half-duplex operation.

3.5.2 Error rate measurement

Block error rates are measured by transmitting a test message and counting the received errors. The test message is usually a pseudo random pattern repeating after 511 or 2047 bits to ensure that all bit combinations in nine or eleven bit groups are transmitted without error. For character-oriented protocols such as Bisync, the text message should consist of typical data such as a 'Quick brown fox jumps over the lazy dog' message which contains all letters of the alphabet.

The bit error rate is calculated by dividing the number of errors received in the test period by the number of bits transmitted in that period. The test period must be long enough to build up a statistically valid figure; this is usually at least 15 minutes. The transmission of special test patterns is called out-of-service testing, but in-service measurement of bit error rates is possible using line code checking or checking a fixed pattern which is always present in the transmitted signal.

At higher data rates a single line impairment can cause more data corruption. For example: a 5 ms dropout may corrupt two bits at 300 bit/s but 24 bits will be corrupted at 9.6 kbit/s. To take account of this, block error rates are commonly quoted for high-speed links with block-oriented protocols while bit error rates are more appropriate for lower-speed links with asynchronous character-oriented protocols.

Block error rate is calculated by transmitting a block of 1000 bits of pseudo random patterns or an alphanumeric test message. Several bit errors in a block result in only one block error. A typical figure for bit error rate on dedicated lines operating between 300 bit/s and 19.2 kbit/s is about 1 in 10^5 while block error rate for lines between 2.4 and 19.2 kbit/s is typically 1 in 10^3.

The error rate is a time-varying parameter so an analysis of error distribution is desirable. CCITT recommendation G.821 sets standards for the limits and method for measuring error distribution. G.821 defines the distribution of errors for the available period on digital speech or data links (where an available period starts with ten consecutive seconds during which the BER was less than 1 in 10^3). During the available period the BER should be:

a) For lines with a BER less than 1 in 10^6: at least 90% of 10 minute intervals should have 38 or fewer errors.

b) For lines with a BER less than 1 in 10^3: at least 99.8% of 1 second intervals should have less than 64 errors.

c) For lines claimed to have zero errors: at least 92% of 1 second intervals should have zero errors.

4 Network topologies, switching and access control

4.1 Network topology and topography

4.1.1 Definition of terms

A communication network is a shared resource used to exchange information between users. A computer network is a distributed collection of computers, viewed by the user as one large computer system which allocates jobs without user intervention. A computer communication network is viewed as a collection of several computer systems from which the user can select the service required and communicate with any computer as a local user.

The ISO definition of a network is an interconnected group of nodes or stations. (*Nodes* are found at the intersection of two or more transmission paths and perform traffic switching but *stations* may attach to a single transmission path in a network.)

The logical manner in which the nodes are linked together by channels to form a network is known as the network topology. Topography is the way in which the cables, which provide channels between stations, are positioned. For the purposes of cable planning, topography is more important than topology. To illustrate the difference between topology and topography, Figure 4.1 shows a ring topology but Figure 4.2 shows a ring topology wired in a star topography.

4.1.2 Alternative topologies

Several forms of topology are used for communication networks including:

a) *Mesh networks* which have multiple message paths between nodes. (See Figure 4.3.)
b) *Star networks* which have dedicated channels between each station and the central hub. (See Figure 4.4.) All communication between stations must pass through the hub.

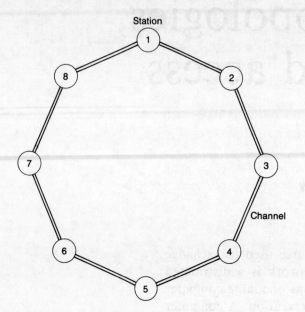

Fig. 4.1 A ring topology

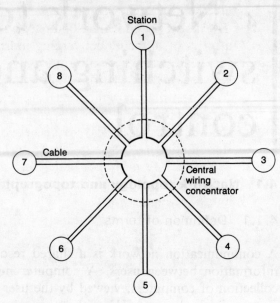

Fig. 4.2 A ring topology
wired in a star topography

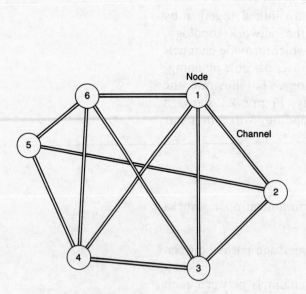

Fig. 4.3 A mesh network

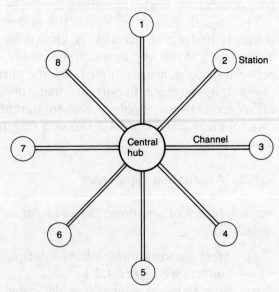

Fig. 4.4 A star network

c) *Bus networks* which have a linear topology and stations attached by taps. (See Figure 4.5.)

d) *Tree networks* which are complex bus networks consisting of a series of branches converging indirectly to a central point (or head end) and offering only one transmission path between any two stations. (See Figure 4.6.)

e) *Ring networks* in which each node is connected to its two adjacent nodes and messages are circulated around the closed ring. A *loop network* is a ring network in which one master station controls transmission. (See Figure 4.7.)

f) *Modified ring networks* which use a central ring of wiring hubs with stations connected in a star topology around each hub. (See Figure 4.8.)

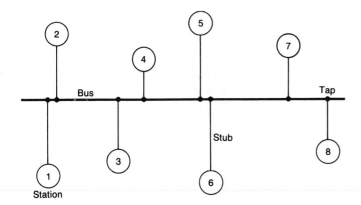

Fig. 4.5 A bus network

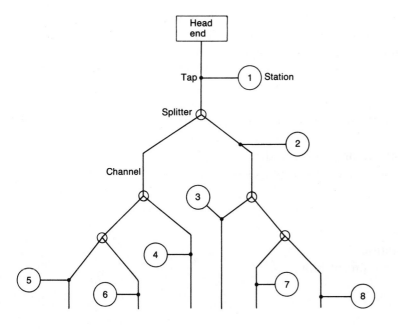

Fig. 4.6 A tree network

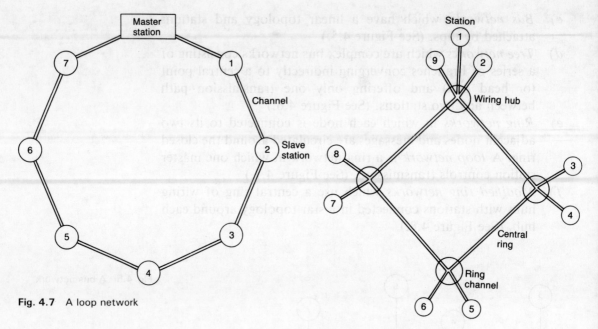

Fig. 4.7 A loop network

Fig. 4.8 A modified ring network using a central ring of wiring hubs to which stations are directly connected in a star topology

All the topologies, except mesh and star networks, generally broadcast all signals to all stations connected; the receiving station or its communications equipment must select only the signals addressed to the station from all the transmissions on the network. In mesh networks, each node inspects incoming messages or packets to establish which ones are addressed to itself; all other messages are routed on an appropriate output channel towards its destination. The central hub of a circuit switched star network routes signals received on one link to the link leading to the addressed station.

Each topology has its advantages and disadvantages; these may be evaluated in terms of:

a) Throughput
b) Maximum distance
c) Maximum number of stations
d) Vulnerability to link or equipment failure
e) Message delay
f) Cost.

104

4.1.3 Mesh networks

Mesh networks are most commonly employed for long-distance transmission of data between nodes which act as message switches, circuit switches or packet switches. A fully connected mesh linking n nodes requires $n(n-1)/2$ links but it is unusual for all the possible connections to be provided. Throughput depends upon the media and the capacity of the switching nodes. Distance may be extended indefinitely and the number of stations may increase up to the limits imposed by the maximum throughput and the size of the address field in the message header. The multiple message paths reduce vulnerability to link or node failure if suitable rerouting facilities are built into the nodes. Message delay may be high because long-distance transmission media have relatively low data rates and the throughput limitations of the nodes may result in queuing for retransmission in store-and-forward nodes. The cost of a mesh network may be optimised by eliminating redundant link capacity.

4.1.4 Star networks

Star networks are most commonly employed to connect remote and local terminals to mainframe computers and in private branch exchanges (PBXs). The throughput of computer-based star networks is constrained by the rate at which the central hub can accept messages and retransmit them if necessary. The distance covered by a star network is determined by the communication bearers; each bearer must have the full length required to link the hub to the station, unlike a mesh which may have lower total cable lengths. The number of stations may be expanded only up to the limits of expansion permitted by the central hub. The central hub is a single point of failure which may cause the entire network to fail; single cable failures affect only single stations. Message delay may be high because of throughput limitations at the central hub which causes queuing. The initial cost of a star network is high because the central hub must be installed with a margin for expansion. Incremental cost for additional stations is low up to the expansion limits of the hub.

4.1.5 Bus networks

Bus networks are used extensively for baseband local area networks, multipoint terminal clusters and military data highways. Throughput is determined by the media and the access control mechanism. Total throughput capability generally decreases as the number of stations increases. The maximum length of the cable is often low because a high bandwidth is required to support many virtual channels. New stations may be added without reconfiguring the network until the throughput and message delay limits are reached. Polled buses have a controller which is a single point of failure capable of rendering the system unserviceable. To prevent the bus cable being a point of vulnerability, dual cables are often used in military systems. Message delay in token passing buses increases with the number of stations and, in contention buses, delay increases with traffic volume. Polled systems have a delay determined by the polling sequence. Cost per station is generally lower than star networks but higher than ring networks and buses do not involve a high initial investment.

4.1.6 Tree networks

Tree networks may be formed from a number of linked linear buses but are most commonly employed by broadband local area networks which have a branching tree topology converging at a head end. Throughput of broadband tree systems is high and limited only by the bandwidth of the cable. The maximum distance covered is greater than linear buses because many branches may be linked using repeaters. Broadband systems may span several kilometres and have extremely large numbers of stations added without reconfiguring the network. The single point of vulnerability in a broadband tree is the head-end equipment which is commonly duplicated. Cable or repeater failure elsewhere in the tree removes all stations in the branches beyond the failure. Message delay in a broadband system is low when independent channels are provided by frequency division multiplexing. Cost is generally similar to linear bus systems.

4.1.7 Ring networks

The ring topology is almost exclusively used by local area networks which use token passing or slotted ring access control. Throughput is determined by the media and the capability of the repeater which is required at each node. The total length of the ring and the distance between nodes is limited but the total span is generally greater than that of a linear bus. The maximum number of nodes is limited by the system design. Each additional node involves system disruption and reduces performance. A ring is vulnerable to a single break in any link or node repeater. Dual ring systems, capable of sustaining two breaks, are available. Message delay increases as more nodes are added to the ring and is greater than for a lightly loaded bus with contention access control. The cost per node is generally lower than other topologies offering similar performance and the amount of cable required is generally less than for a star topology.

106

4.1.8 Modified rig networks

Modified ring topologies are used by the more recent ring local area networks such as IEEE 802.5 and FDDI to simplify expansion and permit less complex station interfaces. Throughput, maximum distances, maximum numbers of terminals, vulnerability and message delays are the same as for standard ring systems but the ease of expansion is improved while wiring hubs have spare connections. Less cable is required than for a star topology. Cost may be lower than for a conventional ring.

4.2 Link switching techniques

4.2.1 Analog telephone exchanges

Since the invention of the telephone in the 1870s there have been several generations of switching technology employed in analog telephone exchanges. Early manual exchanges used patching cables to link jack sockets leading to subscriber lines or trunk lines to other exchanges. The use of rotary dials (with ten finger holes) to indicate the required connection was introduced about 100 years ago. This made automatic routing of telephone circuits possible.

One of the first automatic switching devices, the Strowger switch, was invented by an American mortician who found that much of his business was lost to a rival mortician whose wife operated the local manual telephone exchange. The Strowger switch is shown in Figure 4.9. The first digit dialled causes the wiper to increment vertically over several banks of contacts depending on the number of dial pulses. The second digit dialled causes the wiper to rotate horizontally over the bank of 10 contacts selecting one output line out of

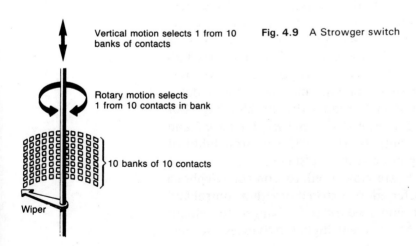

Vertical motion selects 1 from 10 banks of contacts

Rotary motion selects 1 from 10 contacts in bank

10 banks of 10 contacts

Wiper

Fig. 4.9 A Strowger switch

100. By cascading several Strowger switches a complex step-by-step circuit switching system was implemented.

The Strowger switch, and other mechanical devices in a step-by-step exchange, had moving parts which required regular cleaning and adjustment, thus making maintenance expensive. The crossbar switch, which has no moving parts (only contacts), was developed to reduce maintenance needs in exchanges. As shown in Figure 4.10, a crossbar switch has horizontal and vertical bars operated by electro-magnetic coils to select a single crosspoint which is at the intersection of the energised horizontal and vertical bars. A matrix of reed relays is a later development which further reduces the maintenance requirement but operates in a similar manner to the crossbar switch. Both these systems require control logic to decode the incoming dialling pulses and to operate the appropriate rows and columns in several crossbar or reed relay matrix switches.

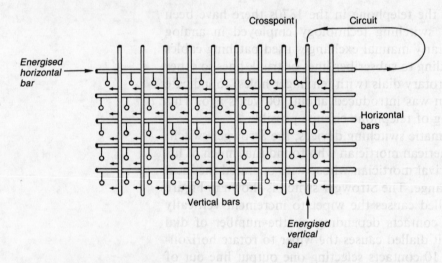

Fig. 4.10 A crossbar switch

To construct larger switching matrices, capable of handling more inputs and outputs, more switching stages are used. Most exchanges use four-stage switching but Figure 4.11 shows two-stage switching to illustrate the principle. A single crossbar or switching matrix with m inputs and n outputs requires $m \times n$ crosspoints. By switching in stages, the total number of crosspoints may be reduced but a two-stage switch results in a high probability of blocking. For example, when input $m1$ is connected to output $n2$, inputs $m2$ and $m3$ cannot be connected to outputs $n1$ or $n3$. The probability of blocking is reduced by using more switching stages.

Highly reliable computers are now used to control telephone exchange switching; this is referred to as stored program control and is used with both crossbar and reed relay exchanges for circuit switching analog channels. More recent digital exchanges use time

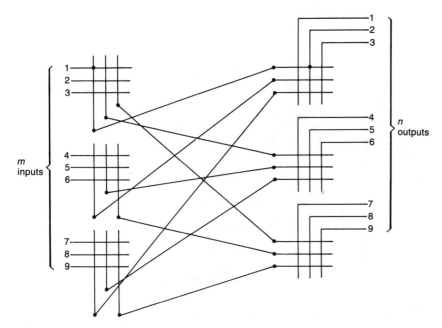

Fig. 4.11 A two-stage switching exchange

division multiplexing under stored program control. These digital exchanges use a separate digital channel or order wire to control the setting-up and supervision of all calls on a trunk cable. The CCITT sets standards for common channel interoffice signalling (CCIS). Advantages of CCIS compared with conventional signalling (which was transmitted through the voice channel) include:

- *a*)   The time to establish a call is reduced.
- *b*)   Rerouting to avoid line or equipment failures is possible.
- *c*)   Less channel capacity is required.
- *d*)   Call forwarding is possible.
- *e*)   Priority can be given to some calls.
- *f*)   Network status information is available.
- *g*)   All types of digital information may be switched.

Analog telephone signals are converted into digital signals for transmission on TDM trunk channels. The analog signal is sampled 8000 times per second and an 8-bit data word, giving signal amplitude, is transmitted in a time slot every 125 microseconds. This process is known as pulse code modulation (PCM) and is illustrated in Figure 4.12. Two different encoding laws are employed to give different analog quantization values for the 256 digital codes. The American μ-law coding law and the European A-law system cannot be directly interworked.

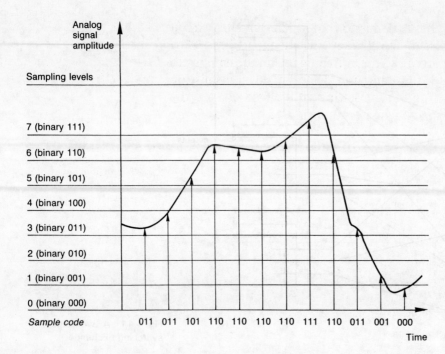

Analog
signal
amplitude

Sampling levels

7 (binary 111)

6 (binary 110)

5 (binary 101)

4 (binary 100)

3 (binary 011)

2 (binary 010)

1 (binary 001)

0 (binary 000)

Sample code   011 011 101 110 110 110 110 111 110 011 001 000

Time

Fig. 4.12 The principle of
pulse code modulation

4.2.2 Switching alternatives

Digital transmission may use dedicated links but, more commonly, a
network of links is shared by several users. There are three primary
methods of switching data from one node to any other node over a
wide area network:

1) *Circuit switching.* An end-to-end transmission path is set up
for the full duration of the call by a switching exchange. The
public switched telephone network and telex networks are
examples of circuit switching.

2) *Message switching.* Store-and-forward techniques are used at
switching exchanges to receive and acknowledge messages
from the originator, then to store these messages until
appropriate circuits are available to forward the message
to its destinations. Private and military teleprinter networks
commonly employ message switching.

3) *Packet switching.* This technique is derived from message
switching but messages are broken down into smaller
elements, known as packets, which are interleaved with
packets from other virtual channels during transmission
through the network. Packets are provided with headers
which enable the complete message to be reassembled by the
recipient.

110

Figure 4.13 compares the transmission of a message by circuit switched, message switched and packet switched networks. The message delay varies according to the switching technique employed. Circuit switching imposes the minimum delay on the transmission once the call has been set up but the setting-up time may be lengthy and it is possible that an inadequate number of circuit stages are

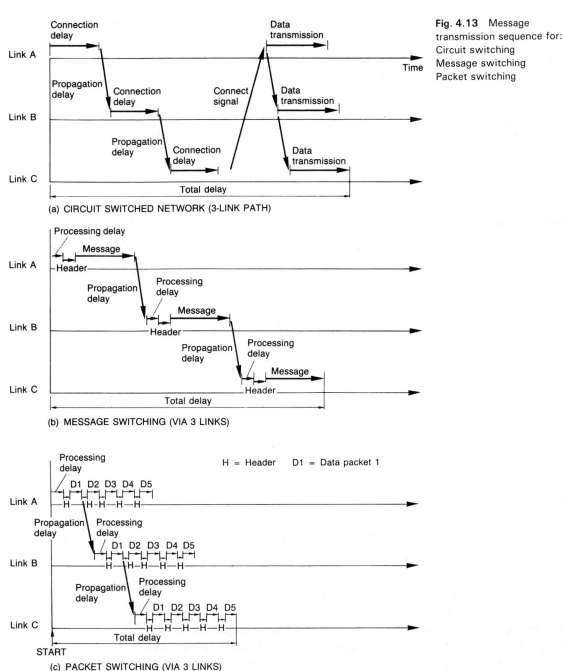

Fig. 4.13 Message transmission sequence for: Circuit switching Message switching Packet switching

(a) CIRCUIT SWITCHED NETWORK (3-LINK PATH)

(b) MESSAGE SWITCHING (VIA 3 LINKS)

(c) PACKET SWITCHING (VIA 3 LINKS)

available when required. When channels are not fully utilised, circuit switching is less efficient than the other techniques in utilising trunk capacity. No addressing data is required in messages sent by circuit switched networks which simplifies the protocol.

Message switching may introduce a long delay because the message is stored at the exchange(s) until suitable circuits are available to transmit the message to the next stage in the transmission path. Each store-and-forward stage must wait until it has received the complete message which is then relayed to the next stage.

Packet switched systems were developed in the 1960s to reduce the long delays inherent in message switching exchanges which had to store entire messages before forwarding them. Message delays are lower in packet switched systems and the trunk capacity utilisation is greater than that of circuit switched systems but the interface equipment is more complex (or an additional, expensive packet assembler/disassembler (PAD) is required). Figure 4.14 compares typical message delay versus trunk capacity utilisation characteristics for the three switching techniques.

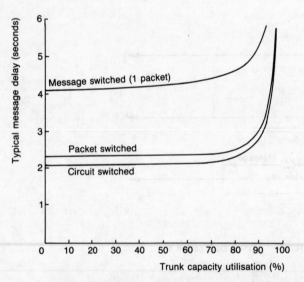

Fig. 4.14 Comparison of message delay/trunk capacity utilisation for circuit switched, message switched and packet switched networks

Assumptions: (1) Many 300 bit/s sources are connected to a 4800 bit/s link.
(2) Average message size = 60 characters, exponentially distributed and arriving with a Poisson distribution.
(3) The packet switched system interleaves data from several sources into one packet.
(4) The circuit switching link is set up in 0.1 seconds.

4.2.3 Circuit switched data transmission

The public switched telephone network (PSTN) is used primarily for temporary connections to computing facilities. Future integrated services digital networks will provide digital circuit switched links between subscribers but the present analog PSTN has many disadvantages for data communication between computers and terminals:

a) Call connection time varies between 10 seconds and several hours (when lines are busy).

b) Bandwidth is limited making high data rates (above about 4.8 kbit/s) impractical without expensive modems.

c) Line quality varies considerably in attenuation, signal-to-noise ratio, bandwidth and phase distortion.

d) Error rates vary between about 1 in 10^3 and 1 in 10^5 which is below desirable standards.

e) The only usage statistic provided is a bill at monthly or longer intervals with no detailed analysis of traffic.

f) Faulty lines may take days to be repaired.

g) Some PSTN systems inject unwanted signals onto the line which causes data corruption.

Private circuit switched networks may be constructed using switching multiplexers or digital private branch exchanges (PBXs) and dedicated digital trunk channels. Switching multiplexers are available to support about 60 subscribers and these can be upgraded to form a network supporting over 25 000 subscribers. Figure 4.15 shows a typical circuit switched digital network using switching

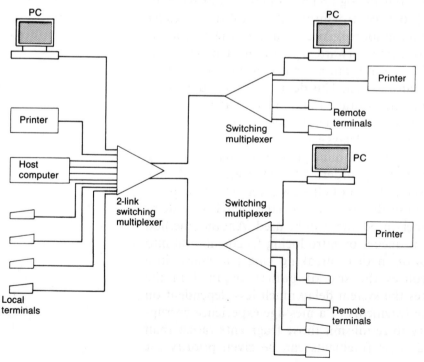

Fig. 4.15 A circuit switched data network using switching multiplexers

multiplexers to connect local and remote terminals to a host computer. Some switching multiplexers and digital exchanges will also support the transfer of data between personal computers and a mainframe computer.

Switching multiplexers transfer data in small segments (typically characters) which contain no address data; therefore a separate signalling channel is commonly employed to set up the circuits. The advantages of circuit switched systems are:

a) The data channel is transparent to protocols used between matched source and destination pairs.

b) The lowest possible network transport delay is encountered.

Because no particular protocol is employed, there is no error detection and correction capability unless this is added at the source and destination. The network is also unable to detect when the link is idle, and therefore trunk capacity utilisation may be low. Hybrid circuit switched systems with packet transport protocols are available to overcome these disadvantages.

4.2.4 Message switched data transmission

In the early 1960s message switching was introduced to make more efficient use of expensive data links and to overcome the problems of data communication over the analog PSTN. A message, or block of data, has an address and some control information added in a header before transmission from the source. At each intermediate node the message is stored before being forwarded to the next node or the destination. To keep the line utilisation high, messages are queued until it is their turn for transmission. This demanded computers with disk storage because the total storage requirement was larger than main memory could support; consequently delays were introduced by the storage system. Message delays were between a few seconds and half an hour or more and it was quite possible for parts of a long message to arrive in the wrong order. Lost messages could take several minutes to recover and a lot of effort was required to manage such systems. To minimise delays in a message switched system, shorter messages or higher-speed lines can be used. Another method is to reduce the length of queues by introducing fragmentation into the system. *Fragmentation* involves breaking longer messages into small pieces which reduces the size of buffers required in the computers, and it makes the system delay much less dependent on message length. If some fragments of a message experience corruption, it is only necessary to retransmit those fragments rather than the whole message and some fragments can be given priority for transmission. The major disadvantages of message fragmentation are:

a) Processing and control procedures are more complex.
b) Transmission overhead is increased because each fragment requires an address and control header.

4.2.5 Packet switched systems

Packet switching was introduced to overcome the problems of analog circuit switching and message switching. In fact, it uses the principle of fragmented message switching but calls the fragments packets. One of the first packet switched systems was Arpanet and this was followed by several other systems, including the French Cyclades network, each using different protocols and interface standards. A major step forward was made in 1976 when CCITT published the X.25 access protocol and interface standard for packet switched systems. This made it possible, in principle, for a piece of equipment to be connected to any network which supports the X.25 access protocol. The X.25 standard was modified in 1977/78 and revised in 1980 and 1984.

Delay in packet switched systems is partly a function of the number of intermediate nodes in the transmission path (because each node performs the storage and retransmission of data) and partly proportional to the packet length divided by the line speed. With a 64 kbit/s line speed, the main component of delay for short packets is the number of nodes but, with long messages which must be broken into many packets, the main component of delay is packet length. For example, it may take 100 ms to send a packet containing 1000 bits of data through an eight-node network path but it may take 20 minutes to transmit a file of 100 million bits through the same network.

Figure 4.16 compares the effective bandwidth (block length/end-to-end delay) versus block length for connecting the Arpanet nodes by (1) a packet switched system, (2) a 50 kbit/s star network, (3) a fully interconnected 2.4 kbit/s network and (4) a 2 kbit/s dial-up system using the Watts public switched telephone network. Figure 4.17 compares the cost per megabit versus delay characteristics of these options for messages 1 to 10 kbits in length. This shows that for messages of 1 to 10 kbits in length the packet switched network was the best compromise between cost and performance.

Packet switched systems may employ dynamic routing which permits packets from the same message to follow different paths, thus avoiding temporary congestion and failed links. At the final switching node the packets are reassembled in the correct order

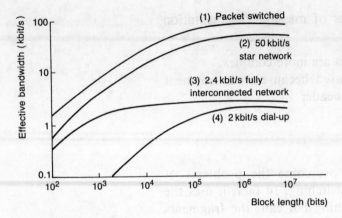
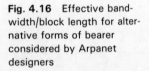

Fig. 4.16 Effective bandwidth/block length for alternative forms of bearer considered by Arpanet designers

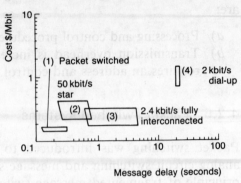

Fig. 4.17 Cost per Mbit/delay for alternative forms of bearer considered by Arpanet designers (messages are 1 to 10 kbits)

before being passed to the destination. Alternatively, packet switching systems may select a path through the network for each session, similar to circuit switching; this is known as a *virtual circuit*. Before a sequence of packets is transmitted through the network, a virtual circuit is set up. The time required to set up the routing and control tables at the entry and exit nodes is typically much less than a second, which compares with several seconds in some circuit switched networks. Speed conversion, code conversion and protocol conversion are provided by some packet switched networks but these require more processing power in the nodes.

Packet switched networks can suffer from congestion when nodes accept more packets than the outgoing links can transmit; to minimise this problem complex control schemes are required in *connection oriented* systems (in which virtual channels for a sequence of packets are set up before transmission). An alternative *connectionless* system can use a *datagram* protocol which transmits single packet messages complete with addressing data. These datagrams are sent through the minimum delay route but, if congestion occurs, the datagram may be lost. The user of a connectionless system must therefore select an appropriate datagram length, provide a mechanism to recover lost datagrams, and put received datagrams into the correct sequence.

Datagrams require more addressing and control overheads per packet. In some datagram systems the source and destination information requires over 200 bits in the packet header; this compares unfavourably with the 12-bit user session identifier in an X.25 packet following the establishment of a virtual circuit. The packets flowing along a virtual circuit are routed along the correct physical path from each node according to a virtual-circuit-to-physical-circuit map (specifying the next node on the path for each virtual circuit) which is stored in each node.

Hybrid packet-circuit switched systems may be used to combine the advantages of packet and circuit switching. The cost and complexity of a hybrid system is however greater than either packet switched or circuit switched systems and the maximum link efficiency is lower than for a circuit switched system. Technological advances will reduce the cost of equipment for hybrid systems compared with the cost of equipment for packet switched systems. Hybrid systems are expected to develop into integrated services digital networks supporting data, voice, facsimile and possibly video transmissions.

Reference 4.1 provides more information on digital communications switching.

4.2.6   Integrated services digital networks

Most of the world's telephone authorities are working towards the replacement of separate telephone, telex and data networks with a single integrated services digital network (ISDN). The ISDN will be a homogeneous network in which transmission and switching will be entirely digital, including local exchange links to subscribers. All network control, signalling and management functions will be performed by computers.

The basic digital channel in ISDN systems will be 64 kbit/s and multiples up to 2 Mbit/s. Each national telephone authority can elect to use a variation on the digital subscriber interface. The CCITT published recommendations for user-network interface standards in 1984; these consist of the I.420 basic interface for subscribers and I.421 primary rate user-network interface standards for PABX and LAN connection. I.420 defines an interface with

a)   Two 64 kbit/s B channels and
b)   One 16 kbit/s D channel.

The B channel is a circuit switched connection capable of carrying digital information from a variety of devices. The D channel is primarily used for signalling but it may also be used to transfer management data and X.25 packet switched data from user devices. The I.421 standard, layer 1, defines the time division multiplexed channels employed in the USA and Europe. In the USA:

a) Twenty-three 64 kbit/s B channels and one 64 kbit/s D channel, or

b) Twenty-four 64 kbit/s B channels and non-associated signalling.

In Europe:

a) Thirty 64 kbit/s B channels and

b) One 64 kbit/s D channel.

(A list of the I series recommendations is given on pages 412–414.) Other aspects covered by the I series recommendations include:

a) I.100 series (*General*) which defines the terminology, modelling methods, evolution, and gives a description of ISDNs.

b) I.200 series (*Service capabilities*) which defines bearer services and teleservices.

c) I.300 series (*Overall network aspects and functions*) which defines: network principles, reference models, numbering, addressing and routing, connection types and performance objectives for circuit and packet switched connections.

d) I.400 series (*User-network interfaces*) which defines the reference configurations, channel structures, access capabilities and applications of basic and primary rate interfaces:

> Layer 1 defines the basic and primary rate interfaces.
> Layer 2 defines the link access protocol on channel D (LAP-D).
> Layer 3 defines the coordinated use of the B channels, multiplexing and support of earlier CCITT interface standards.

e) I.500 series (*Internetwork interfaces*) defines international internetwork interfaces. It is intended that international connections between ISDNs will be provided.

f) I.600 series (*Maintenance principles*).

The user-network interface reference model shown in Figure 4.18 designates various points at which physical interfaces may be provided to an ISDN. The functional groupings are:

a) NT1 (network termination 1) which is equivalent to layer 1 of the OSI reference model (the physical interface) and specifies contention resolution for multipoint connections.

b) NT2 which is equivalent to layers 1, 2 and 3 of the OSI reference model (physical, datalink and network interfaces). This grouping of functions will be provided by PABXs, LANs and terminal controllers.

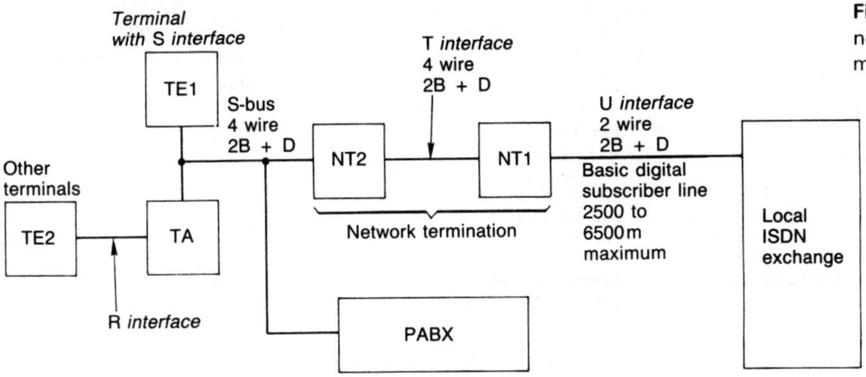

Fig. 4.18 The ISDN user-network interface reference model

c) TE (terminal equipment) which includes functions which are equivalent to all layers of the OSI model. These functions will be provided by digital telephones and multi-function workstations. TE1 interfaces employ the I series interface standards while TE2 interfaces employ other interface standards such as RS-232.

d) TA (terminal adaptor) which is necessary to convert interfaces other than the I series (R interfaces) into the standard (S) interface. A TA is required only by TE2 interfaces.

The S (subscriber) interface permits up to eight subscriber terminals to be connected in a passive bus or star configuration using 4-wire copper cable. I.430 contains the specification for the S interface and the means of resolving contention between terminals on the bus. Power for the first telephone on the S bus is supplied from the exchange in the event of a local power failure but a local mains power supply is required to feed more telephones or terminals on the S bus. The network termination, which converts the 2-wire U interface (from the exchange) to the 4-wire S bus, is powered from the exchange.

The U interface (exchange interface) defines the (physical) layer 1 specification for the subscriber loop to the exchange. Full-duplex transmission of two B and one D channels may be provided on a standard 2-wire twisted-pair by using echo cancellation. The method of encoding is specified as 4B/3T which provides a data rate of 144 kbit/s, an 11 kbaud synchronisation channel, and 1 kbaud maintenance channels from a 120 kbaud symbol rate baseband signal.

The D channel protocol is defined in I.441 and I.451. At layer 2 (the data link layer), a multiple-frame mode and a single-frame mode are available. The HDLC variable-length message format is used. This has an 8-bit flag at the start and end of each frame, a control field, CRC, and a 16-bit address field (which defines the terminal's

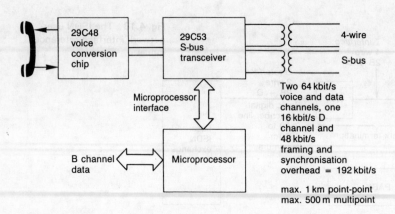

layer 2 address and identifies the information field contents to be signalling, message or packet data).

To make equipment with S interfaces available at low cost for use on the user premises, a variety of integrated circuits have been developed (see Figure 4.19). Most telephone authorities will employ echo cancellation techniques to transmit in full-duplex on a two-wire circuit. Signals are transmitted simultaneously in both directions within the same frequency band (baseband). Cancellation techniques are used to separate received data from transmitted data and reflections of transmitted data. Using this technique, an 80 kbit/s link up to 5 km in length is possible on standard twisted-pair cables leading from subscriber's premises to the exchange (local loops). Alternatively, two 64 kbit/s B channels and one 16 kbit/s D channel may be accommodated on a 4 km local loop. Many private digital PABX systems are adopting time division multiplexing techniques on local loops because it is currently less expensive than echo cancellation.

European telephone authorities expect to have more than 5% of their subscribers served by digital exchanges by 1993 and eventually to completely replace the analog telephone network. Some telephone authorities intend to introduce broadband services such as video telephones by 1990 but most authorities will not offer these services until well into the 1990s. Broadband services use bit rates above 2 Mbit/s and include:

a) Communicative services (video telephony, video conferencing, high-speed data transmission, message handling, moving picture mail, high-resolution images and audio information).

b) Retrieval services (for film, high-resolution images and audio information).

c) Broadcast services for television and audio programmes.

Reference 4.2 contains more on ISDNs.

120

4.3 Network access control

4.3.1 Overview

Time division multiplexed networks require a method of controlling the access of individual users to the transmission medium. Without such an access control mechanism, many users will attempt to transmit simultaneously and the result, without some means of resolving this contention, will be that the medium will carry a large proportion of corrupt data which is of no use to any receiver.

Methods of access control were first developed for radio nets where several users want to share a single frequency channel. A common method of access control on radio nets is to use a control station which invites each user in turn to transmit. This technique, known as polling, is also used in multipoint configurations of terminals where each responds to a polling message from the central computer. When polled, a terminal with nothing to transmit responds with a short 'nothing to transmit' message but a terminal wishing to send a message can transmit when polled.

Early communication satellites used frequency division multiple access (FDMA) to share a microwave link between many users. In the late 1970s an alternative technique, time division multiple access (TDMA), was developed to make more efficient use of the microwave link capacity and to simplify the groundstation equipment. All TDMA groundstations transmit bursts of data at predetermined times (in time frames) which are synchronised by a reference burst from the TDMA controller.

An alternative method of access control was developed for a two-channel UHF packet radio system which linked a central computer to terminals distributed throughout the Hawaiian Islands. This system, known as Aloha, was the first application of the random access method of giving multiple access to a shared medium. On the random access channel linking terminals to the computer, each station transmits when ready. After transmission, the terminal waits for an acknowledgement. If no acknowledgement is received within a timeout period, the terminal retransmits after a random delay.

Slotted Aloha improves the channel utilisation and reduces the probability of a collision compared with pure Aloha by starting all message transmissions at the beginning of a time slot. Figure 4.20 shows messages sent by two stations, A and B, which result in two collisions when pure Aloha is used because the possible collision period is twice the length of a message. Slotted Aloha experiences only one collision because the collision period is equal to the message length when all messages start at the beginning of a time slot (see Figure 4.21).

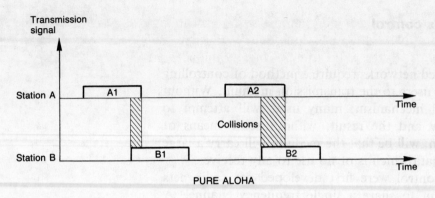

Fig. 4.20 Comparison of Pure Aloha and Slotted Aloha

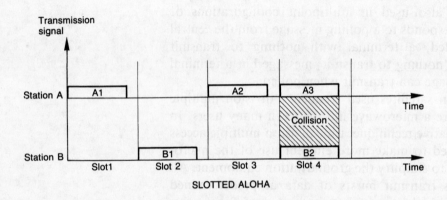

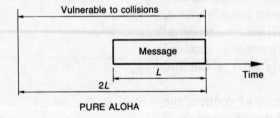

Fig. 4.21 Periods during which Pure Aloha and Slotted Aloha are vulnerable to collisions

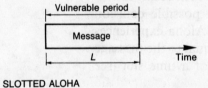

A random delay before retransmission minimises the probability that random access stations will cause subsequent collisions by attempting to retransmit at the same time. This technique was developed into the Carrier Sense Multiple Access with Collision Detection (CSMA/CD) technique (used by Ethernet and other local area networks) by making stations listen for other transmissions before transmitting themselves (CSMA) and detecting collisions as they occur (CD).

In an attempt to avoid the probabilistic nature of transmissions on CSMA/CD local area networks, two popular forms of deterministic access control method have been developed, token passing and slotted rings:

1) *Token passing* distributes the right to transmit on the medium by circulating a token or special bit pattern which gives the right to transmit to the station which receives the token. A station which wishes to transmit waits until it receives the token, then transmits the data and passes the token onto the next station. Token passing is a distributed form of polling in which each station acts as the controller when in possession of the token (by polling the next station in the sequence). Token passing may be employed on ring and bus topologies.

2) *Slotted rings*, such as the Cambridge ring developed at Cambridge University in the UK, pass empty slots from one station to another around a circular ring network. Stations which wish to transmit data deposit it in the first empty slot which arrives. Access to the slot is determined by a token bit in the packet header which indicates whether the slot is being used or is vacant. A destination address is added and the slot is passed from station to station in the ring. Each station inspects the address on the packet and if it matches its own address the data is copied and the empty slot continues around the ring to the sender which changes the token bit. The sender is not allowed to reuse the slot because this would permit it to monopolise the system. This procedure is illustrated in Figure 4.22.

Access control is implemented on half-duplex data links by using a coordinated line turnaround procedure. This is a form of data link or channel access rather than media access control. A station could, in some cases, obtain media access but be denied access to the data link channel because the station with which it intends to communicate has control. Line turnaround may be classified as hard (such as when the modems signal turn around on half-duplex point-to-point links) or soft (where a station is unable to transmit until it receives permission

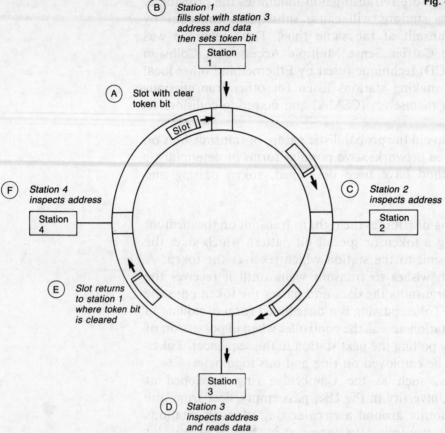

Fig. 4.22 A slotted ring

B — Station 1 fills slot with station 3 address and data then sets token bit

Station 1

A — Slot with clear token bit

Slot

F — Station 4 inspects address

Station 4

C — Station 2 inspects address

Station 2

E — Slot returns to station 1 where token bit is cleared

D — Station 3 inspects address and reads data

Station 3

to transmit from the other end of the link, through the data link protocol).

Access techniques may be classified as:

a) *Centralised* (e.g. a single master station controls network access to the slave stations by polling).

b) *Distributed* (e.g. the stations in a token passing system are temporary masters while they hold the token. The sequence in which the token is transferred on a bus topology creates a logical ring for the purposes of distributed network access).

c) *Decentralised* (e.g. CSMA/CD in which all stations are in contention for media access on an equal basis. An algorithm is employed to resolve conflicts for media access).

4.3.2 Centralised access control

Time division multiple access is a form of centralised access control in which time slots are allocated to individual users and the controller maintains synchronisation of the transmission frames. Typical TDMA terminals for satellite links are capable of operation at

124

62 Mbit/s over a 36 MHz channel transmitting a total of 40 T1 channels (1.544 Mbit/s each).

Figure 4.23 illustrates the operation of a satellite switched TDMA system. A series of frames are received by the satellite from several groundstations. These frames are destined for a number of different groundstations. The satellite has an on-board matrix switch which routes individual frames received from several uplink channels to the particular downlink channels which are received by the appropriate groundstations. The switching matrix is under the control of the switch control earth station and may perform Demand Assignment Multiple Access (DAMA).

SWITCHING MATRIX			
	First slot to	Second slot to	Third slot to
Groundstation A	1	2	3
Groundstation B	2	3	1
Groundstation C	3	1	2

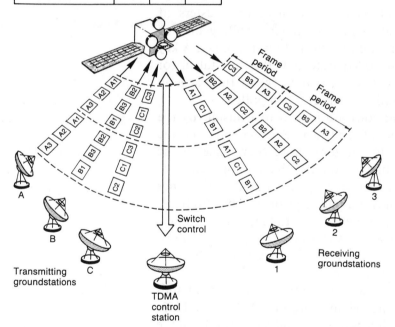

Fig. 4.23 Operation of a satellite switched TDMA system

Figure 4.24 shows the composition of a typical TDMA frame. The frame period is 2 ms and each frame commences with a reference burst generated by the TDMA controller. All the groundstations synchronise their transmissions to this reference burst and each burst of traffic begins (after a guard time) with a preamble containing a synchronisation sequence, the groundstation identification code and an optional voice order wire. The preamble is followed by data from several time division multiplexed data channels.

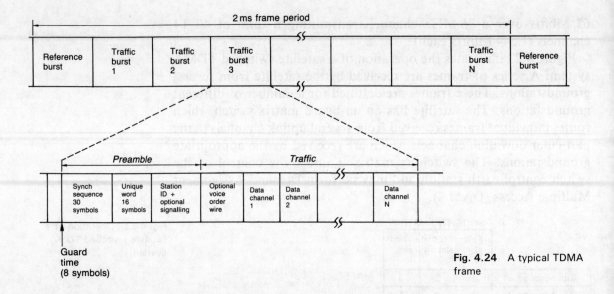

Fig. 4.24 A typical TDMA frame

A common form of centralised access control for clusters of terminals associated with a single master computer is polling and this has frequently been used in a multipoint form of bus topology. A key element in the performance of polled systems is the time taken for the modem (or other terminal interface circuitry) to turn around from reception mode to transmission mode when polled.

In a polled system, slave stations are invited to transmit by the master station (or controller) in a fixed order. The controller has the option of inserting high-priority stations more than once in the polling table and it is possible to modify the polling sequence dynamically. When a station is assigned a priority based on the order in which it is polled, this is known as static priority arbitration. If, once the message transmission sequence is initiated, it is not interrupted, non-pre-emptive arbitration is employed. Figure 4.25 illustrates the transmission of messages in a polled system with static priority and non-preemptive arbitration.

Another form of centralised access control is the command-response system employed in the avionic data bus, MIL-STD-1553. The need for tight control of all message transmissions results in the controller instructing the remote terminals when to transmit and how much data to transmit. It also instructs the recipients of point-to-point messages that they must receive the message. The sequence of control, status and data messages involved in a single point-to-point transmission between two remote terminals with a static bus controller is illustrated in Figure 4.26. A variant of the command-response system permits dynamic bus control by which the control function may be transferred between terminals for the duration of their peak

126

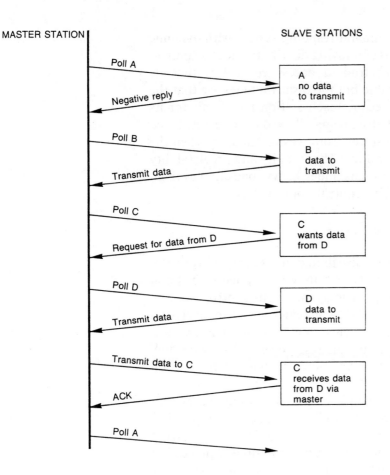

Fig. 4.25 Message sequence for a polled system with static priority and non-preemptive arbitration

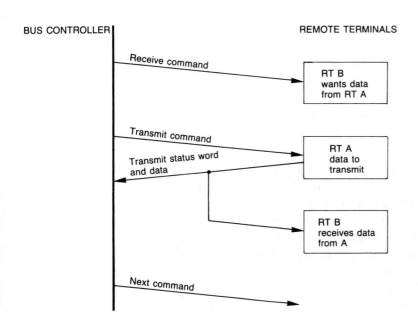

Fig. 4.26 Message sequence for a point-to-point transmission between two MIL-STD-1553 B remote terminals

activity. The variant of the command-response system with dynamic bus control may be classified as employing distributed access control.

The main advantage of centralised access control is that its performance is highly predictable but the disadvantages are that the average access delay is high because each station must wait for its time slot or wait to be polled before being allowed to transmit. Fixed time slot TDMA systems also suffer from wasted capacity when the traffic on a channel is not continuous. The stability and predictability of centralised access control systems under heavy loads makes them popular in real time defence and control applications.

4.3.3 Distributed access control

The two most common forms of distributed access control for local area networks are token passing (which may be applied to bus and ring topologies) and slotted rings. The dynamic bus control mode of MIL-STD-1553 and reservation TDMA schemes may also be classed as distributed access control systems. Reservation TDMA uses distributed control by having terminals reserve time slots according to demand. The request for a slot is made through a reservation subchannel.

Figure 4.27 illustrates the principle of token passing access control. The token gives the holder the right of access to the physical medium and a set of rules determine how the token is passed from one node to the next. The token is passed in a ring-like sequence but the medium need not physically be a ring. Token passing rules can be designed to give priority to particular nodes such as those with synchronous transfer or real time constraints. The IEEE 802.4, IEEE 802.5 and FDDI token passing local area networks provide several levels of priority which may be selected by a node. The token rotation time is monitored by each node and when certain thresholds are exceeded, messages of lower priority may not be transmitted.

On a physical ring the logical token passing ring is composed of all the active nodes on the medium with the order of token passing identical to the sequence in which the nodes are connected to the ring.

A token is a special bit pattern and bit stuffing may be employed to prevent the same pattern occurring in the data. When in listen mode, the nodes copy the bits received from the ring to the output leading to the next node with a typical delay of one bit period. In transmit mode, when the last bit of the token appears, the station inverts it to signify that data follows, then breaks the straight-through path and enters its own data onto the ring.

The node to which the data packet is addressed copies the data and reverses the last bit of the token as an acknowledgement of receipt.

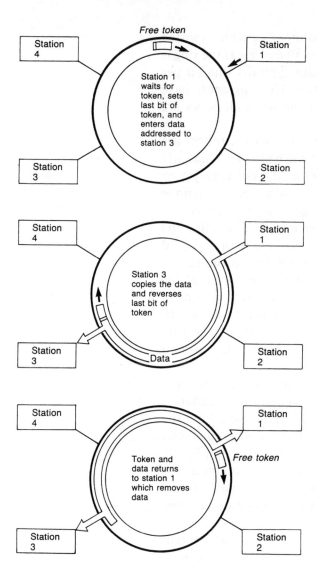

Station 4

Free token

Station 1

Station 1 waits for token, sets last bit of token, and enters data addressed to station 3

Station 3

Station 2

Station 4

Station 1

Station 3 copies the data and reverses last bit of token

Station 3

Data

Station 2

Station 4

Station 1

Token and data returns to station 1 which removes data

Free token

Station 3

Station 2

Fig. 4.27 A token passing ring

The packet then returns to the originator which removes the data. There is no theoretical limit to the length of the packets because the entire packet never appears on the ring at the same instant. When the complete packet has been transmitted the token is regenerated by the transmitting node. When the last bit of the packet has returned to the transmitting node it returns to the listen mode.

The number of bits which may be accommodated on the ring at one time is limited by the length of the cable and the number of nodes. Each bit may be given an equivalent length equal to the propagation delay (typically 200 metres per microsecond), divided by the bit rate transmitted. For example, a 4 Mbit/s ring with a twisted pair cable has an equivalent length of 200/4 = 50 metres. If the ring is 1 km in circumference, 1000/50 = 20 bits plus typically one bit per node may be contained on the ring at once. The ring must have sufficient delay to let a complete token circulate when all nodes are idle.

Slotted rings are similar to token passing rings but the tokens are accompanied by an empty data packet or slot which continuously rotates around the ring. A bit indicates whether the slot is empty or full, performing a similar function to a token. When empty, a node may fill the slot with data and an address, then change the token bit.

The slot circulates from node to node, each node examining the address and, when it matches the node number, the data is copied and an acknowledgement bit is set. The slot returns to the source node where the acknowledgement bit is checked to ensure that the data reached its destination and the token bit is cleared. A control node is required to generate the packets and in some systems to provide a buffer which increases the effective length of the ring making it possible for several slots to rotate simultaneously around the ring.

Token passing systems are more flexible than slotted rings and have therefore become the subject of several international standards. Token passing and slotted ring systems are deterministic in that the performance under all loading conditions is stable and predictable. The disadvantage is that the average transmission delay in a lightly loaded system is higher than that of a contention or random access system. A slotted ring system is more deterministic than a token passing system because a fixed amount of data may be transmitted each time the slot is acquired.

Deterministic access control methods perform better than contention systems under heavy loading conditions but message delay is degraded as the number of stations on the system increases.

4.3.4 Decentralised access control

The first decentralised access control system, Aloha, was a radio-based packet data network sharing a common, multi-access radio channel with no central control of channel access. The random access procedure permitted each terminal to decide independently when to transmit. The resulting collisions were resolved by each terminal waiting for a random time before retransmitting. With a light load on such a system, access time is low, but, as the number of stations transmitting increases, the number of collisions increases and much of the available bandwidth is lost. Pure Aloha systems can only utilise about 18.4% of the channel transmission capacity and, as the total offered load increases, the throughput decreases to zero resulting in total deadlock.

Modified versions of Aloha have been used for access to satellite communication channels. The slotted Aloha system permits contention between groundstations for each time slot but, once allocated, no contention for a time slot is permitted. As shown in Figure 4.28, the channel utilisation of Slotted Aloha can reach 36.8%. By comparison the CSMA/CD system employed by Ethernet can achieve up to 96% channel utilisation with 512 bytes/packet (and without collision detection, up to 60% channel utilisation may be achieved). As the offered load increases, the throughput increases almost linearly to about 90% channel utilisation, then flattens out; this is the ideal situation for system stability.

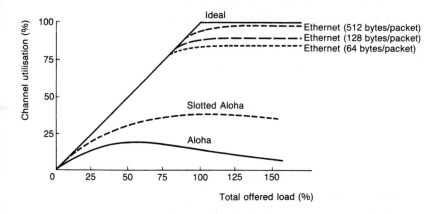

Fig. 4.28 Channel utilisation of decentralised access control methods

Ethernet and IEEE 802.3 employ the CSMA/CD access control method which requires a station to defer transmission while other transmissions are in progress. Using a carrier sense capability, a station detects when no other stations are transmitting before attempting to transmit. In lightly loaded conditions message delay is often zero.

Because there is a propagation delay of about 5 microseconds per kilometre in coaxial cable, and the carrier detection circuitry involves some delay, there is a probability, for about 3 μs at the beginning of each transmission, that more than one station will sense an idle channel and attempt to transmit simultaneously. Each sender continues to monitor the channel during transmission and has a collision detection capability which detects when the signal on the channel does not match its own output. Collision detection is not practical with radio-based systems because the receiver cannot monitor distant signals on the same frequency when a local transmitter is in operation.

When a collision is detected during a frame transmission, the transmission continues for between 32 and 48 additional bits. This collision enforcement or jam ensures that the collision duration is long enough to inform other distant stations which may not have detected the collision. The colliding stations may attempt to retransmit later but, to avoid repeated collisions, each station waits for a pseudo-random period before attempting retransmission. A truncated binary exponential backoff algorithm is used to increase the retransmission interval under conditions of heavy channel loading to prevent overload and possible instability or lock out of stations.

The delay before the nth attempt is 51.2 μs (the slot time) times a uniformly distributed random integer from 0 to 2^k where k lies between n and 10.

Carrier detection (or detection of activity on the channel) is performed by detecting data transitions. If a transition is not detected between 0.75 and 1.25 bit times since the last transition of the Manchester encoding, the carrier is assumed to have disappeared, indicating the end of the packet.

The CSMA/CD system in Ethernet, under 30% load conditions, on average, causes:

a)   97.3% of messages to be transmitted immediately,
b)   2.5% of messages to wait,
c)   0.2% of messages to result in collisions.

The use of these mechanisms in a CSMA/CD system minimises, but does not eliminate, the possibility that packets of data are lost. For this reason it is necessary to employ a transport level protocol to ensure that any missing packets are retransmitted.

5 Layered network architectures

5.1 Introduction

A network architecture is the set of rules which govern the connection and interaction of the network components; it includes the data formats, protocols and logical structures for the functions which provide effective communication between data processing systems connected to the network. Layering separates the functions into distinct levels which communicate individually with like levels in distant nodes.

Network architectures may be classified as hierarchical or peer-coupled as shown in Figure 5.1. In a *hierarchical* network architecture, such as SNA, a master system is aware of the entire network configuration and performs network management and control. A *peer-coupled* (or distributed) network, such as DNA, gives each system information on the network topology and all sessions take place between peer systems which offer a range of services to the users and share the network management functions.

Additional classifications which may be applied to network architectures are end-user-oriented (which offers user services to the end users) and communication-oriented (which offers transport facilities and protocol conversion facilities which make the network transpar-

Fig. 5.1 Comparison of hierarchical and peer-coupled network architectures

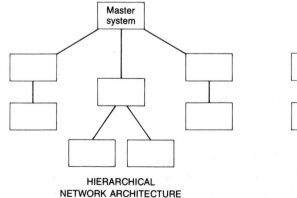

HIERARCHICAL
NETWORK ARCHITECTURE

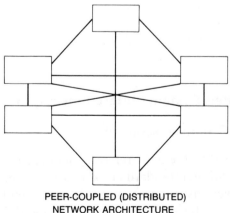

PEER-COUPLED (DISTRIBUTED)
NETWORK ARCHITECTURE

133

ent to the user). SNA and DNA are end-user oriented but a public X.25 data network is communication oriented.

Public networks such as the British Telecom PSS packet switching network offer services to a wide range of users but private networks provide services to a single company or organization. Networks may also be proprietary (controlled by one company) or open. An open communications system may be a combination of: legally open, open to the user, and technically open. A legally open system permits every user to communicate with other users. A system which is open to the user permits any user to decide when and where to take advantage of the services. A technically open system permits a wide variety of equipment to use the communications services without extensive modifications; this can be achieved either by standardisation of interfaces and communications protocols or by providing converters which adapt each user's characteristics to those of the communications system. A network which conforms to the OSI standards is technically open.

The development of distributed data processing, first introduced in the 1960s, has been made practical on a large scale by the introduction of layered network architectures by the major computer manufacturers. These products such as IBM SNA and DEC DNA place severe constraints on the equipment which may be connected to the network. It is necessary for any non-proprietary equipment to emulate the functions of a proprietary equipment in order to take advantage of many network facilities.

The CCITT (Comité Consultatif International Telegraphique et Telephonique) was founded in 1965 to make recommendations for open standards for text, data and telephone communications. The most significant work in establishing international standards for open systems interconnection of computers has been undertaken by the International Standardization Organisation (ISO). The first step towards establishing an open network architecture as an alternative to the proprietary architectures was taken in 1977 by the ISO/TC97/SC16 committee who developed a reference model for Open System Interconnection (OSI); this forms a basis for the co-ordination of developments in layered network communications standards.

5.2 Open Systems Interconnection reference model

5.2.1 General description

In spring 1983 the basic reference model for OSI (ISO 7498) became an international standard and the task of defining standards for each of its seven layers commenced. It was intended that existing standards at the lower layers (1 to 3) should be integrated into the seven-layer model and that new standards would be developed in accordance with the model.

The ISO 7498 reference model is a framework for co-ordinating the development of OSI standards. It uses a layered architecture to break up the problem into manageable pieces. The OSI reference model identifies the functions required in order for computers to transfer information and to interwork in order to achieve common distributed goals. The functions were arranged into seven layers and the functions which each layer must perform were identified in an implementation-independent manner. Later ISO standards defined the implementations for each layer to ensure that full compatibility is achieved at each layer. (These ISO standards for layers of the open systems interconnection reference model are included in the standards section, page 404.)

The layered approach ensures modularity and the facility for networking software to be upgraded incrementally without introducing a revolutionary change. The modularity makes it possible for hardware and software from one vendor to work with products from other vendors who support the same standards at each layer. Modularity also makes it easier to interface one form of media with another, for example to interface X.25 to IEEE 802.3, without changing layers 4 to 7.

The basic functions and ISO standards for the seven layers of the OSI model are shown in Figure 5.2. Two interconnected systems each implement the same standards at each layer and any two entities belonging to the same layer in the corresponding systems communicate by a common protocol. When a message is transmitted, it passes from layer 7 to layer 1 at the sending system with each layer adding its own header to the message or processing the message in some way. The frames which make up the message are transmitted over the interconnection media to the receiving system where they travel through layers 1 to 7, having the headers removed and being reassembled into the message. Where the functions of a particular layer are unnecessary, a null layer is employed.

Each layer offers specific services to the higher layers and logical communication takes place between corresponding layers in the two systems. Data is not passed directly between layers except at the physical layers which are linked by the physical medium. As shown in Figure 5.3, layer interfaces are provided to define the services which layer N expects from layer $N - 1$ below and which layer N provides to layer $N + 1$.

Layers 1 to 3 provide the low-level protocols, mostly implemented in hardware or by dedicated controllers, while layers 4 to 7 provide the application protocols or higher-level protocols which are mostly implemented by software on the host computer.

To illustrate the functions of the layers in the OSI model an analogy may be made between an OSI session and a telephone call:

i)   A physical medium (telephone line) links the two communicators and layer 1 (physical) ensures that the voice signal is converted into an electrical signal which is suitable for transmission at one end of the line and that the received electrical signal is converted back into an audible voice signal at the other end of the line. Layer 1 defines the type of connector on the telephone outlet, the purpose of each connector pin, and the signal levels at the interface to the telephone system.

ii)   Layer 2 (data link) ensures that any words which are not clearly received are notified to the sender and are retransmitted. The words used to request retransmission are previously agreed to avoid misinterpretation. If the telephone system supports conferencing, layer 2 defines the procedure for controlling who speaks. A person who has finished may say 'over' or just stop speaking. Then anyone wishing to speak does so, possibly resulting in contention. If the last speaker invites the next person to speak this contention is avoided.

iii)   Layer 3 (network) establishes the call by providing a mechanism for dialling the number of the person the caller wishes to communicate with. On hearing the telephone bell ring the called person picks up the handset and if the telephone system has routed the call correctly the communication begins; otherwise the called person informs the caller that it is the wrong number and the caller redials. If the called person has an extension on a PABX, the telephone operator routes the received call to the appropriate extension on the private network. If a message is read at different times from several sheets of paper, layer 3 procedures are responsible for ensuring that the complete message is received with the pages in the correct order, possibly by checking the previous page received before reading the next one.

iv)   When the call has been established, layer 4 (transport) is used to ensure that the required messages are conveyed without loss. If the line quality degrades, both parties will agree to hang up their handsets and one will redial to set up another network connection. If the person answering the telephone is not the person required, the correct person will be brought to the telephone. If the person has a changed number the new one will be found. When the transport connection is no longer required, both parties will say goodbye and hang up their handsets.

				CCITT OR ISO STANDARD FOR EACH LAYER.
Application Layer (7)	Application-specific protocols	Application Layer (7)		CCITT X.400 ISO 8571 (FTAM) ISO 8650 (CASE)
Presentation Layer (6)	Messages, Format translation, Codes, Languages, Encryption.	Presentation Layer (6)		ISO 8823 ISO 8825 (ASN.1)
Session Layer (5)	End-to-end dialogue between processes, One-for-one connection (no multiplexing), Accounting and billing, Half/full duplex.	Session Layer (5)		ISO 8327
Transport Layer (4)	Reliable end-to-end message transport, Multiplexing and flow control, Message sequencing.	Transport Layer (4)		ISO 8073 class 0 to class 4
Network Layer (3)	Switching and routing of messages, Ordering of packets.	Network Layer (3)		ISO 8473 CCITT X.25 packet level protocol (ISO 8208)
Data-link Layer (2)	Sending and receiving of frames, Error detection and correction, Media access.	Data-link Layer (2)		ISO 8802/2 (IEEE 802.2 LLC) ISO (HDLC) X.25 LAP
Physical Layer (1)	Transmission and reception of raw bits, Mechanical, electrical and functional compatibility.	Physical Layer (1)		ISO 8802/3 (IEEE 802.3) ISO 8802/4 (IEEE 802.4) ISO 8802/5 (IEEE 802.5)
	Interconnection Media (0)			

Fig. 5.2 The OSI 7-layer model applied to two interconnected systems, showing the basic functions and ISO standards for each layer

Fig. 5.3 OSI layer interfaces

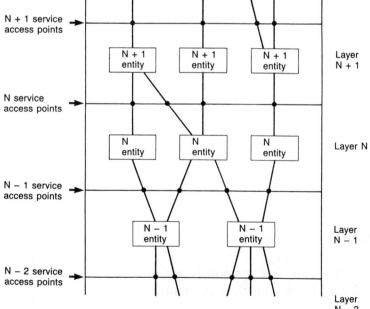

N + 1 service access points

N service access points

N − 1 service access points

N − 2 service access points

Layer N + 1

Layer N

Layer N − 1

Layer N − 2

137

v) At layer 5 (session) protocols are provided which permit the caller to set up a session with another person in the office by asking for the person to be brought to the telephone and provide identification. If one party is called away to attend to other business, the same session may be re-established later, using a different transport connection. Because both parties to a telephone call cannot talk simultaneously, flow control is provided by each party observing when the other has stopped talking; alternatively they may say 'over' to invite the other person to talk.

vi) At layer 6 (presentation) the language problems are resolved. If both parties do not speak the same language but they both speak Esperanto then layer 6 must specify that Esperanto will be spoken. If the subject under discussion is confidential there may be an agreed use of codewords to identify key aspects, e.g. Country A for the USA and Country B for the USSR.

vii) Layer 7 (application) is dependent upon the way in which the two communicators wish to pass the message and work together. If the application is to convey the betting odds for a horse race, a standard application protocol may consist of the horse's name followed by the odds for each horse in turn.

5.2.2 Layer 1, the physical layer

Layer 1 ensures compatibility of the physical interface and provides:

a) Physical transmission of the data stream through the media, defining connectors, control signals, data rates, and interface signal levels.
b) Physical layer management.
c) Activation and deactivation of the physical connection.
d) Collision detection for CSMA/CD access systems.

Services provided for the *data link layer* include:

a) Physical connections, data units and end points.
b) Recognition of equipment location.
c) Sequence indication.
d) Error indication.
e) An indication of quality of service.

5.2.3 Layer 2, the data link layer

Layer 2 ensures compatibility of the data link protocols which provide error-protected transmission and access to the communications media. Functions include:

a) Establishing and releasing the link.
b) Framing and synchronisation including the means of distinguishing data from flags.
c) Sequence control.
d) Detection of transmission errors.
e) Retransmission or other forms of transmission error correction.
f) Flow control.
g) Identification and exchange of parameters.
h) Supervision of the physical connection.
i) Link-layer management.
j) Access control for local area networks.

Services provided for the *network layer* include:

a) Transmission of data in data link service data units.
b) Provision of a data link connection end-point identifier.
c) Sequence control.
d) Notification of transmission errors.
e) Flow control.
f) An indication of quality of service.

5.2.4 Layer 3, the network layer

Layer 3 establishes the transmission path and the network connection using error-protected links, possibly via intermediate switching nodes and possibly to several end systems. It also defines how several network connections may share a link by determining the switching and routing of messages and the ordering of packets in a packet switched system.

Functions of the network layer include:

a) Selecting primary and alternate routes or establishing virtual circuits.
b) Selecting network connections by addressing intermediate nodes.
c) Multiplexing of network connections.
d) Forming data blocks and segments plus reassembly at the destination.
e) Detection and correction of errors.
f) Sequence and flow control.
g) Ensuring the satisfactory transfer of data.
h) Resetting of network connections.
i) Selection of services.
j) Network layer management and communication with adjacent layers.
k) Internetworking.

Services provided for the *transport layer* include:

a) Provision of network address.
b) Provision of network connections.
c) Identification of network end points.
d) Transfer of network-service data units.
e) An indication of quality of service.
f) Notification of unrecoverable errors.
g) Sequence and flow control.
h) Satisfactory transfer of data.
i) Reset.
j) Releasing the network connection.

5.2.5 Layer 4, the transport layer

Layer 4 is responsible for establishing, controlling and releasing transport connections between the application entity, presentation entity and session entity of communicating systems. A transport connection is an end-to-end connection between the communicating systems and it may make use of several network connections provided by layer 3 in the course of one transport connection.

Functions of the transport layer include:

a) Establishing transport connections without concern for intermediate nodes.
b) Data transmission error detection (end-to-end) and retransmission when necessary.
c) Releasing the transport connection.
d) Transport layer management and communication with adjacent layers.
e) Mapping addresses to user names (users may change location).
f) Monitoring quality of service.

Services provided for the *session layer* include:

a) Data transmission.
b) Establishing and releasing transport connections.

Data is passed to the transport protocol entity which encapsulates the data in a transport protocol data unit (TPDU). The transport layer shields the higher layers from the details of the underlying communications service. Three network service types may be defined:

1) Type A: connections with acceptable residual error rate (errors not detected by the network layer) and an acceptable

140

rate of signalled failures (failures detected but not corrected by the network layer).

2) Type B: connections with acceptable residual error rate but an unacceptable signalled failure rate.

3) Type C: connections with a residual error rate which is not acceptable to the transport service user.

Five classes of transport protocol are defined to handle a variety of user service requirements and available network services:

1) Class 0   Simple
2) Class 1   Basic error recovery
3) Class 2   Multiplexing
4) Class 3   Error recovery and multiplexing
5) Class 4   Error detection and recovery.

Classes 0 and 2 are intended for use with Type A networks; Classes 1 and 3 are for use with Type B networks; and Class 4 is intended for use with Type C networks.

The Class 0 transport protocol is the CCITT standard for teletex (a text transmission system) and provides the simplest transport protocol for use with connection-oriented Type A networks. No particular ordering and error control requirements are specified because occasional errors in text transmission are acceptable.

The Class 1 transport protocol is the CCITT standard intended for use with an X.25 network and offering minimum error recovery facilities. Unlike Class 0, the TPDUs are numbered to permit the transport level entities to inform each other of the last TPDU received before a virtual circuit was reset and to retransmit any lost TPDUs. Class 0 and 1 protocols handle each user data block as a separate entity when interacting with the network layer.

The Class 2 transport protocol is a Class 0 protocol with enhancements including multiple transport connections multiplexed onto a single network connection and individual flow control facilities for each transport connection. Class 3 is a combination of Class 1 and Class 2 capabilities offering multiplexing and resynchronisation capabilities for Type B network services. The Class 4 transport protocol has many facilities which make it suitable for use with Type C network services. Out-of-sequence, lost or damaged packets are detected making Class 4 suitable for use with datagrams. It also includes a positive acknowledgement for each TPDU although a single ACK may be used for accumulated TPDUs.

Ten types of TPDU are employed, each consisting of a fixed header, including a length indicator, an optional variable header and on optional data field. Flow control involves the interaction of transport users, transport entities and the network service and restrains the transmission of TPDUs when the receiving transport entity cannot keep up with the flow of TPDUs or if the user is unable to keep up with the flow of data.

5.2.6 Layer 5, the session layer

The session layer establishes and terminates the communication relationship (session or dialogue) in an orderly manner, thus synchronising the communication and determining which transport connection will be associated with the session. Session control includes the passing of the right to transmit in half-duplex systems.

The functions of the session layer include:

- *a*) Association of sessions with transport connections.
- *b*) Flow control for the session.
- *c*) Performing data exchange between tasks.
- *d*) Opening, terminating and re-establishing session connections.
- *e*) Session layer management and communication with adjacent layers.
- *f*) Dialogue control (who, when, how long, half- or full-duplex).
- *g*) Recovery from communication problems during a session without data loss.

Services provided for the *presentation layer* include:

- *a*) Establishing and terminating the session.
- *b*) Performing data transfer.
- *c*) Dialogue control.
- *d*) Synchronisation of the session connection.
- *e*) Notification of unrecoverable errors.

5.2.7 Layer 6, the presentation layer

Layer 6 adapts the data from the application to a form suitable for the communications system. The presentation protocol defines the rules on how the data will be presented and exchanged in a common neutral language, e.g. it may be required to translate ASCII data to EBCDIC or from fixed to floating point format.

The functions of the presentation layer include:

- *a*) Requesting the opening, closing and implementation of a session.
- *b*) Performing data exchange.
- *c*) Co-ordination of syntax and presentation profiles.
- *d*) Syntax translation for character sets, text strings, data display formats, graphics, files and data types.

e) Translation of the presentation profile.
f) Data encryption and decryption, if required.
g) Data compression, if required.

Services provided for the *application layer* include:

a) Data formatting.
b) Selection of syntax.
c) Syntax translation.
d) Selection of presentation profile.
e) Data encryption.

5.2.8 Layer 7, the application layer

Layer 7 brings network services to the end user defining how two communication partners work together. This is the highest layer and is the only one which is not completely transparent to the user. Application software in the host computer is not part of the application layer but common application service elements such as FTAM (file transfer, access and management) and X.400 electronic mail standards are included in layer 7. Network services may include password checks, a distributed database, document or file transfers, log in and file access checks.

The application layer may provide services for the application process including:

a) Identification of the communication partners and establishing availability.
b) Authorisation and validity checks.
c) Allocation of costs.
d) Agreeing available resources.
e) Accepting services.
f) Synchronising applications.
g) Error correction.
h) Selecting the dialogue.
i) Checking data integrity.
j) Complying with the data syntax.
k) File requests and file transfers.
l) Downline loading.
m) Graphics procedures.
n) Database queries, insertions and deletions.
o) Virtual terminal service.
p) Job manipulation and remote job entry.
q) Electronic mail.

For further information on the OSI architecture see reference 5.1.

5.3 Alternative network architectures

5.3.1 General

While most manufacturers of computer communications systems and equipment suppliers are evolving their products towards the ISO standards as they are agreed for each layer of the OSI model, there are a variety of alternative network architectures and protocol layers currently in use. It is unlikely that all these alternatives will be abandoned when all the ISO standards have been finalised and in many cases it will be necessary to provide gateways between systems which comply with the ISO standards and those which use other standards. Many networks are committed to alternative standards and replacement would be a long process.

Alternative network architectures include:

a) IBM, SNA
b) DEC, DNA
c) DARPA, TCP/IP
d) Xerox, XNS
e) Honeywell, DSA
f) Hewlett-Packard, Advancenet
g) Burroughs, BNA
h) ICL, IPA
i) Data General, Xodiac
j) Wang, WSN.

The low-level communications standards supported by several network architectures are shown in Figure 5.4. At the physical, data link and network layers, most architectures will support a variety of different local area network and wide area network standards. IEEE 802.2 (LLC), IEEE 802.3 (CSMA/CD), IEEE 802.4 (token bus), IEEE 802.5 (token ring) and ANSI FDDI (fibre optic token ring) local area network standards define layers 1 and 2 with X.25 covering layers 1, 2 and 3.

Many local area networks installed before the higher OSI layer standards were finalised made use of the IEEE 802.2 common logical link control standard within the data link layer and either the Xerox XNS protocols or DARPA TCP/IP protocols for higher layers. The IBM SNA architecture is probably the dominant network standard, particularly in the USA, with DEC DNA as a second favourite. Because of their common usage the four standards, XNS, TCP/IP, SNA and DNA, will be described in more detail.

Many system manufacturers do not wish to offer the full range of facilities included in the seven OSI layers and have selected a set of functional standards, or a standards profile, which will ensure

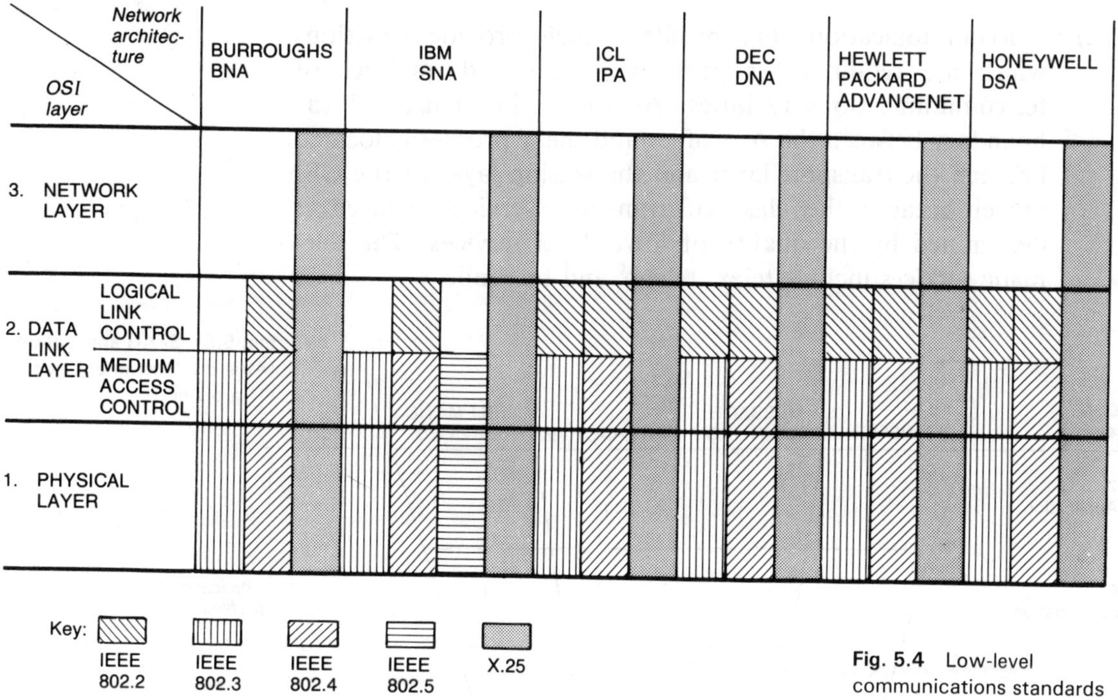

Network architecture / OSI layer

OSI layer	BURROUGHS BNA	IBM SNA	ICL IPA	DEC DNA	HEWLETT PACKARD ADVANCENET	HONEYWELL DSA
3. NETWORK LAYER						
2. DATA LINK LAYER — LOGICAL LINK CONTROL / MEDIUM ACCESS CONTROL						
1. PHYSICAL LAYER						

Key: IEEE 802.2   IEEE 802.3   IEEE 802.4   IEEE 802.5   X.25

Fig. 5.4 Low-level communications standards supported by proprietary network architectures

compatibility with other participating suppliers in the same industry. The objective is to restrict the number of subsets which are allowable within each relevant standard and to adopt a grouping of standards required to support a particular function.

Five groups of users or standards organisations have established functional standards profiles:

1) The European Standard Promotion and Action Group (SPAG).
2) General Motors and other automotive manufacturers which established the Manufacturing Automation Protocol (MAP).
3) Boeing Aerospace and other industries which established the Technical and Office Protocols (TOP).
4) US government and the UK Central Computer and Telecommunications Agency (Government OSI Protocol, GOSIP).
5) CCITT which has established the Teletex standards (CCITT F.200).

SPAG has defined two primary classes of profile:

1) Application (A) profiles which provide user-accessible functions and details of data function and content but do not address any associated telecommunications facilities.

2) Telecommunications (T) profiles which provide functions which are required for particular types and qualities of telecommunications facilities. As shown in Figure 5.5 the boundary between the A profiles and the T profiles is located between the transport layer and the session layer of the OSI model because the class of transport service required is determined by the quality of lower-level services. The telematic services include telex, teletex and facsimile.

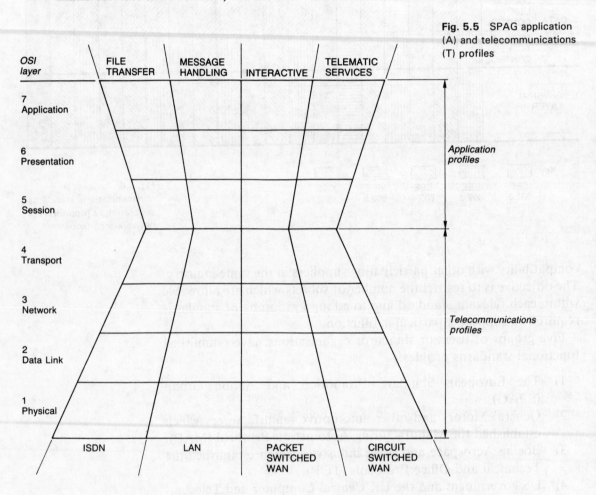

Fig. 5.5 SPAG application (A) and telecommunications (T) profiles

5.3.2 Teletex

Teletex is an international public telecommunication service intended for text transmission. It is expected to replace the telex service and uses a terminal with a message store which permits the text to be modified before transmission. Transmission is 40 times faster than telex, message reception is acknowledged automatically, and it can

146

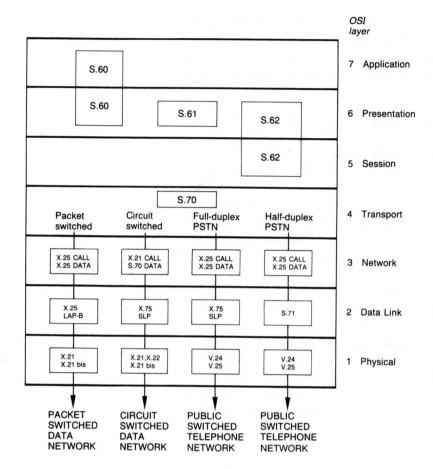

				OSI layer	
S.60				7	Application
S.60	S.61	S.62		6	Presentation
		S.62		5	Session
S.70				4	Transport
Packet switched	Circuit switched	Full-duplex PSTN	Half-duplex PSTN		
X.25 CALL X.25 DATA	X.21 CALL S.70 DATA	X.25 CALL X.25 DATA	X.25 CALL X.25 DATA	3	Network
X.25 LAP-B	X.75 SLP	X.75 SLP	S.71	2	Data Link
X.21 X.21 bis	X.21,X.22 X.21 bis	V.24 V.25	V.24 V.25	1	Physical
PACKET SWITCHED DATA NETWORK	CIRCUIT SWITCHED DATA NETWORK	PUBLIC SWITCHED TELEPHONE NETWORK	PUBLIC SWITCHED TELEPHONE NETWORK		

use the full 7-bit character set unlike telex which was restricted to a 5-bit character set.

The CCITT F.200 teletex standard lays down the provisions for the operation of the automatic international teletex service. Technical details are included in five CCITT recommendations which span the OSI 7-layer model as shown in Figure 5.6:

1) S.60 defines the functional characteristics of the terminals and specifies the requirements for international compatibility between teletex terminals.
2) S.61 defines the international character set for teletex.
3) S.62 defines the network-independent end-to-end control procedures for the teletex service which include the OSI session layer protocol.
4) S.70 defines the network-dependent procedures forming a network-independent transport protocol which has been adopted in OSI as the Class 0 transport protocol.
5) S.71 defines the LAP-B data link layer with extensions for half-duplex operation.

OSI layers 1 to 3 may vary in different countries but an X.21 interface with an HDLC link protocol is used by the Deutsche Bundespost circuit switched system which was the first teletex system in operation. Existing telex systems may be interconnected with teletex systems.

5.3.3 Manufacturing Automation Protocol (MAP)

General Motors estimated that 50% of their automation cost was for networking, in particular for protocol translators between propriety equipment. In 1980 General Motors conceived the Manufacturing Automation Protocol and proposed it as a standard for communication protocols in multivendor manufacturing automation systems. MAP has been adopted by many US manufacturers and in 1984 the US MAP users group was formed. The European MAP users group was formed in 1985.

As shown in Figure 5.7 the physical and data link layers employed are defined in IEEE 802.4 with the IEEE 802.2 (Type 1, connectionless) logical link control standard as part of the data link layer for the 10 Mbit/s broadband backbone network. Connectionless logical link control leaves the detection of missing or duplicated messages to the higher layers; it simply discards messages with faulty frame check sequences. A form of logical link control which provides immediate acknowledgements is used on 5 Mbit/s sub-nets within the MAP

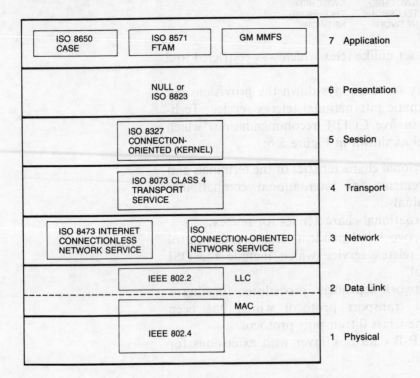

Fig. 5.7 MAP standards

network. The sub-nets employ single-channel transmissions using carrier band modulation as defined in IEEE 802.4.

The network layer has connection-oriented and connectionless options; the connectionless option discards the whole message when errors are detected. An ISO 8073 Class 4 transport protocol is employed at layer 4 to provide a connection-oriented service which detects missing or duplicated messages and initiates a retransmission to provide guaranteed message delivery and correct sequencing.

The ISO 8327 session layer is employed and the MAP version 2.1 specification includes a null layer 6. Later versions will use the ISO 8823 presentation layer. The application layer supports:

a) ISO CASE (Common Application Service Element), which allows user-written applications to interface at layer 5 (ISO 8650). One task requests association with another by simply using its name.

b) ISO FTAM (File Transfer, Access and Management) specific-application service element (SASE). (ISO 8571.) Allows transfer of files between machines with otherwise incompatible file formats.

c) GM MMFS (Manufacturing Message Format Standard) which defines interactions between programmable controllers and numerically controlled machines or robots. Replaced in version 3.0 by ISO 9506 Manufacturing Message Services (MMS).

d) Directory Services (DS) which allows users to access network services.

e) Network Management (NM) Protocol to retrieve network management statistics and modify network parameters.

Specific application service elements may be added when required.
MAP products fall into three categories:

1) OSI end systems including MAP end systems (MES), which implement a MAP subset of OSI, and MAP/combination systems (MCS), which implement the MAP subset and other OSI protocols which may be used by systems which do not implement the full MAP protocol.

2) OSI relays including MAP routers and MAP bridges.

3) Special systems, including gateways.

As shown in Figure 5.8(a), a MAP router may be used to join two OSI subnetworks which may have different lower-level protocols. The ISO 8473 internet protocol is used to link the dissimilar protocols. As shown in Figure 5.8(b), a MAP bridge may be used to join two network segments which have different physical layers. As shown in Figure 5.9, a MAP gateway may be used to permit a MAP network to communicate with a network which does not use

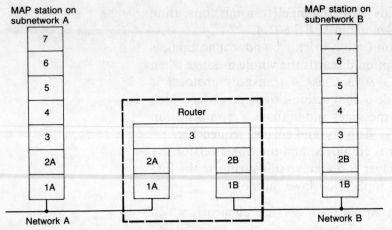

(a) A MAP ROUTER SHOWING OSI LAYERS

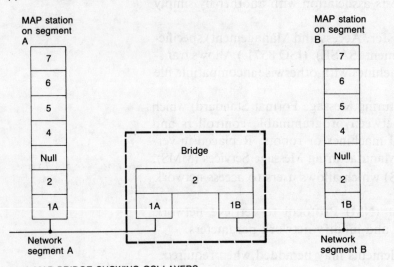

(b) A MAP BRIDGE SHOWING OSI LAYERS

OSI protocols. Both networks remain independent with regard to network management.

5.3.4 Technical and Office Protocols (TOP)

Boeing Aerospace first proposed a subset of OSI protocols for use in offices to enable office computers to communicate with MAP systems. In 1985 the Society of Manufacturing Engineers (SME) was established as secretariat of the MAP/TOP users group. The TOP protocols are the equivalent of MAP protocols but optimised for business and office applications. As shown in Figure 5.10 a core set of protocols is common to MAP and TOP:

a) Network layer (3). c) Session layer (5).
b) Transport layer (4). d) Presentation layer (6).

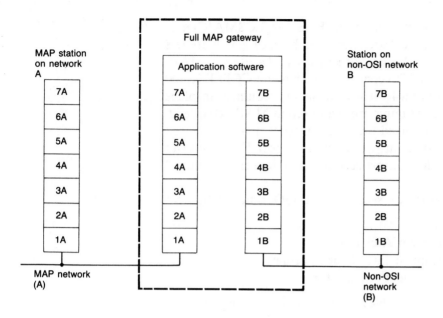

Fig. 5.9 A MAP gateway used to link a MAP network to a non-OSI network

MAP	MAP and TOP	TOP	OSI layer	
EIA RS-511 REAL-TIME MESSAGING	ISO 8650 CASE ISO 8571 FTAM ISO DIRECTORY SERVICES ISO NETWORK MANAGEMENT ISO VIRTUAL TERMINAL	X.400 ODS ODIF DCA	7	Application
	ISO 8823 or NULL		6	Presentation
	ISO 8327 CONNECTION-ORIENTED		5	Session
	ISO 8073 CLASS 4		4	Transport
	ISO CONNECTIONLESS ISO CONNECTION-ORIENTED		3	Network
LLC	IEEE 802.2		2	Data link
	IEEE 802.4 TOKEN BUS / IEEE 802.3 CSMA/CD IEEE 802.5 TOKEN RING			
MAC	IEEE 802.4 BROADBAND IEEE 802.4 CARRIERBAND / IEEE 802.3 IEEE 802.5		1	Physical

Fig. 5.10 MAP and TOP protocols compared with OSI layers

At layers 1 and 2, TOP specifies either in IEEE 802.3 CSMA/CD, or an IEEE 802.5 token ring, local area network, both of which are less expensive than the IEEE 802.4 broadband networks used in MAP. At the application layer, TOP version 3 specifies the CCITT X.400 electronic mail and store-and-forward messaging standard in place of the RS-511 real-time messaging protocol used in MAP because an office environment does not need the speed of transmission required in a manufacturing environment. In order to support X.400 services the TOP session layer includes more services than the kernel included in MAP.

TOP includes standards for security and ISO office document protocols including:

a) ODA, Office Document Architecture.
b) ODIF, Office Document Interchange Format.
c) DCA, Document Content Architecture.

Various document content profiles are supported including OSI text files, graphics files to the International Graphics Exchange Standard (IGES), and the ANSI X.12 Electronic Data Interchange Standard for business documents such as invoices.

A Product Data Exchange Specification (P-DES) has been developed because the IGES standard is unable to meet the demands of product data definitions which replace engineering drawings. Product data definitions may use three-dimensional graphics representations and include all the information required throughout the life of a product from design to manufacturing, quality assurance, sales and maintenance.

5.3.5 Transmission Control Protocol/Internet Protocol (TCP/IP)

The IEEE 802.3 local area network standard came into service several years before the ISO standards for layers 3 to 7 of the OSI model. When the LAN was used with equipment manufactured by a company with a proprietary network standard, the physical and data link layers were made to accommodate IEEE 802.3 and possibly IEEE 802.2; thus manufacturers like DEC assimilated IEEE 802.3 into DECnet. In 1981 Xerox introduced the XNS network system, a development of TCP/IP, based on the use of Ethernet for the physical and datalink layers. Other LAN equipment manufacturers and users wanted a non-proprietary set of standards above layer 2 and adopted the US Department of Defense TCP/IP protocol. TCP/IP has been in use since about 1975 on defence data networks and it is supported by many US computer manufacturers. Some manufacturers used TCP/IP for the network and transport layers with proprietary protocols for layers 5 to 7.

Development of TCP/IP began in the early 1970s when DARPA (the US Department of Defense Advanced Research Projects Agency) awarded several development contracts and it was rapidly adopted as the standard network architecture for many US government networks (a subset is used by Arpanet). TCP/IP has also been incorporated into the Berkeley Unix version 4.2 operating system (together with an address resolution protocol which maps TCP/IP addresses into IEEE 802.3 addresses) which has encouraged its use in local area networks. The Unix–TCP/IP combination became a popular choice for LAN users who wanted to retain an open architecture because TCP/IP protocols are nonproprietary.

As shown in Figure 5.11, the network layer is called the internet protocol (IP); this datagram protocol addresses messages and routes them across the network and exchanges data between systems independent of the network topology and the media used. An additional internet control message protocol (ICMP) is available to provide network layer management and control functions.

OSI layers	TCP/IP layers
7 Application	FILE TRANSFER PROTOCOL (FTP) REMOTE JOB ENTRY
6 Presentation	TELNET VIRTUAL TERMINAL PROTOCOL
5 Session	
4 Transport	TRANSMISSION CONTROL PROTOCOL (TCP) OR USER DATAGRAM PROTOCOL (UDP)
3 Network	INTERNET PROTOCOL (IP) ICMP 1822 NETWORK FOR ARPANET
2 Data Link	NETWORK DEPENDENT (e.g. Ethernet/1822)
1 Physical	NETWORK DEPENDENT (e.g. Ethernet/1822)

Fig. 5.11 TCP/IP layers compared with OSI layers

The transport layer is called the transmission control protocol (TCP, also known as MIL-STD-1778) and is a connection-oriented transport protocol which sequences messages into transactions and provides an end-to-end transport service similar to the ISO 8073 Class 4 protocol. TCP has only one TPDU type and the header requires 20 octets compared with 5 to 7 for the ISO 8073 Class 4 header. A connectionless protocol, user datagram protocol (UDP), is also available. UDP includes all routing information with each message and is used for remote network management and for name service access which lets users assign a name to each protocol address.

The session and presentation layers, called the Telnet protocol, supports virtual circuits between terminals and host computers, allowing a user on one machine to log onto another machine. The file transfer protocol (FTP), which corresponds roughly to the presentation and application layers, provides file transfers between dissimilar machines and operating systems.

5.3.6 Xerox Network System (XNS)

XNS was developed from DARPA funded work at Stanford University but unlike TCP/IP it has been optimised for use with local area networks and can achieve up to twice the performance of TCP/IP in LAN applications. This improvement is achieved because XNS is packet oriented (whereas TCP/IP is byte-oriented) and XNS has excluded the checksums which are mandatory in TCP/IP.

XNS low-level protocols were published in 1981. The datagram concept used by TCP/IP is retained in the layer 3 internetwork datagram protocol (IDP) but internetworking and dynamic routing

OSI layers	XNS layers
7 Application	CLEARINGHOUSE SERVICE FILE TRANSFER SERVICE PRINTER SERVER
6 Presentation	COURIER
5 Session	
4 Transport	SEQUENCED PACKET PROTOCOL (SPP)
3 Network	INTERNETWORK DATAGRAM PROTOCOL (IDP)
2 Data link	ETHERNET
1 Physical	ETHERNET

Fig. 5.12 XNS layers compared with OSI layers

facilities are improved. As shown in Figure 5.12 the transport layer is called the sequenced packet protocol (SPP) and the session/ presentation layer is called the courier but this is not standard in all applications. Xerox published layer 5, 6 and 7 standards for XNS in 1984; these layers conform functionally to the OSI reference model with differences in areas which were not specified by ISO at the time.

Fig. 5.13 XNS headers and tailers applied to a file transfer service message

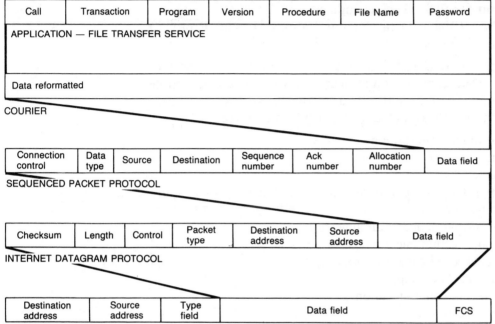

Figure 5.13 shows how headers and tailers are added to a file transfer service message as it passes from the application layer through the lower layers of XNS. The message plus the headers and tailers added at one layer become the data field in the next lower layer. The higher layers of XNS have become common in Ethernet and IEEE 802.3 local area network systems developed before the full set of ISO standards were finalised. The reason for this is that XNS was the only open standard available which offered performance improvements over TCP/IP.

5.4 DEC Digital Network Architecture (DNA)

5.4.1 DNA phases I to IV

DEC and IBM announced their network architectures in the mid-1970s and both have introduced additional functions, in subsequent releases of SNA and in later phases of DNA. DNA is a peer-to-peer communications network (without central control) introduced in 1976. The software products which implement DNA are known as DECnet. Phase I provided:

a) Program-to-program communication.
b) File transfer.
c) Downline loading.
d) Support for PDP 11 minicomputers.
e) DDCMP (Digital Data Communications Message Protocol) communications.

DECnet phase II, introduced in 1978, extended the support to all the major DEC computers and operating systems, added remote file and resource access, and enhanced the network management functions. Phase III was introduced in 1980 and added:

a) Adaptive message routing.
b) Upline dumping.
c) Loopback testing.
d) Network terminal communication between systems running the same operating system.
e) Terminal-to-terminal communication.
f) Multipoint communication.
g) X.25 packet switched network support.
h) Stand-alone SNA support.
i) Task-to-task communication.
j) Remote file access.

DECnet phase IV was introduced in 1983 and added:

a) Ethernet (IEEE 802.3).
b) Larger networks.
c) Dedicated communications servers to offload the general-purpose nodes.
d) DECnet–SNA gateways.
e) Enhanced network management and network routing, including support for up to 64 000 nodes.

Each phase remains compatible with earlier phases and the process of ensuring compatibility with the ISO layer standards has begun with the lower layers.

5.4.2 DNA layers

In DNA terminology, a node is a network entity, an identifiable unit capable of processing, sending and receiving network information and possessing a unique numerical address. The node address includes a 6-bit area number and a 10-bit node number. Data is transmitted between nodes in packets, along lines (or physical data paths). Circuits are logical connections which carry information between nodes. Each tributary on a multipoint line has a separate circuit.

OSI layers	DNA layers
7 Application	USER
	NETWORK MANAGEMENT
6 Presentation	NETWORK APPLICATION
5 Session	SESSION CONTROL
4 Transport	END-TO-END COMMUNICATION
3 Network	ROUTING
2 Data Link	DATA LINK
1 Physical	PHYSICAL LINK

Fig. 5.14 DNA layers compared with OSI layers

Figure 5.14 compares the layers of DNA with the OSI model. The *physical layer* defines the way in which communications hardware and device driver software are implemented to transfer data on lines. The *data link layer* defines the mechanism for error-free communication between adjacent nodes for three link types (DDCMP, X.25 or Ethernet) and supports the maintenance operation protocol. The *routing layer* software transports and routes user data from the sending node to the receiving node (intra and inter-area routing) providing the shortest path or least-cost route and alternative routes if the primary route is impractical. It also provides network congestion control and packet lifetime control.

The *end-to-end communication layer* software is responsible for the system-independent aspects of communication and communication through the network services protocol including:

a) Connection management (creation and disconnection of logical links).
b) Data flow control.
c) End-to-end error control.
d) Segmentation and reassembly of user messages.

The *session control layer* defines the system-dependent aspects of process-to-process communications including:

a) Name-to-address translation.
b) Process addressing.
c) Access control.
d) Requesting logical links for the end user.

The *network application layer* defines network functions required by the user and the network management layer including:

a) Remote file and record access.
b) Remote file and record transfer.
c) Remote terminal capability, including the network virtual terminal function.
d) Access to X.25 systems by using the PSI software of the X.25/X.29 extension package.
e) Access to SNA gateways.
f) Resource sharing among heterogeneous systems using a universal I/O language.

The *network management layer* defines the functions used by the operators and network manager to plan, control and maintain the network. Data on network performance is collected from lower layers and commands are issued to change network operation parameters. The network information and control exchange protocol is used for:

a) Downline loading and upline dumping of remote nodes.
b) Loopback testing of lines.
c) Link service functions.

The *user layer* includes:

a) User-produced software.
b) User-level services which access the network.
c) Network services which directly support user and application tasks.
d) Overall system management.

Utilities include resource sharing, file transfer, remote file access, database management, task-to-task communication, terminal-to-terminal communication and command language interpretation.

The layers within DNA interact vertically and within each node. Each DNA layer provides services which are required to support modules in higher layers and uses services provided by lower layers. As shown in Figure 5.15, several protocols exist between the individual layers of DNA within two communicating nodes:

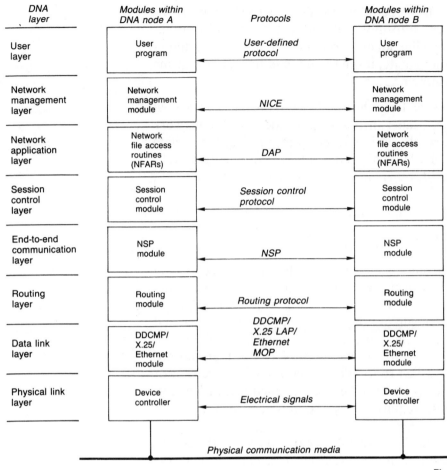

DNA layer	Modules within DNA node A	Protocols	Modules within DNA node B
User layer	User program	User-defined protocol	User program
Network management layer	Network management module	NICE	Network management module
Network application layer	Network file access routines (NFARs)	DAP	Network file access routines (NFARs)
Session control layer	Session control module	Session control protocol	Session control module
End-to-end communication layer	NSP module	NSP	NSP module
Routing layer	Routing module	Routing protocol	Routing module
Data link layer	DDCMP/ X.25/ Ethernet module	DDCMP/ X.25 LAP/ Ethernet MOP	DDCMP/ X.25/ Ethernet module
Physical link layer	Device controller	Electrical signals	Device controller

Physical communication media

Fig. 5.15 Protocol communications between two DNA nodes

a) NICE (network information control exchange) protocol exchanges network, node and configuration data between nodes and services requests by modules in the network management layer.

b) DAP (data access protocol) performs remote file access and remote file transfer for software modules in the network management and user layers.

c) The session control protocol defines messages sent on a logical link as: connect data, reject data, and disconnect data.

d) NSP (network services protocol) sets up and maintains logical links between modules residing within the higher layers of the same or different nodes.

e) The routing protocol, which is part of the transport layer, routes data by the most suitable path to any node in the network.

f) MOP (maintenance operation protocol), which is part of the data link layer, transmits data over the communications channel for downline loading to remote nodes, upline dumping from a remote node, testing nodes and links, and starting unattended remote nodes.

As data packets are passed from the user layer to the physical layer at the transmitting node, header information is added at the network application layer, network services layer, transport layer and data link layer. The data link layer also adds a tailer containing a cyclic redundancy check and other information defined in DDCMP, Ethernet or X.25.

5.4.3 Network routing

DECnet phase III introduced automatic multihop routing of data across the network via intermediate nodes. Network users need only specify the name of the remote nodes with which they wish to communicate. At intermediate nodes only the data link layer and transport layer are used. The transport packet header is used at each node to determine the onward routing path. Nodes with an onward routing capability are called routing nodes and require a version of DECnet software which supports all phase III functions. End nodes, or non-routing nodes, require a less comprehensive version of DECnet.

A single link is provided between a pair of nodes but the source and destination nodes need not be adjacent if a path through the network is available via other routing nodes. Apart from point-to-point connections, multipoint and switched connections are supported.

DECnet routing nodes can select the lowest path cost or the shortest path length through the network. A routing algorithm uses the node routing tables and routing parameters, as defined through the network management layer, to evaluate the alternative paths through the network against the minimum cost or length criteria. Each node maintains routing databases which store the results of the routing algorithms.

In an area-based network, the level 1 routers (which are only responsible for communication within an area) include information on path length and cost to every node and level 2 router in its area. A level 2 router (which is responsible for communication between areas) includes an area routing table which permits the least-cost path to other areas in the network to be determined.

When a packet is received at a routing node, the routing layer consults the routing databases to find the least-costly path to its destination. If the destination is not accessible from the routing node, the packet is discarded or returned to its sender.

If the network changes, possibly as a result of a link failure, each routing node executes the routing algorithm again and passes on the revised contents of its routing database to all adjacent nodes. Thus any network change is incorporated within the routing databases of all network nodes.

Routing will operate over paths consisting of many types of data link circuits. Features are provided to control congestion and packet lifetime. The ratio of packets forwarded through a node is regulated in relation to the number of packets generated by the same node, to produce a balance between incoming and outgoing traffic. The number of nodes through which a packet has been routed is tracked and packets are discarded when a predefined limit has been exceeded.

Verification passwords are exchanged with adjacent nodes when required by the network management layer. Counters and event data are collected for network management purposes. This enables the network manager to identify and locate network problems such as congestion.

5.4.4   Remote file and record access

Using DECnet, a program in one node can access a file in another node, despite differences in the operating systems and file systems. Remote file access enables user-written programs to open and close remote files, create and delete remote files, and read from and write to remote files by use of DECnet I/O calls. Users can also use a terminal to transfer files to or from remote nodes, delete remote files, submit and execute command files at a remote node, append files to local and remote files, list remote directories, and queue files to a remote printer.

Remote file access calls from the source program are translated into one or more DECnet messages by the local DECnet software. These messages are sent to a DECnet program in the remote node where a target program translates the messages to a form which is recognizable by the file system. The source programs may use the Network File Transfer (NFT) utility but the target program is always a version of the File Access Listener (FAL) utility. FAL translates incoming requests into calls to the remote file system and sends the resulting file data back to the accessing program at whose node special routines reformat the data to make it conform to local file structures.

The FAL at the target node and the accessing program exchange data access protocol (DAP) messages to perform remote file access operations. To access a remote file, a user with a terminal must supply the same access-control information as an accessing program; this must include a user identification password and optional account data. The remote file system compares the user's identification with the protection code associated with the file being accessed and, if authorized, the access to the file takes place.

5.4.5   Network terminal facilities

DNA provides several facilities which allow users at one node to communicate interactively with remote nodes and with terminal users at remote nodes; these facilities include:

a) Interactive terminal-to-terminal communication.
b) Network virtual terminal which allows direct access to a remote node's operating system.
c) Remote file access from a terminal.
d) Local area transport (LAT) protocol which enables terminals connected through a terminal server to an Ethernet LAN to establish links with any host on the same Ethernet. Terminals may also be connected to remote hosts not on the same Ethernet via a DECnet host on the same Ethernet.

Interactive, terminal-to-terminal communication may take place through either the phone or TLK utilities. Phone is an operating system utility and TLK is a DECnet utility. Network virtual terminal facilities in DECnet phase IV permit connections to be established between local and remote systems with different operating systems through the Network Virtual Terminal (NVT) utility. NVT enables programmers to use the resources of any system in the network and to log onto any remote node which is most appropriate to their needs.

5.4.6   Internetwork connections

Systems on a DECnet network can communicate with systems on other networks, specifically X.25 packet switched data networks (PSDN) and IBM SNA networks. To communicate over a PSDN, a DECnet node must install either the Packetnet System Interface (PSI) software or the X.25/X.29 extension package which enables the DECnet node to be connected logically to a DECnet Router/X.25 Gateway.

DECnet-to-SNA communication requires a gateway which resolves the protocol differences. The SNA network environment sees the gateway as a physical unit (PU) type 2 cluster controller. The DECnet node and gateway may be located on a wide area network or on an Ethernet LAN.

162

The DECnet-SNA gateway access functions reside in the network access layer of the DECnet node and make the SNA data flow control, transmission control and path control layers available to user programs residing anywhere in a DECnet network. The DECnet system and the PU2 system exchange Gateway Access Protocol messages over the logical link; these include:

a) Connect — Requests that a session be established with a primary logical unit (PLU) in an SNA host.

b) Listen — Waits for a session to be established by a PLU.

c) Bind data — Indicates that a Bind has been received for a session solicited with Connect or Listen. (A Bind is a DNA logical connection between a remote terminal and an application.)

d) Bind Accept — Requests that the session being established with the Bind be accepted and placed in the running state.

e) Normal Data — Carries data on the SNA session's normal flow to and from the PLU.

f) Interrupt Data — Carries data on the SNA session's expedited flow to and from the PLU.

g) Disconnect — Requests orderly session termination.

h) Disconnect Complete — Indicates that normal session termination has been completed successfully.

i) Abort — Requests abnormal termination of a session, or indicates an Unbind has been received from the PLU.

For further information on DNA see reference 5.2.

5.5 IBM Systems Network Architecture (SNA)

5.5.1 SNA releases

Before SNA was introduced in 1974 IBM supported over 200 communications products using over 35 access methods and over 15 protocols. SNA is a design standard for IBM products to resolve incompatibility within IBM product lines and it is constantly evolving to meet market demands. SNA has become an extremely complex set of rules developed to accommodate IBM products.

Before SNA, most IBM communications included separate networks for each data processing application and most networks used

Bisync protocols with 3270 terminals or RJE with HASP software. In the early 1970s independent suppliers introduced multiplexers and intelligent communications front-end processors which increased the flexibility of the networks and offloaded some data communications from the mainframes. The lack of standards made it difficult to interconnect a wide range of computers and terminals, special communications equipment being necessary for most new computer types.

The SNA architecture was developed to support teleprocessing networks and a layered approach was adopted to minimise the impact of changes which are inevitably required in such a network. Other objectives were to make the network able to handle data in a transparent manner and to move communications control functions away from the applications software.

Version 1 of SNA supported only single host networks and introduced a new type of SNA terminal cluster controller. It made the terminals capable of accessing any applications program but the established 3270 terminals and other Bisync terminals would not operate under SNA version 1; only terminals or cluster controllers which used the SDLC protocol were compatible. SNA version 2, introduced in 1976, supported Bisync, SDLC and some asynchronous devices in the same network but Bisync terminals and SDLC terminals could not share the same lines. A dial-up link capability was added for use with asynchronous terminals.

SNA version 3, introduced in 1978, made multihost networking possible and made it possible for terminals to access databases and programs on more than one host machine. The SNA network was organized into regions or domains, each controlled by a host computer. To establish a connection with a host in a different domain, a terminal has first to obtain permission from its own host. These facilities are provided by the Virtual Telecommunications Access Method (VTAM) and Network Control Program (NCP) software.

Adding and deleting terminals became complex because every host in the network requires the address of all devices which may want to communicate with it. Fixed routing rules were employed in version 3 and the network had to be restarted to activate an alternative path if a link failed. A Communications Management Configuration (CMC) was introduced to permit network control and fault diagnosis from a central host machine.

The network job entry facility allowed batch jobs to be entered at any host computer in the network and to be executed and output on any selected host computers in the network. By this means load balancing could be achieved across the host computers in the network.

164

SNA version 4.1, introduced in 1979, extended the support for non-SNA devices such as teletypes and supported the 8100 and 4300 series. Version 4.2, introduced in 1980, provided alternate routing capabilities which were predefined (the alternative path was selected automatically if the main path failed). Modems with diagnostic facilities and a Network Problem Determination Application (NPDA) program were introduced to collect network error data and generate problem statistics. Line, terminal and modem errors may also be isolated by NPDA.

Users of version 4.2 could select separate network transmission paths for different applications or could run multiple links in parallel to provide redundancy in case one link failed. The 3863, 3864 and 3865 modems introduced a remote site loopback capability activated from the 3705 front end by SDLC command sequences. Terminal operation across domains was also simplified.

SNA version 5, introduced in 1984, extended the SDLC frame addressing capability, provided facilities for interconnecting SNA networks, and introduced peer-to-peer communications with logical unit 6.2 (LU 6.2) via Advanced Program-to-Program Communications (APPC). The Document Interchange Architecture/Document Content Architecture (DIA/DCA) was introduced for office applications and supports text, data, voice, image and graphics elements.

5.5.2 SNA layers

Figure 5.16 shows how SNA is separated into seven layers. These layers differ from the OSI layers in two key areas:

1) SNA combines the OSI network and transport layers in its path control layer.
2) The OSI session layer combines the SNA data flow control and transmission control layers.

The physical control layer defines standards for the data terminal equipment (DTE)–data circuit-terminating equipment (DCE) physical interface including the electrical, mechanical, functional and procedural aspects. This layer may be defined by RS-232-C or IEEE 802.5.

The data link control layer initialises and terminates logical links between adjacent nodes, handles error detection and retransmission, and transfers data using the SDLC protocol or IEEE 802.5 token ring protocol. The path control layer provides primary and secondary route selection, multiple active routing, virtual route placing, class of service selection, and message segmentation/blocking.

The transmission control layer provides end-to-end connectivity, session activation/deactivation, session pacing, sequencing of messages and encryption, if required. The data flow control layer is responsible for the correlation of data exchange, flow synchronisation during sessions, and high-level error control.

The presentation services layer formats data for various media and is responsible for syntactic and semantic transformations where necessary. The transaction services or application layer provides the end-user logical interface. The transaction services architectures were formalised in 1986 and provide common command-language formats.

Fundamental SNA messages (or request/response units, RU) are generated by layers 4 to 7 and have headers/tailers provided by the lower three layers before being transmitted. Field-formatted binary data forming a response unit (RU) is assembled by any of layers 4 to 7 in a transmitting node. Layer 6 may add a function management header (FMH) which passes control information within sessions. The request/response header (RH) is assembled by layer 4, 5 or 6 to transmit session-unique profiles. As shown in Figure 5.17 these elements make up the basic information unit (BIU).

Layer 3 adds a transmission header (TH) for path control and node routing based on virtual route or transmission priority criteria. The path information unit (PIU) thus formed has a link header (LH) and link tailer (LT) added by layer 2 to form the basic link unit (BLU) which forms the frame in an SDLC link. If an IEEE 802.5 token ring network is used, the PIU is encapsulated with an IEEE 802.5 header and tailer and possibly an IEEE 802.2 logical link control frame.

5.5.3 Access methods

Two access methods are supported by SNA:

1) VTAM which is intended primarily for specialised communications monitoring and supporting IBM application subsystems.
2) TCAM which is intended primarily for message switching systems and transaction switching networks.

TCAM is a queued access method and is suitable for systems in which jobs require queuing or message switching. Systems with high application subsystem activity use VTAM.

5.5.4 Addressing

Network addresses consist of a subarea address and an element address. Each subarea may contain a number of logical units, each with an element address in the subarea. The original SNA address

Fig. 5.16 SNA layers
compared with OSI layers

OSI layers	SNA layers
7 Application	7 TRANSACTION SERVICES/APPLICATION
6 Presentation	6 PRESENTATION SERVICES
5 Session	5 DATA FLOW CONTROL
	4 TRANSMISSION CONTROL
4 Transport	3 PATH CONTROL
3 Network	
2 Data Link	2 DATA LINK CONTROL
1 Physical	1 PHYSICAL CONTROL

Fig. 5.17 SNA Basic Link
Unit elements

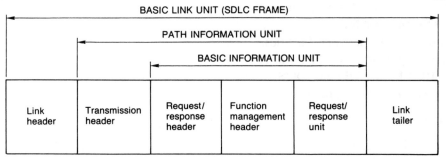

field was 16 bits with the relative size of the subarea and element addresses left to the customer but all nodes in the network had to use the same split.

The increased size of SNA networks made it necessary to expand the addressing field and in 1985 Extended Network Addressing (ENA) was introduced. ENA increased the address from 16 to 23 bits and defines the subarea field to be 8 bits and the element address 15 bits long, making the maximum number of subareas 255 and the maximum number of logical units in any subarea 32K. The maximum number of applications and users in an SNA network has therefore increased from 64K to 8M.

5.5.5 SNA Distribution Services (SNADS)

SNADS was introduced in late 1983 to provide a non-interactive data distribution facility. It uses either store-and-forward or switching to route files and documents to their destinations in a peer-to-peer SNA system (using LU 6.2). SNADS is closely linked to the Document Interchange Architecture (DIA) and Document Content Architecture (DCA). DIA specifies the envelope, the addresses of the sender and receiver, and selects services such as delivery confirmation but does not impose limitations on the envelope contents.

DCA specifies the data which is placed in the DIA envelope using either revisable form text (which defines how revisable documents are constructed) or final form text (which defines how devices can exchange final form documents for printing etc.). Distributed Office Support System (DISOSS), a mainframe program, provides Document Distribution Services (DDS) which create a foundation for worldwide distribution of documents over an SNA network.

For further information on SNA see reference 5.3.

5.6 Comparison of DNA and SNA

The advantages of DNA include:

a) It uses distributed peer-to-peer communication.
b) It integrates LANs and WANs.
c) It provides many end-user network facilities.
d) It provides gateway functions to SNA and X.25.
e) It supports the IBM PC by DECnet DOS.
f) It will converge with the ISO standards.

Its disadvantages include:

a) It is a closed network standard.
b) It does not offer synchronous terminal connections.
c) Facilities are dependent on DEC computers and operating systems.

The advantages of SNA include:

a) It provides inter-IBM compatibility.
b) In the USA it is the dominant network standard.
c) It provides intensive network management.
d) It includes many office applications facilities.

Its disadvantages include:

a) It is not distributed and does not integrate LANs.
b) It is a closed architecture with no gateways provided.

168

c) It requires complex system generation and maintenance.
d) No dynamic routing and dynamic error recovery facilities are provided.
e) The facilities are highly dependent on the IBM computers and operating system release in use.

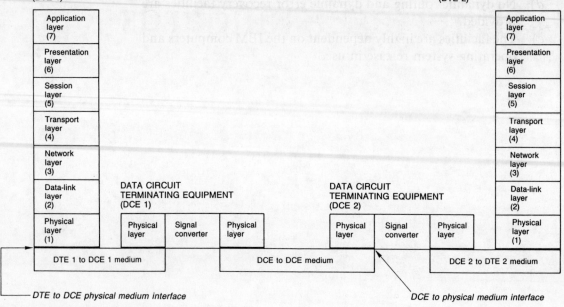

(a) INTERCONNECTION USING A PAIR OF DTEs

Fig. 6.1 (a) Interfaces in a DTE to DTE connection using DCEs; (b) Interfaces in a direct interconnection of two DTEs

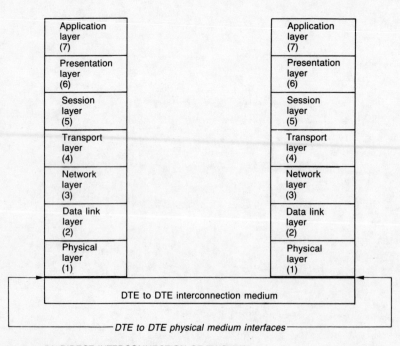

(b) DIRECT INTERCONNECTION OF TWO DTEs

170

6 Interface standards

6.1 Introduction

The communication media and the physical aspects of interfacing were the first to be standardised. Standardisation at this level is essential in any communications application because without an agreement on the electrical (or optical) signal characteristics, communication of any form is impossible. Without an agreed physical interface specification, manufacturers of communications equipment, such as modems, cannot make their equipment operate with a wide range of computer and terminal equipment and terminal manufacturers would be unable to connect their products to a wide range of computers.

An interface is used between dissimilar (non-peer) entities and involves the direct physical transfer of data. A protocol is used for peer-to-peer communication and for indirect physical transfer of data.

The interconnection media provides the physical transmission path for electrical or optical signals and is not concerned with the communications protocol. It must have an agreed interface which specifies the design, dimensions and pin assignments of the connector plus the signalling voltages and signalling sequences for data transmission and control.

Different interfaces may be used between two data circuit-terminating equipments (DCEs) and between the DCEs and the data terminal equipments (DTEs) as shown in Figure 6.1(a). The interfaces in a direct interconnection of two DTEs are shown in Figure 6.1(b).

The physical interface (OSI layer 1) defines:

a) An electrical interface between the DTE and the DCE. The electrical interface between the media and the DTE is also subject to standardisation and in some cases no DCE is employed, the media being directly connected to the DTE.

b) The procedures required to establish, maintain and release the physical connections using the transmission media.

171

c) The means of transmitting a transparent (not influenced by data content) bit stream over the media.

d) A means of monitoring failures of the transmission path and notifying the DTE and/or DCE.

Physical interface standards commonly have four parts:

1) Mechanical specifications for the cable and connectors.
2) Electrical specifications including voltages impedances and waveforms.
3) Functional specifications including signal-pin assignments and signal definitions.
4) Procedural specifications for control and data transfer.

The most popular serial interface standard, RS-232, was published in 1962 and was revised in 1969, 1972 and 1987. The higher-performance serial interface standards, RS-422 and RS-423, were published in 1975. RS-449, a general-purpose functional and mechanical standard which incorporates RS-422 and RS-423, was published in 1977. This was intended to supersede RS-232-C as the preferred serial interface standard between a DCE and DTE.

The CCITT standard X.21 is a general-purpose DCE-DTE interface intended for synchronous operation on public data networks. Figure 6.2 compares the data-rate—distance capabilities of RS-232-C, RS-422, RS-423, RS-449 and X.21. The X.21 bis standard specifies interim interface standards which may be used as alternatives to X.21; these are V.24 (which together with V.28 is equivalent to RS-232-C) and, for higher-speed circuits, CCITT V.35. For asynchronous devices connected to a packet switched data network

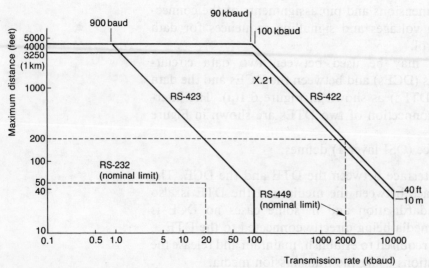

Fig. 6.2 Data rate/dista capabilities of RS-232-C RS-422, RS-423, RS-44! and X.21

via a PAD (packet assembler/disassembler), three CCITT standards were defined:

1) X.3 which defines the PAD parameters.
2) X.28 which defines the terminal-PAD interface.
3) X.29 which defines the communications procedures between a PAD and a packet mode DTE via the network.

High-speed interfaces for connection of local peripherals are usually parallel in order to keep the switching speed of each signal line within the limits of inexpensive cables and interface circuitry. A wide variety of special parallel interface standards are available for line printers and disk drives but until 1978 there was no open, general-purpose parallel interface standard suitable for computers. The IEEE 488 parallel interface bus standard was published in 1978, developed from the Hewlett Packard General Purpose Instrument Bus (GPIB).

6.2 RS-232-C and V.24/V.28

6.2.1 General

RS-232-C was published by the American Electronic Industries Association to standardise the interface between data terminal equipment and data circuit-terminating equipment employing serial binary data interchange. The interconnection media and physical interface are defined in its four main sections:

Section 2 defines electrical signal characteristics.
Section 3 defines the interface mechanical characteristics.
Section 4 provides a functional description of interface circuits.
Section 5 defines standard interfaces for selected communications system configurations

The CCITT equivalent of RS-232-C consists of V.24, which defines the mechanical characteristics and functions of the interchange circuits, and V.28 which defines the electrical signal characteristics. Table 6.1 shows the interchange circuits with their RS-232-C designations and their V.24 designations. Pin numbers and circuit operation is the same for RS-232-C and V.24.

6.2.2 The connector

The connector is a 25-pin D-type as shown in Figure 6.3. Only 21 pins are assigned to interchange circuits. It is conventional to use a male plug on cables with a female socket on the DCE or DTE. There are however exceptions to this convention.

Table 6.1 RS-232-C and V.24 interchange circuits

Pin	RS-232-C Interchange	CCITT V.24 Equivalent	Description	Gnd	Data From DCE	Data To DCE	Control From DCE	Control To DCE	Timing From DCE	Timing To DCE
1	AA	101	Protective Ground	X						
7	AB	102	Signal Ground/ Common Return	X						
2	BA	103	Transmitted Data			X				
3	BB	104	Received Data		X					
4	CA	105	Request to Send					X		
5	CB	106	Clear to Send				X			
6	CC	107	Data Set Ready				X			
20	CD	108.2	Data Terminal Ready					X		
22	CE	125	Ring Indicator				X			
8	CF	109	Received Line Signal Detector				X			
21	CG	110	Signal Quality Detector				X			
23	CH	111	Data Signal Rate Selector (DTE)					X		
23	CI	112	Data Signal Rate Selector (DCE)				X			
24	DA	113	Transmitter Signal Element Timing (DTE)							X
15	DB	114	Transmitter Signal Element Timing (DCE)						X	
17	DD	115	Receiver Signal Element Timing (DCE)						X	
14	SBA	118	Secondary Transmitted Data			X				
16	SBB	119	Secondary Received Data		X					
19	SCA	120	Secondary Request to Send					X		
13	SCB	121	Secondary Clear to Send				X			
12	SCF	122	Secondary Rec'd Line Signal Detector				X			

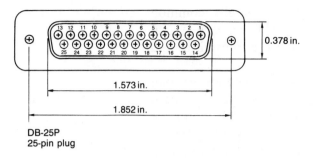

Fig. 6.3 An RS-232-C connector

DB-25P
25-pin plug

When it is necessary to connect a computer directly to a terminal without a modem, the normal definition of interchange signals is no longer applicable because both the computer and terminal are DTEs and both are transmitting on pin 2 and receiving on pin 3. In many applications both DTEs expect particular voltage levels on various control pins before data transmission can take place.

To overcome this problem a null modem may be interposed between the computer and terminal. A less expensive method is to construct an interconnection cable with several transposed connections as shown in Figure 6.4. Linking a computer or terminal to a modem requires a cable with all pins which are used linked to the equivalent pin number at the other end of the cable.

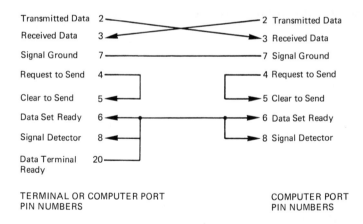

Fig. 6.4 Cable wiring to link the RS-232-C interface on a computer to a terminal or second computer

TERMINAL OR COMPUTER PORT
PIN NUMBERS

COMPUTER PORT
PIN NUMBERS

6.2.3 The electrical interface

The electrical interface uses unbalanced circuits, all referenced to the signal ground. A positive signal between 3 and 25 V is interpreted as on for control circuits or as binary 0 (space) for data circuits. A negative voltage between -3 and -25 V is interpreted as off or binary 1 (mark). The use of relatively high voltages and unbalanced circuits makes RS-232-C highly susceptible to crosstalk, common mode noise (noise which is injected into the signal line and the signal ground), and differences in ground potential at the transmitter and receiver.

The standard was based on discrete transistor logic rather than integrated circuit technology and performance is not up to modern standards. The maximum data rate specified is 20 kbit/s and the maximum cable length specified is 50 ft (15 m for V.24/V.28). In practice it is often possible to exceed the distance limitation with low-capacitance cable in a low-noise environment.

RS-232-C is only suitable for point-to-point interfaces, although the DCE may support multipoint operation. Synchronous or asynchronous baseband signalling may be used. Synchronous operation is supported by the Transmitter Signal Element Timing signal (clock from the DTE), or Transmitter Signal Element Timing (clock from DCE) and Receiver Signal Element Timing (clock from DCE) interchange signals. Modems with out-of-band signalling channels may use Secondary Transmitted Data and Secondary Received Data. Other circuits are provided to change the modem operating speed and to control automatic calling equipment.

6.2.4 Operation with modems on leased lines

For operation with modems on leased lines it is common to use three control circuits:

(CA)   Request to Send
(CB)   Clear to Send (Ready for Sending in V.24)
(CF)   Received Line Signal Detector

Request to Send turns the modem transmitter on and off.

In a polled multipoint network, a terminal which recognises its own address turns on Request to Send and waits for the Clear to Send signal to be received from the modem before sending its response. Before turning on Clear to Send, the modem establishes a link with the receiving modem. When the terminal has finished the data transmission it turns off the Request to Send signal which causes the modem to turn off its transmitter, leaving the line free for other modems to transmit.

Received Line Signal Detector is switched on by the modem when it receives a signal from the modem at the other end of the line. The terminal will not accept data before Received Line Signal Detector is switched on in order to reject spurious data which may be caused by line disturbances.

6.2.5 Operation with modems on dialled connections

For operation with modems on dialled connections it is common to use three control circuits in addition to those used on leased lines; the additional circuits are:

(CE) Ring Indicator (Calling Indicator in V.24)
(CD) Data Terminal Ready
(CC) Data Set Ready

A ringing signal on the line turns the Ring Indicator on and if the terminal is ready to receive data it will have Data Terminal Ready switched on which causes the modem to connect itself to the line and then switch on Data Set Ready. The terminal turns on Request to Send, the modem responds with Clear to Send, and the terminal user will hear the carrier tone in the telephone earpiece. The user connects his modem to the line by a pushbutton on his telephone and the Received Line Signal Detector is turned on by the modem.

After data transmission is complete, the user places his telephone handset on the hook thus disconnecting the modem from the line and switching off Received Line Signal Detector. The terminal turns off Request to Send and Data Terminal Ready which disconnects the modem from the line and causes it to turn off Data Set Ready. The terminal may then turn on Data Terminal Ready in preparation for the next call.

6.3 RS-449, RS-422, RS-485 and RS-423

6.3.1 Improved electrical interface standards

In the early 1970s serial interface standards which made use of the capabilities of integrated circuits were developed; these overcame the severe limitations in speed and cable length imposed by RS-232-C. RS-422 defines the electrical characteristics of balanced voltage digital interface circuits and RS-423 defines the electrical characteristics of unbalanced voltage digital interface circuits.

Table 6.2 compares the performance and major characteristics of RS-232-C, RS-422 and RS-423.

6.3.2 RS-422 (CCITT X.27 or V.11)

RS-422 uses a balanced driver and differential signalling over a pair of conductors. A positive voltage on one line with respect to the other line transmits a mark while the reverse polarity transmits a space. Because no reference voltage is required, the balanced

Table 6.2 Comparison of RS-232-C, RS-422 and RS-423

Parameter	RS-232-C	RS-422	RS-423
Maximum length	50 ft	1200 m (4000 ft)	1200 m (4000 ft)
Maximum speed	20 kbaud	10 Mbaud	100 kbaud
Mark (Data 1)	− 3 V	A < B	A Negative
Space (Data 0)	+ 3	A > B	A Positive
Maximum common mode voltage		− 7 V to + 7 V	
Open-circuit output voltage	3 V to 25 V (5 V to 15 V with 3 to 7 kΩ load)	< 6 V	4 V−6 V
Minimum receiver input	± 3 V	200 mV differential	200 mV differential

interface is immune to errors caused by differences in a reference voltage and common mode signals up to ± 7 V are ignored. Crosstalk is considerably improved by differential signalling through wire pairs and the maximum data rate is increased to 10 Mbit/s with a 10 m cable. The maximum cable length is 1200 m which may be achieved with data rates up to 100 kbit/s.

6.3.3   RS-423 (CCITT X.26 or V.10)

RS-423 uses an unbalanced driver and transmits the signal on one wire with a common signal return wire for all transmitted signals and an independent common signal return wire for all received signals. RS-423 does not have the same cable length and speed capability as RS-422 but it is considerably superior to RS-232-C. The maximum data rate is 100 kbit/s with a 13 m cable and 1200 m cables may be used at data rates up to 3 kbit/s. Although RS-423 does not use a balanced transmission system, the crosstalk in cables is better than RS-232-C because the driver voltages are generally much lower (4−6 V compared with 3−25 V for RS-232-C). The greater cable length is achieved by increasing the receiver sensitivity from ± 3 V in RS-232-C to 200 mV in RS-422 and RS-423.

6.3.4   RS-485

Some driver and receiver chips may be configured to provide either

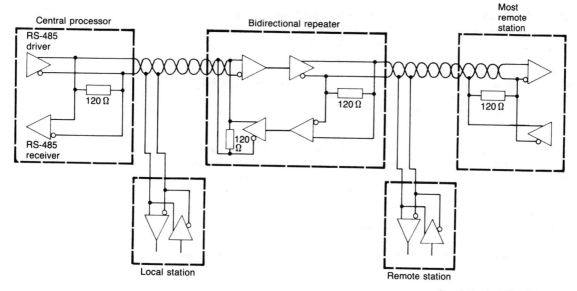

Fig. 6.5 An RS-485 multipoint configuration

RS-422 or RS-423 interfaces and with suitable voltage levels an RS-423 interface maybe connected to an RS-232-C interface. RS-422 and RS-423 interfaces are designed to operate with one driver and up to 10 receivers but a tri-state version of the RS-422 driver is available for use in multipoint or party-line buses with up to 32 driver/receiver pairs (see Figure 6.5). The tri-state version has become the RS-485 standard. In other respects RS-485 is similar to RS-422 with a 10 Mbit/s maximum data rate. Most RS-485 driver chips are compatible with earlier RS-422 types to permit easy upgrading. RS-485 includes current limiting in cases where contention occurs and the common mode voltage range is extended to $+12$ V, -7 V on outputs and ± 12 V on inputs.

6.3.5 RS-449

RS-449 was published in 1977 by the US Electronic Industries Association with the objective of correcting many of the problems associated with the RS-232-C interface by making use of the later RS-422 and RS-423 electrical interfaces. RS-449 is a general-purpose 37-pin and 9-pin interface for data terminal equipment and data circuit-terminating equipment employing serial binary data interchange.

RS-449 specifies the use of a 37-pin D-series connector with an additional 9-pin D-series connector for the secondary channel when required. The dimensions of the connectors are specified in more detail than was the case with the 25-pin D-series connector used

179

Table 6.3 RS-449 interchange circuits and RS-232-C equivalents

Circuit mnemonic	Circuit name	Circuit direction	Circuit type		RS-232-C equivalent
SG	Signal Ground	—	Common		AB Signal Ground
SC	Send Common	to DCE			—
RC	Receive Common	from DCE			—
IS	Terminal in Service	to DCE	Control		—
IC	Incoming Call	from DCE			CE Ring Indicator
TR	Terminal Ready	to DCE			CD Data Terminal Ready
DM	Data Mode	from DCE			CC Data Set Ready
SD	Send Data	to DCE	Data		BA Transmitted Data
RD	Receive Data	from DCE			BB Received Data
TT	Terminal Timing	to DCE	Timing	Primary channel	DA Transmitter Signal Element Timing (DTE source)
ST	Send Timing	from DCE			DB Transmitter Signal Element Timing (DCE source)
RT	Receive Timing	from DCE			DD Receiver Signal Element Timing
RS	Request to Send	to DCE	Control		CA Request to Send
CS	Clear to Send	from DCE			CB Clear to Send
RR	Receiver Ready	from DCE			CF Received Line Signal Detector
SQ	Signal Quality	from DCE			CG Signal Quality Detector
NS	New Signal	to DCE			
SF	Select Frequency	to DCE			
SR	Signalling Rate Selector	to DCE			CH Data Signal Rate Selector (DTE source)
SI	Signalling Rate Indicator	from DCE			CI Data Signal Rate Selector (DCE source)

for RS-232-C. Ten additional circuits plus the signal returns for balanced electrical connections are included. Table 6.3 lists the interchange circuits in RS-449 and gives the RS-232-C equivalents.

RS-449 will support data rates up to 2 Mbit/s with timing signals up to 4 Mbit/s when using RS-422 and 60 kbit/s when using RS-423 with exponential waveshaping or 138 kbit/s with linear (ramp) waveshaping. The maximum cable length is 60 m for either RS-422 or RS-423 implementations but tailored applications may exceed this distance. RS-449 may be configured to interoperate with RS-232-C at all bit rates and cable distances covered by RS-232-C. Adaptors are required to convert 25-pin RS-232-C interfaces into the 37-pin (with optional 9-pin) connector used by RS-449.

Table 6.3 (*continued*)

Circuit mnemonic	Circuit name	Circuit direction	Circuit type		RS-232-C equivalent
SSD	Secondary Send Data	To DCE	Data	Secondary channel	SBA Secondary Transmitted Data
SRD	Secondary Receive Data	from DCE			SBB Secondary Received Data
SRS	Secondary Request to Send	to DCE	Control		SCA Secondary Request to Send
SCS	Secondary Clear to Send	from DCE			SCB Secondary Clear to Send
SSR	Secondary Receiver Ready	from DCE			SCF Secondary Received Line Signal Detector
LL	Local loopback	to DCE	Control		—
RL	Remote Loopback	to DCE			—
TM	Test Mode	from DCE			—
SS	Select Standby	to DCE	Control		—
SB	Standby Indicator	from DCE			—

Each control function has a dedicated pin on the RS-449 connector. A minimum of 10 circuits, designated category 1, are required in all implementations. The rest of the 30 circuits are optional, making it possible for devices which claim RS-449 compatibility to be incompatible (as in the case of RS-232-C).

RS-449 has not been adopted extensively because it was introduced too late and its connectors have too many pins. For telecommunications applications X.21 is becoming popular while RS-232-C is retained for most lower-speed computer and terminal interfaces.

6.4 X.20, X.21 and X.21 bis

6.4.1 X.20 and X.21 bis

The CCITT standard X.21 is a general-purpose interface between data terminal equipment and data circuit-terminating equipment for synchronous operation on public data networks. X.21 is the physical interface specified in the X.25 public packet switched network interface standard but the X.21 bis standard permits V.24 and V.35

physical interfaces (which were developed for use on analog networks) to be used in the interim period until X.21 interfaces become generally available. These interfaces are however unable to take advantage of facilities such as call progress monitoring and facility requests which are available to users with X.21 interfaces.

X.20 is similar to X.21 but for asynchronous terminals; its official title is 'Interface between data terminal equipment and data circuit-terminating equipment for start-stop transmission services on public data networks.' X.20 has a 15-pin connector, balanced or unbalanced electrical circuits and is V.24/V.28 compatible.

X.21 bis specifies V.24/V.28 interfaces for operation up to 9.6 kbit/s and V.35 for rates above 9.6 kbit/s. The V.24/28 interface is equivalent to RS-232-C and V.35 uses a balanced interface with two pins assigned to each circuit for data and clocks but unbalanced signals for control. V.35 uses a 34-pin connector and makes possible high data rates and long cable lengths. The use of V.35 is limited to a small number of high-speed interfaces.

6.4.2 X.21

At the physical level, X.21 employs a 15-pin connector and control signals use the same circuits as user data, rather than separate pins. A separate control circuit identifies data or control signals. This facility reduces the number of pins and permits future extension of control signals.

The electrical characteristics are determined by the X.26 (unbalanced) or X.27 (balanced) interface standards. X.27 is capable of data rates up to 10 Mbit/s with 10 m of cable and up to 100 kbit/s with 1000 m of cable.

X.21 not only specifies the physical interface but also specifies data link and network layer functions for circuit switched networks; these include network control procedures for link establishment and disconnection. After the establishment of the circuit switched connection, X.21 is transparent to the data link. X.21 has been adopted by many circuit switched public digital networks throughout the world.

6.4.3 X.21 operation

Figure 6.6 shows the functions of the six signals in the X.21 interface. The DTE sends data and control information on the Transmit line using the Control line to differentiate data from control information. The DCE uses the Receive line for data and control with the Indication line to differentiate data from control

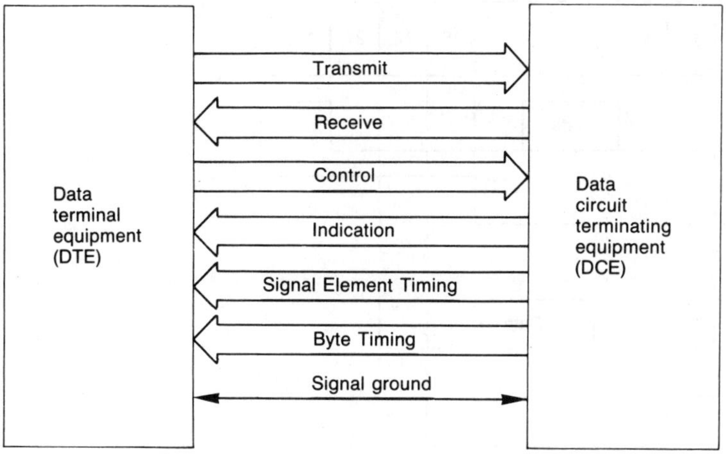

Fig. 6.6 X.21 interface signals

information. The Signal Element Timing line provides bit timing from the DCE and the Byte Timing line may optionally be used to group bits into 8-bit frames. The DTE must begin each character on a frame boundary. If the Byte Timing line is not used, each control sequence must be preceded by at least two SYN characters to identify frame boundaries.

Each call on a circuit switched network goes through four phases:

1) The quiescent phase before transmission or reception.
2) The call establishment phase in which the DTE establishes a circuit switched connection.
3) The data transfer phase in which a full-duplex transmission path is maintained.
4) The clearing phase, initiated by either the DTE or the network, in which the connection is released.

Figure 6.7 shows the progress of a call which is established and cleared by the DTE. The sequence of states through which the interface passes is:

State no. (1)   Ready
         (2)   Call request
         (3)   Proceed to Select
         (4)   Selection Signals
         (7)   Call Progress Signals (DCE sourced)
         (11)   Connection In Progress
         (12)   Ready for Data
         (16)   DTE Clear Request
         (17)   DCE Clear Confirmation
         (21)   DCE Ready
         (1)   Ready

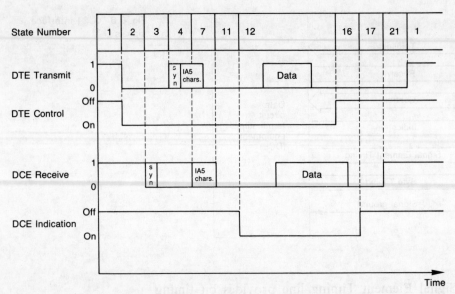

Fig. 6.7 X.21 call progress

6.5 X.3, X.28, X.29

6.5.1 Triple X interface

CCITT have defined three interface standards to permit an asynchronous terminal which does not support the X.25 interface to access an X.25 packet switched network through a packet assembler/disassembler (PAD). The three standards are X.3, X.28 and X.29, sometimes called the triple X interface or interactive terminal interface.

A PAD is a unit which accepts asynchronous, serial character strings from the DTE and converts them into X.25 packets. The packets are delivered by the network to a remote DTE which may have a resident X.25 interface or may use a PAD. Packets received by a PAD are converted into character strings and passed to the DTE via a serial interface such as RS-232-C. The triple X standards support the use of a PAD and define procedures to establish virtual circuits on the network.

6.5.2 X.3

CCITT X.3 defines the basic functions of the PAD; its title is: 'Packet assembly/disassembly facility (PAD) in a public data network.' The 1984 version of X.3 defines 22 user-selectable parameters for the PAD; these are used to specify terminal characteristics, control the assembly and disassembly of packets and to define options for terminal control.

The parameters may be defined when the PAD is configured or may be selected each time a terminal logs onto the PAD. The parameters are:

1) PAD recall (selects the control character which escapes from data transfers).
2) Echo (switches local echo on or off).
3) Data forward (selects the characters which cause the PAD to forward a packet).
4) Idle timer (value of the timer which causes the PAD to forward a packet).
5) Device control (selects the use of X-on and X-off flow control).
6) Service signals (determines whether to send service signals).
7) Break option (determines action when a break is received).
8) Discard data (selects or inhibits discarding of data).
9) Padding (selects a delay after carriage return).
10) Line folding (selects carriage return/line feed at end of lines).
11) DTE speed (selects terminal bit rate).
12) PAD flow control (selects use of X-on and X-off towards the PAD).
13) Line feed insertion (selects line-feed insertion after carriage return).
14) Padding after line feed (selects delay after LF).
15) Editing (selects local editing in the data transfer state).
16) Character delete (causes a character to be deleted).
17) Line delete (causes a line to be deleted).
18) Line display (causes a line to be displayed).
19) Edit PAD service signals (selects editing characters).
20) Echo mask (selects which characters are to be echoed by PAD).
21) Parity treatment (selects use of parity by PAD).
22) Page wait (determines the number of line feed characters at page ends).

6.5.3 X.28

X.28 is a 'DTE/DCE interface for a start-stop mode data terminal equipment accessing the packet assembly/disassembly facility (PAD) on a public data network situated in the same country.' CCITT recommendation X.28 defines handshake procedures between the DTE and the PAD. It defines the character strings which the DTE must employ in order to communicate via the PAD through the network. It also defines the procedure to establish a call to the PAD, setting the PAD parameters, and exchanging data between the PAD and the terminal.

X.28 commands from the DTE to the PAD include:

a) Establishing and resetting virtual calls.
b) Selecting a standard set of PAD parameters.
c) Selecting individual PAD parameters.
d) Requesting the current values of specific PAD parameters.
e) Transmitting an interrupt packet.

The X.3 PAD recall parameter defines which character is used to enter the command mode. Command mode permits X.28 commands to be used for PAD control.

The X.3 PAD to DTE service signals include:

a) Call progress signals to inform the DTE of the call status.
b) Responses and acknowledgements to PAD commands.
c) PAD status signals.

6.5.4 X.29

X.29 defines 'procedures for exchange of control information and user data between a packet mode DTE and a packet assembly/disassembly facility (PAD)'. CCITT recommendation X.29 defines the procedures which exchange data and control information between a PAD and either a DTE with an X.25 interface or another PAD. X.29 PAD messages are contained in the user data field of special X.25 packets.

X.29 also defines procedures for a DTE with an X.25 interface or another PAD to set and read the PAD parameters. PAD control messages, typically consisting of 3 octets, are used for this purpose.

The PAD constructs X.29 packets from data input by the DTE; these include an X.29 header in which a Q bit defines user data or a PAD message. PAD messages perform functions such as setting the X.3 parameters of remote PADs. The X.29 packet is accommodated within an X.25 packet.

6.6 IEEE 488 (IEC 625)

6.6.1 Purpose

IEEE 488 was the first general-purpose parallel interface to be the subject of an international standard. Hewlett Packard submitted their HPIB bus standard to the American Institute of Electrical and Electronic Engineers and in 1975 it was approved as IEEE 488-1975 (the IEEE 488 Standard Digital Interface for Programmable Instrumentation). The standard was revised in 1978 to allow the use of Schottky technology in the drivers and receivers.

The standard is intended to interconnect both programmable and nonprogrammable electronic measuring apparatus with other apparatus and accessories necessary to assemble instrumentation systems. IEEE 488 standard defines device-independent mechanical, electrical and functional interface requirements that the apparatus must meet in order to be interconnected and communicate unambiguously.

6.6.2 Electrical interface

IEEE 488 has two groups of data lines, eight lines are for data transfers (DIO_1 to DIO_8) and eight are for control. A further eight lines provide signal ground returns and shielding. Up to 15 devices may be connected to the IEEE 488 bus and data transfers can take place at up to 1 Mbyte/s with a maximum length of 20 m. The bus cable links devices in a daisy chain typically using 2 m cable lengths.

Negative logic TTL voltage levels are specified. When 48 mA open-collector line drivers are used, the data rate may be up to 250 kbyte/s and the total distance may be up to 20 m with an equivalent standard load on each 2 m length of cable. With 48 mA tri-state drivers the data rate may be increased to 500 kbyte/s. To achieve 1 Mbyte/s with tri-state drivers the capacitance on each interface lead must be less than 50 pF per device and with all instruments in the system turned on the cable length is limited to 15 m (with one equivalent load per metre of cable).

Data transfers are asynchronous, bit-parallel, byte serial, co-ordinated by three interlocked handshake lines, DAV, NRFD and NDAC. The DAV (Data Valid) line indicates the availability and validity of data on the Data Input/Output lines DIO_1 to DIO_8. The NRFD (Not Ready For Data) line signals whether a device is ready to accept data and the NDAC (Not Data Accepted) line indicates that a device is receiving data.

There are five general interface management lines:

1) IFC (Interface Clear) which is issued by the controller to bring all active bus devices to a known quiescent state.
2) ATN (Attention) which is issued by the controller to gain the attention of bus devices before beginning a handshake sequence. It also specifies how data on the DIO lines is to be interpreted and which device must respond. While ATN is held true by the controller the specific response of devices on the bus is obtained by sending talker or listener addresses from

the controller down the DIO lines. All devices listen to the addresses and, when ATN goes false, only the devices which were addressed receive or transmit data, one talker at a time.

3) SRQ (Service Request) which is issued by any device needing service from the controller. This causes an interruption in the current sequence of events.

4) REN (Remote Enable) which is issued by the controller in conjunction with other messages to select between two alternate sources of device programming data.

5) EOI (End Or Identify) which is issued by a talker to notify the listener(s) that the data byte currently on the DIO lines is the last one. EOI together with ATN is issued by the controller to initiate a parallel poll sequence.

6.6.3 Functional specification

As shown in Figure 6.8 devices are able to perform one or more of the three basic functions:

1) Talking
2) Listening
3) Control.

A listener only accepts data from the bus, a talker sends data over the bus, and the controller addresses other devices and grants permission for talkers to use the bus. Only one bus controller and one talker may be active at any time.

Devices all have unique addresses and the controller may address as many listeners as required in broadcast transmission but typical operation is from one talker to one listener. A talker may initiate a serial poll sequence by sending a service-request message to the system controller. The controller responds by obtaining a status byte from all the devices in sequence to determine which one requested the bus. A parallel poll is also possible, in which devices on the bus report their status simultaneously to the controller.

Figure 6.9 shows the 3-wire control handshake required to transfer each byte of data. When the talker has checked that the listeners are ready, it puts data on DIO_1 to DIO_8 and takes DAV low. The listener with the fastest response takes NRFD low to indicate that it is busy. The slowest participating listener raises NDAC (which it has held low since the previous transfer) when it has accepted the data. When the talker detects NDAC is high, it removes the data and takes DAV high which causes all the listeners to prepare for the next transfer. The listeners take NDAC low to indicate that they are ready to accept another byte. The talker may then repeat the handshake for the next byte of data.

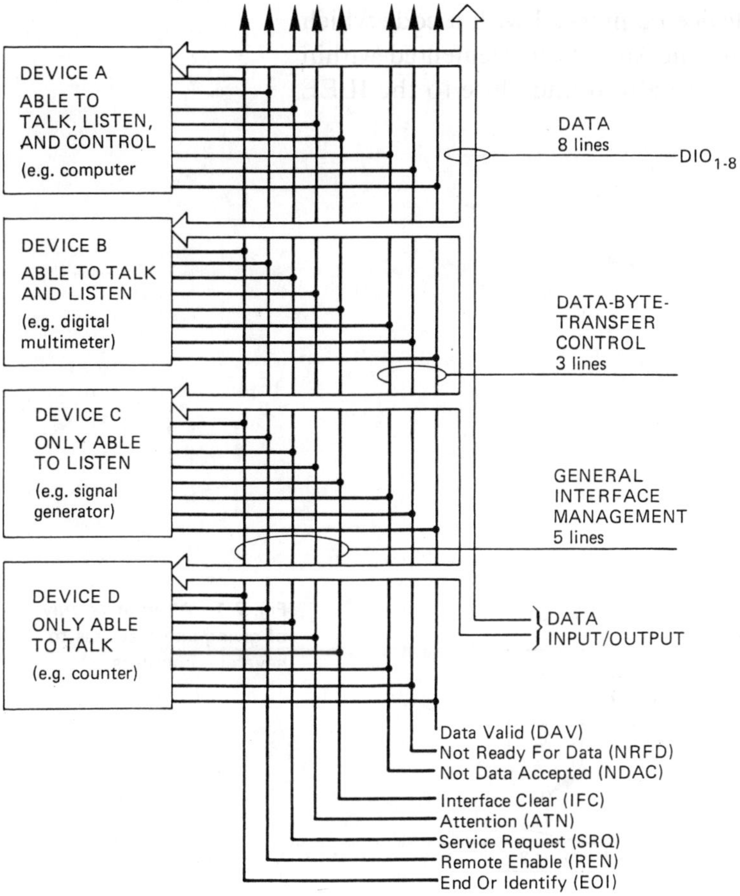

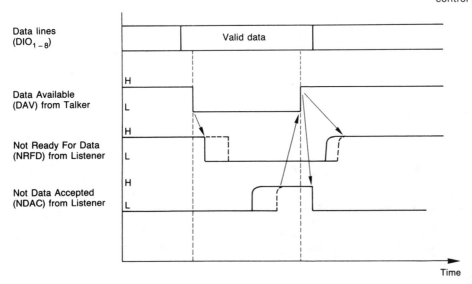

Fig. 6.8 IEEE 488 basic functions and interface lines

DEVICE A
ABLE TO TALK, LISTEN, AND CONTROL
(e.g. computer

DEVICE B
ABLE TO TALK AND LISTEN
(e.g. digital multimeter)

DEVICE C
ONLY ABLE TO LISTEN
(e.g. signal generator)

DEVICE D
ONLY ABLE TO TALK
(e.g. counter)

DATA
8 lines
DIO$_{1-8}$

DATA-BYTE-TRANSFER CONTROL
3 lines

GENERAL INTERFACE MANAGEMENT
5 lines

} DATA
} INPUT/OUTPUT

Data Valid (DAV)
Not Ready For Data (NRFD)
Not Data Accepted (NDAC)
Interface Clear (IFC)
Attention (ATN)
Service Request (SRQ)
Remote Enable (REN)
End Or Identify (EOI)

Fig. 6.9 IEEE 488 3-wire control handshake

Data lines
(DIO$_{1-8}$)

Valid data

Data Available (DAV) from Talker

Not Ready For Data (NRFD) from Listener

Not Data Accepted (NDAC) from Listener

Time

189

It is recommended that each device be marked with a code which identifies those interface functions and subsets implemented within that device. The capability code is usually found close to the IEEE 488 standard connector.

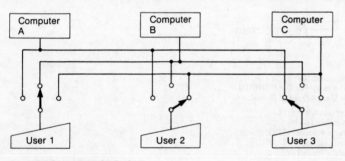

(a) DIRECT CONNECTIONS

Fig. 7.1 Alternative ways of giving users access to several computers

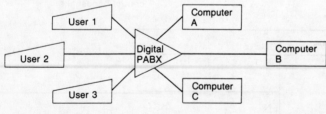

(b) DIGITAL PABX

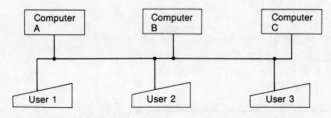

(c) LOCAL AREA NETWORK

190

7 Local area networks

7.1 Local communication alternatives

A Local Area Network is a data communication system which allows a number of independent devices in moderate geographic proximity to communicate with each other.

Local Area Networks (LANs) are employed to interconnect computers, terminals, printers, file servers, etc. located in the same building or within a group of buildings. Metropolitan Area Networks cover larger groups of buildings or a metropolitan area up to 50 km in diameter.

Because the cable lengths in a LAN do not generally exceed about 3 km, it is possible for a LAN to transmit data at much higher data rates than a Wide Area Network (WAN) which may extend across entire continents and have intercontinental links. Error rates are much lower on local area networks than on wide area networks and transmission delays are much lower. Metropolitan area networks fall between LANs and WANs in their data rates, error rates and propagation delay characteristics.

Interest in local area networks began in the mid 1970s, the main motivations being

a) To provide users with access to several computers (see Figure 7.1).
b) To share files.
c) To share hard disks and printers between users with small processors which could not justify provision of dedicated peripherals.
d) To share access to wide area networks.
e) To provide electronic mail and other communications services in office systems.

By 1987 there were 24 600 LANs in the UK with a total of 255 000 station connections.

The relatively short distance covered by LANs makes high data transmission speeds (up to 100 Mbit/s) possible and this together with low error rates opens up a range of LAN applications which are not practical with modem links. These applications include large file transfers, distributed databases and distributed processing systems in which the functions are shared between several host computers.

Because a LAN is usually owned and operated by one organisation, the LAN may not be constrained by the need to conform to international standards and many different varieties of LANs have evolved. Table 7.1 summarises the major characteristics of a relatively small sample of the proprietary LANs available.

The need to offer the latest communications technology and to take advantage of the predicted boom in LAN sales led many companies to develop unique LAN products from scratch. The resulting plethora of incompatible LAN products can confuse the prospective purchaser and can result in systems being abandoned after short periods of use when the required expansion and integration cannot be provided. The development of a limited number of standards for the more significant classes of LAN is helping to rationalise the market for LAN products. The most significant classes of LAN which have evolved are:

a) Broadband
b) CSMA/CD
c) Token bus
d) Token ring
e) Fibre optic
f) Low-cost LANs for personal computers.

Broadband LANs provide many separate data channels for point-to-point or multiple access use together with analog channels such as speech or video. Broadband LANs have become popular for industrial applications and, particularly in the USA, for large office and business complexes.

CSMA/CD permits stations to gain access to a shared channel on a broadband LAN or to a baseband LAN which provides only one channel. The first popular baseband LAN standard, Ethernet, uses CSMA/CD access control and is ideal for office systems where the load is unpredictable and transmission delays do not need to be tightly controlled. The availability of VLSI chips to implement the Ethernet interface heralded a surge in the popularity of Ethernet and its equivalent, the IEEE 802.3 standard.

Following the definition of the IEEE 802.4 standard, *token bus* LANs have been developed to meet the needs of manufacturing automation systems where highly predictable message delays are required. Many LAN types have been developed based on a *ring* topology. Some use a rotating slot of a fixed size (such as the Cambridge Ring, developed at Cambridge University), others use the

192

register insertion principle, but the most popular access control mechanism for baseband rings is token passing. The development of a token passing ring LAN by IBM quickly led to the introduction of the IEEE 802.5 standard and VLSI chips which reduce the size and cost of the LAN interface. The IEEE 802.5 standard is now in widespread use for business applications.

Fibre optic versions of Ethernet and various ring systems are available but the first LAN standard to offer the high data rate (100 Mbit/s) which is possible with optical fibres is the ANSI FDDI dual token passing ring which was adopted as a standard in 1987. A ring topology is most suited to the use of optical fibres because the links between stations do not require optical taps or star couplers, which severely constrain the number of stations on a fibre optic bus or star-wired LAN.

Many proprietary LANs have been developed to interconnect personal computers. The cost of an interface to such a LAN must be low and the design of microcomputer operating systems often constrains its data transfer capabilities to those required for sharing access to disks or printers. The rudimentary LANs developed for use with personal computers often simply allow several machines to share a disk controller. Some LANs simply route data from a standard serial port to a designated port on another interface box. To overcome some of these limitations imposed by single-user operating systems on personal computers, network operating systems have been developed. These are described in Chapter 10.

As described in Chapter 2, four types of transmission media are commonly employed for local area networks:

1) Twisted-pair electrical cable which is limited to data rates of around 3 Mbit/s and has typical error rates around one in 100 000 when not screened. Screened twisted-pair can carry signals up to 10 Mbit/s with error rates better than one in 100 million over distances up to about 1 km but it is much more expensive than unscreened twisted-pair.

2) Baseband coaxial cable for data rates up to 50 Mbit/s and typical error rates of 1 in 10 million.

3) Broadband coaxial cable for data rates (the sum of many FDM channels) over 300 Mbit/s and typical error rates of 1 in 1000 million.

4) Fibre optic cable for total data rates of more then 150 Mbit/s and extremely low error rates. The number of devices which may be attached to a fibre optic bus is small and therefore the ring topology which uses fibre optic links between access points is most suitable.

Table 7.1 Selection of proprietary LANs

Name	Date introduced	Topology	Media	Access method	Transmission speed (Mbit/s)	Max. length per segment/ overall (m)	Max. number of stations
APPLETALK	1985	BUS	TP,BASEBAND	CSMA/CA	0.23	153/763	32
BICC ISOLAN	1985	BUS/STAR	COAX/FO,BASEBAND	CSMA/CD	10.0	500/4000	255
CORVUS OMNINET	1981	BUS	TP,BASEBAND	CSMA/CA	1.0	305/1220	63
DEC NET (ETHERNET)	1980	BUS/TREE	BASEBAND/BROADBAND	CSMA/CD	10.0	500/2800	64 000
DMS HI-NET	1981	BUS	TP/FO,BASEBAND	POLLED	0.5	305/10 000	45
DIGITAL RESEARCH MS/ARC NET	1985	STAR	COAX/BROADBAND	TOKEN	2.5	458	255
IBM TOKEN RING	1985	RING+ STAR	TP/FO BASEBAND	TOKEN	4.0	200/2000	250
IBM PC NETWORK	1984	BUS/TREE	BROADBAND	CSMA/CD	2.0	305 radius	72
ICL OSLAN	1986	BUS	COAX,BASEBAND	CSMA/CD	10.0	500/2000	255
MITEL SX 2000	1983	STAR	TP,BASEBAND	CIRCUIT SWITCHED	0.064	2000/∞	400
NESTAR PLAN	1983	STAR	COAX/FO BASEBAND	TOKEN	2.5 and 4.0	6440	100
NSC HYPERCHANNEL	1982	BUS	TP/COAX/FO BASEBAND	TOKEN CA	50 or 10	1610/8050	10 000

Table 7.1 (continued)

Name	Date introduced	Topology	Media	Access method	Transmission speed (Mbit/s)	Max. length per segment/overall (m)	Max. number of stations
GATEWAY G-NET	1984	BUS	COAX, BASEBAND	CSMA/CA/CD	1.43	2135	15
NOVELL S-NET	1983	STAR	TP/FO BASEBAND	POLLED	0.5	2440	24
ORCHID PC-NET	1983	BUS	COAX BASEBAND	CSMA/CD	1.0	2135	16
RACAL PLANET	1982	RING	COAX/FO BASEBAND	SLOT	10.0	22 000	500
RANK XEROX XC 80	1981	BUS	COAX BASEBAND	CSMA/CD	10.0	500/1500	200
RTD CLEARWAY	1981	RING	COAX BASEBAND	REGISTER INSERTION	0.056	800/80 000	99
3 COM 3 PLUS	1986	BUS	COAX/FO BASEBAND	CSMA/CD	10.0	1000/3000	∞
UNGERMAN-BASS NET/ONE	1984	BUS/RING	BASEBAND/BROADBAND	TOKEN/CD	4.0 or 10.0	500/44 000	1000
WANG LOCAL INTERCONNECTION	1985	BUS	COAX BASEBAND	TOKEN	2.5	610/6440	64
WANGNET	1982	BUS/TREE	BROADBAND COAX	FDM + CSMA/CD	12.0	9662	65 000
XIONICS XINET	1984	RING + STAR	TP BASEBAND	TOKEN	10.0	32 208	250

As described in Chapter 4, four types of network topology are commonly employed for local area networks:

1) Star networks with either an active switch or a passive fibre optic star coupler at the hub, directly connected to each station. A passive star coupler broadcasts data to all connected stations.

2) Bus networks in which stations tap into a single cable. Several segments may be interconnected by repeaters or gateways to increase the distance covered or the number of stations. Information is broadcast to all connected stations.

3) Ring networks in which each node is connected to two adjacent nodes and information is passed around the ring from one node to the next

4) A tree network such as employed in a broadband system with a head amplifier (which changes the transmit frequencies to receive frequencies) connected by successive branches to a large user population.

Local area networks which time division multiplex a shared communications channel must have a protocol which controls access to the channel. As described in Chapter 4 there are three basic forms of access control in common usage.

1) The use of a bus controller to poll each station in turn and invite/command transmission. This form of access control is most common on military data buses such as MIL-STD-1553.

2) Carrier sense multiple access with collision detection (CSMA/CD) as used by Ethernet (IEEE 802.3). In this contention system, each station listens to the traffic on the bus. A station wishing to transmit waits until no traffic is detected before transmitting. If another station transmits simultaneously, both packets of data will be corrupted so a mechanism is included to detect the collision and abort both transmissions. Both stations then wait for a random period before transmitting again to minimise the probability of repeated collisions. Some CSMA systems have access control procedures which avoid collisions (CSMA/CA). Contention ring systems, such as those using register insertion, place packets of data on the ring when a gap is detected.

3) Token passing may be applied to a ring or a bus topology and employs a unique data packet (token) which allows the holder to transmit information. Any station wishing to transmit must wait until it receives the token. It then transmits its data and passes the token onto the next station in the sequence. The rotating slot ring is similar to a token passing ring but each

slot is accompanied by a fixed-length data field which may be used by a node which finds the slot occupancy token clear.

Limiting the options available to a small number of standard LANs will benefit equipment manufacturers by encouraging larger production requirements. The users should benefit from lower equipment costs and a wider range of compatible equipment to chose from. In an attempt to introduce standardisation into local area networks, in 1980, IEEE set up the 802 project which has defined a reference model and a set of standards for the major forms of LAN with data rates below 40 Mbit/s. These standards include:

a)   IEEE 802.1 (A). Local and Metropolitan Area Network Standard. Overview and architecture
b)   IEEE 802.1 (B). Addressing, internetworking and network management
c)   IEEE 802.2. Local Area Network Standard, Logical link control.
d)   IEEE 802.3. CSMA/CD. Access method and physical layer specification.
e)   IEEE 802.4. Token passing bus. Access method and physical layer specification.
f)   IEEE 802.5. Token passing ring. Access method and physical layer specification.
g)   IEEE 802.6. Metropolitan Area Network standards.
h)   IEEE 802.7. Broadband Local Area Network standards.
i)   IEEE 802.8. Fibre optics standards.

Figure 7.2 shows how the IEEE 802 standards fit together and relate to the OSI model. The standards which define the access method and physical layer specification need the logical link control specification to complete OSI layers 1 and 2. IEEE 802.1 (B) provides a minimal network layer. The IEEE 802 standards have been adopted by ISO as ISO/8802.1 to ISO/8802.5.

The American National Standards Institute (ANSI) focuses on standards for LANs with data rates above 40 Mbit/s. The ANSI X3T9 committee has the charter to define input/output interfaces. The X3T9.5 subcommittees have defined two LAN standards:

1)   Local Distributed Data Interface (LDDI) based on the DEC 70 Mbit/s coaxial cable star network (CI).
2)   The ANSI Fibre Distributed Data Interface standard (FDDI), which is a dual 100 Mbit/s fibre optic token passing ring with the ability to reconfigure when one ring fails.

The USA has dominated LAN standardisation. However, the

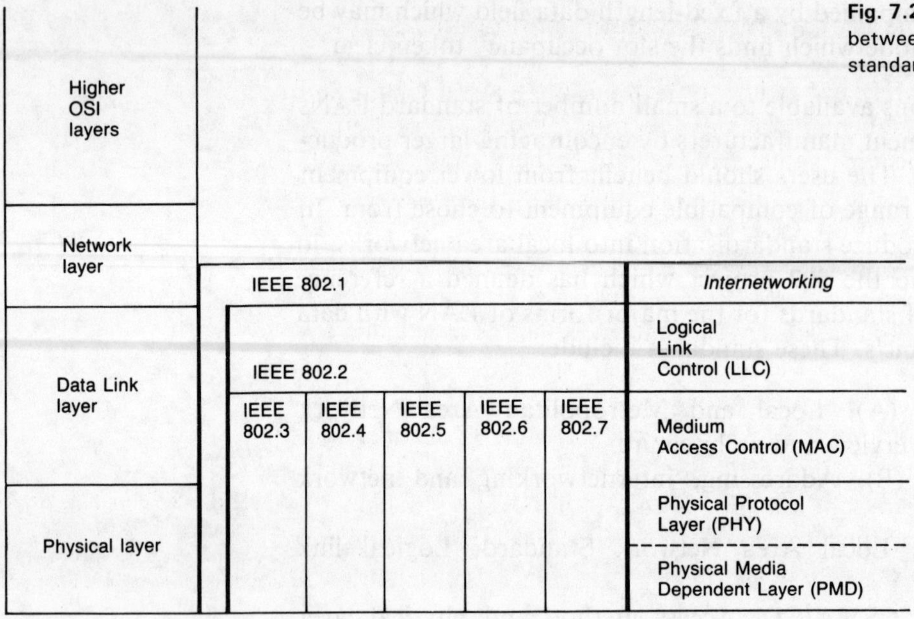

Fig. 7.2 Relationships between the IEEE 802 standards and the OSI model

Higher OSI layers							
Network layer	IEEE 802.1					*Internetworking*	
Data Link layer	IEEE 802.2					Logical Link Control (LLC)	
	IEEE 802.3	IEEE 802.4	IEEE 802.5	IEEE 802.6	IEEE 802.7	Medium Access Control (MAC)	
Physical layer						Physical Protocol Layer (PHY)	
						Physical Media Dependent Layer (PMD)	

British Standards Institution has issued BS 6531 which defines a 10 Mbit/s slotted ring LAN, based on the improved Cambridge ring, and BS 6532 which defines data terminal equipment for attachment to 10 Mbit/s slotted ring LANs.

7.2 Broadband local area networks

7.2.1 Background

Broadband LANs use coaxial cable of the type which was developed for cable television systems (sometimes called community antenna TV, CATV) about 30 years ago; this is relatively inexpensive and can support radio frequency bandwidths up to 400 MHz. Frequency division multiplexing is used to transmit several independent frequency channels down the cable using radio frequency modems to convert the digital information into analog waveforms for transmission.

The topology of broadband LANs typically consists of a bus which branches where segments are connected together by a splitter or directional coupler. The overall topology is a branching tree with terminals connected through RF taps. The bit error rates achieved are typically between 1 in 10^8 and 1 in 10^{11}.

7.2.2   Channel allocation and system configurations

The 300–400 MHz bandwidth is divided into several channels, into which several subchannels may be multiplexed. Television video signals may occupy some bands while others may be used for point-to-point data transmission or local area networks such as a broadband version of IEEE 802.3.

Most broadband LAN systems employ different allocations of channel frequencies but the IEEE 802 and TR 40.1 committees have specified a standard frequency allocation scheme for broadband LANs. As shown in Figure 7.3 the IEEE standard specifies a single cable with 6 MHz channel frequencies defined for transmission (5.75 to 107.75 MHz) and reception (198 to 300 MHz). The 6 MHz channel width is the bandwidth of a television video signal but can typically accommodate about 75 point-to-point data links at 9.6 kbit/s. The broadband LAN channels defined for reception have a 0.25 MHz offset compared with the standard CATV channels. For a 10 MHz CSMA/CD channel, three adjacent 6 MHz channels are used.

Fig. 7.3   The IEEE 802.7 standard frequency allocation scheme for broadband LAN channel pairs

INBOUND	(FORWARD OR TRANSMIT)	OUTBOUND	(REVERSE OR RECEIVE)
Channel designation	Lower edge of channel frequency (MHz)	Channel designation	Lower edge of channel frequency (MHz)
T7	5.75	11	198
T8	11.75	12	204
T9	17.75	13	210
T10	23.75	J	216
T11	29.75	K	222
T12	35.75	L	228
T13	41.75	M	234
T14	47.75	N	240
2'	53.75	O	246
3'	59.75	P	252
4'	65.75	Q	258
4A'	71.75	R	264
5'	77.75	S	270
6'	83.75	T	276
FM1'	89.75	U	282
FM2'	95.75	V	288
FM3'	101.75	W	294

☐ Channel pairs recommended for IEEE local area networks.

Broadband systems generally use amplifiers which limit transmissions to one direction so separate send and receive channels must be provided. Two methods are used: the single-cable mid-split approach and the dual-cable approach. The single-cable mid-split system splits the 300 MHz bandwidth into transmit and receive bands, with a guard band (108 to 198 MHz) to prevent interference between the inbound and outbound frequency bands. In this case the signal amplifiers separate and amplify the two bands in different directions and a central retransmission equipment or 'head end' is used to receive the signals in the transmit band and retransmit them on the receive frequencies (see Figure 7.4).

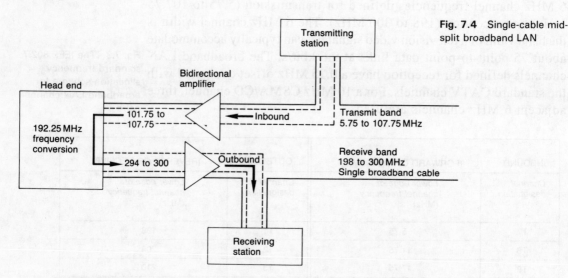

Fig. 7.4 Single-cable mid-split broadband LAN

The IEEE standard reserves frequencies from 107.75 to 216 MHz for television transmission. A frequency offset of 192.25 MHz exists between related transmit and receive frequencies. Thus the last channel of the transmit band (101.75 to 107.75 MHz) corresponds to the last channel of the receive band (294 to 300 MHz). Other offsets and frequency splits are in use: sub-split which may use 5–32 MHz for transmit frequencies and 54–300 MHz for receive frequencies and high-split which may use 5–174 MHz for transmit frequencies and 232–300 MHz for receive frequencies. The use of other than a mid-split may be desirable when a system is mainly used for video applications.

The dual-cable system makes the entire cable bandwidth available for data transmission, one cable transmitting all outbound signals and the other cable conveying all inbound signals as shown in Figure 7.5. There is no central retransmission equipment; the outbound and inbound cables are simply looped around at the head end.

Each terminal is connected to two cables, sending all data on one cable and receiving on the other, using the same frequency. The cost

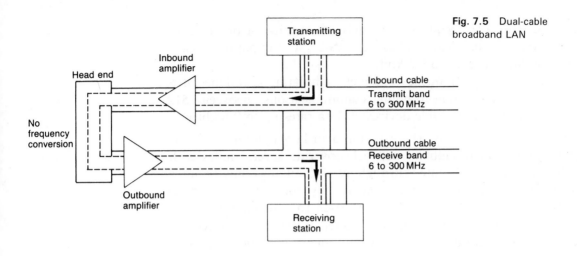

Fig. 7.5 Dual-cable broadband LAN

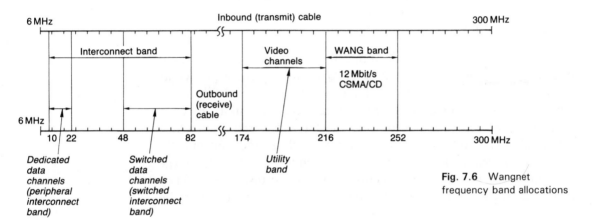

Fig. 7.6 Wangnet frequency band allocations

of a two-cable system is at least 20% higher than that of a single-cable system but twice the bandwidth is available. The most popular two-cable system is Wangnet which uses the frequency band allocations shown in Figure 7.6.

Wangnet allocates part of the spectrum to four services:

1) Wang band which carries a 12 Mbit/s CSMA/CD channel.
2) Peripheral interconnect band which supports dedicated channels.
3) Switched interconnect band which supports terminals and computers.
4) Utility band which contains video channels.

The interconnect bands have three channel groups:

1) 16 dedicated frequency channels for multipoint or point-to-point communications between RS-449/V.35 compatible devices at rates up to 64 kbit/s.

201

2) 32 dedicated frequency channels for multipoint or point-to-point communications between RS-232-C compatible devices at data rates up to 9.6 kbit/s.
3) 256 switched frequency channels, emulating a switched network, for point-to-point communications between 512 RS-232-C compatible devices at data rates up to 9.6 kbit/s.

Amplifiers are used only where required in larger broadband networks. A typical broadband network covering several miles with 3000 connections distributed throughout six buildings only requires six amplifiers to support connections to any point within 7 metres of the main cable. The amplifiers are used to compensate for the changes in cable attenuation at frequency extremes caused by changes in temperature. Some modems incorporate pilot tones to ensure a constant signal level at extremes of temperature.

7.2.3 Communications interface units

Broadband LAN communications interface units incorporate a radio frequency modem tuned to the assigned frequency for a particular channel. Point-to-point data channels employ fixed-frequency modems and, because only one device can transmit at each frequency, no contention resolution mechanism is required. On a single-cable system the modems have one cable connection but use different transmit and receive frequencies. On a two-cable system the modems have two-cable connections but the transmit frequency from one modem is the receive frequency for the other modem in the link.

To handle switched data or voice transmissions in a manner similar to that of a circuit switched network, variable-frequency or frequency-agile modems are used. Control of the frequency used by these modems may be manual or automatic (selected by an intelligent switching device). The automatic switching device keeps track of all available channels. A station may request a frequency channel or the control device may poll all the stations for channel requests using a secondary control channel. When a frequency is assigned, the modems tune to that frequency and establish a link if the receiving device is available. Frequency-agile modems are much more expensive than fixed-frequency modems and the switching control device represents a single point of failure in such systems. Once the modems have been allocated a frequency they are however independent of the switching control device.

A CSMA/CD channel may be implemented on a broadband LAN for applications where several terminals wish to communicate or share resources such as a database server or high-speed printer. The IEEE have approved a standard 10 Mbit/s CSMA/CD channel for

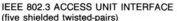

IEEE 802.3 ACCESS UNIT INTERFACE
(five shielded twisted-pairs)

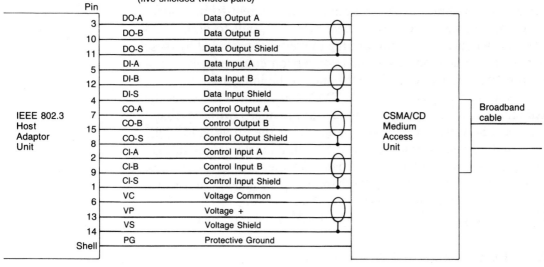

Fig. 7.7 A CSMA/CD channel interface (AUI) for a broadband LAN

broadband LANs. The access unit interface (AUI) is identical to that of a baseband IEEE 802.3 LAN but a special broadband Medium Access Unit (MAU) replaces the conventional baseband one as shown in Figure 7.7.

The location of the head end in the broadband LAN with a CSMA/CD channel is extremely important because the signal propagation time for all stations to become aware of a collision may be extended as a result of the signal having to travel to the head end and back out to all stations.

The reliable detection of collisions on broadband CSMA/CD channels requires a special 4 MHz bandwidth collision enforcement band adjacent to the 14 MHz bandwidth data band, making the total bandwidth for a 10 Mbit/s IEEE 802.3 channel 18 MHz. Baseband IEEE 802.3 detects collisions either by the detection of a direct current voltage, two or more times that of a single transmitter on the cable, or by analog subtraction of the transmitted waveform from the received waveform. Collision detection based on DC level sensing is not possible on broadband systems because only alternating current waveforms are transmitted by amplifiers, splitters, etc. In addition the stronger of two colliding broadband signals may still be received uncorrupted in spite of the presence of another signal.

The broadband Ethernet transceiver (IEEE 802.3 Medium Access Unit) developed by DEC is available in two versions: the single-cable version transmits at 54 to 72 MHz and receives at 210.25 to 228.25 MHz; the dual-cable version transmits and receives at the same frequencies (54 to 72 MHz).

Broadband LANs make it possible to transmit several channels simultaneously. These may be in a number of different forms: video, analog speech, CSMA/CD data channels, or point-to-point data channels. The potential for integrating the services provided by these channels is available but additional conversion equipment is necessary to permit services on different bands to be integrated.

The use of broadband LANs for CSMA/CD channels increases the maximum size of the network from 2.5 km diameter with baseband IEEE 802.3 networks to 3.75 km diameter for the broadband IEEE 802.3 standard and in practice about 5.5 km diameter is possible on some systems. The cost of the broadband medium access unit is however greater than that of a baseband medium access unit or of a fixed-frequency broadband modem.

For more information on broadband LANs see reference 7.1.

7.3   IEEE 802.2 logical link control

The IEEE 802.2 logical link control (LLC) standard together with a medium access control (MAC) standard performs the functions of the OSI data link layer. The 802.2 standard is broadly based on the HDLC data link control protocol but not the HDLC frame structure. HDLC procedures for bit stuffing, flags and abort sequences are not suitable for use on a local area network and are therefore excluded.

As shown in Figure 7.8 the LLC communicates with the network layer by using link service primitives, with the medium access control sublayer using medium access primitives and with the LLC in the communicating subsystem by transfer of LLC protocol data units.

Two types of operation are possible:

1) Type 1 which is a minimum connectionless service.
2) Type 2 which is a connection-oriented service.

The type 1 service transfers messages to specified network addresses or broadcasts them to groups of addresses. No acknowledgements are provided but two classes may be selected to indicate the transmission priority.

Type 2 operation uses an extensive set of primitives for reset, flow control, connection set-up, connection-oriented data transfer and connection termination. A service class may be used to request priority if this facility is available on the particular LAN used. The data transfer primitive makes provision for acknowledgements. The HDLC window mechanism is used; this permits several messages to be transmitted before an acknowledgement must be received and several messages may be acknowledged at once. A flow control primitive is used between peer entities on a connection to indicate the

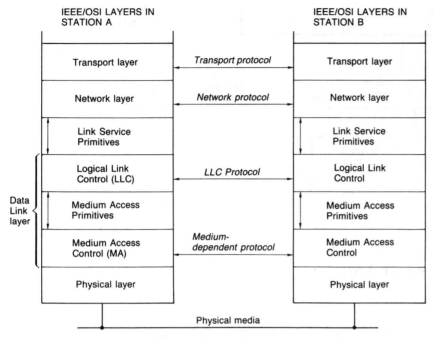

Fig. 7.8 IEEE 802.2 logical
link control (LLC)
communication

Transport layer	*Transport protocol*	Transport layer
Network layer	*Network protocol*	Network layer
Link Service Primitives		Link Service Primitives
Logical Link Control (LLC)	*LLC Protocol*	Logical Link Control
Medium Access Primitives		Medium Access Primitives
Medium Access Control (MA)	*Medium-dependent protocol*	Medium Access Control
Physical layer		Physical layer

Data Link layer

Physical media

amount of data which may be outstanding. This allows the MAC
layer to specify the maximum amount of data which may be sent
without losing data.

The datalink service provided by the LLC to the higher layers is
defined by two classes:

1)   Class 1 which provides type 1 operation.
2)   Class 2 which provides type 1 and type 2 operations.

These services are provided by a protocol which transfers LCC
protocol data units (PDUs) or frames across the LAN. Information
frames are used for connection-oriented (type 2 operation) and
unnumbered information (UI) frames are used for connectionless
(type 1 operation) data transfer which does not require acknowledgements.

LAN frame formats do not match the HDLC frame format and,
therefore when IEEE 802.2 LLC is used, the HDLC address and
control fields are included at the beginning of the data field in the
LAN frame format (see Figure 7.9). Several changes have been made
to the HDLC asynchronous balanced mode including:

a)   Extended format (modulo 128 sequencing) is used for address
and control fields.
b)   A 16-bit address field is used to hold source and destination
addresses plus a group destination address if required.
c)   Three new commands (UI, Test and XID) have been added.
d)   The SREJ and CMDR control commands have been deleted.

205

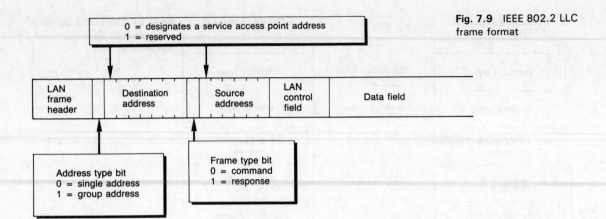

Fig. 7.9 IEEE 802.2 LLC
frame format

7.4 IEEE 802.3 CSMA/CD LAN

7.4.1 Background

The IEEE 802.3 standard was published in 1985, based upon the Ethernet standard for a CSMA/CD LAN. Ethernet was developed in 1981 by Xerox, DEC and Intel, primarily for commercial applications. The data rate is 10 Mbit/s in the majority of applications but operation from 1 Mbit/s to 20 Mbit/s is envisaged (using baseband coaxial cable with a bus topology) in IEEE 802.3. An IEEE 802.3 channel may be implemented on a broadband LAN by replacing the baseband medium access unit with a broadband medium access unit (described in 7.2.3).

As shown in Figure 7.10, the data terminal equipment (DTE) is connected to the cable by a medium attachment unit (MAU) (known as a transceiver on Ethernet). An attachment unit interface (AUI) cable links the standard 15-pin connector on the DTE to the MAU. The MAU is connected to the medium which may consist of up to 500 m of coaxial trunk cable in each segment. Repeater units may be used to extend the system topology by connecting trunk cable segments together up to the limit of 2.5 km between any two MAUs.

The maximum number of DTEs which may be connected to a single IEEE 802.3 network is 1024, but gateways may be used to link several networks together in order to exceed the length and DTE quantity limitations. A less-expensive (type 10 BA SE2) version of the physical layer specification (sometimes referred to as Cheapernet) is available which permits a standard BNC-T connector to be used in place of the MAU and RG58 coaxial cable to be used in place of expensive trunk coax. This reduces the distances which may be supported on each segment but all other parameters are unchanged.

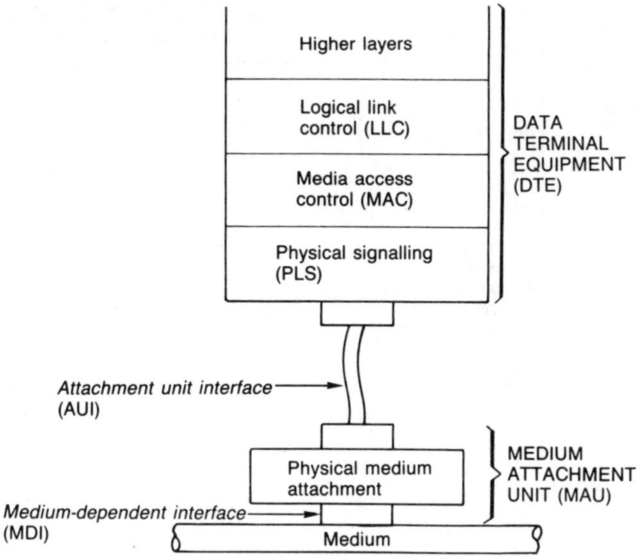

Fig. 7.10 IEEE 802.3 data terminal equipment (DTE) interface

Cheapernet dispenses with the separate MAU; to reduce costs the MAU is an integral part of the DTE.

7.4.2 Media access control frame format

The IEEE 802.3 frame format is shown in Figure 7.11. The preamble consists of 7 octets, each 1010101, which allow the physical signalling system circuitry to reach its steady state synchronisation with the received frame timing. The start frame delimiter consists of the bit sequence 10101011 and indicates the start of a frame.

Separate destination address and source address fields are provided. Each address field consists of either 16 bits or 48 bits; the same source and destination address size is used for all stations on a particular LAN. The first bit of the destination address field designates the destination address as either an individual or a group address. The first bit of the source address field designates whether the source address field contains an individual address or a group address which identifies none, one or more, or all the stations on the LAN.

For 48-bit addresses, the second bit distinguishes between locally or globally administered addresses. Globally administered addresses are used on Ethernet systems. Group addresses indicate a multiple destination and are either

a) A multicast group address which is an address associated by a higher-level convention with a group of logically related stations, or

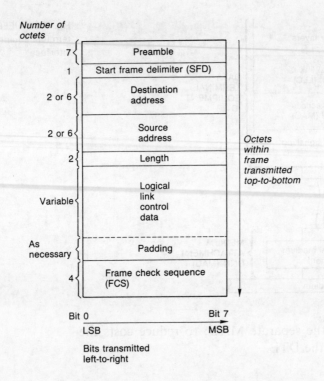

Fig. 7.11 IEEE 802.3 frame format and address field formats

Number of octets

7 — Preamble

1 — Start frame delimiter (SFD)

2 or 6 — Destination address

2 or 6 — Source address

2 — Length

Variable — Logical link control data

As necessary — Padding

4 — Frame check sequence (FCS)

Octets within frame transmitted top-to-bottom

Bit 0 — LSB

Bit 7 — MSB

Bits transmitted left-to-right

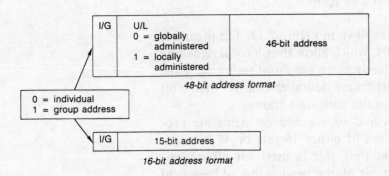

I/G | U/L
0 = globally administered
1 = locally administered | 46-bit address

48-bit address format

0 = individual
1 = group address

I/G | 15-bit address

16-bit address format

b) A broadcast address which sends the message to all stations on the LAN. A broadcast address is defined as all the bits in the destination address field set to 1.

The length field identifies the number of octets in the data field. If the number of data octets is less than the minimum number required for proper operation of the CSMA/CD protocol, pad octets are added. The data field is fully transparent. The minimum and maximum size of the data field is determined for a particular application; Ethernet specifies a data field of 46–1500 octets. The 10 Mbit/s IEEE 802.3 baseband implementation (type 10 BA SE5) assumes a minimum frame size of 64 octets and a maximum frame size of 1518 octets.

The frame check sequence is the last field in the frame. It consists of four octets containing a cyclic redundancy check. The CRC value is a function of the contents of the address fields, length field, data and padding fields. The polynomial used is:

$$x^{32} + x^{26} + x^{23} + x^{22} + x^{16} + x^{12} + x^{11} + x^{10} + x^8 + x^7 + x^5 + x^4 + x^2 + x + 1$$

7.4.3 Transmission procedure

When the LLC sublayer requests transmission of a frame, the MAC sublayer uses the data from the LLC to construct a frame by adding a preamble, start frame delimiter, address fields, a length count field, pad field and frame check sequence.

The carrier sense signal produced by the medium access unit is used to defer transmission until the medium is clear. After an interframe delay (9.6 μs for 10 MHz baseband) to permit recovery of receiving circuits, the serial bit stream is Manchester-encoded and placed on the medium. Throughout the transmission, the collision detected signal is monitored; if no collision occurs the MAC sublayer informs the LLC sublayer and awaits the next request for frame transmission.

At each receiving station the preamble is used to synchronise the internal Manchester decoder. Decoded binary data is passed by the physical layer signalling (PLS) to the MAC sublayer which discards the preamble and start frame delimiter. Bits are collected as long as the carrier sense signal remains on. When the carrier sense signal is removed, indicating the end of the frame, the frame is truncated to the end of an octet boundary if necessary and is decapsulated.

The frame's destination address is checked to decide whether the frame is destined for the station. If so, the destination address, source address and LLC data unit is passed on to the LLC sublayer along with status information for message completeness and correct length. Invalid MAC frames are detected by inspecting the frame check sequence and the octet boundary alignment for the end of the frame.

7.4.4 Collision recovery

When multiple stations initiate transmissions almost simultaneously, after deferring until the medium is free, a collision occurs. Collisions can occur in the initial part of a transmission known as the collision window or slot time (512 bit times for 10 MHz baseband systems), in which time the transmitted signals could propagate to all stations on the medium and back again. Once the collision window has passed, the station is said to have acquired the medium.

The slot time is:

a)   An upper bound on the acquisition time of the medium.
b)   An upper bound on the length of a frame fragment generated by a collision.
c)   The scheduling quantum for retransmission.

To meet all these requirements, slot time must be made larger than the sum of the physical layer round-trip propagation time and the media access layer maximum jam time. These parameters are determined by the medium and interface circuitry.

A collision is detected by the medium access unit which turns on the collision detected signal. The MAC sublayer responds to the collision detected signal by enforcing the collision to ensure that all stations are aware that the collision has occurred.

Enforcement requires a jam bit sequence (32-bit periods for 10 Mbit/s baseband systems) to be transmitted in order to lengthen the duration of the collision. The transmission is then terminated and another transmission attempt is scheduled after a random time interval. The use of a random interval prevents a large number of repeated collisions in a busy system by backing off (delaying retransmissions by progressively larger intervals on the second and successive retransmissions). Up to sixteen attempts at retransmission (the attempt limit) may be made by a 10 MHz baseband system before either the retransmission succeeds or the attempt is abandoned on the assumption that the medium has failed or become overloaded.

A truncated binary exponential back-off process is used to schedule retransmissions. The delay is an integer multiple of the slot time. The number of slot times delay before the nth retransmission attempt is chosen as a uniformly distributed random integer r in the range:

$$0 \leqslant r \leqslant 2^k$$

where $k = \min(n, 10)$.

The algorithm used to generate the integer r is designed to minimise the correlation between the numbers generated by any two stations at the same time.

7.4.5   Implementation of an IEEE 802.3 DTE

Several chip sets are available to construct an IEEE 802.3 DTE. Figure 7.12 shows a typical DTE constructed from the LANCE chip set. The LANCE chip transfers data packets to and from the media access unit and manages the data buffers in local memory, sharing

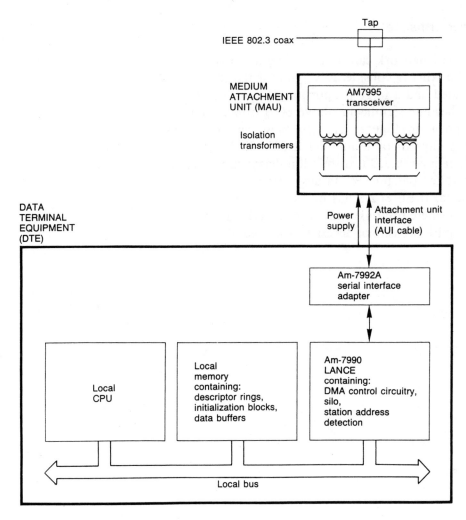

Fig. 7.12 IEEE 802.3 DTE construction using the LANCE chip set

DMA access to this memory with other bus master devices. In the transmitting mode, the LANCE chip transfers data from the current buffer to a 48-byte internal FIFO buffer. The output from this FIFO is serialised and sent to the serial interface adapter which encodes the data and passes it to the coax cable through the transceiver chip in the media access unit.

In the receiving mode the serial interface adapter decodes data and passes it to the FIFO buffer in the LANCE chip. The LANCE chip transfers the data from the FIFO buffer to the current buffer in local memory. The local CPU must provide the functions of OSI layers 3 to 7 and the logical link control part of layer 2 because IEEE 802.3 covers only the access method and the physical layer.

7.4.6   Network performance

A 10 Mbit/s IEEE 802.3 network can transfer data at burst rates up to about 9 Mbit/s but this is considerably reduced if the network becomes heavily loaded and a large proportion of collisions occur. Repeated collisions become significant above 60% offered load on most systems as shown in Figure 7.13. In these circumstances, transmission delay is unpredictable making IEEE 802.3 unsuitable for applications where guaranteed transmission delays are required. Polled systems and token passing techniques with priority mechanisms are more suitable. IEEE 802.3 has become extremely popular for office automation where response times are less critical and large numbers of users require occasional access to the media.

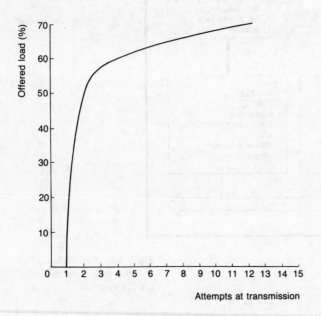

Fig. 7.13 Typical numbers of transmission attempts against offered load for a 10 Mbit/s Ethernet system

Figure 7.14 shows the percentage loading imposed by various user numbers on a large university Ethernet system and the change introduced by different forms of data transfer. Figure 7.15 shows the mean waiting time imposed by various numbers of users with different forms of data transfer.

The transfer rate which may be sustained by an IEEE 802.3 user is frequently limited by the ability of the local processor to carry out the functions of OSI layers 2 to 7 rather than the ability of the network to transmit data or the DTE interface circuitry to transfer data into, or from, local memory.

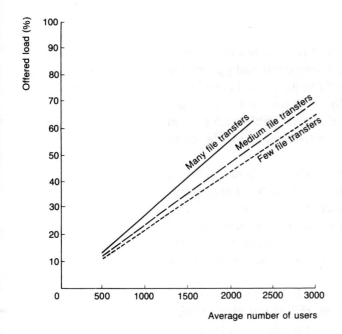

Fig. 7.14 Typical offered load against number of users on a large Ethernet system

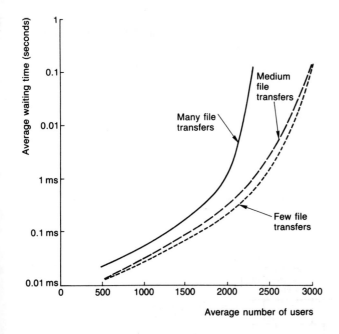

Fig. 7.15 Average waiting time against number of users and data transfer type on a large Ethernet system

213

7.5 IEEE 802.4 token bus LAN

7.5.1 General

The IEEE 802.4 token passing bus standard is intended for factory automation applications and forms layer 1 (physical) and part of the layer 2 (the medium access control part of the data link layer) in the Manufacturing Automation Protocol, MAP. Two forms of media are supported by IEEE 802.4; broadband coaxial cable with several channels (each up to 10 Mbit/s) or a single-channel media using carrierband modulation.

The main network in a MAP system is the backbone network which covers the greatest distances around the factory, interconnecting large computers, gateways and subnetworks (see Figure 7.16). Subnetworks are used to connect small areas of automation and tend to use the less-expensive single-channel carrierband technology whereas the backbone network tends to use the more costly broadband technology.

A token passing bus may be considered as a logical ring. A station which receives a token has control over the medium and may transmit data frames. When the station has completed its transmission it passes on the token to the next station in the logical ring; thus each station in turn is given an opportunity to transmit.

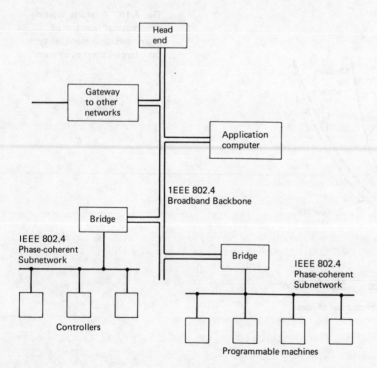

Fig. 7.16 A MAP network in a factory

The medium is used alternately for data transfer and token passing phases. Ring maintenance functions include token initialisation, recovery from token loss, and addition of new stations. The overhead imposed by the token passing phase and ring maintenance functions is high but the bus is prevented from becoming saturated (as may happen with collision detection access control), and transmission delay is predictable. A priority scheme prevents low-priority frames delaying high-priority transmissions.

7.5.2 Frame format

A standard frame format is used for data, tokens and ring maintenance (see Figure 7.17). The preamble is used to synchronise the decoding circuitry and is followed by a start delimiter octet. The frame control octet determines the frame type which may be a control frame or MAC maintenance frame.

Fig. 7.17   IEEE 802.4 frame format

Preamble	Start delimiter (1 octet)	Frame control (1 octet)	Destination address (2 or 6 octets)	Source address (2 or 6 octets)	Data	Frame check sequence (4 octets)	End delimiter (1 octet)

Octets transmitted in left-to-right order

Control frames may be of several types:

a) Token
b) Claim token
c) Set successor
d) Solicit successor
e) Resolve contention
f) Who follows.

The data frame includes bits which determine the level of priority which should be given to the frame (from 8 priority levels).

The destination address and source address fields may be either 16 or 48 bits long. Multicast group address and broadcast addresses are provided as for IEEE 802.3. The data field can accommodate a logical link control data unit, a medium access control management data frame, or a control field related parameter. There is no minimum data field length but the maximum number of octets between the start and end delimiters is 8191.

The frame ends with a four-octet frame check sequence, as employed by IEEE 802.3, which protects all the packets between the start delimiter and the end delimiter. The final byte is an end delimiter. A bit in the end delimiter may be set to indicate that more frames will be transmitted. Another bit may be used by relays to indicate that an error was detected in the frame. A start delimiter immediately followed by an end delimiter indicates that the frame was aborted.

An information frame has a fixed number of overhead octets for a specific implementation of a token bus. Implementation dependences occur for:

a) Preamble, which varies according to bus bit rate. Its duration is at least 2 μs and it comprises an integral number of octets. This yields 1 octet for a 1 Mbit/s bus and 3 octets for a 10 Mbit/s bus.

b) The source and destination address field size depends on whether the 16-bit or the 48-bit addressing option is in use.

The information frame overhead and the token passing frame size are identical and are summarised for various bit rates in Table 7.2.

Table 7.2 Information frame overheads and token frame sizes

Bit rate (Mbit/s)	Overhead/token size (octets)	
	16-bit addressing	48-bit addressing
1	12	20
2.5	12	20
5	13	21
10	14	22

7.5.3 Transmission procedure

All stations are ready to receive frames at any time except when holding the token. A station wishing to transmit must wait until it receives the token before transmitting; it may then transmit as many frames as it likes subject to the limitations imposed by the priority systems and the maximum token hold time which may be imposed for a particular system.

The priority system requires each station to measure the time taken for a token to pass around all the stations in the logical ring. Messages are allocated an access class (6, 4, 2, 0 and ring maintenance) and a target token rotation time is defined for each access class, apart from class 6 (because class 6 is the highest priority which must be transmitted regardless of the token rotation time) and ring maintenance. Data is only transmitted when the token rotation time measured at the station for the last iteration of the token is less than the target token rotation time for the priority level allocated.

The transmission frames are received by all stations but only the addressed stations will read the data from the bus. After the data has been transmitted the token is passed to the next station in the logical ring.

There is no central monitor station to generate the token. Initialisation takes place when the ring is inactive, either when the ring starts up or if the token is lost by a station failing. One or more stations may send a claim token frame to restart the ring. The station with the largest address number claims the token by transmitting the longest length of claim token frame. By detecting silence after its transmission of a claim token, the station with the longest transmission will become aware that it has the largest address number and will claim the token.

Initialisation continues by repeating the process for adding new stations to the logical ring until all the stations are included in the token passing sequence. The station which holds the token issues a solicit successor frame and any new stations respond with a frame which request the next position in the logical ring. The station with the token waits for the duration of the response window, then decides which of the responding stations has the best address (in ascending or descending order) to be next in the logical ring. The token is passed to the successful station; unsuccessful stations must wait for another solicit successor frame.

Each station knows the address of the next station in the logical ring. After transmitting the token to that address the sender listens for a valid frame to be transmitted but, if none is detected within the token loss timeout period, it sends the token again. If no valid frame results from the second attempt to pass on the token, the station sends a who-follows frame with the address of the station it expected was next in the logical ring. The next station but one in the logical ring should respond with a set successor frame and the token holder sends the token to the indicated address, thus bypassing the failed station.

If no station responds to the who-follows frame, the token holder waits until it has data to transmit before transmitting a claim token frame and waiting for a response. As a last resort, a station holding the token may stop transmitting and listen for activity. If a station holding the token monitors no valid frame from the next station in the logical ring and assumes the station has failed when it has not, duplicate tokens will be generated and the resulting contention must be resolved.

7.5.4 Steady state operation

Normal or steady state operation of the token bus occurs when initialisation is complete. All stations wanting to join the logical ring have done so and frames are being transmitted and received without errors, and without loss.

In order to describe normal operation, we will use the examples given in Figures 7.18 and 7.19. Each figure shows the operation of a particular station from receipt of the token to passing the token to the next station. Notation for these figures is explained below:

a) The horizontal axis represents arbitrary time units.
b) Frames on the bus are shown as rectangular blocks:

  T = Token frame
  D = Data or Information frame with access class indicated
      by the suffix
  S = Solicit successor
  R = Response window

c) The durations of timers are shown as horizontal lines.
d) Labelling of timers is as follows:

  T_H = high priority token hold time.
  $TRT_a(n)$ = token rotation time for priority access class 'a'
         and for rotation 'n'.
  Access class 'm' is for ring maintenance.

In Figure 7.18, the station is IDLE while the token is being passed to it. On recognition of the token, the station loads its token hold timer with the value hi-pri-token-hold-time, sets access class to 6, and changes to USE TOKEN state. This occurs at time 0 in Figure 7.18.

The station has high-priority (access class = 6) data to send and sends three data frames (D_6). The data frames could be of different lengths and could be addressed to different destinations. When re-entering the USE TOKEN state for the fourth time, the station finds that its token hold timer has expired and it is therefore not permitted to send any more D_6 frames. The station changes its access class to 4 and changes to the CHECK ACCESS CLASS state. This occurs at time 9 in Figure 7.18.

On entry to CHECK ACCESS CLASS state, the station loads its token hold timer with the residual value of the token rotation timer for access class 4 (TRT_4), restarts TRT_4 with the corresponding target token rotation time, and returns to the USE TOKEN state. In Figure 7.18, we are now fractionally after time 9.

The station has access class 4 data to send and transmits two D_4 frames. It then finds that its token timer has expired (previous TRT_4) and must stop sending, changes to access class 2, and enters the CHECK ACCESS CLASS state. This occurs at time 17 in Figure 7.18.

Figure 7.18 shows that the token rotation timers for access classes

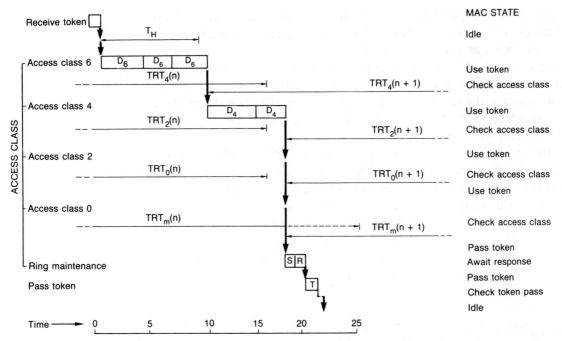

MAC STATE

Idle

Use token
Check access class

Use token
Check access class

Use token
Check access class
Use token

Check access class

Pass token
Await response
Pass token
Check token pass
Idle

Fig. 7.18 Message frames and timers at the end of token rotation n

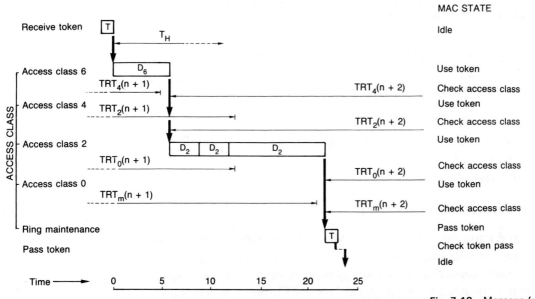

MAC STATE

Idle

Use token
Check access class
Use token
Check access class
Use token

Check access class
Use token

Check access class

Pass token
Check token pass
Idle

Fig. 7.19 Message frames and timers at the end of token rotation $n + 1$

2 and 0 have expired by time 17, and therefore the station 'drops through' these access classes without sending any frames. When the access class has reduced to that of ring maintenance, the station enters the CHECK ACCESS CLASS state with some remaining ring maintenance token rotation time. The station restarts the ring maintenance token rotation timer and enters TOKEN PASS mode at the substate level of 'solicit successor'. In Figure 7.18 we are now fractionally after time 17.

In TOKEN PASS (solicit successor) substate, the usual action is to send a solicit successor-1 control frame and to start a single response window delay. This allows any new station with an address between those of this station and the next station to identify itself.

A special case occurs for one station in the token ring when the next station address is higher than this station (i.e. where the descending address ring returns to the top address). In this case a solicit successor-2 control frame is sent and a double response window delay is started.

The station waits out the response window timer in AWAIT RESPONSE state. In the normal case there are no new stations and therefore no responses will occur. The station returns to the PASS TOKEN (pass token) substate. The token frame is sent and the station ensures (in CHECK TOKEN PASS state) that a valid frame has been transmitted by the successor. In the normal case the station would then return to the IDLE state having successfully handed on the token.

Figure 7.19 shows what might occur at the same station when it next receives the token. The differences from Figure 7.18 are as follows:

a) High-priority data does not need all of T_H.
b) TRT_4 expires before access class 4 is entered and no class 4 data can be sent.
c) TRT_2 allows some access class 2 frames to be sent.
d) TRT_0 prevents access class 0 frames from being sent.
e) TRT_m prevents ring maintenance so the PASS TOKEN state begins with the pass token substate and omits the solicit successor stage.

7.5.5 Carrierband modulation

Broadband transmission of 5 or 10 Mbit/s IEEE 802.4 channels are frequently used for backbone connections in a MAP system but a less-expensive carrierband technology may be used for local connections and is included in the physical layer IEEE 802.4 specification. Carrierband is a single-channel system implemented by digital circuitry rather than analog RF circuitry. Two types of modulation are included in the specification for carrierband, phase continuous FSK and phase coherent FSK.

A single carrierband segment can accommodate up to 30 stations and 1 km of cable but repeaters may be used to extend these limits. Phase coherent modulation (a form of frequency shift keying) with data rates of 5 or 10 Mbit/s is most commonly used at carrierband. A single-chip carrierband modem has been developed by Motorola and this may be connected to the MC68824 Token Bus Controller chip to implement the IEEE 802.4 phase coherent physical layer standard (see Figure 7.20).

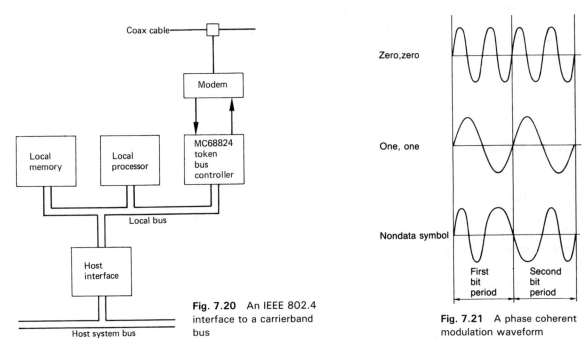

Fig. 7.20 An IEEE 802.4 interface to a carrierband bus

Fig. 7.21 A phase coherent modulation waveform

The physical media is 75 Ω broadband trunk cable with isolating transformer-coupled passive taps connecting more flexible drop cables up to 100 ft in length leading to the stations. Phase coherent modulation is a form of FSK in which the zero crossing points are in phase at the beginning and end of each bit period (see Figure 7.21). A logic 1 consists of a full cycle of the lower frequency in the bit period and a logic 0 consists of two full cycles of the higher frequency in the bit period. The higher signalling frequency is twice the lower signalling frequency.

A nondata symbol is used in frame delimiters and occurs only in pairs. A pair of nondata symbols consists of one full cycle of the higher frequency followed by one full cycle of the lower frequency, then another full cycle of the higher frequency. The silence symbol has no signal present during the bit period and pad-idle symbols, used in the preamble at the beginning of each data frame, consist of alternating 0 and 1 symbols. The preamble is used to provide clock and phase reference information to the modem receiver prior to data transmission.

A station interface constructed from a modem and a token bus controller chip requires a local CPU to handle the logical link control part of layer 2 and all the higher MAP layers. The MC68824 handles medium access control and the modem chip handles the physical layer. If the local CPU handles all the higher MAP layers, between 0.5 and 1 Mbyte of local memory may be required. If the host system provides some of these functions or if only a collapsed set of MAP services is required, the local processing and storage requirements will be reduced.

7.6 IEEE 802.5 token ring LAN

7.6.1 Background

IEEE 802.5 defines a token ring access method and physical layer specification. The standard is based upon the IBM token ring, which is a token passing ring linking multistation access units (MAUs) which support star-wired connections to the stations. Each star-wired station is in series with the ring wiring which joins MAUs. The bit rate on the IBM ring is typically 4 Mbit/s. Up to 100 m lengths of twisted-pair cable may be used to link stations to the MAUs and either shielded twisted-pair or optical fibre may be used to link the MAUs in the ring with a maximum length of 200 m.

IEEE 802.5 emphasises the externally visible characteristics needed for interconnection compatibility while avoiding unnecessary constraints on the processing equipment which is to be interconnected. The data signalling rate may be 1 Mbit/s or 4 Mbit/s. Shielded twisted-pair cable is used with the error rate on the interconnection medium specified to be better than 1 in 100 million. Type 1 cable has a large oval cross-section; type 6 cable is smaller and more flexible but has a greater attenuation.

IEEE 802.5 specifies a standard medium interface connector linking the station to the trunk coupling unit (TCU) which is attached to the trunk cable (see Figure 7.22). An insertion/bypass switching mechanism is incorporated in the TCU, which permits the station to switch itself into the ring when necessary. Transmission is by 50% differential Manchester encoded baseband modulation on shielded twisted-pair trunk cables linking successive stations in the ring. The 50% differential Manchester encoding system has a

222

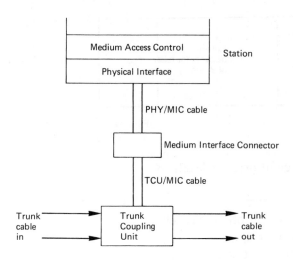

Fig. 7.22 An IEEE 802.5 station interface

transition in the middle of each bit period. A zero has a transition at the beginning of each bit period while a 1 does not (see Figure 3.8). Repeaters may be used to extend the length of the trunk links but each repeater counts as one station from the maximum of 250 which may be connected. Bridges may be used to interconnect up to seven rings.

7.6.2 Token format and frame format

Different formats are used for the token and the information frames. As shown in Figure 7.23 the token starts with a 1 octet start delimiter (SD) and ends with an end delimiter (ED). These are defined bit patterns and are used on all tokens and frames.

The access control (AC) octet is used in the token and in frames; as shown in Figure 7.24 it consists of four fields:

Start delimiter (1 octet)	Access control (1 octet)	End delimiter (1 octet)

TOKEN FORMAT

Fig. 7.23 IEEE 802.5 token and frame formats

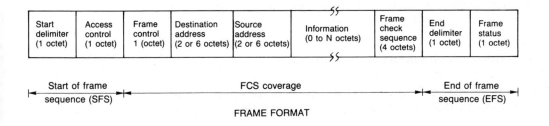

Start delimiter (1 octet)	Access control (1 octet)	Frame control 1 (octet)	Destination address (2 or 6 octets)	Source address (2 or 6 octets)	Information (0 to N octets)	Frame check sequence (4 octets)	End delimiter (1 octet)	Frame status (1 octet)

Start of frame sequence (SFS)	FCS coverage	End of frame sequence (EFS)

FRAME FORMAT

223

				Token bit 0 = token 1 = frame	Monitor bit 0 modified to 1 by monitor			Reservation bits (request for token at 8 priority levels)	
	Priority bits (8 priority levels)									

Fig. 7.24 IEEE 802.5 access control octet

1) Priority field which allocates one of the eight priority levels to the token or frame.
2) Token bit, set to 0 for a token and 1 for a frame.
3) Monitor bit which is used by a monitor station to prevent frames circulating continuously around the ring.
4) Reservation field which requests a high priority token.

The frame format includes start and end delimiters and an access control octet. The frame control field identifies the frame type (LLC level frame or a MAC level ring control frame) and the priority for LLC frames or control information for MAC level frames. MAC control frames include:

a) Claim token
b) Standby monitor present (transmitted periodically)
c) Beacon
d) Purge (which is used for reinitialisation and after a claim token).

The destination address and source address may be either 16 or 48 bits long and may identify individual or group destinations with universal or local significance. The information field may be of any length but this will be limited by the token holding time which is selected for each individual station.

The frame check sequence (FCS) which accommodates a CRC protects all the preceding fields following the start delimiter. The frame status field (FS) is not protected because it follows the FCS. The FS field is used by the receiving station to indicate to the originator what actions it performed on receipt of the frame. Fields include an address recognised field, a packet copied field, and an error bit which is set if the FCS did not match the locally calculated CRC or if other faults were detected. If the fields are unchanged, a faulty or non-existent station is indicated.

7.6.3 Transmission procedures

Each station in the token ring transfers information bit-by-bit from one active station to the next. Upon receiving the token, a station transfers information onto the ring where it circulates. The addressed destination station copies the information as it passes and finally the station which transmitted the information removes the information from the ring and, after checking that the data was not corrupted in transmission, it initiates a new token which provides other stations with the opportunity to gain access to the ring.

A token holding timer controls the maximum period of time a station can use the medium before passing on the token. Eight levels of priority may be assigned to each frame and a station may request tokens of various priority levels as required by the waiting frames. When a token of suitable priority level is received the message may be transmitted.

A station receiving a token may convert the token into one or more frames and the frames must do a trip around the ring before being removed by the sender. The sender may inspect the frame status field to see if the recipient satisfactorily copied the frame. Once the transmitting station has seen the start of the transmitted frame return and has finished transmitting the last frame, it forwards the token to the next station in the ring. If the next station has nothing to transmit, it forwards the token to the next station on the ring.

The token ring procedures differ from those of the token bus because all stations are not aware of the traffic simultaneously. The control of the ring must therefore reside with a single station. All stations have a monitor capability and one will be designated to be the active monitor station while the others put their monitor functions in standby, ready to take over if the active monitor fails.

The active monitor station is responsible for ring maintenance which must detect three possible causes of ring failure:

1) Loss of the token, which is detected by a timeout period and corrected by regenerating the token. Tokens should not be lost when a station fails or is switched off because the bypass relay should come into effect.

2) Failure to reissue the token, which is detected because the monitor bit remains unchanged. The monitor station changes the monitor bit to prevent the frame circulating continuously.

3) Breaks in the ring caused by a node and a node bypass failure or a cable break, which are detected by the next station in the ring. The standby monitor in this station transmits a beacon control frame which is detected by the active monitor station.

The failure of the active monitor station is only detected by standby monitor stations if the token is lost and no action is taken to reissue the token within a defined period. The standby monitor stations which detect the failure transmit a claim token control frame and a claim token resolution procedure results in only one station becom-

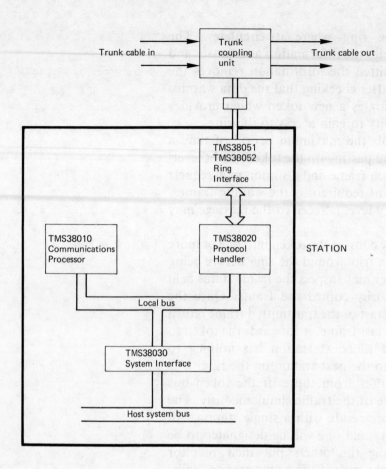

Fig. 7.25 A typical IEEE
802.5 station interface

Trunk cable in

Trunk
coupling
unit

Trunk cable out

TMS38051
TMS38052
Ring
Interface

TMS38010
Communications
Processor

TMS38020
Protocol
Handler

STATION

Local bus

TMS38030
System Interface

Host system bus

ing the new active monitor. A ring poll is transmitted around the ring
by the active monitor every seven seconds to let new stations enter
the ring.

A typical station interface for IEEE 802.5 is shown in Figure 7.25.
The TMS38030 manages the transfer of data between the host system
memory and the LAN adapter bus. The TMS38010 processes and
buffers data while the TMS38020 manages the IEEE 802.5 protocols.
The TMS38051 and TMS38052 monitor cable integrity, control
network insertion, and perform clocking and signal conditioning. A
further chip is available to perform the logical link control if this is
not performed by the host processor. Later versions of the TMS380
family integrate all functions onto two chips and will operate at
16 Mbit/s. Figure 7.26 shows the throughput of the TMS380 chip set
and an IBM PC-AT for a 4 Mbit/s ring with variations in frame size,
internal buffer size and host transfer type.

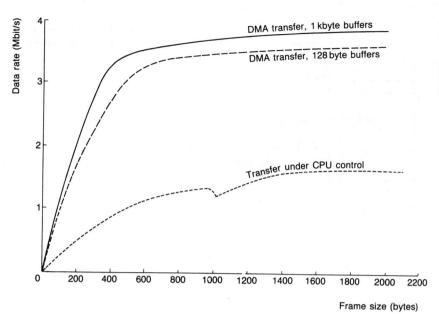

7.7 ANSI FDDI dual fibre optic ring

7.7.1 General

The ANSI Fibre Distributed Data Interface standard specifies a fibre optic timed token passing ring with a signalling rate of 100 Mbit/s. The 100 Mbit/s data rate is the practical maximum which can currently be achieved using relatively inexpensive PIN photodetector diodes and light-emitting diodes with a highly efficient 4B/5B encoding scheme. This encoding scheme requires only 125 Mbaud pulses on the medium whereas the Manchester encoding scheme used on IEEE 802.3 and IEEE 802.5 would require 200 Mbaud for 100 Mbit/s data transmission.

An FDDI network can work with 2 km of fibre between stations, a total circumference of 200 km of fibre, and a maximum of 1000 stations. Two classes of connection are defined. Class A nodes can take advantage of the dual ring fault tolerance capability but class B nodes support only a single ring and may be routed to a wiring concentrator for connection to a dual ring (see Figure 7.27). If a class B node fails, the wiring concentrator bypasses the node and keeps the ring operating. Class A nodes may use both rings simultaneously giving the system a maximum effective bit rate of 200 Mbit/s. The term 'node' is used to describe the part of a station which is concerned with the routing of data and cable interfaces.

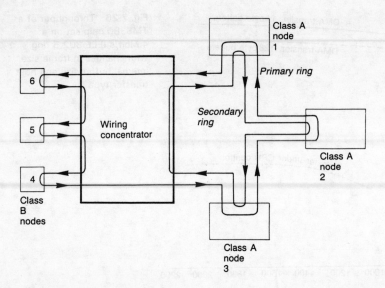

Fig. 7.27 FDDI class A and class B node connections

Fibre optic cables permit higher data rates than other baseband media and, because attenuation is lower than with electrical cables, larger distances may be covered. Further benefits include the immunity of the cable to electrical noise and lightning strikes (or the electromagnetic pulse associated with a nuclear explosion). FDDI interfaces will inevitably be more expensive than IEEE 802.3 interfaces and the initial applications will probably be as a backbone network connecting high-performance computers and linking spur networks via gateways. Later applications may include the linking of high-performance CAD workstations which require high data rates to transfer graphics data.

FDDI uses the IEEE 802.2 logical link control standard and ISO standards for high layers. The FDDI medium access control layer is based on IEEE 802.5 but incorporating modifications for higher-speed operation including:

a)   Use of a distributed elastic buffer.
b)   The use of a timed token priority scheme.

A hybrid system combining a slotted ring within the FDDI system has been proposed to handle digital voice and data. This proposal, known as FDDI II, would permit many time division multiplexed voice channels to be transmitted in fixed time slots without imposing excessive transmission delay variation. FDDI II produces sixteen dynamically programmable 6.144 Mbit/s channels and a 1.024 Mbit/s control channel from the 100 Mbit/s capacity.

228

7.7.2 Token format and frame format

Separate token and frame formats are used (see Figure 7.28). Both the token and the frame start with a preamble consisting of idle symbols, to synchronise the local clock. The one-octet start delimiter (SD) consists of the symbols JK. The one-octet frame control field contents are shown in Table 7.3. The frame control field contents are

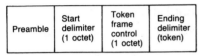

Fig. 7.28 FDDI token and frame formats

Preamble	Start delimiter (1 octet)	Token frame control (1 octet)	Ending delimiter (token)

FDDI TOKEN FORMAT

Octets transmitted in left-to-right order →

Preamble	Start delimiter (1 octet)	Frame, frame control (1 octet)	Destination address (2 or 6 octets)	Source address (2 or 6 octets)	Information (0 or more octets)	Frame check sequence (4 octets)	Ending delimiter (frame)	Frame status (1.5 octets)

FDDI FRAME FORMAT

Table 7.3 Contents of the FDDI frame control field

X000 0000	Void frame
1000 0001 to 1000 1111	SMT frame
0100 0000	Token
1100 0000	Void frame
L100 0001 to L100 1111	MAC frame
LC01 0000 to LC01 1111	Reserved
LC01X 0000 to LC1X 1111	LLC frame

different for a token and a frame and indicate frame type plus address length. The token is terminated by an end delimiter but the frame is terminated by an end delimiter followed by a 12-bit frame status field which is used by the nodes through which the frame passes to signal to the transmitting node.

The frame destination address field may be either 16 or 48 bits long and the source address field is the same length as the destination address field. The total frame may be up to 9000 symbols (about 4500 octets) and the data field may contain from 1 to a maximum number of octets which is compatible with the maximum frame size. More than one frame may be transmitted when the token is received. The 32-bit frame check sequence field accommodates a cyclic redundancy check code which covers all the packet between the start and end delimiters.

7.7.3 Physical layer

The physical layer specification includes the optical and mechanical characteristics of the fibre and the optical power levels and dynamic range of optical receivers plus the 4B/5B encoding method.

These fibre options are included:

1) 62.5/125 μm diameter (core/cladding)
2) 85/125 μm diameter (core/cladding).

The wavelength used is 1300 nm and bulkhead mounted optical connectors are specified. Two fibres, for transmit and receive, are contained within one outer jacket.

The 4B/5B encoding method provides an efficiency of 80% compared with 50% for Manchester encoding. Thus a 100 Mbit/s data rate requires 125 Mbaud transmission compared with 200 Mbaud if Manchester encoding was used. Four-bit nibbles of data are encoded into 5-cell symbols, as shown in Table 7.4. The

Table 7.4 4B/5B encoding

Symbol	Code	Assignment
0	11110	0000
1	01001	0001
2	10100	0010
3	10101	0011
4	01010	0100
5	01011	0101
6	01110	0110
7	01111	0111
8	10010	1000
9	10011	1001
A	10110	1010
B	10111	1011
C	11010	1100
D	11011	1101
E	11100	1110
F	11101	1111
J	11000	Start delimiter
K	10001	Start delimiter
T	01101	End delimiter
R	00111	Reset
S	11001	Set
Q	00000	Quiet
I	11111	Idle
H	00100	Halt (forced break)

symbols are transmitted in a non-return to zero inverted (NRZI) line transmission format.

The assignment of 4-bit nibbles to 5-cell symbols is selected to ensure that a transition occurs at least once every three cells; this makes clock recovery practical. The eight possible symbol combinations which violate this requirement are prevented from occurring in a correctly functioning FDDI system.

Of the 24 valid code groups, 16 are allocated to 4-bit nibble data values and the rest are used for special physical layer line states (quiet, idle, halt) and control functions (J, K, T, R, S) which have special functions:

JK   =   start delimiter
T with R and S   =   end delimiter

7.7.4   Transmission procedures

Packets are transmitted by the next node holding the token, then from one node to the next in the ring. At each node the packets are retimed and regenerated except when a station is idle, in which case the station may have an optical bypass or be configured to function as an active repeater.

The station to which the packet is addressed copies the packet which is returned to the originator for removal from the ring. The originating station follows the packet(s) by a new token which the next station can use to transmit its data.

FDDI uses a timed token access control method which permits the originator to specify message priorities. Each node measures the time the token takes to return and compares this with the eight target token rotation times for frames of various priority levels. When the ring is heavily loaded the token rotation time will increase and only messages with a target token rotation time less than the last measured token rotation time may be transmitted when the token is acquired.

As shown in Figure 7.29, the ring load is proportional to the token rotation time (TRT). An operative TRT (Topr) is specified, above which only synchronous transmissions (such as voice) may be transmitted. In a normally functioning system the TRT never exceeds 2 Topr, giving synchronous nodes the opportunity to transmit in each period of duration 2 Topr. Local buffers are required to store synchronous data for a period up to 2 Topr. When the TRT is less than Topr, asynchronous traffic with various priority levels may be transmitted.

If the TRT exceeds 2 Topr a ring fault is implied. An early warning timer, TVX, initiates recovery before 2 Topr is reached. The recovery procedure requires each station to transmit claim token packets which contain the TRT value required by the station to

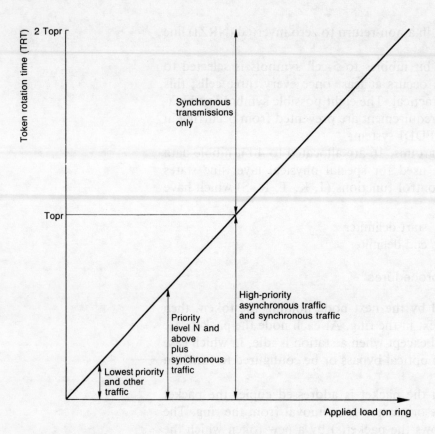

Token rotation time (TRT)

2 Topr

Synchronous
transmissions
only

Topr

High-priority
asynchronous traffic
and synchronous traffic

Priority
level N and
above
plus
synchronous
traffic

Lowest priority
and other
traffic

Applied load on ring

support its synchronous traffic. The station with the lowest TRT wins the token or, if more than one station has the same value, the one with the highest address wins.

When the ring is broken, stations transmit beacon packets which are repeated by each node. By inspecting the beacon packets the fault location may be identified and reconfiguration of the rings takes place. Loss of power at a station may cause an optical relay to operate thus bypassing the station. Cable breaks or link faults cause the dual ring to reconfigure into a single ring within a few milliseconds (see Figure 7.30(a)). Station management facilities permit the dual ring to be restored automatically when the fault is repaired.

A second ring failure causes the ring to split into two smaller independent networks as shown in Figure 7.30(b). A fault in a cable to a class B node causes the wiring concentrator to cut the node out of the network.

7.7.5 Implementation of an FDDI DTE

Figure 7.31 shows an FDDI interface constructed using the AMD Supernet family of chips. The station processor offloads the host

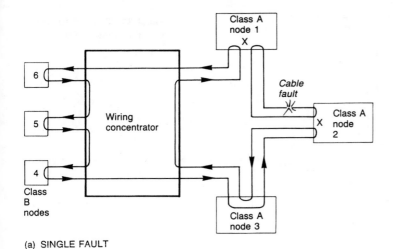

(a) SINGLE FAULT

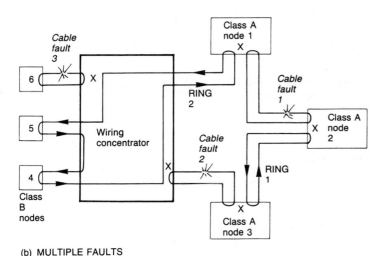

(b) MULTIPLE FAULTS

Fig. 7.30 (a) FDDI reconfiguration when a cable breaks; (b) FDDI reconfiguration with two failures on the dual ring and one class B node cable fault

system and must be a high-performance microprocessor in high-performance stations. Its functions are to initialise and control the other chips and to handle higher OSI layers. The RAM buffer controller generates buffer memory addresses, configures the RAM to perform as FIFO buffers, and arbitrates for access to the buffer memory. The data path controller converts data formats, performs reception and transmission of packets, generates/checks parity and counts packet length, when necessary generating error status and interrupts.

The FORMAC 1 chip is the fibre optic ring media access controller which implements the FDDI protocol. The encoder/decoder performs clock recovery, converts serial to parallel data, generates/

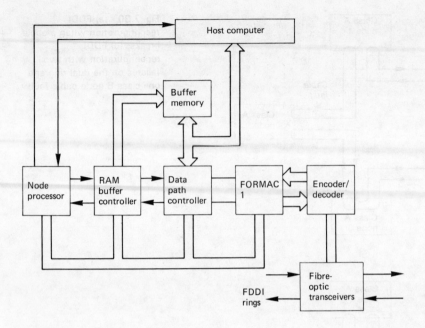

Fig. 7.31 FDDI interface using Supernet chips

checks parity, performs 4B/5B encoding and decoding, provides an elastic buffer, and implements the connection management (CMT) interface.

7.8 MIL-STD-1553 B avionic data bus

7.8.1 Background

MIL-STD-1553 B is a data bus standard intended for use in aircraft but now widely adopted throughout the NATO countries in military aircraft, ships, submarines and armoured vehicles. The first version, MIL-STD-1553, was published in 1975 by the US Department of Defense, followed by an improved version, MIL-STD-1553 B (aircraft internal time division command/response multiplex data bus), in 1978. The British version of MIL-STD-1553 B is known as DEF.STAN.00-18 Part 2.

The use of MIL-STD-1553 B in military aircraft has simplified the specification of interfaces between avionic subsystems and goes a long way towards producing off-the-shelf interoperability. The simplified cable requirements produce volume and weight benefits and have reduced the time to develop and test avionic systems. Figure 7.32 shows the distributed avionics architecture of the F-18 fighter using three pairs (main and redundant cables) of MIL-STD-1553 buses.

MIL-STD-1553 B is a serial, time division multiplexed data bus using a single screened twisted-pair cable to transmit data at

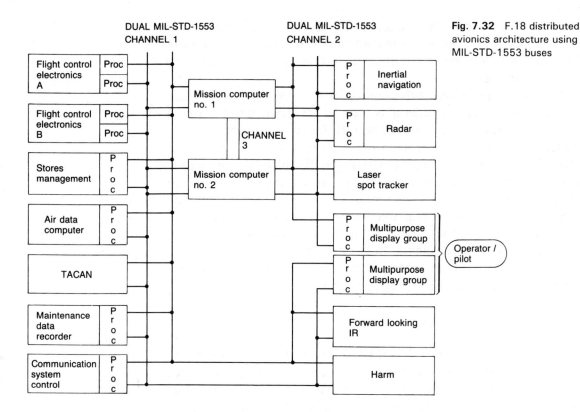

Fig. 7.32 F.18 distributed avionics architecture using MIL-STD-1553 buses

1 Mbit/s. Data is transmitted in 16-bit words with a parity bit and a 3-bit-period synchronisation signal, the whole word taking 20 micro-seconds to be transmitted. Transformer-coupled baseband signalling with Manchester encoding is employed. A maximum of 31 terminals may be connected to the bus and one must be designated as the bus controller.

Most avionic applications of MIL-STD-1553 B require a duplicate, redundant bus cable and bus controller to ensure satisfactory system operation if the first bus or controller fails or is damaged. MIL-STD-1553 B is intended primarily for systems with central intelligence and less intelligent terminals in applications where the data flow patterns are predictable.

Three types of device may be attached to the bus:

1) The bus controller (BC).
2) Remote terminals (RTs).
3) The bus monitor.

The bus controller is in complete command of the bus traffic. It indicates for each transaction the source device address, the destination device address and the message length. The bus controller

235

therefore has to know the sequence and content of all transactions between devices on the bus. The controller can conduct transactions between itself and remote terminals or transactions between two remote terminals.

There can only be one active controller in the system at any time. However, an active controller may offer to pass control to a dormant controller. Remote terminals connect devices to the system and can transmit/receive data to/from other remote terminals or the bus controller. The bus monitor is a passive device which takes no part in any data transactions; it merely listens to bus traffic and extracts selected information for use at a later time. The monitor is optional.

Several chips sets are available to reduce the size of MIL-STD-1553 B interfaces; these may be used with processor-based or unintelligent remote terminals. Bus controllers require a processor, possibly the main system processor, with a special interface capable of transmitting command words and receiving status words.

7.8.2 Bus control

All messages are transmitted at the command of the bus controller. This method of access control is called command/response which ensures that data is not corrupted by more than one terminal transmitting simultaneously and no terminal has to wait for more than a predetermined time to transmit its message. Two forms of bus control are supported, stationary and dynamic bus control. A dedicated bus controller can be called a stationary master but a system in which bus control is passed from one unit to another according to a predefined procedure has dynamic bus control.

MIL-STD-1553 B defines a procedure for issuing a bus control offer to the next potential bus controller which can accept or reject control by using a bit in the returning status word. Dynamic bus control requires all potential bus controllers to have additional capabilities, and the algorithms which determine the identity of the next bus controller, or the controller at system start-up, must be rigorously tested.

A dedicated bus controller with a backup (in case of failure) requires an effective method of detecting failure of the active bus controller and of activating the standby. This transfer procedure does not usually rely on monitoring the data bus but preferably employs a watchdog circuit in the bus controller directly wired to the standby bus controller.

7.8.3 Word formats

Information flow on the data bus comprises messages which are

236

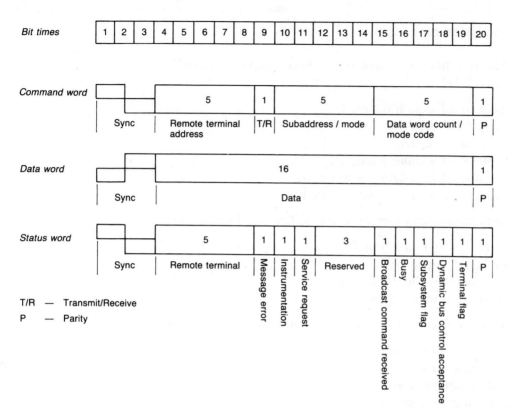

Fig. 7.33 MIL-STD-1553 B word formats

formed of three types of words (command, data and status), as shown in Figure 7.33. The maximum amount of data which may be contained in a message is 32 data words, each word containing sixteen data bits, one parity bit and three synchronisation bits (which permit decoding of the word).

Command words are issued by the bus controller only, and their content and sequence determine which of the four possible data transfers are to be undertaken:

Point-point between controller and remote terminal
Point-point between remote terminals
Broadcast from the controller
Broadcast from a remote terminal.

Status words are the response from a remote terminal after the receipt of a command word. Both command words and status words may be followed by data words, depending upon whether the controller or a remote terminal is the source of the data.

7.8.4 Transmission procedures

MIL-STD-1553 B defines six formats for point-to-point transmissions (see Figure 7.34):

1) Controller to RT data transfer.
2) RT to controller data transfer.
3) RT to RT data transfer.
4) Mode command without a data word.
5) Mode command with data transmission.
6) Mode command with data word reception.

Four broadcast transmission formats are specified (see Figure 7.35):

1) Controller to RT(s) data transfer.
2) RT to RT(s) data transfer.
3) Mode command without a data word.
4) Mode command with a data word.

The command words issued by the bus controller may be divided into three types:

1) Receive command words.
2) Transmit command words.
3) Mode command words.

The receive command identifies the recipient of a message (either a single remote terminal or all remote terminals). The number of data words in the message is also specified. The receive command word is immediately followed by the data words if the controller is the source of information (Figure 7.34 (a) and Figure 7.35(a)). If, however, the source is to be another remote terminal, the receive command word is followed by a transmit command word (Figures 7.34(c) and 7.35(b)).

The transmit command identifies the source of the data (a single remote terminal) and the number of data words. If it is not preceded by a receive command word then the recipient is the controller itself (Figure 7.34(b)). If the transmit command word is preceded by a receive command word then the message is either to be received by another terminal (Figure 7.34(c)) or it is to be broadcast and received by all devices (Figure 7.35(b)). The identified source will respond with a status word followed by the specified number of data words (Figures 7.34(c) and 7.35(b)).

The mode command word is used to communicate with the highway interface hardware in remote terminals and to assist in self-test or transmitter shutdown. Mode commands may be issued alone (Figures 7.34(d) and 7.35(c)) or immediately followed by a data word (Figures 7.35(e) and (f) and 7.35(d)). The remote terminals may

238

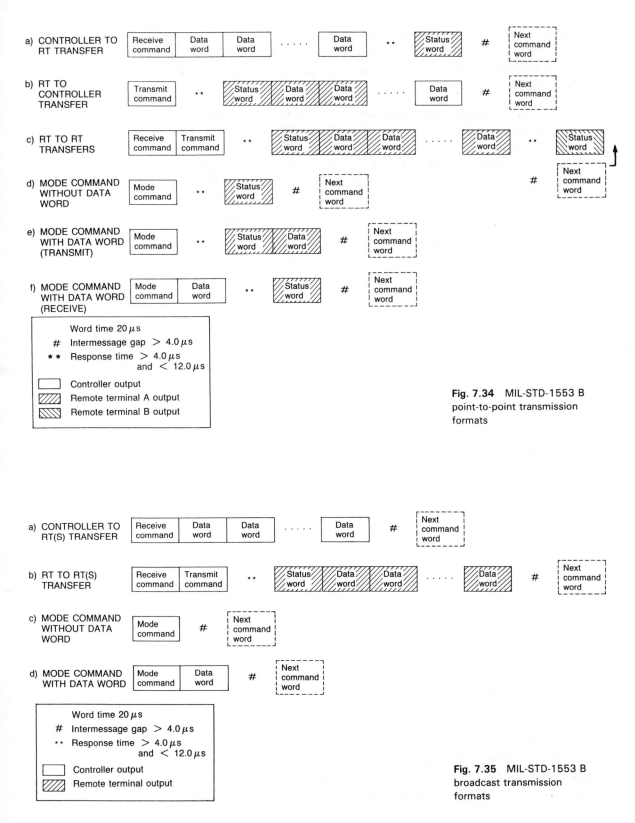

Fig. 7.34 MIL-STD-1553 B point-to-point transmission formats

Fig. 7.35 MIL-STD-1553 B broadcast transmission formats

239

respond to a mode command with either a status word (Figures 7.34(d) and (f)) or a status word and data word (Figure 7.34 (e)).

Status words are output by remote terminals under the following circumstances:

a) At the head of a stream of data words following receipt of a transmit command word (Figures 7.34(b) and (c) and 7.35(b)).

b) As a single word after the receipt of a data word in response to a directly addressed (i.e. not broadcast) mode command word (Figures 7.34(d) and (e)) or a directly addressed mode command word plus single data word (Figure 7.34(f)).

Status words are not output in response to either broadcast data streams or broadcast mode commands. The broadcast address in the command word suppresses the response.

7.8.5 Calculating average bus load

Analysis of average bus loading is a relatively simple matter for MIL-STD-1553 B. The message transmission overheads are (in microseconds):

Command word	20
Status word	20
Response time	4–12 (assume 8)
Intermessage gap	4–30+ (assume 20)
Mode code	20 (40 with a data word)
Data word	20

If N is the number of data words, the durations of the message types are:

a) Bus controller to remote terminal and remote terminal to bus controller:
   $20N + 68$

b) Remote terminal to remote terminal:
   $20N + 116$

c) Broadcast from bus controller to remote terminal:
   $20N + 40$

d) Broadcast from remote terminal to remote terminal:
   $20N + 88$

e) Mode code without data word: 68.

f) Mode code with data word: 88.

g) Mode code without data word (broadcast): 40.

h) Mode code with data word (broadcast): 60.

The average bus loading is the sum of the message durations transmitted per second, divided by 1 000 000 (which is the number of bits per second) multiplied by 100 to express the bus load as a percentage. During development the calculated bus loading should not exceed about 40% to allow for growth throughout the system's life.

MIL-STD-1553 B does not specify any explicit techniques for the handling of acyclic message transfers, message transfers between buses, broadcast checking schemes, data formatting or error detection and correction techniques for critical data (e.g. weapon release commands).

Extended message protocols are required to standardise the higher levels of subsystem interaction. No international avionic standards have been agreed and therefore these standards must be specified for all subsystems in each aircraft.

8 Wide area network standards

8.1 Long-distance communication alternatives

8.1.1 Introduction

A wide area network may be arbitrarily defined as a network which interconnects computers, terminals and local area networks at a national or international level. The most significant standards which apply to wide area networks are concerned with:

a) The media (modems, lines, etc.).
b) The physical interfaces.
c) The data link control protocols.
d) The network architecture standards.

Wide area networks have different requirements from local area networks:

a) The propagation times are much longer because of greater distances, particularly when satellite relays are used.
b) The data transmission rates are usually much lower than those employed by LANs.
c) The error rate is usually much higher than found on LANs making more effective error detection and recovery procedures necessary. The transport protocols must be designed to cope with uncorrected errors.
d) Several parties are often involved in providing bearers, terminals or computers on the network and in defining standards. A LAN is often privately owned and administered by one organisation.
e) The links are more prone to failure and network reconfiguration must be considered.
f) The network may store data, introducing unpredictable delays, and may deliver the data in different-sized packets and in a different order to that in which it was sent.
g) The cost of using the network may be related to the amount of traffic whereas a LAN involves fixed costs.

h) There may be gateways which undertake protocol conversion in the transmission path. Different protocols may have different addressing requirements.

Chapter 2 described the media used in wide area networks and Chapter 6 described the physical interface standards (OSI layer 1) which are applicable to wide area networks. This chapter describes the more significant data link control protocols (OSI layer 2) and the CCITT X.25 interface for packet switched systems which incorporates standards covering OSI layers 1 to 3 (the network layer). Network architecture standards were described in Chapter 5.

The International Standards Association (ISO) defines a data link control protocol as a set of rules for orderly information interchange between physically connected stations. Data link control protocols have evolved over the last 20 years. Early wide area networks used the IBM Bisync character-controlled protocol. In the mid 1970s DEC introduced the more versatile DDCMP character-count protocol while IBM introduced the more efficient SDLC bit-oriented protocol and ISO established the HDLC bit-oriented protocol standard.

Many other data link control protocols have been developed but the four most popular standards are Bisync, DDCMP, SDLC and HDLC. Table 8.1 summarises the main features of these data link protocols and compares their capabilities. Sections 8.2 to 8.5 describe these protocols in more detail.

Wide area networks may be circuit switched, packet switched, constructed from non-switched lines, or of a hybrid construction. Chapter 4 described switching techniques and Chapter 6 described the X.21 circuit switched network interface and the X.3, X.28, X.29 interfaces for packet assembler/disassemblers. Section 8.6 provides a description of X.25, the most popular interface for packet switched data networks which was first adopted by CCITT in 1976.

Table 8.1 Comparison of data link protocols

	BISYNC	DDCMP	SDLC	HDLC
Originator	IBM	DEC	IBM	ISO
Full-duplex	No	Yes	Yes	Yes
Half-duplex	Yes	Yes	Yes	Yes
Serial	Yes	Yes	Yes	Yes
Parallel	No	Yes	No	No
Data Transparency	Character stuffing	Count	Bit stuffing	Bit stuffing

244

Table 8.1 (*continued*)

	BISYNC	DDCMP	SDLC	HDLC
Asynch Transmission	No	Yes	No	No
Synch Transmission	Yes	Yes	Yes	Yes
Point-to-Point	Yes	Yes	Yes	Yes
Multipoint	Yes	Yes	Yes	Yes
Station Addressing (Multipoint)	Optional header	Header	1 or extended number of octets	
Error Detection:	CRC-16/12 (VRC/LRC)	CRC-16 (Hdr + Data)	CRC-CCITT	CRC-CCITT
Error Detection On	Text messages only	Header + data separately	All frame	All frame
Error Recovery	Stop and wait	Go back N	Go back N	Go back N or Selected reject
ACK Window Size	1	255	7/127	7/127
Bootstrapping	No	Yes	Yes	Yes
Character Codes	ASCII EBCDIC Transcode	ASCII (control characters only)	Any	Any
Control Characters	Many	DLE, ENQ SYN, SOH	Flag	Flag
Frame Formats	Numerous	1 (3 types)	1 (3 types)	1 (3 types)
Link Control	Optional header	Header	1 or 2 octets	1 or 2 octets
Data Field Length	$n \times L$	$n \times 8$	$n \times 8$	Unrestricted
Framing start end	2 SYN FTX/ETB	2 SYN count	Flag Flag	Flag Flag
Flow Control	Control characters	None, data discarded	Control field formats and window mechanism	RNR frame, window mechanism

Section 8.7 describes protocols for mobile radio links. Data transmission from vehicles is becoming popular where cellular radio is available and protocols with strong error-correction capabilities are required.

Section 8.8 describes videotex, a form of information distribution which permits modified domestic television sets to display information pages from a central database, accessed through the public switched telephone network.

8.1.2 Services available in the UK

The selection of long-distance communications network types is largely determined by the cost–traffic relationship. As shown in Figure 8.1, a leased (dedicated) line has a relatively high fixed annual cost but dial-up lines on the public circuit switched network have a cost which is directly proportional to the traffic and which increases rapidly, making them suitable only for low traffic volumes. Packet switched networks have a fixed cost element and a cost element which is directly proportional to the number of packets transmitted.

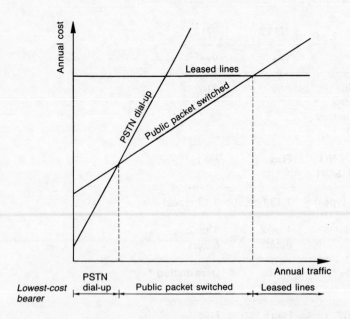

Fig. 8.1 Cost/traffic relationships for wide area network bearers

The choice between dial-up, packet switched and leased lines in relation to annual costs can clearly be seen in Figure 8.1. The choice of leased lines is dependent upon the charges of the local telephone companies. In the UK, the X-stream, digital services offered by British Telecom include:

246

a) *MegaStream*. A point-to-point private service which may be used to link private telephone exchanges (TDM) or for 2 Mbit/s data transmission.

b) *KiloStream*. A private service which will provide direct links between two or more points. Simultaneous two-way transmission is available at 2.4, 4.8, 9.6, 48 and 64 kbit/s.

c) *SwitchStream*. A packet switched public data service with international connections.

d) *SatStream*. A private satellite data link service covering Western Europe using small antennae close to the customer's premises to relay data using communications satellites.

KiloStream network terminating units (NTUs) provide an X.21, V.35 or V.24 interface and link the customers premises over a 4-wire local circuit to the nearest exchange where the KiloStream multiplexers form 2 Mbit/s channels. Each KiloStream circuit occupies a 64 kbit/s time slot regardless of its data rate. This digital service is less expensive and more reliable than analog leased lines.

Standard forms of Value Added Network (VAN) are now available including:

Telex
Teletex
Facsimile
Videotex
Mailbox
Mobile communications

Operators of VANs are licenced in the UK by the Department of Trade and Industry which grants managed data network licences. In 1986 there were 782 VAN licences issued to 195 different operators.

8.2 Bisync (BSC) character-controlled protocol

8.2.1 Origins

Binary Synchronous Communications (BSC or Bisync) provides a set of rules for synchronous transmission of binary-coded data. Bisync was developed by IBM and has been in use with IBM computer systems since 1968, primarily to link remote batch mode terminals and video display terminal cluster controllers to IBM mainframes.

Bisync is a character-controlled protocol and it has been replaced in many applications since the introduction, in the mid 1970s, of SNA and the bit-oriented SDLC protocol. Character-oriented protocols use ASCII or EBCDIC coded characters for link control and special characters are used to separate the various message fields. Character-oriented protocols are more complex and less efficient than bit-oriented protocols but could be implemented with simpler interface hardware in the days before VLSI semiconductors were available.

Bisync may only be used on synchronous half-duplex serial data links in point-to-point and multipoint configurations. The point-to-point link may be established over switched or dedicated lines. On a switched network, the data link is disconnected after each transmission. Error recovery procedures requires the transmitter to stop and wait for an ACK after each block transmitted.

For multipoint operation, one station in the network is designated to be the control station and other stations are designated tributary stations. Multipoint operation usually employs dedicated lines. The control station initiates all transmission by polling (sending an invitation to transmit to) a tributary station. Transmission on the network takes place between the designated control station and one of the tributary stations while the other stations remain in the passive monitoring mode. Selection is a request to received notification from the control station to the tributary station, instructing it to receive the following message.

8.2.2 Message format

The Bisync message format is shown in Figure 8.2. Control characters are used as field delimiters and the text portion of the field is variable in length. The data portion may be defined as containing transparent data, in which case it is delimited at the start of the frame by DLE STX and at the end of the frame by DLE ETX (or DLE ETB characters). Interframe time fill is indicated by continuous pads (e.g. mark on the line).

Fig. 8.2 Bisync message format

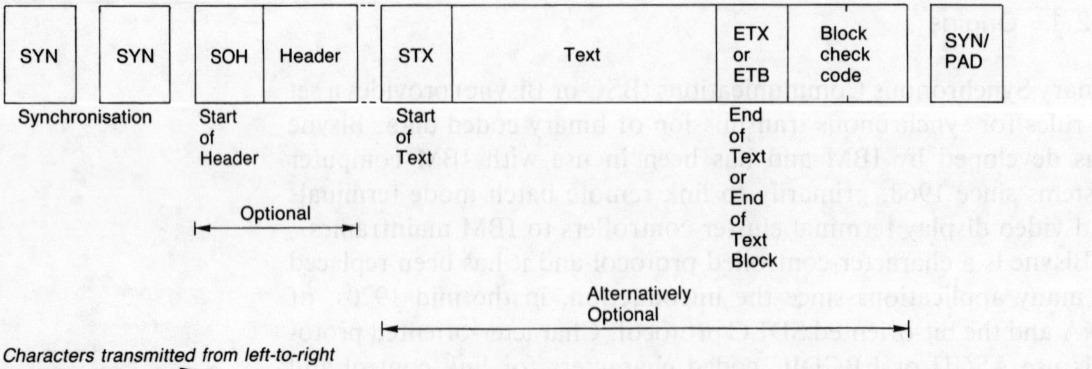

Characters transmitted from left-to-right

248

The control characters are:

DLE = Data link escape
SOH = Start of header
STX = Start of text
ETX = End of text
ETB = End of transmission block
ITB = End of intermediate transmission block
EOT = End of transmission
NAK = Negative acknowledgement
ENQ = Enquiry
ACK 0, ACK 1 = Positive acknowledgement
WACK = Wait before transmit positive acknowledgement
RVI = Reverse interrupt
TTD = Temporary text delay.

The character codes may be ASCII, EBCDIC or 6-bit Transcode. Certain bit patterns are reserved for the control characters: SOH, STX, ETX, ITB, ETB, EOT, NAK, DLE and ENQ; and two character sequences are used for ACK 0, ACK 1, WACK, RVI and TTD.

The header is optional and, if used, it commences with SOH and ends with STX, the contents being defined by the user. Polling and addressing on multipoint lines are handled by control messages, not by the message header field.

8.2.3 Error detection and recovery

The frame ends with a block check code which may be either a longitudinal redundancy check or a cyclic redundancy check. The block check code used depends upon the character code being used; for ASCII code, each character has a parity bit and the block check code is a single 8-bit longitudinal redundancy check character (LRC8). EBCDIC code and 6-bit transcode include no parity bits but a cyclic redundancy check is added. For EBCDIC, two 8-bit CRC characters are added (CRC-16) and for 6-bit transcode, two 6-bit CRC characters are added (CRC-12).

When the transmitted CRC or LRC does not match the check calculated at the receiver, a NAK is returned to the sender in a separate control message. When the block checks match, the receiver returns a positive acknowledgement, in a separate control message. ACK 0 is used for even-numbered blocks and ACK 1 for odd-numbered blocks. The use of different ACK characters for alternate blocks identifies duplicated or missing blocks.

If a NAK sequence is received, the originator retransmits the entire block in which the error occurred. If further NAKs are returned, the

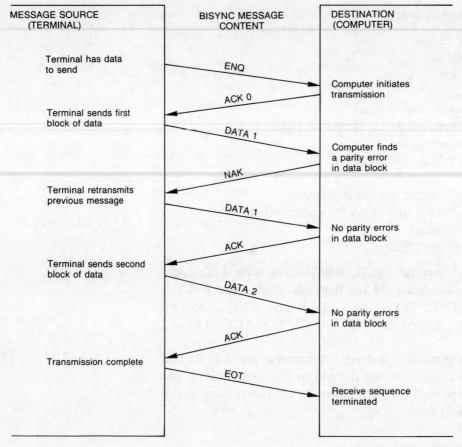

MESSAGE SOURCE (TERMINAL)	BISYNC MESSAGE CONTENT	DESTINATION (COMPUTER)
Terminal has data to send	ENQ	Computer initiates transmission
	ACK 0	
Terminal sends first block of data	DATA 1	Computer finds a parity error in data block
	NAK	
Terminal retransmits previous message	DATA 1	No parity errors in data block
	ACK	
Terminal sends second block of data	DATA 2	No parity errors in data block
	ACK	
Transmission complete	EOT	Receive sequence terminated

Fig. 8.3 Message sequence in a Bisync, point-to-point data exchange with a retransmission caused by data corruption

transmitter will assume that the link is faulty and suspend transmission. Figure 8.3 shows the sequence of messages in a typical Bisync point-to-point data exchange with a single retransmission caused by data corruption.

8.2.4 Transparency and synchronisation

Transparent mode is initiated by commencing the text field with DLE STX; the only control character which is recognised when found in the data field is then DLE (data link escape). All control characters transmitted in transparent mode must be preceded by a DLE in order to be executed. At the transmitter, any data bit patterns which correspond to the DLE character have a DLE character added (known as character stuffing). These additional DLE characters are removed from the transparent data at the receiver.

A minimum of two SYN (synchronisation) characters are transmitted before each block or control sequence. SYN is a unique bit pattern which is recognised by the interface hardware to obtain character synchronisation. In the text and Figure 8.4 the symbol Ø represents SYN characters.

Character synchronisation is re-established for each transmission by the receiver recognising the SYN character. Character synchronisation is maintained until a line turnaround character or the end of transmission character is received or until a timeout is complete.

Bit synchronisation must be established before character sync or the transmission will not be recognised. Where the modem is self-clocked, bit phase is automatically established by the modem but, when the computer internal clock is used, a special bit-phase sync pattern must precede the character sync sequence. Bit sync requires two consecutive hexadecimal 55 characters or four consecutive SYN characters to be transmitted before the character synchronisation SYN characters.

To maintain synchronisation during message transmission, the sync-idle sequence is automatically inserted in header and text data at one-second intervals. For normal data the sync-idle sequence is SYN SYN but for transparent data it is DLE SYN. When in normal mode, this sequence permits stations to verify that they are in sync and to get into sync if they are not in character sync. Sync-idle characters are excluded from the block check code calculation.

Multipoint operation is initialised by the control station transmitting Ø EOT Ø PAD (polling or selection address) ENQ. This sequence ensures that all tributary stations are in control mode and are ready to receive a poll (invitation to send) or a selection (request to receive) from the control station. The polling and selection sequences consist of from one to seven characters defining the station's address and the desired component of the station followed by ENQ. The possible replies from a polled tributary station are:

a) Heading data (Ø SOH...).
b) Text data (Ø STX text...).
c) Transparent text data (Ø DLE STX transparent text...).
d) Negative reply when station has nothing to send (Ø EOT).
e) Temporary text delay when the station is unable to transmit its initial block within two seconds (Ø STX ENQ).

The possible replies from a selected tributary station are:

a) Affirmative reply indicating that the tributary station is prepared to receive (Ø ACK 0).
b) Negative reply indicating that the tributary station is not ready to receive (Ø NAK).
c) Reply indicating that the tributary station is temporarily not ready to receive (Ø WACK).

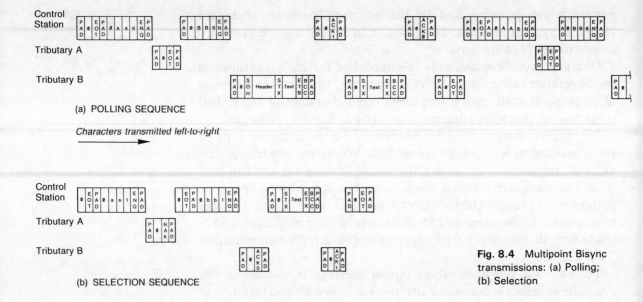

Control
Station

Tributary A

Tributary B

(a) POLLING SEQUENCE

Characters transmitted left-to-right

Control
Station

Tributary A

Tributary B

(b) SELECTION SEQUENCE

Fig. 8.4 Multipoint Bisync transmissions: (a) Polling; (b) Selection

Figure 8.4 illustrates the operation of a typical centralised multipoint Bisync transmission. For more information on Bisync see reference 8.1.

8.3 DDCMP character-count protocol

8.3.1 Origins

Digital Data Communications Message Protocol (DDCMP) was developed by Digital Equipment Corporation for operation over a large range of wide area network bearers (synchronous, asynchronous, dedicated or switched, full-duplex, half-duplex, point-to-point or multipoint). DDCMP even has the ability to work on serial and parallel interfaces; the parallel interfaces are intended to be local interprocessor links.

DDCMP, introduced in 1975, was initially the only standard DEC protocol and is now one option, along with X.25, supported by DNA. DEC set out to develop a proprietary wide area network protocol to give much greater flexibility than IBM Bisync. To avoid the complicated procedures required for data transparency in Bisync, DEC used a protocol which keeps track of the byte count in the message block. This provides transparency without the use of control characters.

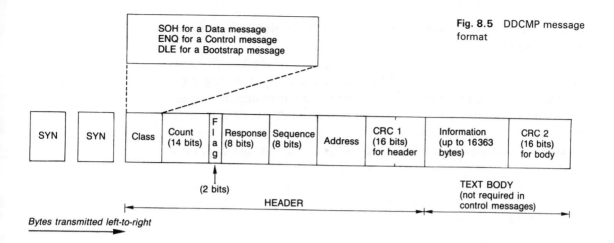

Fig. 8.5 DDCMP message format

| SYN | SYN | Class | Count (14 bits) | Flag (2 bits) | Response (8 bits) | Sequence (8 bits) | Address | CRC 1 (16 bits) for header | Information (up to 16363 bytes) | CRC 2 (16 bits) for body |

SOH for a Data message
ENQ for a Control message
DLE for a Bootstrap message

HEADER

TEXT BODY (not required in control messages)

Bytes transmitted left-to-right

8.3.2 Message format

Figure 8.5 shows the message format which consists of a header and a text body. The header contains essential control information including the message sequence number and character count for the text body. The header has its own 16-bit cyclic redundancy check which precedes the text field. The text field may contain up to 16 363 8-bit characters and is followed by a 16-bit cyclic redundancy check. Control messages may only consist of the header without the text body and its cyclic redundancy check.

The ASCII control characters, SOH (start of header), ENQ (enquiry) or DLE (data link escape) following the SYN characters, are used to distinguish between the three message types:

1) Data
2) Control
3) Maintenance.

The 14 count bits and 2 flag bits are contained in the second and third characters following the SYN characters. The 14 count bits are used in data and maintenance messages to indicate the number of information characters following the header. In control messages the first eight bits are used to designate the type of control message and the remaining six bits are zero except for NAK messages which use the six bits to identify the cause of the negative acknowledgement.

The 2-bit flag field contains the quick sync and the select flags. The quick sync flag indicates that the message will be followed by SYN characters. The receiving station is warned to employ sync stripping to prevent its buffers being filled with SYN characters. The select flag indicates that the message is the last one to be transmitted and the receiver may now transmit in a half-duplex or multipoint configuration.

The 8-bit response field contains the number of the last correctly received message for use with data messages and acknowledgement messages. The 8-bit sequence field is used in data messages to contain the sequence number for the message; it is assigned by the transmitting station. A REP message uses the sequence field to enquire whether all the messages with numbers up to the number contained in the sequence field have been received correctly.

The 8-bit address field identifies the tributary station addressed or responding in multipoint operation. In point-to-point systems the address field is set to 1.

8.3.3 Error detection and recovery

DDCMP employs more complex error detection and recovery facilities than Bisync. When a transmission error is detected by the CRC, a special negative acknowledgement (NAK) message is returned to the transmitter by the receiving station. Positive acknowledgements are not transmitted for all messages because the number in the response field of data and acknowledgement messages specifies the sequence number of the last message which was correctly received. When operating in full-duplex mode, the NAK message is added to the sequence of messages being transmitted. It is therefore not necessary to stop and wait for a retransmission when an error has been detected. A go-back N block retransmission scheme is used which permits transmission to continue and the faulty block plus successive blocks (which may be N blocks back in the transmission sequence) will be retransmitted. DDCMP permits up to $N = 255$ unacknowledged messages outstanding; this maintains high efficiency when operating over circuits with high delays such as satellite links.

All messages transmitted from each end of a link are given an 8-bit sequence number. In multipoint systems with five tributaries there will be five message number sequences for messages from the tributaries to the control station and five for messages from the control station to each tributary.

When a station receives a message which does not have the correct sequence number, no response is given and the transmitting station will detect this by inspecting the response field of received messages. If a reply wait timer expires before an acknowledgement is received, the transmitting station sends a REP message which contains the sequence number of the most recently unacknowledged message transmitted. If the receiving station has correctly received all messages with sequence numbers up to, and including, the one in the REP message, it sends an ACK message and if it has not received the message(s) it sends a NAK message containing the number of the last message it received correctly. The transmitting station must then retransmit all data messages following the sequence number specified in the NAK message.

Figure 8.6 shows a message sequence for a unidirectional data transmission link; this sequence is duplicated for a bidirectional data transmission link. The only dependency between the links in each direction of a full-duplex system is the placing of acknowledgements in the response field of the next message sent in the opposite direction to that which is being acknowledged.

Fig. 8.6 DDCMP transmission with sequence and CRC errors

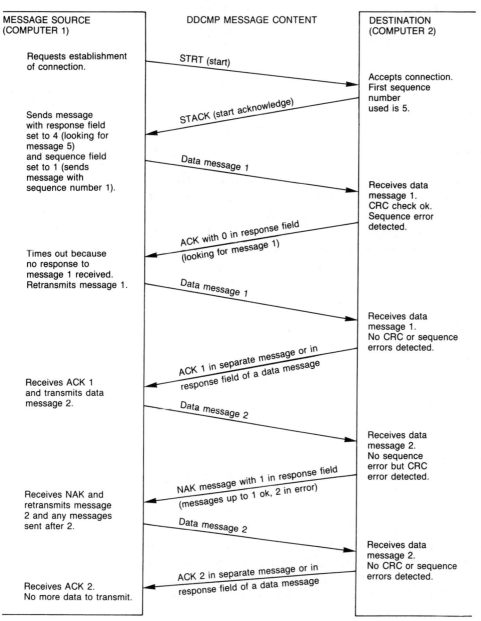

MESSAGE SOURCE (COMPUTER 1)	DDCMP MESSAGE CONTENT	DESTINATION (COMPUTER 2)
Requests establishment of connection.	STRT (start)	Accepts connection. First sequence number used is 5.
Sends message with response field set to 4 (looking for message 5) and sequence field set to 1 (sends message with sequence number 1).	STACK (start acknowledge)	
	Data message 1	Receives data message 1. CRC check ok. Sequence error detected.
Times out because no response to message 1 received. Retransmits message 1.	ACK with 0 in response field (looking for message 1)	
	Data message 1	Receives data message 1. No CRC or sequence errors detected.
Receives ACK 1 and transmits data message 2.	ACK 1 in separate message or in response field of a data message	
	Data message 2	Receives data message 2. No sequence error but CRC error detected.
Receives NAK and retransmits message 2 and any messages sent after 2.	NAK message with 1 in response field (messages up to 1 ok, 2 in error)	
	Data message 2	Receives data message 2. No CRC or sequence errors detected.
Receives ACK 2. No more data to transmit.	ACK 2 in separate message or in response field of a data message	

255

8.3.4   Synchronisation and bootstrapping

Two SYN characters precede each message block and it is not necessary to resynchronise between messages if no gaps exist. DDCMP links are therefore often run continuously in heavy traffic conditions to minimise the control overhead. Character synchronisation is unnecessary with serial asynchronous and parallel channels. Transmitting stations must not place SYN characters in messages because that causes an incorrect character count and causes the cyclic redundancy check to indicate a fault.

A maintenance message is available to perform bootstrap down-line loading of programs. The maintenance message begins with a DLE control character and the information field contains the program which is to be loaded.

8.4   SDLC bit-oriented protocol

8.4.1   Origins

Synchronous Data Link Control (SDLC) was announced by IBM in 1973 and came into use as part of IBM SNA systems from 1974 onwards. SDLC was the first popular bit-oriented protocol and is similar to ISO HDLC. Bit-oriented protocols use one standard frame format (rather than a header field) which specifies various control parameters and an information field which contains control characters. The main advantage of bit-oriented protocols is that software is not required to interpret control characters and character sequences or to maintain character counts.

SDLC is suitable for full-duplex or half-duplex operation over serial synchronous dedicated or switched links but asynchronous operation is not possible because bit stuffing varies the character length. Point-to-point and multipoint operation is possible. In unbalanced configurations such as multipoint networks, the stations are designated either primary or secondary stations. The balanced modes available in HDLC are not supported by SDLC. SDLC permits a secondary station to initiate message transmission. In full-duplex operation, SDLC is highly efficient and it has a lower control character overhead than Bisync and DDCMP.

8.4.2   Frame format

Figure 8.7 shows the SDLC frame format. The only control code is the flag which is a bit pattern 01111110 used to begin and end the SDLC frame. When frames follow immediately after another frame,

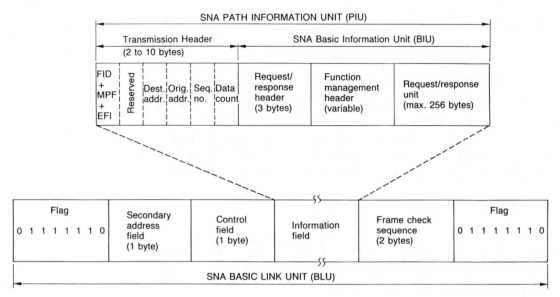

SNA PATH INFORMATION UNIT (PIU)

Transmission Header (2 to 10 bytes)

FID + MPF + EFI	Reserved	Dest. addr.	Orig. addr.	Seq. no.	Data count

SNA Basic Information Unit (BIU)

Request/ response header (3 bytes)	Function management header (variable)	Request/response unit (max. 256 bytes)

Flag 0 1 1 1 1 1 1 0	Secondary address field (1 byte)	Control field (1 byte)	Information field	Frame check sequence (2 bytes)	Flag 0 1 1 1 1 1 1 0

SNA BASIC LINK UNIT (BLU)

Bytes transmitted left-to-right

Fig. 8.7 SDLC frame format (SNA basic link unit)

only one flag is required because it functions as the end flag of one frame and the start flag of the next frame.

To prevent data patterns being interpreted as the flag, any sequence of five ones has a zero inserted at the transmitter. This technique of bit stuffing maintains transparency of data. At the receiver the additional zero bits are removed and they are not included in the frame check code calculation.

The information field may be any length from zero to an upper limit which is determined by the error rate of the link. There is no restriction on message format or content and therefore any information code is permitted.

The information field is preceded by 8 address bits and 8 control bits. The address field is extendable and the control field may be extended to 16 bits. The address field identifies the secondary station to which the command from the primary station is addressed in a multipoint system. The control field may have three formats:

1) Information transfer format
2) Supervisory format
3) Non-sequenced format.

The information transfer format is used for data transmission and uses frame sequence numbering. The supervisory format, in conjunction with the information transfer format, is used to initiate and control information transfer. The non-sequenced format is used to set operating modes and initialise stations.

257

The first two bits in the control field determine the format used:

00   indicates information transfer format.
10   indicates supervisory format.
11   indicates non-sequenced format.

The P/F or poll/final bit is used in all three formats to identify whether the frame is being sent from the primary station (P/F bit set to 1) to a secondary station or if the frame is being sent from a secondary station in response to a poll (this has the P/F bit set to 0 for initial response frames but set to 1 for the final response frame).

8.4.3 Error detection and recovery

A 16-bit cyclic redundancy check (CCITT standard) is applied to the entire frame (except the CRC and flags). This CRC differs from those used on character-oriented protocols and improves the probability of detecting multiple-bit errors.

All frames transmitted in the information transfer format have a frame sequence number $N(s)$ transmitted in three bits within the control field. The receiving station using the information transfer format stores the error-free frame sequence number $N(r)$ which should agree with the next $N(s)$ count received. The $N(r)$ count which indicates the next expected frame sequence number is transmitted in three bits within the control field.

Supervisory format frames are used for three commands:

RR   (Receive ready)
RNR   (Receive not ready)
REJ   (Reject)

RR indicates that all frame sequence numbers up to $N(r) - 1$ have been received correctly and the originator is ready for more data. RNR acknowledges messages up to $N(r) - 1$ but indicates that the originator is busy and can accept no more data. REJ requests transmission or retransmission of $N(r)$ and the following frames.

RR and RNR perform a similar function to ACK in character-oriented protocols but a go-back-N transmission scheme is used with a maximum of 7 frames outstanding before acknowledgement is required (a window of 7 frames). Some equipment used with satellite links has an extended window of 127 frames. When an error is detected, the REJ format is used on the next message bound for the message originator. The originator checks the $N(r)$ field and, after a timeout period, retransmits the message and all subsequent messages.

A link may be terminated by the abort procedure. The transmitting station sends eight consecutive 1 bits followed by a flag or a minimum of seven additional 1 bits to idle the link.

258

8.5 HDLC bit-oriented protocol

8.5.1 Origins

High level Data Link Control (HDLC) is a bit-oriented protocol standardised by ISO and adopted as the data link layer of CCITT X.25 where it is known as either Link Access Procedure (LAP) or Link Access Procedure Balanced (LAP-B).

ISO began developing protocols in 1962. First they developed a character-oriented protocol known as basic mode but they went on to develop a bidirectional transparent data transport mechanism using a single delimiter (flag) and a bit stuffing method of ensuring transparency. This became the HDLC standard in 1976.

Bit-oriented data link control protocols use a single-frame format, have an unrestricted information field length, can use any character codes, and have few reserved bit sequences. All these aspects simplify software design. Subsets of ISO HDLC are found in ECMA HDLC, ANSI ADCCP (which is almost identical to HDLC), CCITT LAP and LAP-B, and IBM SDLC (which contains additional commands and responses). Bit-oriented protocols are now the favoured type of data link control protocol. HDLC was designed for operation over full-duplex synchronous links and it has a half-duplex capability.

8.5.2 HDLC configurations

HDLC may have three logical link configurations:

1) Unbalanced
2) Balanced
3) Symmetrical.

A primary station transmits command frames to and receives response frames from secondary stations on the link which may be point-to-point or multipoint. An unbalanced link configuration, which may be point-to-point or multipoint, has a primary station and one or more secondary stations as shown in Figure 8.8. Two modes of operation are possible: normal response mode (NRM) in which the primary station polls the secondary station, and asynchronous response mode (ARM) in which the secondaries may transmit point-to-point in turn. The configuration is unbalanced because the primary station is in control of each secondary station.

A balanced configuration consists of two combined stations with a point-to-point connection and both stations have equal data transfer and link control capability (see Figure 8.9.) Only point-to-point operation is supported. With asynchronous balanced mode (ABM),

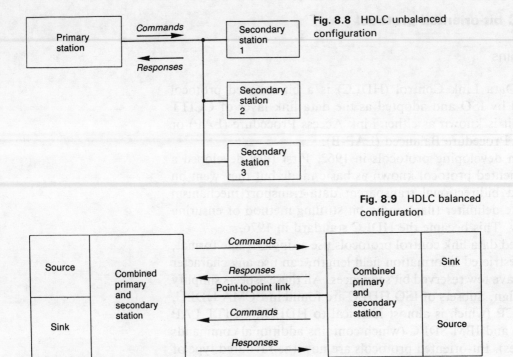

Fig. 8.8 HDLC unbalanced configuration

Fig. 8.9 HDLC balanced configuration

only one station may transmit at a time. The balanced configuration is used in X.25 LAP-B.

Two unbalanced point-to-point logical station configurations may be connected together symmetrically and multiplexed on a single physical data link as shown in Figure 8.10. Two primary-to-secondary station logical channels are required and each primary station has responsibility for mode selection. This configuration is used in the X.25 LAP.

Fig. 8.10 Two unbalanced point-to-point logical station configurations connected symmetrically by a multiplexed link

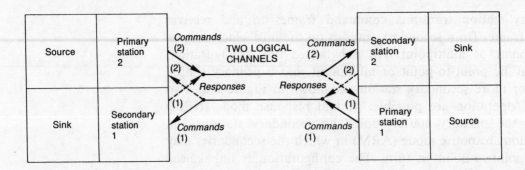

8.5.3 Logical states and modes

Communication between HDLC stations takes place in one of three logical states:

1) Information transfer state (ITS).
2) Initialisation state (IS).
3) Logically disconnected state (LDS).

While in ITS, a secondary or combined station can transmit and receive information frames. ITS may be entered when the logical link is set up in either NRM, ARM or ABM mode. In initialisation state, communications are under the control of a higher-level system procedure (above HDLC). The secondary or combined station is initialised by receiving parameters from the remote station. The logically disconnected state prevents the secondary or combined station from transmitting or receiving data and uses NDM or ADM mode.

The modes of operation are:

a) NRM (normal response mode) which is used in unbalanced configurations and permits the secondary to transmit only after receiving explicit instructions to do so after being polled by the primary (i.e. when receiving a frame with the poll bit set).

b) ARM (asynchronous response mode) which is used in unbalanced configurations to permit a secondary to transmit without being polled by the primary. ARM may be used to indicate status changes.

c) ABM (asynchronous balanced mode) which is used in balanced configurations only for point-to-point communications. The secondary may transmit at any time without being polled.

d) NDM (normal disconnected mode) which is used when in the logically disconnected state by the secondary station in either balanced or unbalanced configurations. The secondary may initiate transmission only after receiving a poll command.

e) ADM (asynchronous disconnected mode) which is used when in the logically disconnected state by the secondary station in either balanced or unbalanced configurations. The secondary station may initiate transmission at any time and may use ADM to indicate status changes.

f) IM (initialisation mode) is used by the secondary station when in initialisation state.

8.5.4 Frame format

The same basic frame format is used regardless of mode, configuration or procedure. The frame composition is shown in Figure 8.11. There are however three frame types:

1) *Information*, I frames (indicated by 0 in the control field).

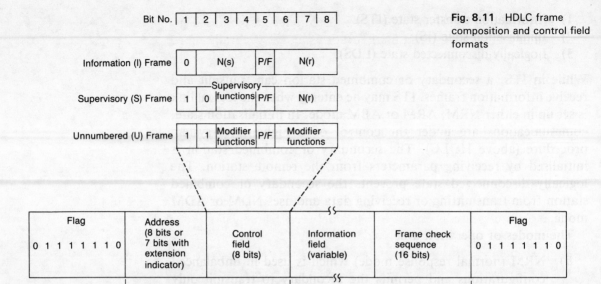

Fig. 8.11 HDLC frame composition and control field formats

Bit No. | 1 | 2 | 3 | 4 | 5 | 6 | 7 | 8 |

Information (I) Frame: 0 | N(s) | P/F | N(r)

Supervisory (S) Frame: 1 | 0 | Supervisory functions | P/F | N(r)

Unnumbered (U) Frame: 1 | 1 | Modifier functions | P/F | Modifier functions

Flag: 0 1 1 1 1 1 1 0

Address (8 bits or 7 bits with extension indicator)

Control field (8 bits)

Information field (variable)

Frame check sequence (16 bits)

Flag: 0 1 1 1 1 1 1 0

FRAME HEADER

BIT STUFFED

Transmitted from left-to-right

2) *Supervisory*, S frames (indicated by 10 in the control field).

3) *Unnumbered*, U frames (indicated by 11 in the control field).

The frame type is specified by the first two bits in the control field. The control field formats are also shown in Figure 8.11. I frames may contain a variable number of bits of user data in the information field, and include a send sequence number N(s), a receive sequence number N(r), and a P/F bit in the control field.

S frames are used to acknowledge correctly received I frames by their receive sequence number and can request transmission of I frames when errors are detected. They can also request temporary suspension in the transmission of I frames. The frame length is normally 6 octets.

U frames are used during link initialisation or disconnection for link control functions. They include five modifier bits which permit up to 32 additional responses depending upon the class of procedure employed.

There are three classes of procedure:

1) UA (unbalanced asynchronous response mode) may be used on a multipoint data link with either unbalanced or symmetrical configurations.

2) UN (unbalanced normal response mode) may be used on a multipoint data link with either unbalanced or symmetrical configurations.

3) BA (balanced asynchronous response mode) may be used on balanced point-to-point configurations and is generally more efficient than class UA.

Each class has a basic set of commands and responses and a receiving station belongs to a class if it can decode and respond to the control field in the received command or response for that class. A primary station receives all responses in a class of procedures but a secondary station receives all commands and a combined station receives both commands and responses.

The frame format always includes all the fields and is delimited by an 8-bit flag sequence 01111110. The flag provides synchronisation and it is used repeatedly to fill the gap between frames. To allow transparent user data, any sequence of five ones causes a zero to be inserted. Whenever five ones are received followed by a zero, the zero is removed. When a sixth one is detected in a sequence the next bit is checked for the flag sequence; if this bit is a one the frame is considered invalid and is aborted.

The address field is an 8-bit sequence but it may be extended if more than 256 secondary terminals are required on a link. The low-order bit (first transmitted) of the address field can be used to indicate extension of the field if this is agreed for the particular system. If the first bit in any octet of the address field is set to 0, the following octet is interpreted as an address extension.

The basic control field is one octet but this may be extended to two octets. The control field is used to contain frame sequence numbers, acknowledgements, retransmission requests and other control functions.

The information field may consist of any number of bits which are completely transparent. The frame check sequence is the V.41 CRC-CCITT 16-bit cyclic redundancy check.

Besides the flag there are two reserved bit patterns:

abort = 01111111
idle = 111111111111111

Abort causes premature termination of a frame and is used when the transmitting station has a problem which prevents the frame being completed. Flags are used to follow an abort in order to keep the link active. The idle pattern indicates an inactive link. Idle is used to invite line turnaround in half-duplex links or it may indicate link failure.

8.5.5 Flow control

The flow control window, which determines how many acknowledged messages may be outstanding, may be set to suit the buffer space available to store frames and the link delay. With a modulo-8 sequence number used for the basic control field format, it is possible to allow up to seven unambiguous unacknowledged frames. The extended control field format permits modulo-128 sequence numbers and it is possible to allow up to 127 I frames to be unacknowledged at any time.

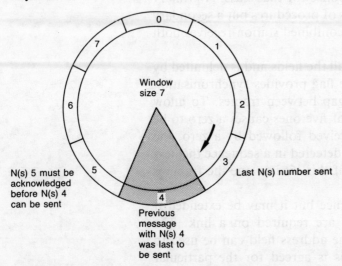

Fig. 8.12 HDLC flow control window (size 7)

Figure 8.12 shows the operation of the flow control window for a basic control field and a window size of 7. I frames with N(s) sequence numbers of 5, 6, 7, 0, 1, 2, and 3 have been sent and acknowledgements are outstanding, thus closing the window and preventing more messages being transmitted until the N(s)5 sequence number frame is acknowledged.

8.5.6 Phases of link operation

There are six phases of link operation:

a) Idle state, in which no signals are exchanged.

b) Active state, in which contiguous flags are exchanged or frames are being transmitted.

c) Link set-up phase, in which the link is initialised by exchanging SABM (set asynchronous balanced mode) or SARM (set asynchronous response mode) commands to reset sequence numbers before information is transferred.

d) Information transfer phase, in which information and supervisory frames are exchanged.

e) Link reset phase, in which irrecoverable errors are overcome by reinitialising the link using the link set-up procedure.

f) Link disconnect phase, in which the information transfer is ended by sending a disconnect command.

In the information transfer phase, when the primary has an I frame to transmit, it sends it with a sequence number, a timer is started, and the frame is stored until either:

a) An acknowledgement is received from the secondary.
b) A reject is received and the stored frame is retransmitted.
c) The timeout expires and the frame is retransmitted.

On receiving an I frame the secondary first checks the CRC. If it is incorrect, the frame is discarded or the sequence number is checked against the receive-state variable. All frames received after a frame has been rejected are ignored apart from acknowledgement in the $N(r)$ field of these frames. The reject condition is cleared by receipt of an I frame with the correct sequence number.

When a station is temporarily busy and unable to receive I frames, it sends an RNR (receive not ready) response but still accepts and processes supervisory frames. It will also send an RNR (with the F bit set) when an I frame is received with the poll bit set. The busy condition is cleared by transmitting an RR (receive ready) or REJ (reject) frame. The P/F bit in the control field is used as a poll bit by a primary to solicit a response from a secondary and as a final bit by the secondary to indicate that the particular frame is a response to a poll.

There are many options permitted in an implementation of HDLC and this may result in minor incompatibilities between two implementations but these may nevertheless prevent correct operation. The parameters which must be defined in an HDLC implementation are:

TI   The timeout for frame retransmission (default 3 seconds).
T3   The timeout for completion of link initialisation (default 90 seconds).
N1   The maximum number of information bits in a frame.
N2   The maximum number of transmissions and retransmissions permitted for a frame before declaring a link failure (default 20).
K   Window size.

8.6 CCITT X.25

8.6.1 Origins

CCITT X.25 is a recommended 'interface between Data Terminal Equipment (DTE) and Data Circuit-terminating Equipment (DCE) for terminals operating in the Packet Mode on public data networks'.

Another CCITT recommendation, X.75, extends the scope of packet switched systems to provide international connections between X.25-based systems. X.75 is a recommendation for 'terminal and transfer call control procedures and data transfer system on international circuits between packet-switched data networks'.

Packet switched networks were first designed and built in the 1960s. These early research networks proved to be technically and economically feasible and this resulted in the construction of several private packet switched networks. A demand for public packet switched networks developed in the early 1970s and this made it necessary to develop network standards.

The CCITT, of which the national postal, telegraph and telephone authorities (PTTs) are voting members, set up a working party to study digital networks in 1972 and this developed into CCITT Study Group viii. By 1974 development work for public networks commenced in the USA, Canada, France, the UK, Spain and Japan and work started on the X.25 standard for accessing these packet switched networks with the final draft recommendation being presented by December 1975.

The X.25 recommendation was approved at the 6th plenary session of the CCITT in October 1976. It was modified in 1977/8 and revised in 1980 and 1984. It is therefore necessary to ensure that equipment used in a system incorporates the appropriate revisions of the recommendation.

The 1976 version of X.25 defined a link access procedure and seven user-selectable facilities, e.g. multi-address calling and closed user groups. The 1980 revision introduced the LAP-B link access procedure (which supports balanced HDLC operation) and several additional user-selectable facilities. The 1984 revision expanded the packet switching capabilities and added the X.21 access specification but deleted the datagram recommendation because it had been found to be inefficient. Study into some alternative form of connectionless service was initiated when the datagram service was deleted.

8.6.2 Structure of X.25

X.25 applies to the interface between a DTE (computer, intelligent terminal or front-end processor) and a DCE (network node or packet switching equipment). The protocol used between the network DCEs is the internal network protocol which maintains the format of X.25 throughout the network. X.25 does not define how the network routes data between nodes within the network or the protocols used between the nodes.

As shown in Figure 8.13, when an asynchronous terminal is connected to the packet switched data network, a PAD (packet

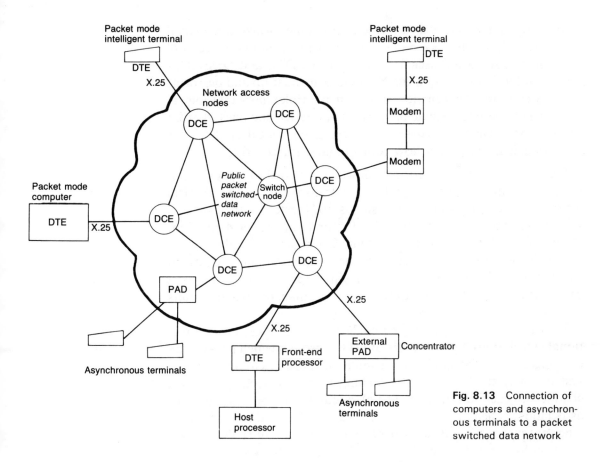

Packet mode
intelligent terminal

DTE

X.25

Network access
nodes

DCE

DCE

Packet mode
intelligent terminal

DTE

X.25

Modem

Modem

Packet mode
computer

DTE

X.25

Public
packet
switched-
data
network

DCE

Switch
node

DCE

DCE

DCE

DCE

PAD

X.25

X.25

Asynchronous terminals

DTE

Front-end
processor

External
PAD

Concentrator

Host
processor

Asynchronous
terminals

Fig. 8.13 Connection of computers and asynchronous terminals to a packet switched data network

assembler/disassembler) is required. The PAD conforms to the triple X (X.3, X.28, X.29) standards as described in Chapter 6 and no X.25 interface is employed.

As shown in Figure 8.14, X.25 is made up of three individual layers or levels:

1) Level 1, the *physical interface*, which defines the mechanical, electrical, functional and procedural specifications necessary to set up and maintain the physical link between the DTE and DCE. Level 1 provides a bit-serial, synchronous, point-to-point, full-duplex service to the higher levels. The level 1 interface standards are X.21 and X.21 bis (see section 6.4).

2) Level 2, the *link access procedure*, which defines the data link control procedure to convert the error-prone physical circuit into a relatively error-free link. A subset of the HDLC protocol, defined in 1980 as LAP-B, is employed. This specifies methods for avoiding errors and procedures for controlling link operations.

3) Level 3, the *packet level*, which defines the format and control procedures for exchange of packets containing control information and user data between the DTE and DCE. This level is defined within the X.25 recommendation and performs a concentrator function in that it multiplexes several logical channels onto a single physical link, interleaving packets from various channels where necessary. Each logical channel has independent packet flow control and error control.

Figure 8.15 shows the information which is added to a packet as it is passed from layer 3 to layer 1 and is transmitted by the physical interface. The maximum packet size is 1024 octets with 2048 and 4096 octet extensions permitted for facsimile in the 1984 revision. Packets are delivered in the order sent. Up to 4095 logical channels may be maintained by the interface, the destination being identified by the logical channel number (LCN) which applies for the duration of the call or permanently in the case of permanent virtual circuits (PVCs).

Virtual circuits are established by X.25 level 3; these are bidirectional associations between pairs of DTEs through which packets are exchanged. The virtual circuits, similar to those in circuit switched systems, may traverse several switching nodes connecting a logical channel in each DTE. The virtual circuits may be a temporary association, called a virtual call (VC), switched virtual call (SVC), or a permanent circuit, called a permanent virtual circuit (PVC). A VC is set up by the exchange of supervisory packets between the called and the calling DTEs. A PVC eliminates the need for call set-up because the DTE is always in data transfer mode.

A fast select facility was made available in the 1984 revision; this permits up to 128 octets of user data to be delivered during call set-up. A switched virtual circuit is usually created, and therefore the fast select facility is not an alternative to the datagram service which was deleted in 1984. A datagram is a connectionless service which permits a packet of data to contain all its routing information, thus reducing the overheads required by a short once-off transmission.

8.6.3 Packet format

There are three packet formats required to support the X.25 phases of operation:

1) Call establishment and clearing packets
2) Data packets
3) Control packets.

One packet is transmitted as the information field of an HDLC link frame. The call establishment and clearing packet establishes

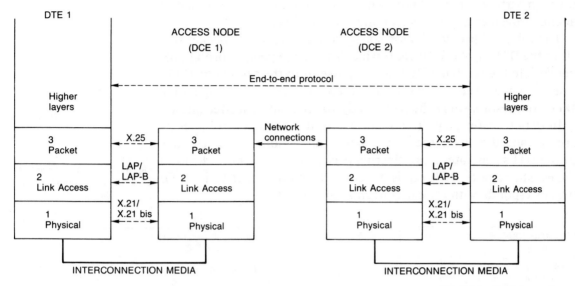

Fig. 8.14 X.25 layers in DTEs and DCEs

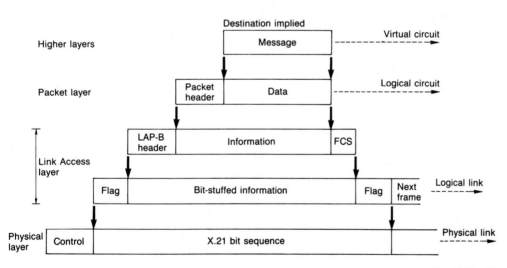

Fig. 8.15 The assembly of an X.25 frame

and clears switched virtual circuits; the data packet carries data through virtual circuits; and control packets are used for packet acknowledgement, flow control and error recovery.

The call establishment phase starts with a call request packet sent from the DTE to the local DCE which routes the packet through the network to the receiving DCE which passes it to the associated DTE. The receiving DTE returns a call accept packet to the originating DTE, thus establishing the SVC ready for the data transfer phase.

In data transfer phase (see Figure 8.16) data and control packets are exchanged between the DTEs. When the session is complete, one of the DTEs generates a call clearing packet which is sent to the local DCE. The remote DCE sends a clear indication packet to its DTE which responds with a clear confirmation packet.

Fig. 8.16 Data and control packets in the three phases of a virtual call

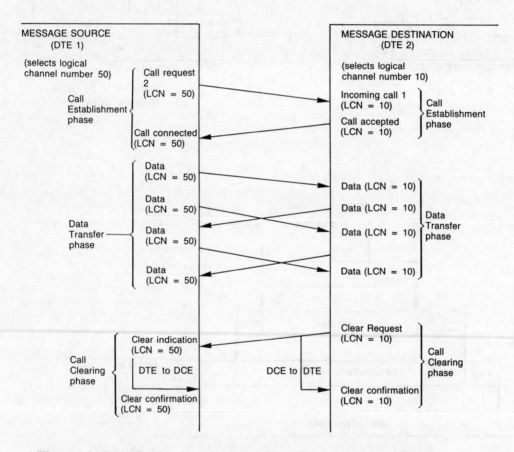

The packet header is the same for all packet types (see Figure 8.17). The general format identifier includes the data qualifier (Q) bit in bit 8, the delivery confirmation (D) bit in bit position 7, and the packet numbering modulo indicators in bit positions 5 and 6. The packet-type identifier uses bit 0 to indicate data packets (set to 0) and control packets (set to 1).

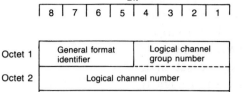

Fig. 8.17 X.25 packet header format

Octet 1	General format identifier / Logical channel group number
Octet 2	Logical channel number
Octet 3	Packet-type identifier (except in data transfer packet)
Octet 4 onwards	Other fields vary with packet type

Each packet type has a different overall format. The call establishment packet follows the header with:

a) The destination DTE address.

b) The source DTE address.

c) Facilities information which allows the network to meet the call requirements.

d) User data.

The call accepted packet is similar to the call establishment packet but has no user data. The data packet consists of a packet header and user data. The call clearing packet has a packet header and a clearing cause field.

Each packet is acknowledged, during the data transfer phase, using a window mechanism similar to that employed by HDLC. This is achieved by including $P(S)$ and $P(R)$ sequence counters for flow control and acknowledgement in the data transfer packet format as shown in Figure 8.18. A different packet format is used for modulo-8 numbering and modulo-128 numbering on the logical channel. No address data is included because this is implied by the logical channel group number.

Fig. 8.18 Data transfer packet formats for modulo-8 and modulo-128 addressing

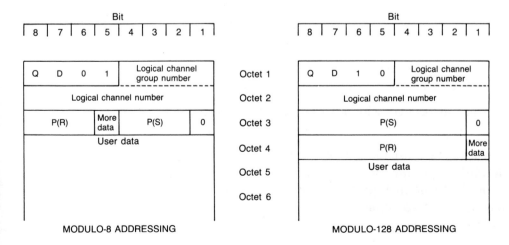

MODULO-8 ADDRESSING   MODULO-128 ADDRESSING

271

The standard maximum data field size is 128 octets but options of 16, 32, 64, 256, 512 and 1024 octets may be selected for different networks. The maximum length may differ at each end of a virtual circuit; to accommodate this the network may have to fragment or assemble packets. The more data (M) indicator may be set in a maximum length packet to indicate that it is part of a logical sequence which may not be combined with subsequent data packets.

Each logical channel or virtual circuit has separate flow control to prevent congestion by limiting the number of packets accepted by the network. The D bit set to 1 indicates an end-to-end acknowledgement and 0 indicates acknowledgement by access nodes only. The acknowledgement window mechanism uses P(R) and P(S) counts in the packet format. Acknowledgement criteria are defined by the call request packet.

Different window sizes may be used by the X.25 interface and the internal network protocol. Three packet types are available to perform acknowledgements and flow control in addition to the frame level procedures.

8.6.4   User facilities

User facilities permit the user to determine the way in which calls are set up and operated. Some user facilities may be permanently available to a DTE and others may be selected when the call is set-up by using three fields in the call request and call accept packets. Essential facilities include call barring and closed user groups. Additional facilities include optional features available to a particular user such as reverse charging which may be requested per call.

Facilities which restrict access include:

a) Call barring to prevent incoming or outgoing calls from the DTE as requested.
b) Closed user groups of seven different types.
c) One-way logical channel outgoing which restricts logical channel use to outgoing calls only.
d) One-way logical channel incoming which restricts logical channel use to incoming calls only.

Facilities which are associated with flow control and throughput include:

a) Nonstandard default list for window sizes.
b) Nonstandard default list for packet size.
c) Flow control parameter negotiation.
d) Throughput class negotiation.
e) Transit delay selection and indication.

272

Facilities which are associated with charging include:

a) Reverse charging request from the DTE for a call.
b) Reverse charging acceptance which authorises a DCE to transmit reverse charged calls to a DTE which requests this service.
c) Local charging prevention to avoid third party call charges.
d) Charging information, giving information on the connection time and call charges to the caller by using a field in the call clearing packet.

Facilities which are associated with routing include:

a) Hunt group which distributes incoming calls to any available member of the hunt group.
b) Call redirection which reroutes calls when the first addressee cannot be contacted.
c) Called line address modified notification which uses the call confirmation packet to inform the caller that the call has been redirected.
d) Call redirection notification which informs the recipient of the forwarded call that the call has been redirected.
e) Registered Private Operating Agent (RPOA) selection which permits one or more networks to be used in call routing.

General facilities include:

a) Extended packet sequence numbering which provides modulo-128 sequence numbers for packets in place of the standard modulo-8 sequence numbers.
b) Fast select request.
c) Fast select acceptance.
d) Packet retransmission which allows the DTE to request retransmission of flow controlled packets from the DCE.
e) Network user identification which provides user identification, online facilities registration and billing.

8.7 Protocols for mobile radio links

8.7.1 Error detection and correction

VHF and UHF radio links to vehicles are becoming available in digital wide area networks where the users are mobile. There are many causes of transmission errors on radio links including:

a) Poor signal-to-noise ratio
b) Multipath fading

c) Interference

d) Shadowing by buildings or natural terrain features.

To detect these errors, error detection codes such as parity and cyclic redundancy checks may be used. A 16-bit CRC used with a radio link may allow, on average, one erroneous block in 65 000 to go undetected. It is common to employ an automatic repeat request (ARQ) system to request the retransmission of blocks of data which contain errors.

Radio links often have high error rates and low data rates which make the overhead associated with requesting the retransmission of a complete block of data take up a large proportion of the link capacity. Forward error-correction codes can reduce the number of blocks which must be retransmitted but they require a large overhead in redundant bits transmitted with the data.

Forward error-correcting codes may be classed as convolutional codes (which convolve the data with a polynomial) or block codes (which add parity bits to each block of data). Block codes may be binary or symbol codes. Symbol codes group the data bits into symbols which may be modulated on the carrier. Binary block codes frequently use polynomial division by a defined bit pattern to generate a remainder which is added to the data block.

Error-detecting codes can detect many random errors in a block but radio links are susceptible to burst errors which occur in rapid succession and cannot be handled by many forward error-correcting codes. Some convolutional codes are capable of detecting burst errors; for example the code used in the Nordic NMT 450 cellular radio system can detect and correct bursts of up to 6 errors. A Reed Solomon (31, 16) block code can also detect and correct up to 7 symbol errors per block where 5-bit symbols are employed.

To avoid the complication of convolution and block codes, a technique known as *interleaving* may be used to separate the burst of errors throughout a block of transmitted data where a simpler random error-correcting code can be used to detect and correct the errors. Interleaving alters the order in which bits are transmitted, typically by reading a block of data into a matrix row after row and taking the data out of the matrix column by column for transmission. At the receiver the reverse deinterleaving process recovers the original data sequence. The greater the dimensions of the matrix are (the depth of interleaving), the longer is the burst of errors which will be spread out.

8.7.2 CDLC

The CDLC protocol is used by Racal in the British TACS cellular radio system. TACS uses burst error correction and ARQ to handle situations when burst error correction cannot cope with a long burst. CDLC is able to operate at 2400 bit/s. Typical multipath fades of 1 to 10 ms and bursts of errors up to 5 seconds must be accommodated when vehicles pass through radio shadows. Error bursts of about 300 ms also occur when the call is handed over from one base station to another. Long bursts of this magnitude cannot be handled by any other mechanism than ARQ.

In normal operation, over 10% of the 512 bit data blocks contain errors while the vehicle is moving. This makes it necessary to use interleaving and a block error-correcting code to maintain system throughput. A 'punctured BCH' (16, 8) code is used; this is able to correct 2 errors in each 16-bit block.

The interleaving depth chosen is a compromise between the length of error bursts handled and delay imposed in the interleaving and deinterleaving process. Delay is about twice the product of the block length and the bit time and the maximum burst error length is about twice the interleaving depth. Because CDLC is intended for use in a wide range of applications, the depth of interleaving is selectable. For a block length of 60 ms and an interleaving depth of 2.5 ms, with 2 information characters per block, the efficiency is 0.14. At the other extreme, for a block length of 473 ms and an interleaving depth of 28.3 ms with 64 information characters per block, the efficiency is 0.56.

The CDLC frame consists of:

a)   48 sync bits
b)   16 address bits
c)   16 control bits
d) N 16-bit information words
e)   Two 16-bit CRC words.

Start and stop bits are removed from asynchronous characters before transmission and 8 data bits are accommodated in each 16-bit information word.

8.8   Videotex (viewdata)

Videotex is an information distribution system which uses a modified domestic television set for information display. Information is stored in a central computer which is accessed on the public switched telephone network. The user may employ a keypad with a modem capable of asynchronous FSK reception at 1200 bit/s and transmission at 75 bit/s to request the relevant page of information. Information pages may be from a variety of sources, some public and some for private users.

Several different videotex systems exist:

Prestel	(UK)
Compuserve	(USA)
Telenet	(France)
Captain	(Japan)
Telidon	(Canada)

In the UK the videotex standard is known as viewdata and the format is the same as that used by Prestel, the public viewdata service provided by British Telecom. Prestel uses an alphamosaic display method in which each character is composed of a 6×10 matrix and graphics are formed from 2×3 cell matrices, which make only crude graphics available. The page consists of 24 lines, each with 40 characters.

The Telidon and Captain systems have improved graphics capabilities, Telidon uses an alphageometric method of character generation in which the character shapes and symbols are stored in the display systems memory. Captain uses a display method based on individually addressing pixels from the 50 592 pixel screen divided into 31×17 sub-blocks which are further divided into a matrix of 8×12 pixels. Sub-blocks are used to generate graphics and characters but pictures may be displayed using an alphaphotographic technique. A trial digital Captain system using the public packet switched network was begun in 1984. It is intended to transmit compressed high resolution video information (using Adaptive Block Truncation Coding) and Adaptive PCM speech over the 64 kbit/s digital network.

Most videotex systems are descendants of the Prestel system which went into service in September 1979, and now has over 250 000 pages of information. Business users can store a private database on Prestel and specialist information providers serve user groups such as travel agents. Where automatic access is required to the database, videotex adaptors may be added to computers.

Private videotex systems may use a private computer to store the central database or a private section of the Prestel database may be used (known as a closed user group). Videotex systems, in which users pay for access to the information provided, are a form of value added network (VAN).

Private videotex systems are applicable to many wide area network applications where remote terminals access a central database (write/read). Videotex is a suitable medium for integrating a range of office automation applications such as electronic mail, text processing, diary, telephone directory and document filing. The characteristics which make videotex suitable are:

a) Support for a family of different terminals.
b) The use of page structured information with linking between pages provided through a simple standardised procedure such as a menu.
c) An explicit basic-level user syntax which is simple and based on a set of rules which match database structure.
d) The provision of assistance to users.
e) Some systems are capable of limited processing to assist in accessing the correct database page.

9 Performance prediction

9.1 Introduction

A point-to-point communication link may be procured with a fair amount of confidence that the link circuitry and protocol will meet the design objectives. To estimate the line throughput (number of information bits correctly received divided by the time taken for transmission) several factors must be taken into account including:

a) Data transmission rate.
b) Transmission block size.
c) Block overheads and other protocol factors.
d) Line error rate.
e) Number of blocks which must be retransmitted when an error occurs.
f) Propagation delay.
g) Modem turnaround and throughput delays.
h) Delays and limitations within the computer/terminal interface circuits.
i) Software-induced delays within the host computers.
j) Transaction characteristics.

A network of links has all the performance uncertainties of each point-to-point link plus many more which arise through polling in a multipoint network, delays at store and forward nodes, different paths through the network, partial network breakdowns, and congestion in message switched and packet switched networks. The design of wide area networks requires an analysis of network throughput, response time, and availability in order to predict performance in the highly complex and uncertain environment. Many analytical and simulation procedures, including queuing theory, may be called upon to help in this analysis.

The topology of a wide area network constructed from a network of point-to-point links between switching/multiplexing nodes may take many forms because the number of combinations of link speed and link connectivity are enormous, even for a relatively small network (about 10 nodes). There is obviously an optimum combination of links which minimises the annual line costs and algorithms are available to perform this topological optimisation.

Local area networks are available in many forms and the choice may be quite bewildering. Manufacturers claims may be difficult to compare and in many cases the information on throughput and delay may not be available for a network of the size anticipated and for the kind of usage envisaged.

The performance of command-response buses such as MIL-STD-1553 B are relatively easy to determine (see section 7.8.5) but comparisons between token passing LANs and contention access control networks such as IEEE 802.3 are more difficult. Fortunately, some simulation studies have been carried out to make these comparisons. However, the results of such simulations must be interpreted with care because the conditions and circumstances assumed in the simulation may not match those in the network under consideration.

Many performance figures quoted for local area networks assume that the transmitting and receiving stations can handle the data with no delays or throughput limitations. In practice the processing necessary to execute the OSI level 2, 3 and 4 software often has a greater influence on response times than the physical and data link aspects of the LAN.

The ability of a network to function when some of the components have failed is often of vital importance. It may be acceptable for one user to lose the communication service occasionally but large numbers of network users must not lose network service together. The impact of network component failures must be quantified and suitable component and line redundancy may be necessary to meet the required network availability. Reliability/availability analysis techniques are available for component parts and for networks as a whole.

9.2 Link performance

9.2.1 Link throughput

A general formula for calculating link throughput taking into account the data transmission rate, protocol overheads, block size and retransmissions when errors occur is:

$$\frac{\text{Number of information bits}}{\text{Time for transmission}} = \frac{I_C I_B (1 - P)}{[B_C(I_B + O_B)/R + T_G] \, (1 - P + N_R P)}$$

where

P = the probability of an error in a block
I_C = the number of bits of information per character
B_C = the total number of bits of information per character
I_B = the number of information characters per block
O_B = the number of overhead characters per block
R = the data rate in bit/s
T_G = the gap between successive blocks in ms
N_R = the number of blocks which must be retransmitted when a block contains any errors.

Any retransmissions or delays caused by errors in sending acknowledgements are ignored because these are generally relatively small compared with the effect of errors on data blocks.

The value of P, the probability of a single-bit error in a block, may be calculated from the line error rate E using the formula:

$$P = 1 - (1 - E)^{B_C(I_B + O_B)}$$

For a typical digital line with $E = 1$ in 10^{-6} and

I_B = 200 information characters/block
O_B = 6 overhead characters/block
B_C = 8 bits/character

then

$$P = 1 - (1 - 0.000001)^{8(206)}$$
$$= 1 - (0.999999)^{1648}$$
$$= 0.00165 \text{ or } 0.165\%$$

T_G, the gap between successive transmissions, may be calculated for half-duplex links by finding the sum of:

a) Two propagation delays (about 1 ms per 100 miles each way).
b) Modem data delay (usually relatively small).
c) RTS/CTS delay in the receiving modem.
d) The time taken to transmit an acknowledgement.
e) RTS/CTS delay in the transmitting modem.
f) Two receiver reaction delays (usually zero).

For full-duplex links, T_G is usually zero.

N_R, the number of blocks which must be retransmitted when a block contains any errors, depends on the retransmission procedure employed by the data link protocol. Selective retransmission procedures, in which only the block containing the error is retransmitted, have an N_R of 1.

Go-back-N retransmission procedures, as employed in SDLC, HDLC and X.25 LAP-B, retransmit all the outstanding blocks from the block containing the error to the block transmitted immediately before the reject message was received by the sender. For go-back-N procedures:

$$N_R = \frac{R}{I_B} = \text{Error notification delay}$$

and for HDLC:

$$N_R = \frac{2 + R(2 \times \text{Propagation delay}) + (\text{Characters in reject message})}{I_B}$$

rounding upwards to the next integer.

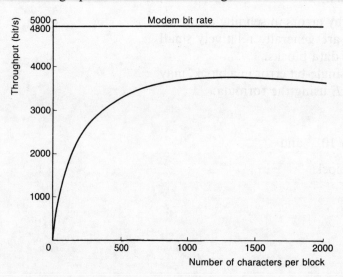

Figure 9.1 shows the relationship between throughput and the number of characters per block for an analog half-duplex link with:

I_C = 8 bits/character
O_B = 6 overhead characters per block
R = 4800 bit/s
Propagation delay = 10 ms
Modem data delay = 0 ms
RTS/CTS delays = 150 ms
Acknowledgement = 6 characters
E = line error rate = 1 in 10^{-5} (0.00001)
Receiver reaction delay = 0 ms

The fall in throughput with longer data blocks is caused by the increase in the overhead imposed by each retransmission when a line error occurs. The low throughput with small blocks is caused by the relatively large overheads per block and relatively large gap between successive blocks. The maximum link efficiency is achieved around 1200 characters per block where throughput is about 78% of the modem data rate.

9.2.2. Transaction response time

Average response time for a point-to-point data link interrogating a processor is the sum of:

a) Input message transmission time (I_T)
b) Host processing time (H_T)
c) Output message transmission time (O_T)

For a terminal accessing a host processor using character mode transmission, the average response time measured from the last character transmitted to the last character received back from the processor (last in, last out) is

$$I_T + H_T + O_T$$

where

$$I_T = \frac{1 \text{ (character)}}{\text{Link speed in characters/s}} + \text{Propagation delay}$$

H_T as defined.

$$O_T = \frac{\text{Number of characters in output message}}{\text{Link speed in characters/s}} + \text{Propagation delay}$$

The variance in response time is given by:

$$\frac{\left(\begin{array}{c}\text{Variance for characters} \\ \text{in output message}\end{array}\right)}{(\text{Link speed})^2} + \left(\begin{array}{c}\text{Variance in host} \\ \text{processing time}\end{array}\right)$$

9.2.3 Multiplexed link capacity

A character-multiplexed time division multiplexer on a point-to-point link can accommodate a wide variety of terminal speeds and codes. Table 9.1 shows the capacity in terms of single asynchronous input rates for various synchronous output rates.

Statistical multiplexers take advantage of the lack of activity on any input channel to provide more than twice the number of input channels, in typical applications, compared with a character multiplexer used with the same output rate. Figure 9.2 shows how a statistical multiplexer uses dynamic bandwidth allocation to increase the input channel capacity (300 bit/s input channels and a 9.600 bit/s output channel) as average input channel activity changes and as output link error rate changes.

Table 9.1 Capacity of a character multiplexer for various asynchronous input rates

Low-speed asynchronous inputs			*Synchronous output rate (bit/s)*		
			Number of asynchronous channels		
Bit/s	Code	Bits per character	2400	4800	9600
50	Baudot(ITA3)	7.5	57	115	128
110	ASCII	11	25	51	103
134.5	EBCDIC	9	18	38	77
300	ASCII	10	7	16	33

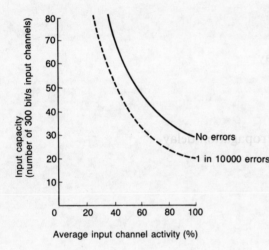

Fig. 9.2 Variation in channel capacity of a statistical multiplexer with changes in average input channel activity and output link error rate

9.3 Wide area network performance prediction

9.3.1 Alternative models

When designing a wide area network, particularly one which uses polling, it is difficult to predict performance unless a detailed analysis of a similar network has been carried out. Suitable information on a similar network is not generally available so performance modelling must be employed.

Three forms of predictive modelling are used:

1) Analytical queuing models
2) Simulation models
3) Hybrid models which incorporate analytical techniques in a simulation model.

Analytical models are mathematical representations which relate the system output to the inputs by defined functional relationships between variables. Analytical queuing models of polled systems are often extremely complex and many simplifications must be made which may result in unpredictable inaccuracies or limitations.

Queuing theory may be used to model the processing of messages arriving at processing nodes but the assumptions about the distribution of input messages may make the results inaccurate. Such analytical models may be used for rapid initial assessment and trade-off analysis where gross answers are acceptable. Simulation models can give more accurate results than analytical models but are often difficult to use and require much computer and human time to run.

Simulation models are computer programs which use software routines to model the relationships between system inputs and outputs. The working of a network may be modelled to any desired level of detail if the necessary system relationships are known but the time and effort required to model the system is directly proportional to the level of detail required. The time required to run simulation models on a computer is also directly related to the level of detail and this makes detailed simulation slow and expensive. Simulation models are usually employed in the later stages of network design where more precise performance figures are required.

The *hybrid model* is a compromise which offers the flexibility and speed of analytical models and the accuracy available from simulation models. Information employed by the hybrid model may be detailed empirical data when available, or statistical approximations when it is not available. Hybrid modelling programs such as Contel Information System's Mind network analysis package include a variety of simulation modules in which the functional equations of the analytical approach are embedded within the simulations approach.

Experience has shown that it is not practical to model an entire complex data communications network in detail. Hybrid models employ simplified analytical models for the operation of communications processors and the central processor within a simulation of the entire system. This allows response times to be examined within the context of the whole network but without excessive complications which make results difficult to interpret. Reference 9.1 discusses communications models in more detail.

9.3.2 Performance of polled multipoint networks

Polled multipoint (or multidrop) networks are commonly used for connecting remote terminals to central data processing systems.

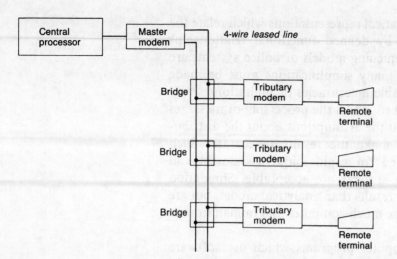

Fig. 9.3 Basic polled multipoint network configuration

Figure 9.3 shows the basic hardware configuration of a polled multipoint network. The central processor has a master modem which is linked to several tributary modems by a dedicated 4-wire multipoint line. The master modem transmits polling sequences and addressing sequences (which send data to the tributary modems); it may therefore leave its carrier permanently on. The tributary modems share the return path and their carriers must be switched on only when the terminal has been polled and wishes to transmit. Line sharing is used to save line costs and is possible when terminal input rates are typically much lower than the transmission rate of the communication line.

The most significant parameter in a polled multipoint system is the response time because this is degraded as more terminals are added to the shared line and as more messages are transmitted. Figure 9.4 shows the typical relationship between response time and input message rate (or utilisation). Beyond a threshold message rate the response time increases rapidly and therefore the system should be designed to operate below this threshold message rate.

Reference 9.2 describes a verified analytical model for polled multipoint networks which is capable of determining response times under criteria and control procedures which are applicable to real systems. A brief summary of this model by Chou, Nilsson and King of North Carolina State University, USA is given.

There are several definitions of response time based on different start and end points. The response time period may begin after the arrival of the message at the terminal or at the time when the message has been keyed in at the terminal. The period may end when an acknowledgement is received from the host computer or concentrator or when the last character of the response is received. It is

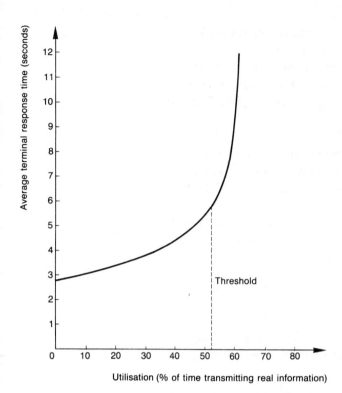

therefore necessary to obtain a precise definition of response time and make any necessary corrections when making comparisons.

Figure 9.5 shows the typical timing sequence for polling or addressing, independent of variations introduced by different link protocols such as Bisync, SDLC, HDLC, etc.

T_P is the average total time for a negative poll.

T_{PB} is the average time associated with a positive poll prior to the transmission of the input message.

T_{PA} is the average time associated with a positive poll after the transmission of the input message.

T_{AB} is the average time associated with addressing before output transmission.

T_{AA} is the average time associated with signalling the end of output transmission.

T_{KI} is the average total time for processing or keying an input message at the terminal.

T_{SI} is the mean input message transmission time (input message size divided by the line capacity).

T_{CPU} is the mean computer (or concentrator) turnaround processing time, from arrival of input at the computer to the time when the corresponding output is sent to the output queue.

T_{SO} is the mean output message transmission time (output message size divided by the line capacity).

T_{WO} is the average total time an output message waits in the output queue at the host computer (or concentrator).

T_{WI} is the average total time an input message waits in the input queue at the terminal.

T_{BTP} is the mean bid to poll time (between the keying-in of the last character of input and the polling of the terminal).

T_{LCFC} is the average terminal response time from the keying-in of the last character of the input to the arrival of the first output character at the terminal.

T_{LCLC} is the average terminal response time from the keying-in of the last character of the input to the arrival of the last output character at the terminal.

Chou's analytical model states that the average response time is

$$T_R = T_{BTP} + T_{SI} + T_{CPU} + T_{WO} + T_{SO}$$

where response time is measured from the keying-in of the last character of the input at the terminal to the last character of the reply or the first page of the reply to the input.

The terms T_{SI}, T_{CPU} and T_{SO} may be considered to be system constants but T_{BTP} and T_{WO} require analysis.

T_{BTP} is expressed as:

$$T_{BTP} = 0.5 \left[1 + V(t_c)/T_c^2\right] T_c$$

where T_c = mean poll cycle time

   $V(t_c)$ = variance in t_c.

$$T_c = \frac{MT_P}{1 - [\rho_I + \rho_O + U(\text{HDX-non}) \, \rho_{CPU} - \rho_I \rho_O U(\text{FDX})]}$$

and

$$V(t_c) = E(n_I) \left[V_{SI} + V_{SO} + U(\text{HDX-non})V_{CPU}\right]$$
$$+ V(n_I) \left[T_{SI}^2 + T_{SO}^2 + U(\text{HDX-non}) \, F_{HDX}\right]/[1 + U(\text{FDX}) \, \rho_I \rho_O]^2$$

where M is the number of terminals sharing the line

ρ_I is the average line utilisation contributed by input messages

$$= \frac{\text{Input message arrival rate} \times T_{SI}}{\text{Line capacity}}$$

ρ_O is the average line utilisation contributed by outputs

$$= \frac{\text{Input message arrival rate} \times T_{SO}}{\text{Line capacity}}$$

288

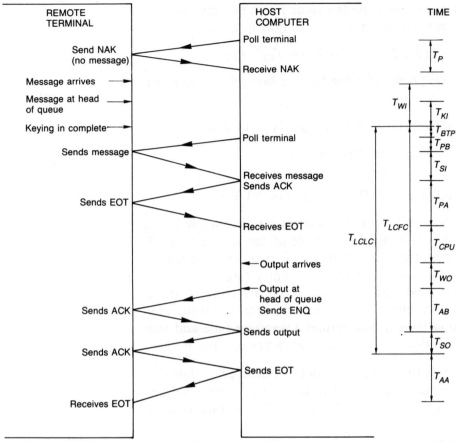

Fig. 9.5 A typical timing sequence for polling or addressing

ρ_{CPU} is the average line utilisation contributed by the CPU turn-around time

$$= \frac{\text{Input message arrival rate} \times T_{CPU}}{\text{Line capacity}}$$

$U(\text{HDX-non}) = 1$ for half-duplex, noninterleaved protocols
$\qquad\qquad\quad = 0$ for any other protocols.
$U(\text{FDX}) = 1$ for full-duplex protocols
$\qquad\quad\;\; = 0$ for any other protocols.
$E(n_I)$ is the expected value for the number of input message arrivals in a specified time interval (often a polling cycle).
V_{SI} is the variance of input message transmission time.
V_{SO} is the variance of output message transmission time.
V_{CPU} is the variance of the computer (or concentrator) turn-around processing time.

$V(n_I)$ is the variance in the expected value for the number of input message arrivals in a specified time interval.

$$F_{HDX} = T_{CPU}^2 + 2(T_{SI}.T_{CPU} + T_{SI}.T_{SO} + T_{CPU}.T_{SO})$$

To derive T_{WO} a non-preemptive head-of-the-line priority queuing model is used:

$$T_{WO} = [1 - U(\text{HDX-non})] [W(\rho_O, V_{SO}, T_{SO}, N) T_{SO}]$$

$$+ \frac{1 - [\rho_I + \rho_O - \rho_I\rho_O U(\text{FDX}) T_P]}{\rho_O}$$

$$+ U(\text{HDX}) (\rho_I/\rho_O) W(\rho_O, V_{SI}, T_{SI}, N) T_{SI}$$

where $W(\rho, V, T, N)$ is the normalised waiting time in a single server queuing system, with V being the variance of the service time, T being the mean service time, and N being the number of terminals for the single entry case (∞ for the multiple-entry case).

Chou's analytical model gives results which are close to those produced by a complex simulation model. Reference 9.2 investigates (using the simulation model) how terminal response time and line throughput behave under various conditions. Some conclusions are:

a) The maximum productive utilisation (percentage of time the line spends transmitting information rather than overheads) is about 0.65 for full-duplex SDLC and 0.2 for non-interleaved Bisync.

b) For a full-duplex SDLC polled system with 0.5 second CPU turnaround time, and a constant (0.4) line utilisation, the average response time may vary between 1 and 4 seconds as the number of terminals sharing the same line increases from 1 to 20.

c) If a polled multipoint network is designed to ensure that the average terminal response time is kept below a specified limit, the line utilisation is not always greatest when the number of terminals is minimised. If no more than one outstanding transaction is allowed per terminal, the line may be idle during the wait for a response from the processor while messages are waiting for input.

d) An effective way of configuring polled multipoint lines is to plot line utilisation against the number of terminals for various values of average terminal response time, i.e. by constraining line utilisation as a function of the number of terminals sharing the line.

e) For a full-duplex SDLC polled multipoint line using a polling frequency which is independent of the traffic volume at the terminals, the mean response time becomes smaller as traffic volume is distributed among the terminals while the line utilisation is kept constant.

   If the polling frequency is made proportional to the traffic volume the standard deviation of the response time becomes larger as the traffic volume is distributed more between the terminals

f) With the same number of terminals and the same utilisation, the response time varies little with different traffic distribution patterns among the terminals.

g) For a full-duplex SDLC line with a line utilisation of 0.3, response time reduces initially as the message size is increased because the percentage of overhead is reduced but, as message size is increased further, the response time increases again because the message transmission time becomes significant.

h) A noninterleaved system which leaves the line idle while the CPU is processing the message has a lower line utilisation than an interleaved system but the response time may be lower and less random when the CPU processing time is small compared with transmission time.

i) Comparison of protocols shows that asynchronous half-duplex procedures can produce lower response times than bit-oriented synchronous full-duplex protocols in some circumstances because they have lower polling overheads but full-duplex protocols are more efficient when transmitting in both directions simultaneously.

j) For full-duplex protocols, response times may be reduced by breaking long messages into blocks with polling messages transmitted between the blocks. This nested polling is most advantageous when line utilisation is high or when input message size is great.

9.3.3   Average network transit delay for most networks

A mesh network has several alternative routes through which messages may pass on the way from the source node to the destination node (see Figure 9.6). Intermediate nodes have a routing algorithm which determines the next node to which packets or messages for each destination should be routed.

   Design of mesh networks is a complex process involving connectivity and determining routing tables and capacity allocation. The connectivity of a mesh network is the least number of disjoint (totally independent with no common elements) paths between any two nodes. A network with a connectivity of n can withstand $n - 1$ failures without disconnecting a node from the network when n is at least 2. The minimum degree for a network is the minimum number

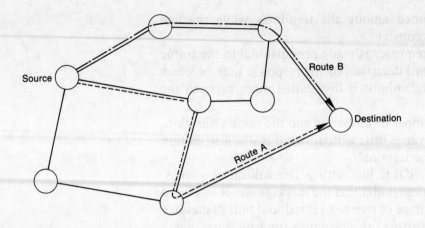

Fig. 9.6 Alternative routes through a mesh network

of links attached to any node; a value of 2 is necessary but not sufficient to provide a connectivity of 2.

The topology of a mesh network may be selected using several strategies:

a) In a fully connected network (which links each node directly to all the other nodes) the largest number of links, which is $0.5\,N(N-1)$ links, is required to fully connect a network of N nodes (see Figure 9.7).

b) Nodes may be connected to 2 or 3 neighbours in the order of least cost.

c) Nodes may be connected to 2 or 3 neighbours in the order of greatest communication requirements.

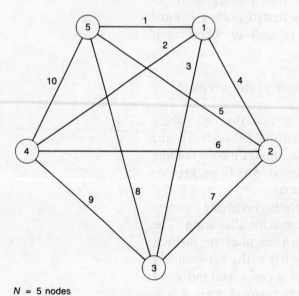

Fig. 9.7 A fully connected network with N nodes

N = 5 nodes

Number of links = $\dfrac{N(N-1)}{2} = \dfrac{5 \times 4}{2} = 10$

This initial connection topology may be subjected to the Kleitman connectivity test to ensure that a minimum connectivity (n) is achieved.

The Kleitman test involves three steps:

1) From any node, check that there are n disjoint paths to all the other nodes; if there are not, modify the network and start again, otherwise go to step 2.
2) Remove the first node checked from the network and make $n = n - 1$.
3) Check that n is greater than zero; if not, stop and modify the network, otherwise go to step 1.

There are many routing algorithms, some are fixed and others adapt to traffic conditions. Adaptive routing may be isolated (affected by the local knowledge of traffic conditions at each node), distributed (which exchanges knowledge of traffic conditions between nodes), or centralised (which uses a central control node to collect traffic information from all nodes and to instruct each node what routing table should be used). For a given routing assignment the traffic expected on each link may be determined for a defined network usage scenario. Link data rates may then be determined allowing an adequate margin for safety and expansion.

Average network transit delay T_D is a good indication of network performance; this may be calculated for connection-oriented networks by using the formula:

$$T_D = T_n + \frac{1}{F_t} \sum_{I=1}^{L} A_p . T_1$$

where

T_n = the processing time at the source and destination nodes
F_t = the total of all packets flowing per second into the network
A_p = the average number of packets flowing per second on link 1
L = the total number of links on the network
T_1 = the delay in seconds on link 1 caused by queuing, propagation delay and nodal processing

For link 1, the value of T_1 is given by

$$\frac{\text{Average message transmission time}}{1 - (\text{Average packets/second}) (\text{Average message transmission time})}$$

+ Propagation delay + Nodal processing delay

Messages are assumed to have a gamma distribution.

9.3.4 Finding the minimum cost topology for multipoint networks and centralised hierarchical networks

Several heuristic algorithms have been developed to find the minimum cost topology for multipoint networks and centralised hierarchical networks with multiplexers and concentrators. These centralised forms of network must connect the remote terminals (or computers) to a central site. The optimum network has the lowest annual line cost consistent with meeting the traffic load requirements. A typical teleprocessing network with multipoint lines terminating at intermediate line concentrators, and connected to the central computer by dedicated lines, is shown in Figure 9.8.

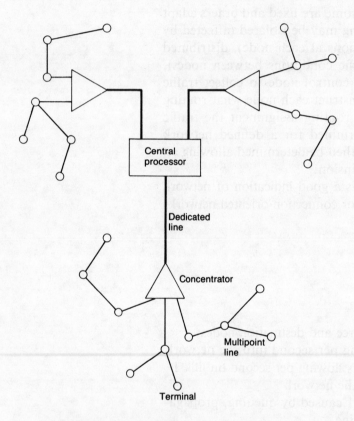

Fig. 9.8 A teleprocessing network using dedicated lines from multipoint line concentrators to the central computer

Heuristic algorithms (named after the Greek *heros*, to enquire) use a try-it-and-see approach with several iterations which converge on the optimum solution but do not always produce the optimum result. Reference 9.3 by Aaron Kershenbaum and Wushow Chou of the Network Analysis Corporation describes a unified heuristic algorithm which can produce the same results as several other algorithms by Prim, Kruskal, Esau and Williams, and Vogel's approximation method (VAM).

The topological design for multipoint lines may be split into five subproblems:

1) Determining the ideal number of concentrators.
2) Selecting the best locations for the central computer and the concentrators.
3) Connecting the concentrators and central computer.
4) Associating each terminal with a concentrator (cluster controller).
5) Connecting the terminals to the concentrators.

All these subproblems are interrelated but can be solved sequentially if adequate care is taken. Subproblems 4 and 5 are the most difficult and may be solved by using the unified algorithm (ref. 9.3).

The starting point for using the unified algorithm is a table of trade-off parameters t_{ij} where

$$t_{ij} = (\text{Cost of connecting location } i \text{ to location } j) - W_i$$

W_i is a weighting factor for terminal i.

When $W_i = 0$ for all terminals, the Kruskal algorithm results.

When $W_i =$ the cost of connecting the terminal i to the central site, the Esau and Williams algorithm results.

When $W_1 = 0$ and $W_i = -\infty$ for $i = 2$ to N (N is the total number of locations including the central site), and if W_i is set to 0 whenever a branch incident to terminal i is selected as a tree branch, a Prim algorithm results.

When $W_i =$ (the cost of the line connecting terminal i to its second nearest feasible neighbour) $-$ (the cost of the line connecting terminal i to its nearest feasible neighbour), the Vogel approximation method results.

Five steps are followed in each iteration:

1) The minimum value for t_{ij} is found.
   If t_{ij} is ∞ terminate; otherwise go to step 2.
2) Check the constraints (e.g. throughput) on link $i-j$. If any are violated, eliminate the link (set t_{ij} to ∞) and go to step 1; otherwise go to step 3.
3) Check whether adding the link $i-j$ forms a loop in the network. If so, eliminate the link and go to step 1; otherwise go to step 4.
4) Add the link $i-j$ to the network and update the constraint parameters W_i and T_{ij}.
5) Check whether the network contains $N-1$ links. If so, stop; otherwise go to step 1.

The unified algorithm may be implemented in many ways and a network of 1673 terminals has been designed in 15 seconds on a

CDC6600 computer. Terminals may be associated with concentrators and a variety of different constraints may be evaluated.

Heuristic algorithms may be used to find the optimum locations for multiplexers or concentrators in centralised hierarchical networks. One algorithm, known as the add algorithm, starts by assuming a network with all terminals connected to the central site, then cycles through two steps:

1) Connect each concentrator to those terminals which result in the greatest cost reduction compared with the connection cost in the previous configuration, subject to the constraints on concentrator throughput. Stop if no cost savings are achieved; otherwise go to step 2.

2) Update the network by incorporating the concentrator which produced the greatest cost saving, then go to step 1.

An alternative algorithm, known as the drop algorithm, starts by assuming that all terminals are connected to concentrators based on least-cost considerations, subject to the constraints on concentrator throughput. Then cycles through two steps:

1) Individually eliminate each concentrator and transfer the terminals to the remaining concentrators using least-cost considerations. Stop if no cost savings are achieved; otherwise go to step 2.

2) Update the network by eliminating the concentrator which produced the greatest cost reduction when eliminated. Go to step 1.

9.4 Local area network performance prediction

9.4.1 Ethernet performance

Reference 9.4 describes the early 3 Mbit/s experimental Ethernet system constructed at the Xerox Palo Alto Research Center. This reference, dated 1976, must be one of the earlier attempts to predict the performance of operational CSMA/CD systems.

A simple set of formulae illustrates Ethernet's distributed contention resolution system under heavy load.

P is the number of data bits in a packet.
H is the number of overhead bits in a packet.
C is the peak capacity of Ethernet in bit/s.
T is the duration of a slot in seconds.

A slot is a contention interval during which stations attempt to gain control of the bus; it is also the time taken to detect a collision after starting a transmission.

It is assumed that Q stations are continuously queued to transmit a packet. Q also represents the total offered load on the bus and is assumed to be greater than one.

If it is assumed that a queued station has a probability of transmitting in a current slot of $1/Q$, the probability of being delayed is $1 - (1/Q)$. To calculate A, the probability that exactly one station attempts to transmit in a slot and therefore acquires control of the bus:

$$A = (1 - [1/Q])^{Q-1}$$

To calculate S, the mean number of slots a station experiences while waiting to gain control of the bus: the probability of waiting no time is A, which is also the probability that only one station attempts to transmit in a slot interval. The probability of waiting for 1 slot interval is $A(1 - A)$ and the probability of waiting for n slots is $A[(1 - A)^n]$. The mean of this geometric distribution of waiting slot periods is:

$$S = (1 - A)/A$$

To calculate E, the efficiency, which is the proportion of time when the bus is transmitting useful data: transmission of a packet takes $(P + H)/C$ seconds and the mean time to gain control of the bus is ST seconds, therefore:

$$E = \frac{(P + H)/C}{[(P + H)/C] + ST}$$

For the maximum data packet length, 1500 octets, $P = 12\,000$ bits.
  $H = 208$ overhead bits per packet.
  $T = 51.2 \times 10^{-6}$ seconds contention slot interval.
  $C = 10\,000\,000$ bit/s.
  $Q = 2$ stations continuously queued to transmit a packet.

$$A = \left(1 - \frac{1}{Q}\right)^{Q-1} = (1 - 0.5)^1 = 0.5$$

$$S = \frac{1 - A}{A} = \frac{0.5}{0.5} = 1$$

Therefore

$$E = \frac{12\,208/10\,000\,000}{(12\,208/10\,000\,000) + (51.2/1\,000\,000)} = 0.96$$

The efficiency of 96% in these circumstances is reduced to 53% when the minimum data packet length, 368 bits, is used. This reduction in efficiency is caused by the increased proportion of packet overheads and contention slot times compared with the amount of data transmitted. The calculation assumed that the two stations were continually queued to transmit a packet but in practice this parameter is difficult to quantify.

9.4.2 Comparison of maximum mean data rate

Reference 9.5 describes the work of an IEEE 802 subcommittee in comparing the maximum mean data rates of the common types of LAN under the same workload. The conclusion of this work is that CSMA/CD offers the shortest delay with a light load but is sensitive to heavy loading, bus length and message length.

Token passing buses have the greatest delay with a light load and cannot carry as much traffic as an equivalent ring under heavy loading conditions. They are also sensitive to propagation delay caused by the bus length. Token passing rings are the least sensitive to workload, offer short delays under light loads, and exhibit controlled delay under heavy load.

The mean throughput rate for a CSMA/CD bus with one station active is the reciprocal of the time spent transmitting data plus control bits:

$$\text{Maximum mean throughput rate} = \frac{1}{T_m + T_i}$$

where T_m is the transmission time for successful messages and T_i is the interframe gap time (which allows for circuit and propagation transients and is 9.6 μs for Ethernet).

The contention slot time T_s is the time required to transmit 512 bits in a 10 Mbit/s Ethernet. This is the time allowed for a signal to propagate to the far end of the bus and back again plus interface circuit delays. The jam time T_j is the time required for a station which detects a collision to transmit a 48-bit pattern in order to reinforce the detected collision.

For 100 active Ethernet stations the maximum mean throughput delay is the reciprocal of the mean transmission time, plus interframe gaps, plus the time spent in collision resolution per successful transmission:

$$\text{Maximum mean throughput rate} = \frac{1}{T_m + T_i + (2e - 1)(T_s + T_j)}$$

This result for 100 stations active assumes that 2e collisions are experienced per successful transmission. (e = 2.718.)

A token passing ring with one active station has a maximum mean data rate which is the reciprocal of the time taken for transmission plus the time required to pass the token around the ring (assumed to be 99 idle stations and one active station):

298

$$\text{Maximum mean throughput rate} = \frac{1}{T_m + T_t}$$

where T_m is the message transmission time (including control overheads) and T_t is the token passing time for the complete ring.

$$T_t = T_p + 100 \, T_{ID}$$

where T_p is the propagation delay around the ring circumference, for a ring with 100 stations. The interface delay time T_{ID} is assumed to be 1 bit transmission time for a token ring.

For a token passing ring with 100 active stations, the maximum mean data rate is the reciprocal of the time to transmit plus the time required to pass the token on to the next station. For 100 stations with equal separation between them, the token must pass one hundredth of the circumference to the next recipient:

$$\text{Maximum mean throughput rate} = \frac{1}{T_m + T_{ID} + (T_p/100)}$$

for 100 active stations.

A token passing bus with one active station has a maximum mean data rate which is the reciprocal of the time taken for a station to transmit a message and pass the token through each of the 99 idle stations and the active station:

$$\text{Maximum mean throughput rate} = \frac{1}{T_m + T_t}$$

where T_t is the time required to pass the token through 100 stations, i.e. $100(T_p + T_{ID})$.

For a token passing bus with 100 active stations, the maximum mean throughput delay is the reciprocal of the time taken for a station to transmit a message and pass the token to the next recipient station:

$$\text{Maximum mean throughput rate} = \frac{1}{T_m + T_p + T_{ID}}$$

9.4.3   Packet delay in LANs with multilevel priority

The introduction of multilevel priority schemes in the more recent LAN standards (IEEE 802.4, 802.5 and FDDI) makes the estimation of packet delay much more complex. Without multilevel priority, delay may be estimated by multiplying the average number of packets in the queue by the average packet transmission time and adding collision, token passing and propagation delays. With multilevel priority schemes, a much more detailed simulation is required where the priority levels are computed for each rotation of the token and the delay is calculated for packets of each priority in a defined scenario of packets waiting at each station.

Simulation programs for multilevel priority LANs have been produced using a personal computer in one or two working weeks. These programs will output minimum, average and maximum delays given the list of packets waiting for transmission at each station and the priority levels associated with each packet.

Jan Thorner of Phillips Elektronikindustriev AB has carried out simulation studies of IEEE 802.5 token ring LANs with multilevel priority and has compared the packet delay with that which may be achieved by IEEE 802.3, with and without multilevel priority in the software up to level 4 of OSI. The IEEE 802.3 (Ethernet) simulation has been shown to reflect accurately the performance of a real network.

Transmission time was measured from the time when the packet was entered into the send buffer of the transmitting station up to the time when it reached the receiving station. When level 3 and 4 software was included in the simulation, the transmission time was measured from the insertion of the packet at the buffer input to level 4 in the transmitting station until it exited the level 4 software in the receiving station. To ensure valid comparisons, both the IEEE 802.3 and IEEE 802.5 networks were assumed to operate at 10 Mbit/s. Simulations were carried out for applied loads up to about 50% of full capacity with the load distributed relatively uniformly over several nodes varying in number from 10 to 80. Packet length was 50 bytes with appropriate overheads.

The results of this simulation were obtained after several hours of processor time representing about 10 seconds of real time. At 20% loading (2 Mbit/s) the performance of IEEE 802.3 and IEEE 802.5 were identical without priority and at each priority level when priority was implemented. Networks with priority were found to give a lower standard deviation in delay than those without priority. At less than 20% loading, IEEE 802.3 was found to be unaffected by the number of nodes active at constant load and packet delay in IEEE 802.5 was found to increase in proportion to the number of nodes.

As shown in Figure 9.9, with applied loads above 40% (4 Mbit/s), token ring was found to be considerably superior to CSMA/CD where collisions take up an increasing proportion of the time if priority is not implemented at OSI level 4. Token ring without priority was found to suffer from only a 50% increase in delay time when the load was increased from 20 to 40%. IEEE 802.3 with priority implemented at OSI level 4 improves the packet delay for highest-priority packets but lowest-priority packets are delayed much more than those on IEEE 802.5 (see Figure 9.10).

The overall conclusions to be drawn from this simulation are:

a) For typical loads up to about 20%, IEEE 802.3 and IEEE 802.5 (with 10 Mbit/s transmission rate) behave similarly.

b) For loads of about 50%, token ring is superior to IEEE 802.3 (without priority) in packet delay but when priority is added to IEEE 802.3 the delay for high-priority packets is considerably improved.

c) Software-induced delays at OSI levels 3 and 4 are most significant in networks with a maximum of 20 to 30 nodes if the packet length does not exceed about 100 bytes.

d) Software-induced delays are much larger than delays associated with an IEEE 802.3 network even when all nodes transmit at their maximum packet rate.

e) Software-induced delays are mostly attributable to the number of packets transmitted rather than their length.

f) When faster processors are available to reduce software-induced delays it will be desirable to implement priority schemes on heavily loaded networks.

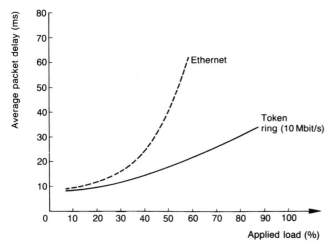

Fig. 9.9 Packet delay/ applied load comparison for Ethernet and a 10 Mbit/s token ring, without priority

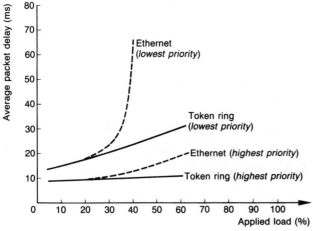

Fig. 9.10 Packet delay/ applied load at different priorities

9.5 Network reliability and availability prediction

9.5.1 Definition of terms and basic calculations

Equipment reliability is defined as the probability (expressed as a percentage) that an equipment will operate within its specification for a defined period of time. Reference 9.6 (section 10.2) describes the prediction of equipment reliability and availability. The usual way of indicating the reliability of a piece of equipment is to quote the Mean Time Between Failures (MTBF).

The MTBF may be calculated from real failure statistics collected over a long period of time or the figure may be predicted using component failure rates given in MIL-HDBK-217. Quoted MTBF figures are only valid for the constant failure rate region of the 'bathtub' reliability curve (see Figure 9.11). The constant failure rate region of the curve applies during the normal life of the equipment, excluding the early life (or burn-in period), and the region when the equipment is wearing out. Many more failures occur outside the constant failure rate region.

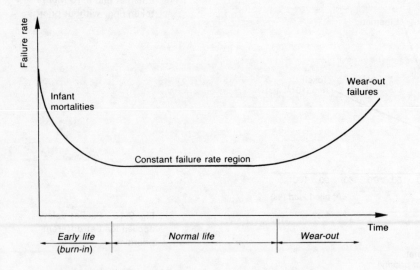

Fig. 9.11 The 'bathtub' reliability curve

The probability of component failure within the time interval t is

$$1 - [\text{Reliability factor } R(t)] = 1 - e^{-t/\text{MTBF}}$$

The probability of failure within a time period equal to the MTBF is typically 63%. Therefore MTBF figures should not be taken out of context with the time period for which the operation is being considered.

Equipment availability is the proportion of time for which the equipment is expected to be fully operational:

$$\text{Availability } A = \frac{\text{MTBF}}{\text{MTBF} + \text{MTTR}}$$

where MTTR is the mean time to repair a fault, including the time required for diagnosis.

The availability of a system consisting of several components wired together in series and parallel combinations may be calculated (assuming that a single failure of a series element causes the system to fail). The availability of several (n) series components (as shown in Figure 9.12) may be calculated by finding the product of all the individual component availabilities. Expressed in mathematical terms this is the product of the series:

$$\prod_{k=1}^{n} A_k$$

where n components are in series.

Fig. 9.12 Series components in an availability network diagram

Fig. 9.13 Parallel components in an availability network diagram

The availability of two components in parallel (as shown in Figure 9.13) may be calculated by finding the sum of the individual component availabilities and subtracting the product of the two component availabilities. When several (n) components are in parallel and only one is required for the system to function satisfactorily, the availability is

$$A_s = 1 - \prod_{k=1}^{n} (1 - A_k)$$

When M out of N identical components are required for the system to function satisfactorily, the availability may be calculated using the formula:

$$\text{System availability } A_s = A^N + \sum_{I=1}^{N-M} \frac{N! \, A^{(N-I)}(1-A)^I}{(N-I)! \, I!}$$

where A = the availability of each individual component.

Figure 9.14 shows several system availability network diagrams consisting of series and parallel elements. The availability of the system may be calculated by breaking the availability network diagram into simple groups of series or parallel elements, calculating the effective availability, and then using that value in a smaller availability network diagram which is eventually reduced to a single

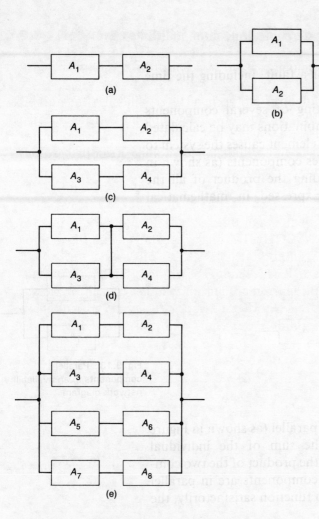

component. If each element in Figure 9.14 has an availability of 0.90 the system availability is calculated as follows:

a) $A_s = A_1 A_2 = 0.81$ or 81%

b) $A_s = A_1 + A_2 - A_1 A_2 = 0.9 + 0.9 - 0.81 = 0.99$ or 99%

c) $A_s = A_1 A_2 + A_3 A_4 - A_1 A_2 A_3 A_4$
    $= 0.81 + 0.81 - 0.6561$
    $= 0.9639$ or 96.39%

d) $A_s = [A_1 + A_3 - A_1 A_3] [A_2 + A_4 - A_2 A_4]$
    $= 0.99 \times 0.99 = 0.9801$ or 98.01%

e) $A_s = 1 - [1 - A_1 A_2] [1 - A_3 A_4] [1 - A_5 A_6] [1 - A_7 A_8]$
    $= 1 - [0.19]^4 = 0.9987$ or 99.87%

9.5.2 Estimating network availability

Communications networks consist of many types of equipment and the availability of the communications service to some users will

304

differ from the availability to other users, depending upon the network configuration. Clearly a means of estimating overall network availability is required which does not assume that any component failure causes a network failure because the service may still be available to some users.

A procedure for estimating network availability may be executed in five stages:

1) Obtain the MTBF and MTTR for each network component.
2) Calculate the sum of device hours per month for each type of component.
3) Calculate the average number of users affected by the failure of each type of component.
4) Calculate the number of hours when users will have no network service due to failure of each type of component, using the formula:

Unavailable user hours =

$$\frac{\text{Device hours (from 2)} \times \text{MTTR} \times \text{Average users affected (from 3)}}{\text{MTBF}}$$

5) Calculate network availability using the formula:

$$A_n = \frac{\text{Total network user hours} - \text{Total unavailable user hours}}{\text{Total network user hours}}$$

To illustrate the procedure for calculating network availability, consider a polled multipoint network with a processor, modems, lines, cluster controllers and terminals as shown in Figure 9.15. The MTBF and MTTR figures are given in Table 9.2.

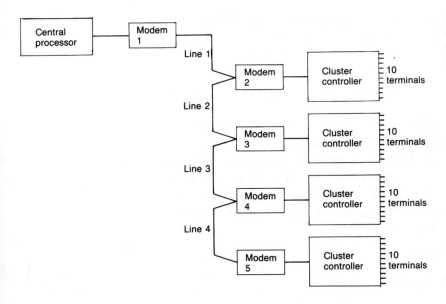

Fig. 9.15 The polled multipoint network configuration used for availability calculations

To calculate the sum of device hours per month for each type of component, multiply the number of hours for which the devices are operational per month by the quantity of devices. If some examples have different numbers of operational hours the products of the number of operational hours and the number of devices with that usage must be summed. Table 9.3 derives the sum of device hours for each type of component.

When calculating the average number of users affected by the failure of each component type it is assumed that only the users downline of the failure are affected.

Line 1 affects 40 users
Line 2 affects 30 users
Line 3 affects 20 users
Line 4 affects 10 users

Total   100

Therefore the average number of users affected by a line failure is $100 \div 4 = 25$.

Failure of modem 1 affects 40 users
Failure of modem 2 affects 10 users
Failure of modem 3 affects 10 users
Failure of modem 4 affects 10 users
Failure of modem 5 affects 10 users

Total   80

Therefore the average number of users affected by a modem failure is $80 \div 5 = 16$.

The average number of users affected by a processor failure is 40 because the network polling mechanism would fail. The average number of users affected by a cluster controller failure is 10 because 10 terminals are connected to each cluster controller. The average number of users affected by a terminal failure is 1 because each user has a dedicated terminal.

The number of unavailable user service hours for each type of network component are calculated using Table 9.4.

The total network availability may now be calculated when the total number of network user hours is known. The total number of network user hours may be calculated by multiplying the number of users (one per terminal) by the number of hours/month when the network is operational, i.e.

$40 \times 400 = 16\,000$ hours

Network availability A_n is

Table 9.2 MTBF and MTTR figures for network components

Network component	MTBF (hours)	MTTR (hours)
Processor	200	2
Modems	5000	3
Lines	3000	4
Cluster controllers	500	2
Terminals	1000	2

Table 9.3 Sum of device hours for network components

Network component	Number of devices	Operational hours/month	Sum of device hours/month
Processor	1	600	600
Modems	5	400	2000
Lines	4	400	1600
Cluster controllers	4	400	1600
Terminals	40	300	12000

Table 9.4 Calculation of unavailable user service hours

Network component	Device hrs/month	MTTR (hrs)	Ave. no. of users affected	MTBF (hrs)	Unavailable user hours
Processor	600	2	40	200	240.0
Modems	2000	3	16	5000	19.2
Lines	1600	4	25	3000	53.3
Cluster controllers	1600	2	10	500	64.0
Terminals	12000	2	1	1000	24.0
				Total	400.5

$$\frac{\text{Total network user hours} - \text{Total unavailable user hours}}{\text{Total network user hours}}$$

$$= \frac{16\,000 - 400.5}{16\,000} = 0.975 \text{ or } 97.5\%$$

If the predicted network availability is lower than required, the network components which contribute most to the unavailable user hours (in Table 9.4) may be identified and, if practical, their MTBF and/or MTTR improved. Alternatively it may be necessary to incorporate redundant components such as a standby processor in order to meet a required system availability figure. The effective MTBF of the parallel processors should be calculated and substituted for the single processor figure in the system availability calculation.

10 Computing and software issues

10.1 Introduction

The evolution of data communications technology and network design is closely allied to the evolution of data processing. The ability to transmit data at high speed over long distances first made remote computer terminals possible and later led to distributed data processing. The needs of distributed data processing systems with satellite processors determined the architecture of many communications networks.

The introduction of personal computers in the 1980s has led to the development of new forms of network, based on local area network technology and network software. Without network software, LANs may improve the cable system required to provide links between computers but they do not provide a new approach to data processing or the way in which computers are used.

Network software based on a file server frequently employs a single central computer with a hard disk and possibly other peripherals. The personal computers connected to the file server via a local area network make use of the hard disk to share files and do not themselves require expensive disk storage. Only the file server requires a multitasking operating system; the satellite processors require only a single-tasking operating system because operation may halt until a record is returned by the file server. The dependence on a single file server limits the expansion capability of the network by the response time to read or write files, a situation similar to that of a single, multiuser, central processor.

The provision of computers with operating systems which support network operation makes possible networks with many additional characteristics:

a) Peer-to-peer connections are available without a central computer.
b) Network computers may be single or multiuser.
c) Any user on any network computer can access any file on any network computer transparent to applications software, but subject to authorisation checks.

d) Any user on any network computer can access any peripheral on any network computer.

e) File and record locking is necessary to permit multiuser operation of the network.

f) Computers from many vendors are able to make full use of the network facilities.

Other computing and software issues addressed in this chapter include:

a) Distributed databases for use on networks.
b) PC-to-mainframe links.
c) X.400 electronic messaging standard.
d) Data compression to reduce the volume of data transmitted.

10.2 Distributed data processing

10.2.1 The evolution of distributed data processing

Distributed data processing decentralises processing resources to where the user is located. The development of minicomputers, then microcomputers, has increased the trend away from centralised mainframe computers towards distributed processing systems. The development of network systems has provided the communications mechanism necessary to realise distributed data processing.

The use of centralised mainframes with remote terminals was intended to take advantage of the economies of scale offered by mainframe computers before inexpensive minicomputers became available. Other advantages included the more straightforward design of a centralised database and the tighter control which is possible with a centralised processing system. Many users of centralised systems have encountered the complexity of scale limitations which arise through the logistics of housing large processing systems in one building and the complexity of the communications processing facilities required to support the information processors.

Three basic functions must be provided in a distributed data processing system:

a) Information processing
b) Database processing
c) Network processing.

Information processing manipulates information as directed by the application programs and produces output in the specified media and format. Database processing stores large amounts of information in a form suitable for rapid access by the users via the network.

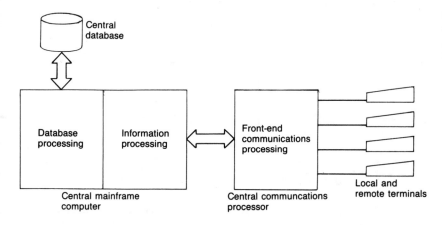

Fig. 10.1 A fully
centralised computer system

Central
database

Database
processing

Information
processing

Communications
processing

Local and
remote terminals

Central mainframe computer

Fig. 10.2 A centralised
data processing system with
a front-end communications
processor

Central
database

Database
processing

Information
processing

Front-end
communications
processing

Local and
remote terminals

Central mainframe
computer

Central communcations
processor

Network processing moves information between nodes within the network and controls the exchange of information between users, information processors and database processors.

Early centralised computer systems executed information, database and communications processing in one mainframe computer as shown in Figure 10.1. All three functions had to compete for computer resources such as the memory and CPU time. To resolve this problem the functions were separated in distributed systems introduced from the mid 1960s. As a first step, communications processing was handled by the front-end communications processor at the central site as shown in Figure 10.2.

Distributed processing began with the distribution of network (communications) processing to front-end processors at remote sites where clusters of terminal users were situated. At this stage the information and database processing remained at the central site (see Figure 10.3). The next step towards distributed processing was the introduction of distributed information processing using satellite processors at remote sites for remote batch or remote job entry processing as shown in Figure 10.4. This satellite processor was

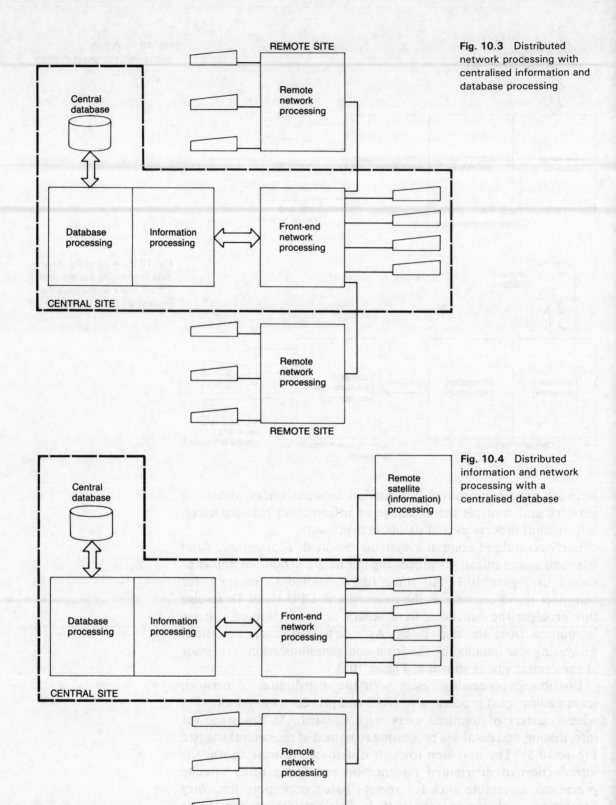

Fig. 10.3 Distributed network processing with centralised information and database processing

Fig. 10.4 Distributed information and network processing with a centralised database

usually a small information processor with a line controller to permit communication with a central host processor. Later versions had multiline controllers or front-end processors which made it possible for local terminals to access the local resources as well as resources located elsewhere via the network.

The next stage in the evolution of totally distributed data processing was the distribution of the centralised database. Many systems find it desirable to retain a central database but a totally distributed system can offer resource sharing in which information and/or database processing may be distributed evenly across currently available network resources. There are many possible configurations for totally distributed data processing. Figure 10.5 shows a system in which the information, database and network processing exists at more than one location, possibly at all locations.

Where the necessary local resources are available in a fully distributed data processing system, these will be used but an evaluation of resource requirements may make the system use remote information processing to balance the load on the overall system. When this redistribution has been made it would probably be maintained until completion unless exceptional conditions occur.

10.2.2 Database distribution

It is most desirable to put the database processing with the application processing which most frequently uses the data. This policy results in a partitioned database where no single site holds a complete copy of the entire database. Each database processing element must be capable of accepting data from and providing data to both local and remote users.

A directory of available database resources is required by a partitioned database; this may be kept at a central site or a copy may be kept at each site (covering the database processing functions for all sites).

An alternative form of database is the replicated database which gives each site a copy of the entire database. A directory is not so important for a replicated database but mechanisms must prevent multiple, conflicting database updates. The design of a distributed database system influences the information and network processing functions. Network traffic for a directory function or a replicated database can be high and it therefore limits communication data capacity and response times for application functions.

10.2.3 Resource allocation

The allocation of application programs to run on a particular site

Fig. 10.5 A fully distributed data processing system

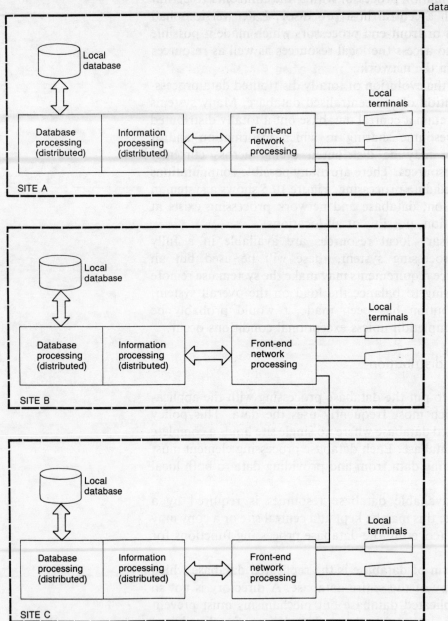

requires a dynamic allocation algorithm. In theory, any application program can run on any site but in practice some sites may not have the necessary peripherals and the required data may not be held locally, making the communications processing load increase.

The dynamic resource scheduling algorithm may be held at a central site or be partitioned with a part resident at each site. The algorithm must assess each assignment of an application program to

314

minimise the effect on the database processing and network processing activities. To simplify resource scheduling, database partitions may be moved with the applications programs which access them. Moving database partitions may however create problems if other application programs are accessing them when they are moved or if application programs at different sites need access to the same partition simultaneously.

Very large application programs which cannot be accommodated within a single processing resource must be partitioned and the partitions assigned to different sites. The co-operation between these partitions may result in the database processing, network processing and network channels being adversely effected.

10.2.4 Advantages and disadvantages of distributed data processing

The use of a single processor to support information processing and database processing limits the capacity in either function. Distributed processing and distributed databases offer greater performance than a single facility can provide. By separating the database processing into a freestanding database processor or processors, the performance may be increased by optimising the design for one function and eliminating the overheads required to schedule both information and database processing.

The distribution of network processing reduces communications costs by reducing the number of trunk links. When the information and database processing is distributed, the network processing must be distributed to give other users on the network access to the distributed resources. By distributing the information and database processing, the high density of data communications facilities around a central site is eliminated.

The advantages of distributed data processing include:

a) Reduced data communications costs.
b) Improved user access to facilities.
c) Improved throughput and response times.
d) Improved resilience and system availability through alternate routing and resource allocation.
e) Improved expansion capability.
f) The impact of system changes is minimised.

The major problems of distributed data processing include:

a) Equipment at different sites is frequently incompatible and requires protocol conversion.

b) Dynamic resource scheduling is extremely complex and may not give optimal results.
c) Operating systems for distributed processing have taken a long time to develop.
d) Distributed database systems have taken a long time to develop.

Distributed data processing was once limited to large systems but the development of network software for personal computers (PCs) on local area networks has made it attractive for small systems. PC networks are essentially composite standalone systems but they have acquired many of the characteristics of distributed multiuser data processing systems by using network software to control the access of each PC to the network resources and to allow PCs to communicate between themselves.

10.3   Network software

10.3.1   Personal computer networks

The widespread use of PCs in the 1980s has caused a revolution in the computer world. Users no longer rely on the data processing department and no longer have to put up with excessive response times from multiuser machines. Users frequently require data from a mainframe database and many companies provide software packages which permit PC connections to mainframes.

Resource sharing by using personal computers and file or print servers on a local area network have become popular in office systems and many other applications in industry and commerce. It is often necessary to interconnect many different types of PC, each type with a different operating system. To do this LAN software or network operating system software may be used; this functions in the network in the way a local operating system functions in a standalone computer. The network operating system can provide a standard connection language and message passing protocol among the individual operating systems of the networked machines as well as providing access to files in other machines.

A PC local area network may use several pieces of hardware:

a) Network interface cards for the PCs.
b) The network cable.
c) Server machines for the database or printers.
d) Gateways to other LANs or WANs.

The LAN software provides the software environment in which the hardware operates. Functions provided by LAN software may include:

a) File and record locking.
b) Security.
c) Print spooling.
d) Electronic mail.

Early network operating systems were based on a disk server. A disk server network operating system (see Figure 10.6) makes the PC operating system think it is accessing a local disk when it is using a disk server elsewhere on the network. The more recent file server network operating systems (see Figure 10.7) use a central machine on the LAN to manage access to a shared disk system and the local disks in the PCs. Files on the central machine are shared in a multiuser environment. PCs send high-level requests to the file server software which provides disk access.

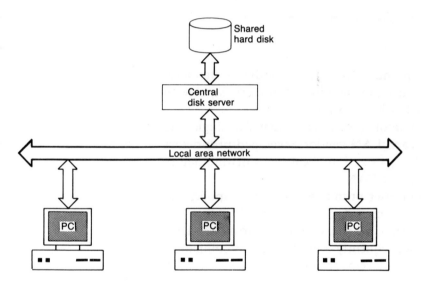

Fig. 10.6 A disk server network operating system

Another form of network operating system is based on message passing. The system behaves like a packet switching network which routes data between PCs. In message passing network operating systems it is common for every node to function as a server, making the system more expensive than file server systems which may have only one server.

10.3.2 File server LAN software

In 1984 Microsoft released MS-DOS 3.1, the first version of the operating system software for IBM PCs which would support PC networks. The use of LAN operating systems with an MS-DOS 3.1

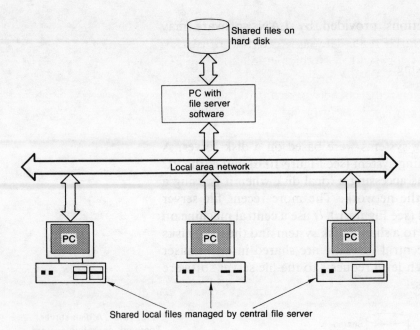

Fig. 10.7 A file server
network operating system

Shared files on
hard disk

PC with
file server
software

Local area network

PC

PC

PC

Shared local files managed by central file server

interface has changed the emphasis from LAN hardware standard-isation to software standardisation, making computers capable of operation with many LAN hardware systems.

MS-DOS is the most common operating system for single-user PCs. Before MS-DOS 3.1 each LAN vendor developed proprietary file and record locking techniques and applications software had to be modified to suit each type of LAN.

MS-DOS 3.1 includes multiuser primitives to control application access to the network. This provides a standard interface for applications software and permits one version to run on all MS-DOS 3.1 compatible networks. Consequently a large range of compatible applications software has been developed for multiuser PC network applications.

Another software standard in PC networks is IBM Netbios (Network basic input/output system) which is a peer-to-peer, session-layer interface for the IBM PC network. For compatibility with the IBM PC, a network operating system must emulate Netbios and, if the IBM PC network program is to be run, a LAN must emulate Netbios because Netbios is implemented in firmware on the PC network adapter hardware.

A file server network operating system resides on a central, shared file server and manages access to the data on the shared disk from any PC on the network. This centralised control makes it possible to incorporate file access controls. Operation of the file server is transparent to the user.

The IBM PC Network program, the operating system for the PC network, was released in March 1985. The same program is used by IBM for the token ring network with a Netbios emulator. The PC Network program includes the PC-DOS 3.1 or 3.2 PC operating system and a redirector which redirects network calls to the network file server via Netbios. The PC Network program's file server runs as an application of PC-DOS in the network server machine. Because PC-DOS is a single-tasking single-user operating system it must complete one task before beginning the next. This considerably slows down the operation of the file server when multiple requests are received from several PCs simultaneously.

Novell Advanced Netware, introduced in 1983, is a higher-performance network operating system than the IBM PC Network program. Advanced Netware is file based and can run on a wide variety of LAN hardware. It uses a multiuser operating system environment suited to a file server on a LAN. When it runs on a single-user IBM PC, the ROM Bios is bypassed to eliminate the single-user limitation. A consequence of this is that Advanced Netware requires special disk driver software.

Figure 10.8 shows the hardware and software components in an Advanced Netware file server system. Figure 10.9 shows a typical

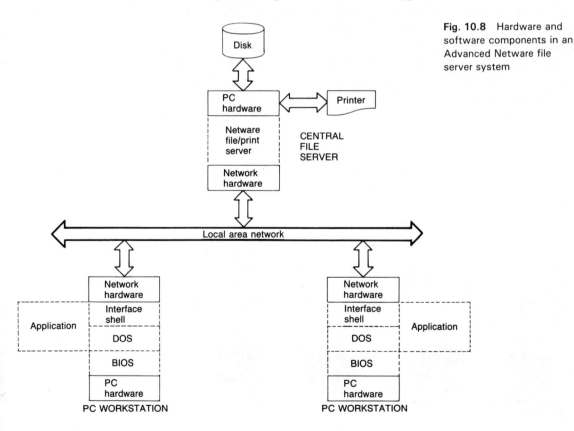

Fig. 10.8 Hardware and software components in an Advanced Netware file server system

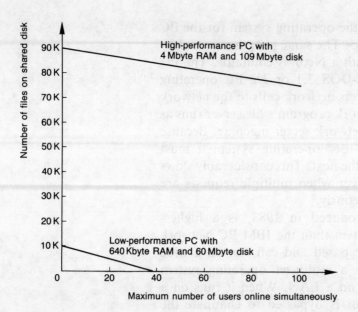

relationship between the number of files which may be stored on a shared disk and the number of users online at the same time using Advanced Netware on low-performance and high-performance PCs.

Fourteen different network adaptor cards are supported by Advanced Netware and all these types of LAN may be internetworked using the internal bridge facility in each network server to simultaneously support up to four network types (see Figure 10.10).

Security facilities in Advanced Netware allow the network supervisor to grant user authorisation and individual access rights to specified network resources such as file servers, printers, application software, and data files in directories and subdirectories. Access

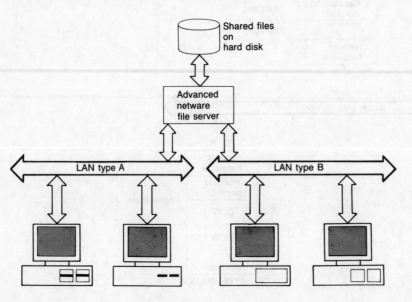

Fig. 10.10 The Advanced Netware internal bridge facility for internetworking

privileges are granted to read, write, open, create, delete, control subdirectories, search and modify files. Files may be designated shareable, nonshareable, read-only or read/write. A user logs into the network by giving a user name and password; when this has been verified, the user is given transparent access to those resources for which access is authorised.

10.3.3 Message passing LAN software

Message passing LAN software provides a standard connection language and message passing protocol for the transfer of message packets between computers on a LAN. Applied Intelligence's PC/NOS is a typical message passing software package which is installed in every node of the network and does not require a central server. It provides an environment for the development of multiuser applications on a network of machines with single-user operating systems.

PC/NOS converts the host operating system on each machine into a message-based system and the network, as a whole, into a multiprocessor system suitable for office automation. Any of the nodes may be designated a superuser which provides overall control with the ability to designate each user's access and update privileges.

A window-based user facility called Netview allows users to 'browse' through the network making linkages between their 'plug' resources and local or remote 'socket' resources.

PC/NOS uses a distributed cache system to quickly distribute and manage data which is shared between all network users. (A cache is an equivalence between one virtual and one physical address space.) Identical copies of data may be placed simultaneously in more than one network address space. An address space may be a physical address in RAM or a disk or it may be a virtual address such as a host operating system file.

Each node may function as a file server making resources available within each node accessible to other nodes, subject to access privileges. PC/NOS is not tied to a particular host operating system or type of computer/network hardware. Initial implementations for machines with CP/M and MS-DOS operating systems used a minimum sector size for transfers between address spaces of 128 bytes. Normal block sizes for network transfers are typically 1K or 2K bytes. The user sends transactions to defined 'plugs' and 'sockets' connected to resources like disk drives and printers. Each network resource is assigned an address when the system is configured.

Data is transferred and manipulated in packets. Data packets may be sent directly to one or more destinations or routed through one or more 'socket' subaddresses. All types of packet have a common header which contains fields for the destination node, 'socket', user number and packet type.

10.3.4 UNIX support for networking

UNIX is a multiuser multitasking operating system which is available for a wide variety of computers and offers a convenient means of standardising applications software for use on many types of host computers. AT&T announced system V release 3 of UNIX in June 1985; this release introduced support for networking.

The support for networking is based on 'streams' which are sets of system calls, library routines, kernel resources and kernel routines to define a standard interface for character input/output between the kernel and the rest of UNIX. A transport level interface is provided to support OSI level 4; this may be circuit-oriented, for use with data transfers which are made up of self-contained units.

Remote file sharing (RFS) is supported, based on a central name server. Once a connection is established, machines communicate through the transport level interface. A client machine accesses files on a server machine by sending a request message to the server which holds the file. Any machine on the network may be a client, server or both.

To establish an RFS connection the server advertises that a subtree of its local file tree is available for remote access. Clients wishing to access this resource mount the remote file system into their local file trees. A name server maintains a central database of unique names representing file trees which are available for sharing. This database is queried by clients to determine which remote resources are available.

Remote resources may be accessed by the RFS message protocol which sends a message to the remote machine via the local process server. The remote process server recreates the client's environment using the contents of the request message and executes the system call. The results of the system call are copied into a response message which is sent to the client machine. Detection of remote resources uses the file system switch (FSS).

Remote file sharing provides:

a) Transparent access to remote files.
b) Binary compatibility with existing applications software permitting existing applications to run without modification on remote machines.
c) Network independence, operating without modification over many types of network.
d) Portability: operating on many different types of hardware.

322

10.4 Distributed databases

10.4.1 Evolution of distributed databases

A database may be defined as 'a common pool of shared data in which the data is interrelated and each item of data is used in a wide range of applications'. The first general-purpose database management software packages become available in the mid 1960s.

The early database management systems were hierarchical, with a branching tree structure. Each record is connected to one parent record as shown in Figure 10.11. To access a record it is necessary to be familiar with the entire record structure.

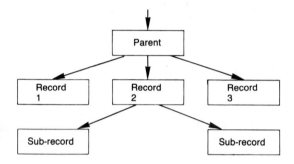

Fig. 10.11 A hierarchical database record structure

In 1969 the Conference on Data Systems Language (CODASYL) produced a model which has led to many database systems for mainframes and minicomputers. The CODASYL or network model permits a record to have more than one parent as shown in Figure 10.12. Physical pointers which identify connections between records are used to access the records one at a time. A database administrator is required to maintain the system.

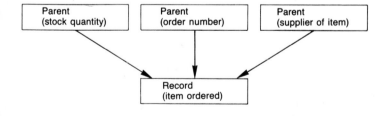

Fig. 10.12 A CODASYL database network record structure

In June 1970, E. F. Cod of IBM published a paper which prompted the development of several relational database management systems. Relational database management systems are structured from records organised in tables. The records are arranged in rows and columns defined according to common data elements as shown in Figure 10.13. Random access is made possible, independent of the storage and index techniques because there are no embedded

323

Date	Customer	Order No.
15	IBM	A36
15	ICL	A37
16	DEC	A38

Order No.	Item ordered	Quantity
A36	DU1	5
A37	DU5	20
A38	DU3	100
A39	DU3	10
A40	DU1	50

Customer	Address
DEC	READING
HP	WINNERSH
IBM	HAVANT
ICL	MANCHESTER

Fig. 10.13 Record structure in a relational database

relationships between the tables. Relationships are determined from the data values themselves.

A relational database management system can look at one attribute of a group of records to create new tables with records which are related to the original fields. A central dictionary keeps track of database contents and is organised to make access dependent only on the information required, not on its location in the database. The SQL query language developed by IBM to access data in relational databases has become an ANSI standard.

The development of relational databases has made distributed databases a practical possibility because the earlier hierarchical and network style databases typically used pointers embedded in the records to define relationships. A distributed database would be difficult to implement with a nonrelational system because pointers within records may relate to records which are only stored at other locations. Records in a relational database system are related to the data contents without the data having to know the geographical location of the record, only its data value is known.

The development of networks and distributed processing has made distributed databases necessary to manage distributed files. A distributed database management system should provide users with the illusion that they are working on a single database, on a single machine. They should not have to know the physical location of files, how files are protected from conflicting updates and network failure, or how copies of any file exist at any instant. A distributed database management system must therefore be transparent in terms of file location, file replication and network failure.

Distributed file management is commonly provided in two ways:

a) By centralised data storage in one or more dedicated servers.
b) By decentralising the data and storing it in several machines.

Both methods require a mechanism to handle simultaneous requests for the same data. This may be done by using a flag to give only one user at a time access to a file or by giving all qualified users access but allowing none to update the file without informing all other users that an update is in progress. This technique, commonly employed in mainframe database systems, uses a copy of the base record to prevent corruption of the original data.

Microcomputer database management systems, such as dBase III/plus, manage the locking and unlocking of files and records in a user-transparent manner. The database query language may be made transparent to the user by employing an application envelope. This can provide consistency across a network without changing the database structure or application software and giving the illusion of working with a single nondistributed database.

The first fully distributed relational database management system, RTI Ingres/Star, was introduced in 1986. The Oracle Star distributed database is similar to the Ingres/Star and was developed in phases over a similar timescale. Ingres Star was first developed for DEC VAX super minicomputers but later versions have been produced for IBM mainframes, Unix-based systems and IBM PC compatible machines. Ingres/Star (the distributed database manager) runs on heterogeneous networks and links individual Ingres relational database management systems.

10.4.2 Organisation of distributed databases

Distributed database management systems store data at physically distributed points; the users may also be distributed but they must see a single unified database. A distributed database management system may be partitioned with little or no replication of data or it may be fully redundant, with a copy of the full database held at each location. Other possible organisations include partitioned databases with full redundancy or with overlapping subsets of the database (some nodes having access to the total database while others store large or small sections).

Nonredundant partitioned databases store the partitions at the location which makes greatest use of that data. By avoiding the need to keep duplicate sets of data in step, the system is simplified but there is no way of recovering the data if the only copy is lost. The need to update multiple copies of data may be satisfied in many ways. A simple updating system may allow only one node to perform updates. To prevent conflicts between versions of the database, each update must be completed before the next one commences. When back-up copies are kept, access to the main copy will be delayed until the back-up copy has been completed.

When more than one node is allowed to perform updates, the order in which updates are received may vary for different copies of the data and inconsistencies may be found at any instant in time.

An updating algorithm may be used to control the concurrency of different copies of data. One solution uses centralised locking of reading and writing. This causes delays in reading and updating and increases the number of messages passed over the communications network.

One noncentralised solution to the concurrency problem is known as majority consensus. This updating algorithm makes it necessary for a majority of nodes which can update the data to agree on the update before it is carried out. This solution delays updates and generates additional messages but reading the database is not delayed. Alternative concurrency control algorithms include ones which permit several timestamped versions of the data to be stored and various distributed locking techniques.

10.4.3 The Ingres/Star distributed database management system

The Ingres relational database system uses the IBM SQL, structured query language, for all local and remote accesses. The network can therefore consist of different computer types and all information passing between individual Ingres databases consists of SQL and data. The use of SQL should permit Ingres to communicate with other SQL-based database management systems.

The Ingres/Star was implemented in three phases:

1) Phase 1 supporting transparent retrieval of data from multiple sites simultaneously, update of data at a site in a single transaction, and transparent update of deferred secondary copies of data.
2) Phase 2 provides full update capabilities across multiple sites simultaneously, concurrent copies, and gateways to other SQL-based systems.
3) Phase 3 has the ability to divide tables into horizontal and vertical fragments which permit rows with different values or columns in the same table to be dispersed over several nodes. It also provides the tools required to generate interfaces to non-SQL-based database management systems and custom applications.

Ingres/Star is a distributed database manager which operates as a local database management system (DBMS) on each node in a network (see Figure 10.14). Each local DBMS regards the other DBMSs as virtual users and all communication takes place in SQL. Queries are handled the same whether they are from a local or a remote user and the user sees a logical database which is transparent to the location of data, the hardware, the operating systems and network protocol.

326

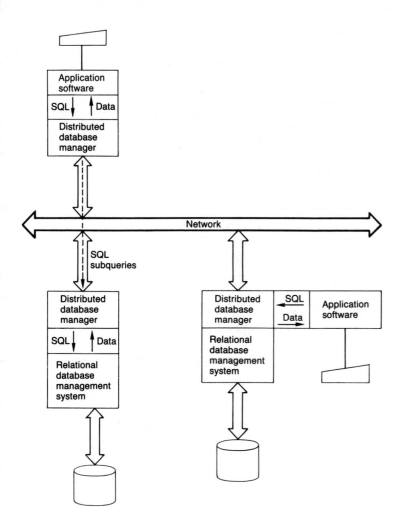

Fig. 10.14 Ingres/Star distributed database structure

A distributed data dictionary automatically locates data in the distributed environment and supports queries which require statistical and other information relating to the distribution of data. For communication between individual nodes which have Ingres/Star, the Ingres/Net communications facility is used. This relies on the host computer having DECnet or TCP/IP network software.

Ingres/Star provides local control over shared data and data access over a network at three levels of transparency:

1)   Location transparency
2)   Replication transparency
3)   Transaction transparency.

Transparent data access is provided by separating queries into subqueries which are transmitted to the appropriate local database for action.

10.4.4 ADDAM distributed database manager for naval applications

In a programme of work spanning ten years, Software Sciences Limited has developed a distributed database manager for the UK Admiralty Research Establishment (ARE Distributed Database Manager, or ADDAM). ADDAM has been designed to provide high-speed (real-time) distributed database facilities for a LAN-based distributed naval command and control system.

ADDAM is probably the first real-time distributed database system. It provides replication and partitioning of the database between nodes to ensure continuous operation when nodes or parts of the network fail, possibly as a result of battle damage. Partitioning and replication is transparent to the applications software and makes the database appear to be a nonreplicated entity wholly resident at each node.

The database is organised into pages and several copies of each page may be held at different nodes. One copy is designated master and the others are slaves. Page replication permits the response times for bulk data users to be improved by providing local access to copies of frequently required data. It also helps improve system reliability

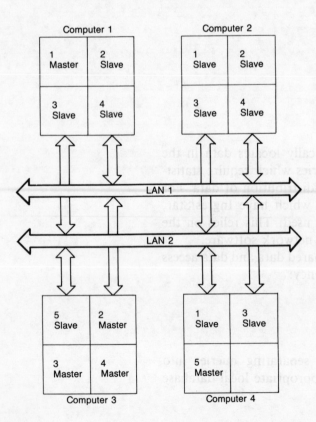

Fig. 10.15 Partitioning and replication of pages in four nodes of the ADDAM distributed database

because the failure of individual nodes does not cause loss of data in the system.

The physical location of database pages is controlled dynamically by the database manager and is governed by the application's demand for data as well as the number of computers which are active in the network. The data structure is relational and facilities are provided to support transaction recovery and to prevent concurrent updates. Figure 10.15 shows how pages are partitioned and replicated on four nodes.

Early versions of ADDAM used M700 or Argus 700 mini-computers at each node sharing applications processing, LAN communication processing and database management processing. A transputer-based module has been developed to provide the database management processing and communications processing functions in an integrated communications and database system (Diomedes). This module may be interfaced to a range of LANs (or data buses) and may be connected to the application host processor by a range of common interface standards.

For further information on distributed databases see reference 10.1.

10.5 PC-to-mainframe links

10.5.1 Alternatives

The rapid increase in the number of personal computers in most organisations has made users less dependent on the corporate mainframe computer but it is often necessary for PC users to access data on the mainframe's database. Personal computers may also be used as a common terminal emulating terminals on several computers and communications systems.

The user demand for mainframe processing power is estimated to be growing at around 60% per annum; to cope with this problem some organisations have adopted personal computers in place of terminals. By using a PC for some local processing the mainframe load may be reduced and the user is no longer totally dependent on the mainframe. The mainframe still has a significant load imposed by terminal emulation, downloading files to the PC, and acting as an information exchange server, but some users estimate that the loading on a mainframe for a PC connection is only a third of that for a terminal.

There are several ways of connecting a PC to a mainframe and many software packages are available to perform this function. Figure 10.16 shows six common ways of linking PCs to mainframes:

1) The PC emulates an asynchronous terminal on the main-frame.

2) Where the mainframe protocol is more complex, a protocol converter may be used to convert the asynchronous interface into the protocol employed by a cluster controller.

3) A card is inserted in the PC to provide the coaxial link required by IBM cluster controllers. Software in the PC makes it behave like a 3278 or 3279 terminal. File transfers may be performed in 3270 screens which are copied to a disk in the PC. This is a common approach and many products are available for IBM mainframe links.

4) A communications card and communications software in the PC may emulate the cluster controller. Alternative emulations may be incorporated to make a PC capable of switching to different mainframe types.

5) To connect several PCs into a mainframe, the PCs may be connected to a LAN with one PC performing the gateway function using cluster controller emulation software and a line interface card. The other PCs emulate the required display devices. This approach is relatively inexpensive and leaves the PCs free to perform local processing.

6) PCs may be connected to a LAN and an X.25 gateway used to communicate with the mainframe. PAD software may be run in each PC to provide dumb terminal emulation. The X.25 interface may be used to interface with any mainframe, or other LANs, but the load imposed on the mainframe is high and the X.25 interface may become a throughput bottleneck.

10.5.2 Advantages and limitations of connection types

Connecting a PC to an IBM mainframe requires a link to the SNA environment, either directly through coaxial links or remotely through a modem using a communications/terminal-emulation board. The board makes the PC appear to the mainframe as an IBM terminal, IBM PC or familiar peripheral. A database query program is used to extract data from the mainframe database for the file transfer program which loads the data into the relevant file in the PC.

The Irma board is a popular communications/emulator link; this gives IBM personal computers direct high-speed access to IBM mainframes using IBM 3274, 3276 and integral terminal controllers. These operate in SNA and Bisync environments emulating IBM 3278 and 3279 protocols. File transfer utilities may be employed to transfer binary data between PCs using the mainframe as an intermediate storage facility.

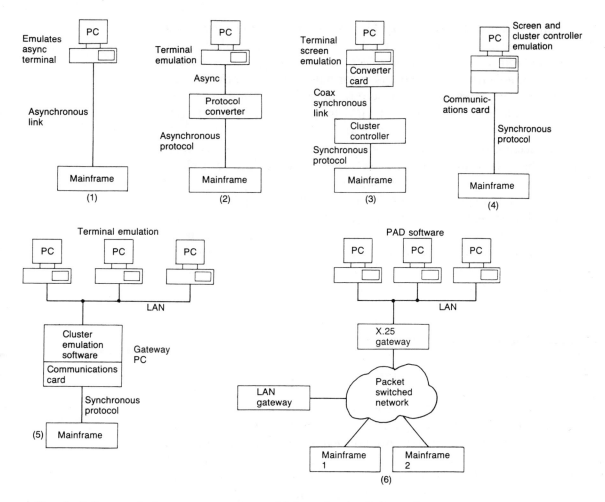

Simple PC-to-mainframe connections which make the PC emulate a mainframe terminal and use a communications board in the PC will allow the PC to view data in the mainframe but limit the PC to dumb terminal functions. No facilities are provided for downloading and uploading and the PC is dedicated to the emulation function.

More complex data transfer systems allow the PC to transfer mainframe files in bulk, making the mainframe database available to the PC user. These nonselective systems require special software in the mainframe and in the PC. The entire file is transferred, often taking a long time, when only a small part may be required.

Systems with selective data access extract the data from mainframe files and transmit only this data to the PC where it is reformatted as required by popular types of PC software. Data from the PC may also be uploaded to the mainframe where no special software is required. No communication with other PCs is supported and access is typically limited to one file at a time making the process slow and inefficient.

Fig. 10.16 Six common ways of linking PCs to mainframes

Fully integrated links with file distribution management can distribute programs and data between PCs with selective data access and the ability to access many files simultaneously. This enables PC communication and extracts information from many files for transfer in one combined block sent from the mainframe to the PC. These facilities are available for IBM mainframes but may not be able to access specific vendor applications or databases.

Connections through an X.25 gateway require specific software at both the mainframe and the PC and often introduce a large overhead. Such systems can be connected to a mainframe in place of a cluster controller and direct PC-to-PC communication can take place without loading the mainframe.

Peer-to-peer communications between PCs, without going via the mainframe, are preferable for office automation. Electronic mail for PCs on a LAN/WAN may require a mail server with telex, teletex and public X.400 messaging system interfaces.

10.6 CCITT X.400

10.6.1 Electronic Messaging

Several forms of electronic mail have evolved, and telex is being replaced by teletex and facsimile for document transmission. Word processors or office workstations may be interconnected by local area networks or wide area networks offering electronic mail facilities. Mailbox services are available to store and forward messages, e.g. (British) Telecom Gold. Interpersonal electronic messaging requires standards which permit computers and terminals of all types to communicate.

CCITT have introduced the X.400 series of recommendations to enable electronic messaging within the OSI framework. Four forms of agreement are required to send messages between terminals:

1) Use of communications facilities.
2) Message envelope and format.
3) Compatibility of message content.
4) Connection of terminals and services to message handling systems.

The use of communications facilities is defined in a range of CCITT and IEEE standards for various media. The OSI session and presentation layers form the main standards for the use of communications facilities. Various agreements govern the use of OSI session and presentation services; these are called Common Application Service Elements (CASE) and include:

a) Remote operations server (ROS) which is used in the P3 protocol for submission and delivery of messages to user agents which are remote from the message transfer agent.

b) Reliable transfer server (RTS) which manages noninteractive bulk message transfers between message transfer agents using an OSI session.

The X.400 recommendations are intended for several purposes:

a) To specify the interconnection of messaging services provided by public telephone and telecommunications authorities.

b) To specify the interconnection of individual function units within a message handling system.

c) To specify the interconnection of private message handling systems and individual function units of private systems.

d) To specify the interconnection of private message handling systems to public message handling systems.

e) To specify the interconnection of existing, dissimilar, non-standard message transfer systems using half-gateways.

10.6.2 X.400 (1984) recommendations

X.400 is implemented at the OSI application layer. As shown in Figure 10.17, X.400 forms additional layers within OSI layer 7; these define standards for message content, message header (P2), standard envelope (P1), and a reliable transfer server (RTS).

The X.400 recommendation 'Message handling systems, system model service elements' describes the functional and administrative models of the message handling system to which the other recommendations apply. It also gives an overview of the architectural

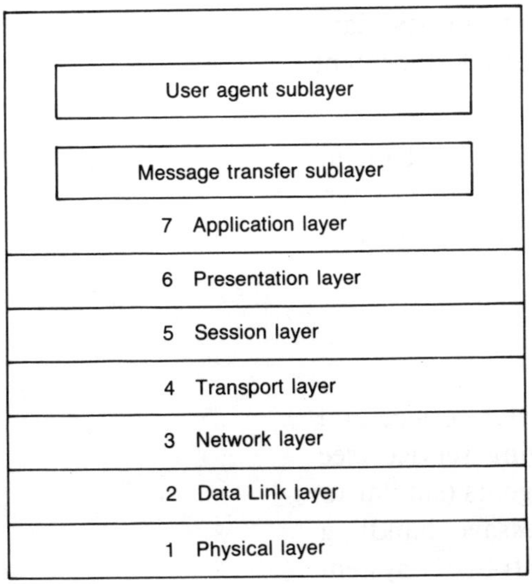

Fig. 10.17 X.400 layers within the OSI model

| User agent sublayer |
| Message transfer sublayer |
| 7 Application layer |
| 6 Presentation layer |
| 5 Session layer |
| 4 Transport layer |
| 3 Network layer |
| 2 Data Link layer |
| 1 Physical layer |

layers for system components and the basic concepts of naming and addressing the service elements. Other recommendations in the X.400 series include:

X.401   Basic service elements and optional user facilities for the interpersonal message service and the message transfer service.

X.408   Encoded information type conversion rules for document types such as telex, ITA 5 text, teletex, G3 facsimile, text interchange format 0, videotex, voice, text interchange format 1, and simply formatted documents.

X.409   Presentation transfer syntax and notation. Defines the expression of protocol elements in other documents of the X.400 series and defines the mapping of elements into data structures of protocol elements.

X.410   Remote operations and reliable transfer server. Defines interactive protocol (P3) using remote operations, the reliable transfer service, and the mapping of the message transfer service layer entities into the presentation and session layers.

X.411   Message transfer layer. Defines the P1 protocol which is used to interconnect message handling systems and message transfer agents within systems. The P1 protocol supports store-and-forward multi-address transfer of messages. Also defines the P3 protocol which is used between a user agent and a remote message transfer agent.

X.420   Interpersonal messaging user agent layer. Defines the P2 protocol which is used between user agents (a standard message header format) and simply formatted document content encoding.

X.430   Access protocol for teletex terminals. The protocol elements and gateway functions required to interconnect teletex terminals and X.400 message handling systems are defined.

10.6.3   P1, P2 and P3 protocols

The P1 and P3 protocols support the message transfer service and the P2 protocol supports the interpersonal messaging service (see Figure 10.18). P1 is used between message transfer agents (similar to message switches) and between interconnected message handling systems. The P1 header determines how the message transfer system

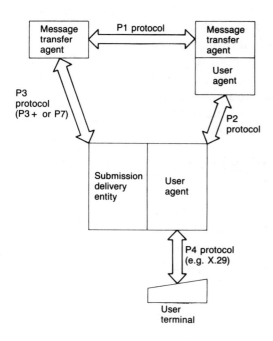

Fig. 10.18 P1, P2 and P3
protocol applications

should route and deliver the message and which facilities are
required, similar to a postal envelope. An alternative routing strategy
is provided to overcome system faults.

The P2 protocol is used between user agents to perform interpersonal messaging. P2 is a standard message header format
containing:

a)   Originators address.
b)   A list of recipients and their addresses.
c)   Primary and copy recipients.
d)   Identification of the originator and the message.
e)   Authorising users indication.
f)   Expiry date indication.
g)   Importance indication.
h)   Obsoleting indication.
i)   Sensitivity indication.
j)   Reply request indication.
k)   Replying interpersonal message indication.
l)   Forwarded interpersonal message indication.
m)   Body part encryption indicator.

This delivery service control message envelope is followed by a
multipart message body.

The P3 protocol is used between submission and delivery entities
in support of a single user agent which is remote from its message
transfer agent. Controlled access to the message transfer service is
provided in a manner which is required by individual terminals.

Problems with the P3 definition have resulted in two alternative mailbox protocols being introduced. The CCITT have introduced the P3 + protocol and ECMA have introduced P7, both of which are expected to be added to the X.400 specification in 1988 together with extensions which permit secure communications and inter-working with physical delivery systems (making it possible to reach people by paper mail when no X.400 facilities are available).

10.6.4 The interpersonal messaging and message transfer services

The interpersonal messaging service carries electronic mail between user agents. User agents represent points through which users can access the interpersonal messaging service and each user agent is identified by an originator/recipient address. User agents may be employed to perform format conversion, making, for example, word processed documents compatible regardless of their origin.

User agents employ the message transfer service to pass inter-personal messages. The message transfer service uses a network of message transfer agents to store and forward multi-addressed messages sent from originating user agents to recipient user agents. Other services, such as directory enquiry or telemetry, may use the store-and-forward, multi-addressed facilities of the message transfer service.

The message transfer service provides elements for:

a) Message submission with a unique message identifier.
b) Message delivery for a specified grade of delivery with a submission time stamp.
c) Deferred delivery (until a defined time).
d) Alternate recipients if the message is not delivered to its user agent.
e) Nondelivery notification.
f) Delivery notification and delivery time stamp.
g) Message content conversion if the user agent cannot accept messages of the type transmitted.
h) Content type which identifies which user agent and protocol type is contained in the message.

The interpersonal messaging service elements include those of the message transfer service and additional services associated with reactions from user agents and standard forms for representing fields in the message body:

a) Blind copy recipient which allows delivery of a message to recipients which are not identified on individual recipient's copies.

b) Autoforwarded indication which informs the alternative recipient that the message has been diverted.

c) Interpersonal message identification and a typed body encoding indication, e.g. Teletex, ITA 5, Fax.

d) Receipt notification.

e) Originator indication.

f) Authorising user's indication.

g) Primary and copy recipient's indications.

h) Expiry date indication.

i) Cross-referencing indication.

j) Importance indication.

k) Obsoleting indication.

l) Sensitivity indication (personal/private/company confidential).

m) Subject indication.

n) Replying interpersonal message indication.

o) Reply request indication.

p) Body part encryption indication.

In simple terms, an X.400 message consists of the body text which uses the X.409 protocol syntax to make it readable by other systems. The body text is passed to a user agent (analogous to placing it in an envelope) and is forwarded to the message transfer agent (analogous to a sorting office) using the P3 protocol (analogous to a postbox). The X.410 reliable transfer service uses the P1 protocol (analogous to the postal delivery van) to deliver the message to a message transfer agent near the user. The user agent (acting like a postman) reads the address and delivers the message using the P2 protocol.

10.6.5 X.400 applications

Public X.400 message handling services are being set up by national telecommunications organisations to provide transparent routing of person-to-person messages between incompatible systems. These services are said to be in the administrative domain but private network services may also be developed (PRMDs). Many large multinational corporations will set up private global message handling services. Most computer manufacturers now offer X.400 capability in their office automation packages, some providing a gateway from a non-X.400 implementation.

One of the major aspects which will be defined in the 1988 version of X.400 is the directory service which provides a directory of subscribers. Many organisations do not want to make a list of their employees and mailbox codes public for security reasons and because they do not want to encourage junk mail. A likely solution is to make part of the directory public and part restricted to internal use.

10.7 Data compression

10.7.1 Data compression alternatives

Data compression is a technique for reducing the bandwidth required to transmit data without loss of information. Data compression techniques include:

a) Data compaction
b) Bandwidth compression
c) Redundancy removal
d) Redundancy reduction by data dependency
e) Source coding
f) Data rate reduction
g) Adaptive sampling
h) Parameter extraction
i) Optimal estimation
j) Universal coding
k) Null suppression by run length coding
l) Null suppression by bit mapping.

Data compression techniques fall into two classes; parametric and waveform representations. Parametric representations treat the signal as the output of a model which best characterises the data generation process. Waveform representations are concerned with preserving the waveshape of the data signal using sampling and quantisation.

Waveform representations are applied to analog transmissions within the communications system but parametric representations may be applied by the data originator and data user, the compressed data being handled transparently by the communications system. Source encoding transforms a message into a corresponding sequence of code words and this may be combined with redundancy reduction techniques such as null suppression.

Typical methods of source encoding involve the allocation of short codes to frequently occurring events and longer codes to infrequent events. Special block codes may be used to represent common blocks of data elements. Techniques for removing redundancy such as data compression, compaction or source coding may be compared by the degree to which they tolerate transmission errors and the ability to cause no changes between the original and the restored data.

One of the most common methods of data compression for alphanumeric data is the Huffman encoding technique. ASCII characters or data words which occur frequently are given shorter Huffman codes and longer codes are assigned to characters which occur less frequently. Huffman encoding may be employed in facsimile, digital video and word processing to reduce the data volume which reduces the storage requirement or transmission bandwidth requirement. Typical data volume reductions are in the range 20–50%.

10.7.2 Huffman codes

Huffman encoding produces optimum variable-length codes representing a finite number of input words for a fixed input word size. The input words may be alphanumeric such as ASCII seven-bit codes which represent 128 alphanumeric characters. To simplify decoding, no two Huffman coded characters may be represented by the same code words and codes must be constructed to prevent multiple short codes appearing as longer codes.

The probability of occurrence must be known for each input word and a Huffman code assigns output code words to the input words according to their frequency of occurrence.

Figure 10.19 shows a code tree for an input wordlength of 3 bits and probabilities of occurrence of:

111	0.5
110	0.3
101	0.1
100	0.03
011	0.03
010	0.02
001	0.01
000	0.01

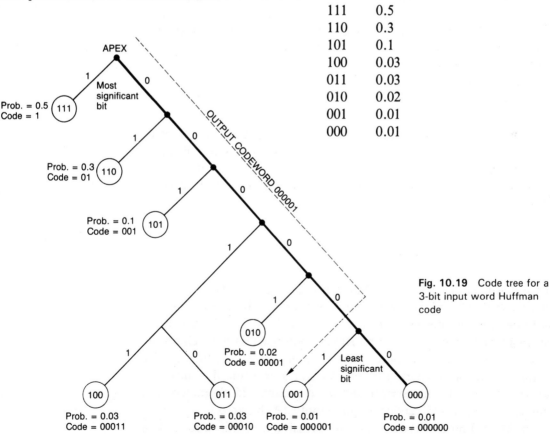

Fig. 10.19 Code tree for a 3-bit input word Huffman code

The average output wordlength is 1.92 bits giving a compression ratio of 0.64. The input word 001, with a 0.01 probability of occurrence, is given a long output code word, 000001. The input word 111 with a 0.5 probability of occurrence is given a short output code word, 1.

To form Huffman codes, the input words are listed in descending order of frequency. The two input words with the lowest frequency of occurrence are selected, a 0 bit is assigned to one and a 1 bit to the other for the least significant bit of the output code word. Other input codes have no bit in the least significant position.

By combining successive lowest-frequency pairs, binary 0 and 1 values are assigned to each branch in the code tree. The Huffman codes are derived by tracing the sequence of bits from the apex of the code tree to each input code branch with the most significant bit first. Decoding of Huffman codes is simply a matter of looking up the input character corresponding to each received output code. Different forms of data require different Huffman codes for optimum efficiency.

The adaptive Huffman encoding procedure may be used when the probability of occurrence for each input word is not known in advance and when input wordlengths are not fixed. A running estimate of source statistics is kept and the code tree is modified accordingly.

10.7.3   Null suppression

The null suppression technique for compressing data is simple to implement; it compresses strings of zero and/or blank symbols into a shorter form for transmission or storage. Null suppression may be used in addition to or as an alternative to Huffman coding. Two techniques for null suppression are commonly used:

1)   Run length coding
2)   Bit mapping.

Run length coding (RLC) uses a unique character to indicate the start of a string of blanks or zeros; this is followed by a count which indicates the number of blanks or zeros in the string. Figure 10.20 compares the uncompressed and RLC compressed data which results from a simple form displayed on a video display terminal. The symbol * indicates a string of blanks and a # symbol indicates a string of zeros. The uncompressed form requires 25 characters and the RLC compressed version requires only 19 characters.

The bit mapping method of null suppression transmits a series of a

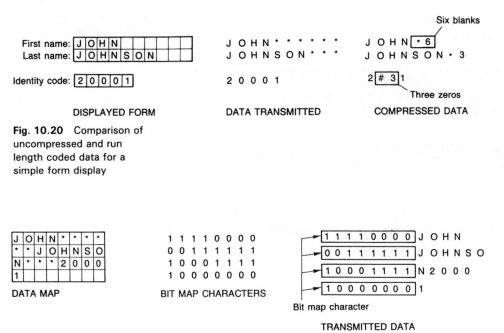

Fig. 10.20 Comparison of uncompressed and run length coded data for a simple form display

DISPLAYED FORM · DATA TRANSMITTED · COMPRESSED DATA

DATA MAP · BIT MAP CHARACTERS · TRANSMITTED DATA

Fig. 10.21 Bit mapped transmission for the form display shown in Fig. 10.20

bit maps in which each bit represents a character. Each 1 bit in the map indicates the presence of a character and each 0 indicates the absence of a character; thus any blanks are suppressed in the transmitted data. Figure 10.21 shows the bit mapped transmission resulting from the simple form display shown in Figure 10.20. Four 8-bit map characters are transmitted with the non-blank characters, making the transmission 20 characters in length.

10.7.4 Data dependency

Redundancy reduction by data dependency is similar to null suppression but it reduces the character length when strings of similar characters, such as numeric characters, are transmitted.

A string of EBCDIC numbers has the first four bits of each character set to 1. The last four bits of each character identify, in binary coded decimal (BCD), the number identity. If more than three EBCDIC numbers are found in succession, a unique character may be transmitted to indicate that numerics follow and this is followed by a four-bit count which indicates the number of numerics, up to a maximum of 16. This is followed by a sequence of four-bit BCD representations of the numbers.

341

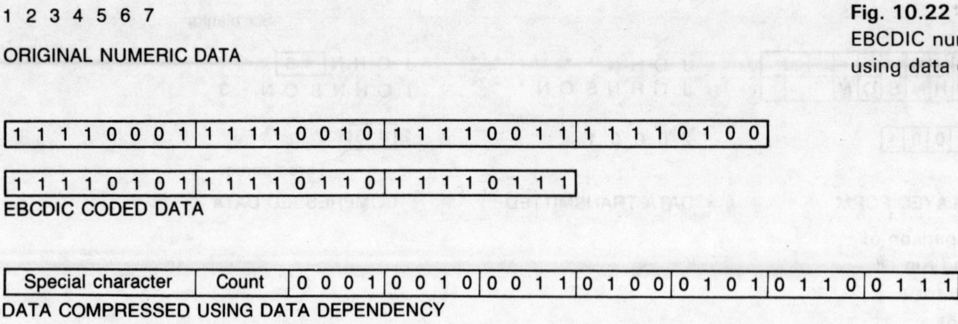

ORIGINAL NUMERIC DATA

Fig. 10.22 Compression of EBCDIC numeric characters using data dependency

| 1 1 1 1 0 0 0 1 | 1 1 1 1 0 0 1 0 | 1 1 1 1 0 0 1 1 | 1 1 1 1 0 1 0 0 |

| 1 1 1 1 0 1 0 1 | 1 1 1 1 0 1 1 0 | 1 1 1 1 0 1 1 1 |

EBCDIC CODED DATA

| Special character | Count | 0 0 0 1 | 0 0 1 0 | 0 0 1 1 | 0 1 0 0 | 0 1 0 1 | 0 1 1 0 | 0 1 1 1 |

DATA COMPRESSED USING DATA DEPENDENCY

Figure 10.22 shows a string of seven EBCDIC numeric characters (56 bits) compressed by using data dependency into a special character and eight four-bit digits, making a total of 40 bits transmitted.

11 Threats to communications security

11.1 Introduction

An autonomous computer, with no external communications links and with all its terminals and peripherals housed within a secure, screened computer room, is vulnerable only to the entry of unauthorised users and users gaining access to information which they are not authorised to receive. These security risks may be reduced by an efficient means of user identification and control on access to the computer room, plus a system of access controls for information within the computer. These aspects are outside the main theme of this chapter because they are computer and physical security issues. This chapter is concerned with security threats which arise when the computer is connected to external terminals or peripherals and to communications networks which provide remote access or file transfers with other computers. Computer and communications security are considered in greater detail in reference 11.1.

There are many ways in which information may be obtained from a computer or the normal service provided by a computer denied to its legitimate users, and the development of open communications standards has made it easier for security to be breached. Communications products incorporating security features specified in the ISO standards are not expected to become available until about 1989 but many countermeasures can be incorporated in communications interfaces and network protocols to reduce their vulnerability.

There are three major forms of attack on computer security:

1) Unauthorised release of information
2) Unauthorised modification of information
3) Unauthorised denial of normal service to users.

The unauthorised release of information is called a *passive attack* and unauthorised modification of information or denial of service is called an *active attack*. Both forms of attack can take place from any point in a communications link or network through which the relevant information can pass.

The main objectives of countermeasures against security attack are:

a) To minimise the probability of intrusion by providing protection devices and procedures.

b) To detect any intrusion as soon as possible

c) To be able to identify the information which has been subjected to attack and to identify the control/status information necessary to recover from the attack.

11.2 Passive attacks

Wiretapping can take place at any part of a communications link or network. Figure 11.1 shows the physical path through which data may pass when a terminal is connected to a host computer through a packet switched system. In addition to wiretapping, the computers and communications equipment in the path may be subverted by modifying their hardware or software. The data may also be obtained by monitoring electromagnetic radiation from the equipment.

Whatever medium is employed to transmit data, it may be tapped with varying degrees of difficulty. Telephone wires may have direct electrical connections made at any inconspicuous point in the link. These invasive taps permit both active and passive attacks but noninvasive taps, such as those which use inductive coupling, are suitable only for passive attacks.

Monitoring equipment may be connected to telephone lines within the building which contains the computer or at any access point or equipment along the link. The data may be recorded locally or transmitted to a nearby receiver and recorder outside the building. If a transmitter is employed, it may be powered from the DC voltage which is present on the public switched telephone system. This, however, makes the device present a low impedance to the line and renders it susceptible to detection. A high-impedance passive monitor is virtually undetectable once it is connected to the line.

Microwave and satellite data links may be intercepted by suitable, highly sensitive radio receivers. The side lobes from microwave antennae make it possible to monitor signals near relay towers without being in the direct path of the main beam. Satellite downlinks are accessible over a wide area on the earth's surface around the intended groundstation. Active attacks on microwave and satellite data links are possible but require complex high-powered transmitters which are likely to be detected if used frequently. Figure 11.2 shows the kind of attacks which may be made on satellite links.

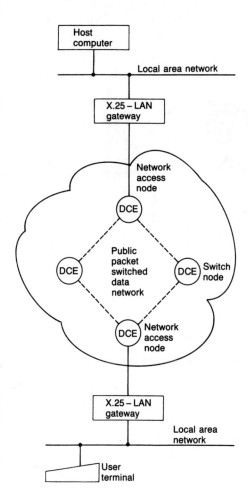

Fibre optic cable may be invasively tapped if a sensitive optical receiver is available. There is no optical or electromagnetic radiation from a sheathed fibre-optic cable but, if the sheath is removed and the fibre bent, a proportion of the optical flux is radiated and may be detected by a sensitive receiver with a high signal-to-noise ratio. The loss of optical flux from such a tap may, however, be detected if a reflectometer is connected to the link and regular measurements are made. If the flux loss is large, the link may fail to operate because the received signal is attenuated.

High-quality coaxial cable emits a negligible amount of electro-magnetic radiation if correctly installed but if a cable with a braided screen is bent past its minimum bend radius the leakage will increase. Sensitive radio equipment may be used as a noninvasive tap but a close coupling is required. An invasive tap may be fitted by piercing the sheath and the screen, leaving few external signs.

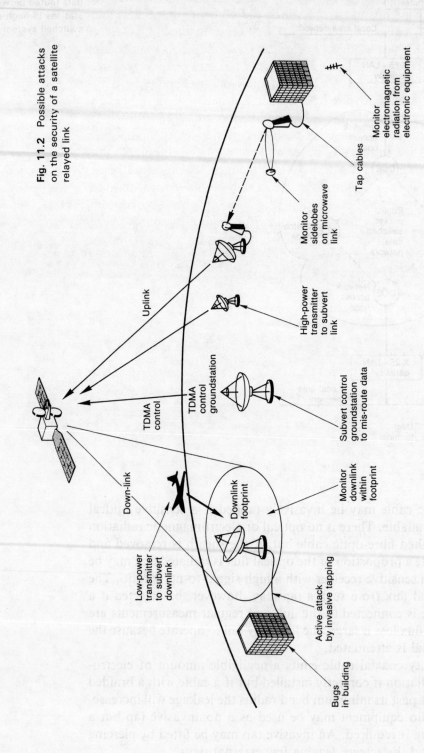

Fig. 11.2 Possible attacks on the security of a satellite relayed link

Monitor electromagnetic radiation from electronic equipment

Tap cables

Monitor sidelobes on microwave link

High-power transmitter to subvert link

Subvert control groundstation to mis-route data

TDMA control groundstation

TDMA control

Uplink

Down-link

Low-power transmitter to subvert downlink

Active attack by invasive tapping

Bugs in building

Monitor downlink within footprint

Downlink footprint

Any electronic equipment which carries data may radiate an electromagnetic emission from which the content of the data may be obtained. A sensitive receiver located close to the equipment or connected to its power lines or other nearby conductors may be used to filter and record the emissions. Telephones make excellent inductive pick-ups for near field radiation from computer equipment. The switch hook can be bypassed by placing a zener diode across the contacts and the signals picked up may be monitored indefinitely by tapping the telephone line outside the secure area. Depending upon the nature of the radiated signal, simple or complex equipment may be required to extract the desired data from the background noise.

Various forms of subversion may be employed to monitor information passing through computers or processor-based communications equipment such as statistical multiplexers, packet assembler/disassemblers, concentrators or gateways. The software in such equipment may have subversive routines incorporated at the design stage or modified versions of the software may be substituted to cause specific information to be rerouted or recorded. This is sometimes called the Trojan horse ploy and has been used to commit many cases of computer crime.

Passive attacks may result in the release of message contents but if data is encrypted it may still be of value to the intruder to obtain the location and identities of the parties who are communicating; this information is generally available in the message or block headers. The length of messages and their frequency of transmission may disclose the nature of the information being transmitted. These forms of passive attack (which do not cause release of message contents), referred to as violations of transmission security, may be used as part of a more sophisticated intrusion. For example, a Trojan horse program may be used to modulate the nondata parameters of messages in order to form a covert communication channel between a protected computer and the intruder.

11.3 Active attacks

An active attack on a communications link may take many forms including:

a) Selectively modifying the data or headers
b) Deleting data or messages
c) Delaying messages
d) Reordering messages
e) Duplicating messages
f) Inserting additional messages.

Active attacks may be subdivided into three categories:

1) Message modification
2) Denial of message service
3) Initiation of spurious association.

Message modification includes attacks on:

a) Authenticity (by modifying the protocol control information causing the message to be sent to the wrong destination or by inserting bogus messages).
b) Integrity (by modifying the data).
c) Ordering (by deleting messages or modifying sequencing information in the protocol).

Denial of message service includes attacks in which the intruder discards or delays messages. Initiation of spurious association includes attacks in which previously recorded message sequences are played back or attempts are made to establish access under a false identity.

Typical examples of active attacks are:

a) The use of authorisation information obtained by line tapping to establish a session using the identity of a valid terminal.
b) Once a session has been established by a valid terminal, intruders can use the idle time for personal use.
c) After a valid terminal has sent a sign-off message to terminate the session, intruders can delete the sign-off message and continue the session with their own traffic.
d) When a terminal is active, intruders can transmit an error message to the terminal indicating that the computer is not available, then continue the session with their own traffic.

11.4 System penetration ploys against dial-up systems

Hackers and more serious computer criminals require only a personal computer and a modem to gain access to many inadequately protected systems which use dial-up access on a public telephone network. Unpublished telephone numbers may be discovered by using an autodial modem to perform a search for numbers which have modems connected. Once the number has been found, it is often necessary only to try a few typical passwords to gain entry.

Some systems retain the passwords which were installed by the manufacturer for test purposes and anyone familiar with the type of computer used can gain access. Where users assign their own passwords they often use a small range of names or dates which may be guessed after a few attempts. In other cases, ex-employees can gain access using privileges and passwords which were not revoked when they left the company.

To prevent the telephone numbers of intruders being traced if their activities are detected, they may employ a telephone rerouter box, or cheese box, which switches calls to another number.

11.5 Countermeasures

11.5.1 Introduction

There are many precautions which may be taken to reduce the probability of breaches in communications security. These counter-measures may, in some cases, be expensive or inconvenient, and it is necessary to select those which are appropriate to the level of risk and the type of threat anticipated.

Risk management is a method for identification, measurement and control of uncertain events and it may be applied to communications security. The elements of risk management are:

a) Risk analysis, which is a systematic investigation of the threat potential and quantification of the impact of the potential actions.

b) Countermeasure alternative design, which is the design of several countermeasures to each threat in order to satisfy the defined security requirements.

c) Implementation and monitoring, which implements an effective security system and monitors that system for continued effectiveness.

The rest of this chapter describes alternative forms of countermeasures for potential threats.

The forms of countermeasures which may be applied against specific threats include:

a) Encryption prevents message contents being released by wiretapping.

b) Port protection devices may be used to prevent unauthorised dial-up access.

c) Passwords may be made more effective and linked to individual access authorisations.

d) Authentication codes may be added to messages which request data in order to prevent some forms of active attack.

e) Sequence numbers may be added to prevent duplication or loss of messages.

f) Physical security measures may be taken to prevent unauthorised access to computers, terminals or communications equipment.

g) Equipment may be screened and installed in a manner which prevents compromising electromagnetic radiation.

h) Audit trails and other operational procedures may be adopted to detect security breaches and speed up recovery.

i) A trusted computer base and trusted network may be implemented to prevent a wide range of subversion ploys.

11.5.2 Defences against wiretapping

Physical and electrical precautions

Where a communications path is entirely under the user's control, it may be possible to run cables through screened metal ducts which cannot be opened by intruders without being detected. This prevents invasive tapping and the detection of compromising electromagnetic emissions. Fibre optic cable or double-screened electrical cable may alternatively be employed to prevent compromising electromagnetic emissions. The computers, terminals and all communications equipment, including junction boxes, may be located in physically secure rooms or enclosures where unauthorised access is prevented.

Compromising electromagnetic emissions from equipment may be reduced by several precautions:

a) Enclosing the equipment within a grounded, screened enclosure which acts like a Faraday cage to prevent electromagnetic radiation passing through.

b) By using equipment which has been designed to meet security requirements or has good internal screening and filtering to prevent electromagnetic radiation.

c) By fitting effective low-pass filters on mains cables and electrical signal cables attached to the equipment.

d) By installing the equipment in an area which does not have cables, conductive pipes or telephones which can conduct the compromising signals outside the secure area.

e) By use of a low-impedance ground for the equipment.

An alternative approach to the suppression of compromising electromagnetic radiation is to mask the radiation with random electromagnetic interference over a similar range of frequencies and with similar characteristics to those which are transmitted by the secure equipment. It is necessary, however, to ensure that the radiation levels from the noise source do not exceed the legal limits set by national standardisation authorities such as the FCC. Emissions from parallel data transmissions within a computer are effectively masked by the many similar noise sources within the computer.

To minimise electromagnetic radiation from electrical cables a number of guidelines should be followed:

a) Use low voltages and currents and make the switching edges as slow as possible by using filters.
b) Use balanced signalling rather than unbalanced transmissions (which use a reference voltage).
c) Use coaxial or twisted-pair cable preferably with one or two external screens.
d) Ensure that all connectors maintain the screen effectively between the cable and equipment without gaps.

The presence of taps on electrical cables may be detected by regular visual inspection along the entire signal path. Power-robbing taps or low-impedance taps may be detected using an electronic voltmeter to check the line at regular intervals. High-impedance taps are almost undetectable but, in some circumstances, balanced-capacitance bridges have been shown to be capable of detecting their presence. Inductively coupled taps are not detectable electrically. Taps on fibre optic cables may be detected by time domain reflectometers or signal-level meters at the receiver.

11.5.3 Authentication codes

Authentication codes (calculated at the sending device and added to the message; then checked at the receiving device) can be performed much more simply than encryption. The algorithm used to calculate the code may simply take part of the data field and use that as the authentication code or a complex algorithm based on many parameters may be used.

Message authentication may be used to prevent:

a) Insertion of false messages by the intruder.
b) Playing back a message from a previous sequence.
c) Playing back a message previously sent in the same sequence but in the opposite direction.

In order to detect (a) and (b) the authentication code should uniquely identify the message sequence and to detect (c) it should include direction information. An authentication code, using message contents, can detect (a) only. An authentication code containing time information may prevent (a) and (b) if the intruder was not aware of the code but unless the time code had great precision it would not prevent (c).

11.5.4 Message ordering

Message sequence numbers for each terminal may be included within the control portion of the message to make each message, on a particular terminal or line, unique for a period of time such as a year. The terminal message sequence number differs from frame sequence numbers which are added by the lower protocol layers. It is usual to employ an input sequence number on all messages sent from the terminal and an output sequence number on all messages sent to the terminal. The sequence numbers may be reset each day and added to a month, day code.

Input message numbers are best incremented for both accepted and rejected inputs but not for bad passwords or failed attempts to log-on. Output message numbers are best incremented on successful message delivery. The host computer checks the input message number and only accepts the message if it is the expected value. If three bad input message numbers are received in sequence, it is usual to lock out the terminal until enabled manually. At the end of each day, the host should send a message to each terminal containing the number of accepted messages, the number of rejected input attempts, and the last input message number which should equal the sum of the other two numbers.

Message sequence numbers for each terminal should detect message ordering attacks including:

a) Deleting messages from the stream.
b) Altering the order of messages in the stream.
c) Duplicating messages in the stream by playing back previously recorded messages.

Message sequence numbers are most suitable for application to links using dedicated lines where terminals are associated with a particular computer port. For dial-up connections, where terminals are not associated with a particular computer port, a port sequence number may be used containing the month, day and an incrementing port connection number.

11.5.5 Operational procedures and audit trails

Communications security requires a combination of automatic and manual procedures. Elementary procedures like logging off terminals at the end of each session should be encouraged and some systems automatically log terminals off after a predetermined quiet period. Network status must be available in order to recover rapidly from a detected security breach or other incident. There is a greater security risk at times when a network is in a state of flux or has a fault condition; therefore, sensitive conditions should be brought to the attention of the network controller.

To reduce the risk of collusion between people working with the system, sensitive functions should be separated, with different people performing part of each operation such as encryption key distribution. Crosschecks may be performed by having someone, who is not directly involved, check the message totals and the log of password violations.

Audit trails permit the sequence of actions to be reconstructed after a security breach or system failure. Information which is typically used in an audit trail includes:

a) Configuration changes.
b) Equipment status changes.
c) A log of transactions with unique identification numbers which appear in the message header and tailer.

These records, in the form of a print-out of events and exceptions plus tapes or floppy disks containing a journal of all transactions, should be kept for later analysis. The transaction journal may be used for recovery of lost messages. The events recorded include input and output message occurrences with user identification, message type, date, time, terminal/port sequence number, and a system sequence number for each occurrence. This information may be used to derive network utilisation statistics and billing data as well as an audit trail. Exceptions recorded include anomalies such as failed passwords and attempts to log-on, unauthorised transactions, terminal lock-outs and message errors.

11.6   Port protection

11.6.1   Passwords

Computer ports on remote terminal access systems make extensive use of passwords and typically also need to know the user identification before granting access. The number of log-on attempts is usually limited to about three unsuccessful tries, after which the terminal is locked out and the user identification is given to the system controller.

Passwords may be generated by the users but this frequently results in trivial passwords which are simple to guess. To increase the number of possible passwords and identification codes, these should be allocated centrally but should not be maintained in a single central directory to minimise the risk of password compromise. With personal identification numbers encoded on magnetic cards, users are not aware of their own code but in other circumstances it may be desirable to let users choose their own password for complete privacy.

Basic precautions which should be taken in using passwords include:

a) When passwords are typed in they should not appear on the screen or in print to prevent the password being compromised.

b) Passwords should be changed at irregular intervals and when employees leave, to prevent ex-employees continuing to use the password and to minimise the period of damage if a password is compromised.

c) Passwords may be accompanied by a user identification which is checked against the password. This may be an employee number or it may take the form of a personal identification number read from a magnetic card which must be inserted into a card reader on the terminal to open a session with the host computer.

11.6.2 Port protection devices

Computer ports on dial-up networks are susceptible to hackers discovering the ex-directory phone numbers. To do this hackers use an autodial modem to try numbers in sequence until the carrier tones from a modem are found. Several port protection devices are available; these are connected as shown in Figure 11.3. Some port protection devices camouflage the line by inhibiting the carrier tone of the modem when first accessed. One device answers with a synthesised human voice. Voice-oriented port protection devices require a telephone to gain access and some use the telephone keypad to enter the password. This may be inconvenient for some terminals with built-in modems which connect directly to a line because the session must be set up on a voice telephone before the modem is connected to the line.

Many port protection devices have a callback facility which calls back the normal telephone number of a user requesting access, to ensure that the request came from a legitimate location. The callback usually occurs after the user has entered a password and was instructed to hang up the telephone. If the password is correct, a callback is made to the telephone number stored with the password

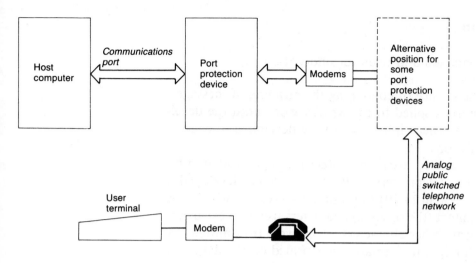

Fig. 11.3 Use of a port protection device in a dial-up computer access system

for each user. Callback usually results in the host being charged for the call and a delay of about one minute is added by the callback procedure. Certain users, such as travelling sales representatives, do not have fixed telephone numbers; therefore a means of circumventing the automatic callback procedure is required in some systems.

Many port protection devices also provide security logging capabilities, storing the number of invalid password attempts and, in some cases, the time and line identity of each failed password attempt is printed on an audit record. These records are additional to any which are provided by the computer operating system and provide a security check which would require collusion between the people controlling each set of records to hide any violations.

Port protection devices provide an additional layer of security in dial-up systems where the computer operating system does not include suitable facilities. Additional security features may be required where there is a risk of line tapping; the use of encryption may, however, render the port protection device unnecessary if access to the computer is not possible without a suitable encryption device and key. Access control devices should be used as part of a comprehensive security programme and should be selected to provide a degree of protection which is commensurate with the value of resources being protected.

11.7 Encryption

11.7.1 Basic principles and uses for encryption

Cryptography is the science of concealing the meaning of messages. Its use was exclusively applied to the written word until the development of telegraphy when cipher codes were developed to encrypt telegraphic transmissions.

In World War I, a need arose to protect messages sent in 5-bit Baudot code between teleprinters. Gilbert S. Vernam developed a suitable encryption system in 1917 by using a secret key which was combined with plaintext (the original) characters using an exclusive-OR function to form cipher characters which were transmitted. (A cipher is an algorithmic transformation performed on the data.) At the receiver, the original plaintext was recovered by combining the same key with the ciphertext using an exclusive-OR function. (See Figure 11.4.)

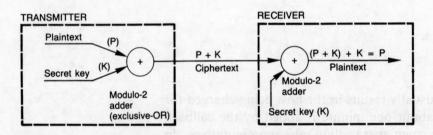

Fig. 11.4 The Vernam cipher

There are two basic methods of encryption:

1) *Data ciphering by transposition* which takes the plaintext characters and encrypts them to form the ciphertext. This changes only the position of the characters in the message and not the characters themselves.
2) *Data ciphering by substitution* which replaces each character in the plaintext by a different character according to a predefined algorithm. The Vernam cipher uses substitution because each bit in a character is modified by the key.

The introduction of computers resulted in the need for cryptographic protection of sensitive data when stored in the computer and when transmitted through public communications systems. Computers also provided a means of more easily breaking the cipher codes so more complex encryption methods were required. The US National Bureau of Standards published the Data Encryption Standard (DES) in 1977 and it has become the most widely used encryption system for commercial applications as well as the nonclassified government applications for which it was intended.

Encryption is primarily a countermeasure against passive attacks (to prevent disclosure of the data) but it can also be used as the basis of countermeasures against active attacks (to prevent modification of data). Encryption may be implemented either:

a) On each data transmission link without regard for message content, or

b) As end-to-end encryption, applied at the user level before data enters the network and decrypted at the destination. End-to-end encryption makes it necessary to put information such as headers, which are required by the network, in plaintext.

Conventional private key ciphers use the same key to decipher the message as used to encipher it. Anyone in possession of the key and a decryption unit which implements the correct algorithm can, therefore, decipher the message.

A public key cipher uses different keys to encipher and decipher the message. Pairs of keys are used, and these define a pair of transformation algorithms, each the inverse of the other and one may not be derived from the other. All users possess a pair of keys; one is publicly known and is used to encipher messages for that user, while the second key is kept secret for use in deciphering messages sent to the user. To verify the identity of the sender, the message is encrypted with the sender's own secret key, then the public key of the receiver. The receiver can strip off the first layer of encryption by using the receiver's secret key and then obtain the original plaintext by using the public key of the sender (see Figure 11.5).

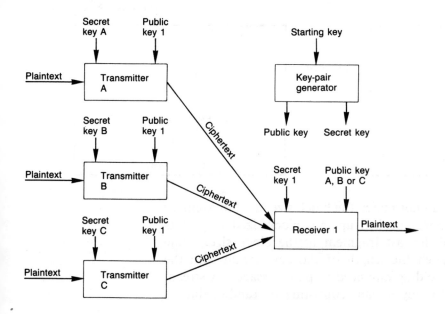

Fig. 11.5 Use of public and secret keys in a public-key cipher

Public key cryptosystems are based on one-way functions which are computationally impossible in the reverse direction. If a solution to the reverse computation were found, the cryptosystem would be compromised.

The major advantage of public key cryptosystems is that only public keys are distributed to potential information sources whereas conventional ciphers require the highly sensitive keys to be distributed, therefore increasing the risk of being compromised and involving frequent key changes. Public key cryptosystems have the disadvantages that they are slow, the integrity of the public key directory must be maintained, and the 'synonym' problem occurs if two users adopt the same prime number to develop their one-way function.

Another form of classification for cipher techniques are the terms 'block ciphers' and 'stream ciphers'. *Block ciphers* transform a block of characters (64 bits or 8 characters for DES) together, making each encrypted output block a functional combination of the complete key and the input block. A *stream cipher*, such as the Vernam cipher, makes each bit of encrypted data a function of only one bit of the original plaintext and one bit of the key (see Figure 11.6). A stream cipher causes only the plaintext bits which correspond to bits of ciphertext which are corrupted in transmission to be lost but, with a block cipher, the entire block of plaintext is lost if any part of the ciphertext block becomes corrupted. Both forms of cipher lose the rest of the message or text block if a whole character is lost or added causing the synchronisation between the key streams at the transmitter and receiver to be lost.

Fig. 11.6 A stream cipher

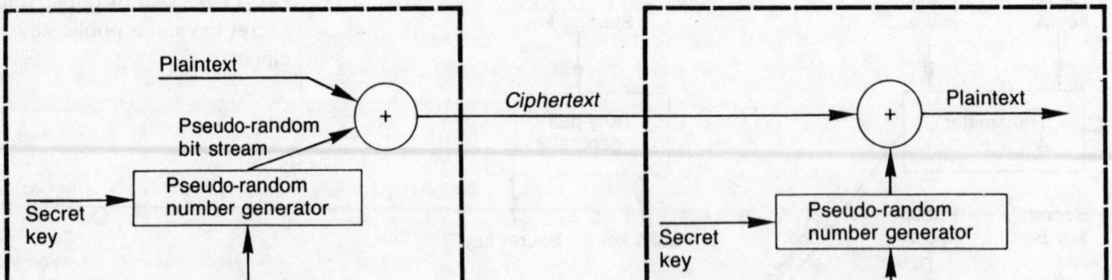

Messages frequently do not match the block size in a block cipher so messages are commonly broken up into block-sized fragments with padding to make the last fragment fit the block size. Some stream ciphers can match the length of the key stream with the message length, thus avoiding any need to pad messages. A stream cipher with a once-only key stream consisting of random bits is known as a Vernam cipher. This uses a keystream which is as long as all the transmitted messages and ensures unconditional security, but requires a constant supply of key streams. Most practical stream ciphers use long pseudo-random key streams which renders them susceptible to being broken by cryptanalysis.

Stream ciphers may use a key stream which is a function of the plaintext, ciphertext or the key stream itself. Key autokey (KAK) ciphers use a key stream which is not related to the plaintext or ciphertext; this makes them less susceptible to errors which occur in transmission but makes them susceptible to message-stream modification attacks. Ciphertext autokey (CTAK) ciphers use transmitted ciphertext as an input to the keystream generator, thus introducing interbit dependence which ensures desirable error propagation properties. CTAK ciphers are self-synchronising, resuming normal operation when a number of uncorrupt ciphertext bits are received following the receipt of corrupt characters.

A bulk encryption unit is a high-speed encryption device which encrypts the complete data stream which may include several multiplexed data channels. The synchronisation and control information for each channel is also encrypted and the use of a bulk encryption unit should have no effect on the data channel apart from the enhanced security provided. Bulk encryption units are available for the common TDM channel standards such as the 1.544 Mbit/s T1 link which can accommodate 24 digitised voice channels at 64 kbit/s each.

11.7.2 Data Encryption Standard

DES was developed by the US National Bureau of Standards with IBM and will be the US government standard for nonclassified data security until 1990 when it is felt the integrity of DES may be questionable. DES is the only encryption standard which is widely adopted by industry and for which several VLSI implementations are available. Several manufacturers have had their DES chips or units validated by the National Bureau of Standards and new algorithms are being developed under the NSA Commercial COMSEC Endorsement Program (CCEP).

The cryptographic strength of DES is determined by the keyspace (the number of possible combinations of bits which could produce the key) which is 2^{56} or 7.2×10^{16}. With an example of ciphertext and the corresponding plaintext available, a computer would be required to try up to 2^{56} different keys by trial and error to discover the true key.

The time and expense required to break a DES key is considered to exceed the value of any information transmitted but advances in computer technology may make this assumption questionable by 1990. To counter this trend, a version of DES with a 128-bit key in place of the present 56-bit key would be a viable alternative. Any user who wants to increase the security of DES could, however, apply DES encryption twice to double the effective key size to 112 bits.

The DES algorithm operates on 64 bits of plaintext to produce 64 bits of ciphertext under the control of a 56-bit key. Figure 11.7 shows the flow of information in the DES algorithm. Four main steps are involved:

1) Initial permutation
2) Key scheduling
3) Cipher function
4) Inverse permutation.

The initial permutation mixes the 64 input data bits to form an 8×8 matrix. The 64-bit word generated is loaded into the L and R registers, each 32-bits. The 64-bit key word meanwhile undergoes similar processing to produce a 48-bit subkey, K. The contents of the R register undergo a cipher function which expands the 32-bit word into a 48-bit word which is modulo-2 added to the selected 48-bit key. The sum is used as an address to the random-function S-box look-up table which goes through another permutation and generates the 32-bit cipher function output. This output is modulo-2 added to the contents of the L register and the output is loaded into the R register while the previous contents are loaded into the L register.

The key scheduling and S-box look-up are repeated sixteen times before the contents of the L and R registers are subjected to the reverse of the initial permutation to generate a 64-bit ciphertext output word. The least significant bit in each byte of the key is used only for parity checking; the remaining 56 bits of the key are left-shifted during encryption (right-shifted during decryption) to select 48 bits for use as a key in the cipher function. Decryption is the reverse of encryption.

DES has four modes of operation which make it suitable for use as either a block or a stream cipher:

1) ECB mode: electronic code book (fundamental mode).
2) CBC mode: cipher block chaining (used in telecommunications).
3) CFB mode: cipher feedback (keystream generator for a CTAK cipher).
4) OFB mode: output feedback (KAK cipher).

ECB mode is a block cipher which takes in 64-bit blocks of plaintext and uses a 56-bit key to produce 64 bits of ciphertext (see Figure

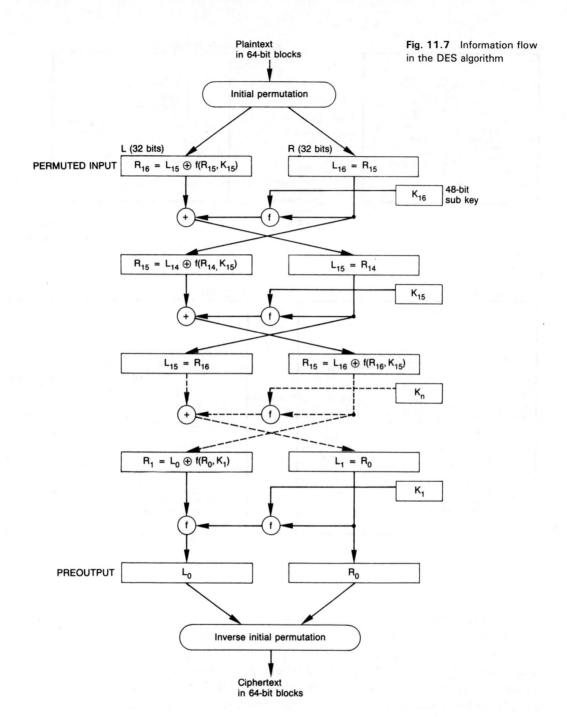

Plaintext
in 64-bit blocks

Initial permutation

Fig. 11.7 Information flow
in the DES algorithm

L (32 bits)   R (32 bits)

PERMUTED INPUT | $R_{16} = L_{15} \oplus f(R_{15}, K_{15})$ | | $L_{16} = R_{15}$ |

K_{16} 48-bit
sub key

$R_{15} = L_{14} \oplus f(R_{14}, K_{15})$ $L_{15} = R_{14}$

K_{15}

$L_{15} = R_{16}$ $R_{15} = L_{16} \oplus f(R_{16}, K_{15})$

K_n

$R_1 = L_0 \oplus f(R_0, K_1)$ $L_1 = R_0$

K_1

PREOUTPUT | L_0 | | R_0 |

Inverse initial permutation

Ciphertext
in 64-bit blocks

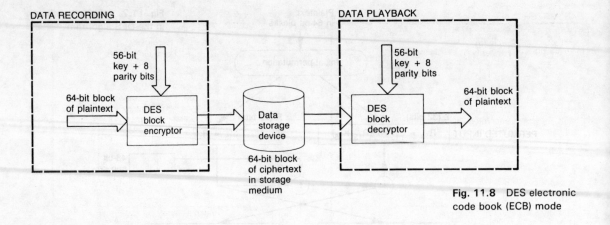

Fig. 11.8 DES electronic code book (ECB) mode

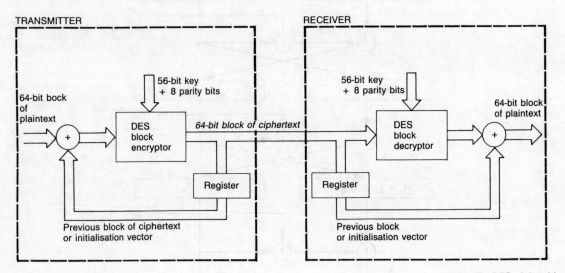

Fig. 11.9 DES cipher block chaining (CBC) mode

11.8). Common applications of ECB mode are for encrypting data in disk or tape stores. CBC mode makes each block a function of the previous block (see Figure 11.9), which prevents message insertion and deletion by removing enciphered blocks in transmission. CBC mode is suitable for use in data communications. CFB mode is used mostly for low-speed message transmission with DES (in ECB mode) used as part of a key-stream generator for a CTAK cipher (see Figure 11.10). This forms a self-synchronising stream cipher operating on data blocks of 1 to 64 bits in length. OFB mode produces a KAK cipher. The lack of protection against message stream modification attacks makes the OFB mode unsuitable for use in data communications. Table 11.1 compares the capability of several DES chips.

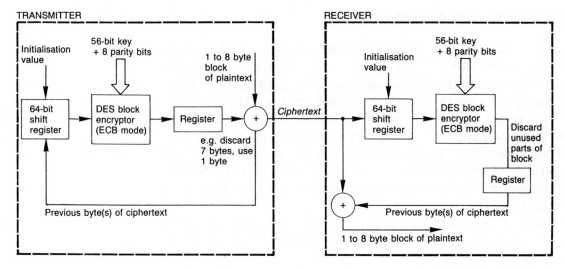

TRANSMITTER

Initialisation value

56-bit key + 8 parity bits

1 to 8 byte block of plaintext

64-bit shift register

DES block encryptor (ECB mode)

Register

e.g. discard 7 bytes, use 1 byte

Ciphertext

Previous byte(s) of ciphertext

RECEIVER

Initialisation value

56-bit key + 8 parity bits

64-bit shift register

DES block encryptor (ECB mode)

Discard unused parts of block

Register

Previous byte(s) of ciphertext

1 to 8 byte block of plaintext

Fig. 11.10 DES cipher feedback (CFB) mode which uses a DES encryptor, in ECB mode, as part of a key-stream generator for a CTAK self-synchronising stream cipher

Table 11.1 Comparison of DES encryption chips

Manufacturer and designation	Maximum data rate (kbyte/s)	Microprocessor bus interface	Micro-programmed	Modes supported	Number of keys
AMD AmZ 8068	1770	Yes	Yes	ECB CBC CFB	3
Fairchild 9414	1670	None	Yes	ECB	1
Western Digital 2001-3	167	Yes	Yes	ECB(2001) CBC(2002) CFB(2003)	1
Motorola MC6859	50	Yes	No	ECB	2
Texas Instruments 9940	0.60	Yes	No	ECB	1
AMI S6894	0.59	Yes	No	ECB	Several
Intel 8294	0.08	Yes	No	ECB	1

11.7.3 Public key cryptography

The RSA public key cryptosystem was developed at the Massachusetts Institute of Technology by Rivest, Shamir and Adleman, from whose names the title was derived. RSA, published in 1977, is the most widely used public key cryptosystem; suitable applications are in electronic mail where a signature may be verified by consulting a directory of public keys, and in data communications for privacy and authentication. The high processing requirement for public key cryptosystems has restricted their commercial use to a few banking applications and to the distribution of keys for the Data Encryption Standard.

RSA uses large data blocks, typically 512 bits, and encryption requires the equivalent of three million sixteen-bit multiplications per block. Software implementations require about 45 seconds to process a 512-bit block on an IBM PC while hardware implementations take at least 0.1 seconds. With these long processing times, RSA is not attractive for many high-speed data communication requirements.

The RSA keys are 200-bit words. The encryption key is the product of two secret prime numbers, each about 100 bits, and the decryption key may also be computed from the two prime numbers. To derive the secret prime numbers, the key may be factored but this would take 3.8 billion years for a 200-bit key, assuming one operation per microsecond.

A plaintext message is first converted into a data block up to 512 bits in length. Encryption of a plaintext block, using the encryption key, produces a ciphertext block of the same size. Decryption is the reverse of the encryption process but using the decryption key. The RSA encryption algorithm is based upon a one-way function which will permit a number u to be transformed to v, but the reverse transformation is computationally unfeasible. A trapdoor is a means of deriving u from v given special information.

Hybrid encryption systems have been produced in which a slow public key cryptosystem is combined with a private key cryptosystem such as DES to take advantage of the speed and availability of VLSI chips. Such a system is much faster than a public key cryptosystem because many more private key encryptions are required per message than public key encryptions. To transmit data, the sender first generates a random key which is used in a fast private key encryption algorithm. The random key is then encrypted using the public key method and both the encrypted key and DES encrypted text are transmitted to the receiver. The receiver first decrypts the key, then uses it to decrypt the ciphered text. A second pass may be used to check the authenticity of the text.

The *Diffie-Hellman* public key cryptosystem may be used for the distribution of DES keys in secure networks. A 32-bit microprocessor can compute the common key in about one second. Station 1 has a secret key SK_1 and computes, using modulo-M arithmetic, a public key PK_1 by means of the relationship

$$PK_1 = C^{SK_1}$$

where C is a well known constant. Station 2 also has a secret key SK_2 and computes, using modulo-M arithmetic, a public key PK_2 from $PK_2 = C^{SK_2}$.

A common key $K_{1,2}$ may be calculated by station 1 using

$$K_{1,2} = PK_2^{SK_1} = (C^{SK_2})^{SK_1} = C^{(SK_1, SK_2)}$$

Only stations 1 and 2 can calculate $K_{1,2}$ because it is necessary to know either SK_1 or SK_2. Station 2 calculates $K_{1,2}$ using

$$K_{1,2} = PK_1^{SK_2} = (C^{SK_1})^{SK_2} = C^{(SK_1, SK_2)}$$

11.8 Trusted computers and networks

11.8.1 Trusted computers

A computer system which has been approved as meeting a specified level of security protection, together with any other parts of the system which are known to be secure, is termed a trusted computer base or TCB. Computers and operating systems which may be considered to be a TCB, together with their applications software, must meet the appropriate security criteria specified in the Orange book, 'Trusted Computer System Evaluation Criteria', published in 1982 by the US Department of Defense, or alternative national requirements (Reference 11.2).

The DOD Orange book specifies three levels of protection, A, B and C, in reducing order of protection, and within each division numbers are given to classify the categories of security protection, and assurance that the protection works. For example, the highest level of protection and assurance achieved is A1, A indicating verified protection and A1 indicating a verified design, while A2 indicates verified implementation which is beyond the present state-of-the-art.

Systems in class A1 are functionally equivalent to those in class B3 but formal design specification and verification techniques are applied. Class B3 systems possess security domains which mediate all accesses of subjects and objects, are tamperproof, and exclude code which is not essential to the security capability.

Class B2 (structured protection) systems are based on a clearly defined and documented formal security policy model which enforces discretionary and mandatory access control enforcement, as found in class B1, but extended to cover all subjects and objects in the system, and including strengthened authentication mechanisms.

Class B1 (labelled security protection) systems have all the features of class C2 systems but include an informal statement on the security policy model, data labelling and mandatory access control over named subjects and objects.

The selection of the appropriate level of security for a system depends upon:

a) The local processing capability (receive only terminal/fixed function interactive terminal/programmable device).

b) The communication path type (receive only/transmit and receive link/interactive network).

c) The user capability (subscriber/transaction processing user/ full programming capability).

d) The data exposure (depending upon indices for user clearance and data sensitivity).

The use of a trusted computer base is extremely expensive and it costs many times more to achieve an A1 system than a C1 system. The DOD Orange book provides a range of security protection from low assurance and low functionality up to high assurance and high functionality but the need for systems with, for example, low functionality and high assurance or high functionality and low assurance are not considered.

11.8.2 Trusted networks

Wide area networks are clearly a potentially insecure means of communication and a range of countermeasures are available to combat the threat. Local area networks are, however, often considered to be less vulnerable because they are on home territory. LANs do, however, have many of the vulnerabilities of wide area networks and many of the vulnerabilities of a computer system. Particular problems include:

a) Most LANs use broadcast transmission which makes all data available to all devices connected to the LAN.

b) The same communication medium may be used for different applications with different security requirements.

c) LANs are frequently connected by gateways to wide area networks making the data remotely accessible.

A trusted network is an extension of the trusted computer base (TCB) where the transmission of information on the network is

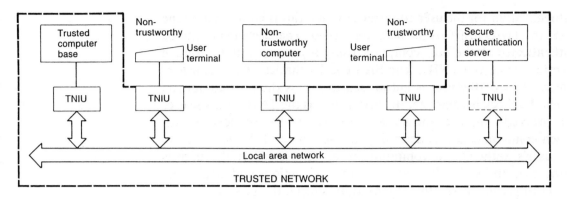

Fig. 11.11 A trusted network

considered secure and each access point includes a trusted network interface unit (TNIU) which prevents users gaining access to information which they are not authorised to receive (see Figure 11.11).

A trusted network provides a service to the trusted computer base by guaranteeing authentication, mutual secrecy and message delivery. The TNIU must contain only trusted computing facilities and software, and may use encryption to provide protection for data transmitted on the network, but physical security measures may alternatively be used to protect data on the network, possibly at a lower cost.

An alternative approach to network security is to employ a secure terminal interface unit between the user and the LAN interface unit. A secure host interface unit is also required between the trusted host and the LAN; both these units include equipment which encrypts only the data, not the network control information. Communication between the host computer and the user is achieved by the user establishing a connection with encrypted address codes and then the host computer authenticating the identity of the user with passwords and checks on users' access rights. This approach is more complex than a trusted network with TNIUs but it may be implemented with any LAN.

A trusted network prevents any communication which is not authorised by the network; this is achieved by using a secure authentication server (SAS) as part of the network. The SAS gives each TNIU permission tokens for each session appropriate to the users' rights and needs. The SAS will also maintain a security file which stores passwords, ideally encrypted using a one-way algorithm.

A user on a trusted network initiates authentication directly with the TNIU, and the TNIU communicates with the SAS to get the authentication for the user confirmed. When this is confirmed by the SAS, the TNIU instructs the user to proceed. The user then has to be authenticated to the host computer using a password and a unique identifier from the TNIU. The SAS checks that the two identifiers match and that the user is authorised to access the host computer. When the check is complete, the SAS informs the TNIU that the user can proceed. The user must then enter the names of devices with which communication is desired in the session and the SAS checks the user's authority to communicate as requested. If the user is authorised, the SAS will arrange for the connections and inform the TNIU to permit these other connections during the session.

The US National Computer Security Center issues the Trusted Network Interpretation of the Trusted Computer System Evaluation Criteria (Reference 11.3).

11.8.3 Multilevel security

Multilevel security systems permit the connection of users with different levels of security access rights and the storage of data with various levels of classification in separate compartments. Systems which raise the level of all information and users to the highest security classification are called system high; these systems are less complicated, but make it impossible for users without the highest clearances to use the system and information with low classification is artificially raised to the highest classification.

Multilevel security systems partition the data into disjoint sets, one for each security compartment, and access is controlled by trusted hardware and software which implements a defined mandatory security policy. To realise a multilevel security system, the security compartments must be isolated and a trusted access control mechanism is required to implement the security policy.

Isolation of security compartments may be provided by one of the following:

a) Physical separation of parts of the system: when communication links are used between physically isolated systems, the information is constrained to flow in a well defined manner.

b) Temporal separation, where information from different security compartments may be stored in the same parts of the system, but at different times and only after all data is purged before loading data from another security compartment.

c) Logical separation, by which data from different compartments is separated using trusted algorithms implemented by a combination of hardware and software.

368

d) Cryptographic separation which uses encryption with different keys for each security compartment to ensure that data can only be read by its intended recipients.

System-high security systems rely on physical and temporal separation while early centralised multilevel security systems rely on trusted computers and operating systems which may use logical separation. The current trend is towards distributed multilevel security systems based upon trusted networks. Such systems may make use of all four separation mechanisms in different places to produce a system with smaller amounts of trusted hardware and software than centralised systems.

The use of a TNIU to connect a single-level part of the system ensures that only data in its specified security compartment may be accessed and that data may only be transmitted to authorised systems of the same, or higher, security classification. By this mechanism, it becomes unnecessary for software in a single-level end-system to be trusted.

11.9 Security in the open systems architecture

11.9.1 Required security services

Various standards bodies are involved in the enhancement of communications protocols to include security features. The International Standards Organisation is developing a Security Addendum to the OSI 7-layer model. The ISO/IS/7498 proposed Addendum 2 on security architecture attempts to identify the security services which users may require to be provided and the security mechanisms which will be required to provide these services.

The objective of the OSI standard is to ensure that a secure system using OSI communications protocols will be no less secure than the host computer or end-systems. The types of security services which may be required are:

a) Confidentiality (protection of transmitted data from accidental or deliberate disclosure to unauthorised persons).
b) Integrity (ensuring that received data contains no duplication, insertions, modifications or replays).
c) Peer entity authentication (the identification of remote entities, eliminating the possibility of previous authentication sequences being replayed).
d) Access control (limiting and controlling the access to host computers via communication links).

Table 11.2 Allocation of security services to OSI layers

Service	OSI LAYER						
	1	2	3	4	5	6	7
Peer entity authentication			O	O			O
Access control			O	O			O
Confidentiality	O	O	O	O		O	
Traffic flow security	O		O				O
Integrity			O	O			O
Data origin authentication			O	O			O
Non-repudiation							O

O = optional service

e) Traffic flow security (disguising or hiding traffic patterns).
f) Non-repudiation (ensuring that the recipient of data cannot deny that it was received or the sender denying that it was sent).
g) Data origin authentication (ensuring that the source of data is the one claimed).

11.9.2 Allocation of services to OSI layers

Security services will be allocated to particular OSI layers where they may be implemented if required (see Table 11.2). Higher layers will be able to make use of security services if implemented in lower layers.

370

12 Network implementation

12.1 Requirements analysis and architectural design

12.1.1 High-level planning

Before embarking upon any communications system design it is necessary to establish a definition of requirements which is agreed by the sponsoring authority or by user representatives. Information systems are often extremely complex and the communications system may be a relatively small part. The more complex systems may not be controlled by one department so it may not be possible for one department to take authority for the definition of the system requirements.

In some circumstances a detailed system requirement definition cannot be established without first establishing a higher-level system architecture which identifies individual subsystems which are in operation or under development and establishes the interfaces between these systems. It is also necessary to identify the development options for the overall system and its subsystems and to involve users and system developers in the requirements definition.

In many cases several project teams may be involved in system definition and it may be impractical or too expensive to replace an entire system at once so a phased approach will be necessary. A high-level management team may therefore be required to develop the system architecture and co-ordinate its implementation. Without a high-level architecture, development may be unco-ordinated and developments may be duplicated in different departments. It may cost about the same to develop a system which supports several departments as to develop a system which supports only one department and it is therefore cost effective to identify any duplication.

High-level strategic planning may include four stages:

1) Assess business objectives
2) Determine what information systems are necessary to meet the

business objectives and develop an information architecture which takes account of subsystem priorities.

3) Conduct a technological planning study in association with other studies to derive an agreed conceptual infrastructure and a list of priorities.

4) Conduct a resource planning study to establish the probable future need for people with various skills.

12.1.2 Architectural design

The logical subsystems and data flows between subsystems may be established with the aid of questionnaire forms and the results displayed on data flow matrices as shown in Figure 12.1. The analysis of intersystem and intrasystem data flows must be performed before the communications architecture may be developed.

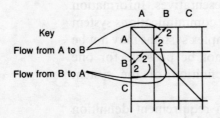

Fig. 12.1 A matrix showing data flows between logical subsystems

In the design phase, the data flows may be translated into file transfers and the means of transferring the files decided. The communications system design may then commence, determining the data flow, transmission capacities and network topology. A decision on the use of centralised or distributed processing may be taken and its influence on the communications system design established.

When the aggregate communications requirements are established and the possible growth requirements agreed, the feasibility of alternative communications architectures may be compared using simple analytical modelling procedures. A cost/benefit analysis may be performed for each viable alternative and the most economical ones shortlisted. The preferred architecture may now be subjected to a more detailed analysis; its topology may be optimised and simulations performed to quantify the anticipated traffic load and response times.

12.1.3 Equipment selection

The communications equipment and bearers may now be selected and calculations performed to confirm that the selected configurations will meet the performance requirements and have an adequate margin for system expansion or offer a means of upgrading performance.

The system availability calculations may be carried out when the equipment MTBF and MTTR figures are known. If the availability targets are not achievable with the initial design, equipment with improved MTBF or MTTR figures may be employed or redundant facilities incorporated.

Figure 12.2 shows how the system availability, project risk and amount of management effort required can depend on the number of suppliers involved. A single supplier without competition may neglect the support provided and it may be impossible to make the supplier keep to timescales or achieve performance requirements. The optimum number of suppliers is generally two or three; more increases the risk of incompatibility, increases delays, and reduces availability because one supplier may blame other suppliers for faults.

It is important that the requirement for compatibility between equipment is specified precisely and forms part of the contract. Where equipment from different suppliers must work together, the suppliers must confirm their compatibility and it is desirable to be present at any discussions between the suppliers. Many facilities may be available only in later versions of the equipment so it is important to witness operation in the relevant circumstances. Second sources should be sought where the application is an essential one.

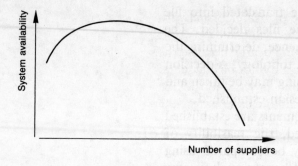

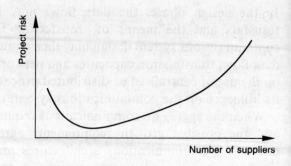

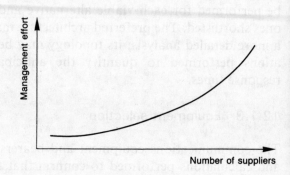

Fig. 12.2 Typical changes in system availability, project risk and management effort required against changes in the number of suppliers

12.2 Implementation options

12.2.1 Network selection

The number of alternatives for a wide area network or a local area network is enormous. Some of these alternatives may be shown to be superior in compatibility, performance and cost and those shortlisted may be evaluated against other criteria such as:

a) MTBF
b) MTTR
c) Proven performance
d) Manufacturer's long-term support
e) Ease of expansion
f) Dimensions of equipment
g) Environmental factors
h) Self-test facilities
i) Security features
j) Delivery dates.

One of the most significant choices is the type of bearer or network service to be employed for a long-distance link or wide area network. An initial analysis may eliminate some forms of bearer because the error rate may not be acceptable, the data rate may not be adequate, the connection time may be excessive, or the service may not be available at all the required locations. After this, the candidates may be subjected to a cost analysis and the results displayed on graphs showing annual costs at various levels of usage.

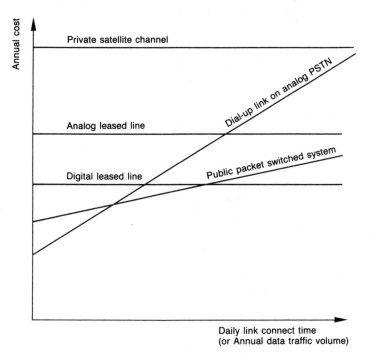

Fig. 12.3 Typical relationships between the cost of communications bearers and the daily link connect time (or annual data traffic volume)

Figure 12.3 shows typical relationships between the cost of bearers and the daily connect time (or annual data traffic volume). Dialled connections over the analog public switched telephone network are generally only suitable for applications where infrequent connections are required. The installation cost and the fixed element of annual cost is the lowest but the cost per minute connected or per Mbyte transferred is highest. Error rates on analog dial-up lines are unpredictable and may be unsatisfactory for many applications.

The use of a public packet switched system offers lower error rates than the analog public switched network but it has a higher fixed element of annual cost. The cost per minute of connect time or per Mbyte of data transmitted is lower than that of the analog public switched network but the total annual cost will be higher than any form of leased line in most circumstances where high data volumes or long connect times are required.

Digital leased lines are likely to be the most cost effective bearers when high data volumes and several hours connect time each day are required. Digital leased lines are generally less expensive than analog leased lines and the error rates are superior. In the UK, British Telecom offer KiloStream circuits at speeds up to 48 kbit/s or 64 kbit/s and MegaStream circuits at speeds between 2 Mbit/s and 140 Mbit/s. Alternatively, digital leased lines are available from Mercury at 64 kbit/s and 2 Mbit/s. The competitive position in the UK and the USA makes it essential to evaluate the costs from different suppliers in detail; installation and standing charges may differ considerably.

The use of private satellite links is becoming popular in the USA where long distances are involved. Private satellite links may also be employed for high-volume international communications. Multi-access satellite systems, based on very small aperture terminals, are becoming popular in the USA but in Europe land-based public data networks are exclusively used.

The number of network termination points in Europe has increased from 393 000 in 1978 to 916 000 in 1982 and over 2 million in 1987. While the number of leased digital lines has increased, the number of leased analog network connections has declined from 50% of the total number in 1978 to 45% in 1982 and around 25% in 1987. Switched analog lines declined from 40% of the total in 1978 to 34% in 1982 and less than 25% in 1987. The number of X.25 packet switched connections were 5% of the total in 1982 but were over 15% of the total by 1987. Digital circuit terminations were 3% of the total in 1982 and over 20% in 1986.

Packet switched data networks offer a more reliable service than analog switched networks and offer greater flexibility than leased lines. Multiple destinations, automatic back-up facilities, rerouting and shared use of redundant resources are available, all of which can contribute to cost reductions. When assessing the suitability of a packet switched service it is necessary to take into account the response time of the network which is higher than that for a dedicated leased line because network resources are shared. It is also necessary to provide a suitable interface for the packet switched network, either a host DTE interface as specified in X.25 or a terminal DTE which interfaces with a packet assembler/disassembler (as specified in X.3, X.28 and X.29).

As an alternative to the use of a public network service or leased lines, a value added network (VAN) service may be used. VANs offer various data processing services, for example electronic mail, videotex or electronic funds transfer. VAN services provide all the necessary network operation and management in addition to providing their value added service but in Europe the VAN suppliers may not act solely as communications carriers.

Larger organisations may find it worthwhile to construct a private packet switched data network using leased lines between proprietary packet switching equipment and user facilities. The use of a private packet switched system can be extremely cost effective for organisations such as banks which require a flexible transmission system linking several facilities in each of hundreds or thousands of locations. Gateways may be used to link the private network to the public packet switched network and value added networks if required. A major commitment to network management is however required to maintain efficient operation of a private packet switched network.

12.2.2 Component sizing

Packet switches, multiplexers, data concentrators and port selectors present a sizing problem because the average response time depends upon the number of ports or channels available and on the data traffic volume. If a similar configuration has not previously been tried in similar circumstances, some form of scientific sizing method based on known data traffic patterns may be used.

Two techniques developed for sizing trunk lines between telephone exchanges may be employed for sizing packet switches, multiplexers, data concentrators and port selectors; these techniques are:

1) The Poisson formula
2) The Erlang B formula.

These formulae may be used to establish the optimum level of service (or number of channels) to minimise total costs while keeping the waiting time within acceptable limits (see Figure 12.4).

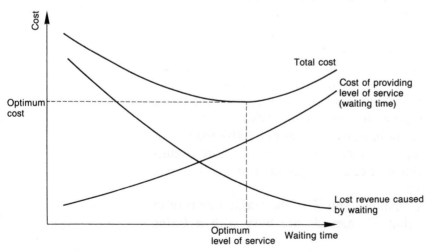

Fig. 12.4 Traffic formulae may be used to establish the optimum level of service in order to minimise total costs while keeping the waiting time within acceptable limits

377

The *Poisson formula* assumes that lost calls are held until a channel is available and that a Poisson distribution of call arrivals per unit time applies (i.e. arrivals are random). The probability of r arrivals is

$$P(r) = \frac{e^{-\lambda} (\lambda^r)}{r!}$$

where λ is the mean arrival rate

e is the base of natural logarithms = 2.71828
$r!$ is $r(r-1)(r-2) \ldots 4 \times 3 \times 2 \times 1$.

A multiplexer with an average of two calls arriving per second during the busy hour has a probability of r arrivals per second:

$$P(r) = \frac{2.71828^{-2} (2^r)}{r!}$$

which gives a probability of

0.1358 for 0 calls per second
0.2707 for 1 call per second
0.2707 for 2 calls per second
0.1805 for 3 calls per second
0.0902 for 4 calls per second
0.0361 for 5 calls per second
0.0120 for 6 calls per second
0.9960

To find the number of channels required to give at least 99% probability that no calls will have to wait (are blocked) the probability of 0, 1, 2, etc. calls are added until the total exceeds 0.99. In this case, with an average of two calls per second arriving, up to six calls could arrive per second and therefore six channels are required to ensure a 99% probability of not having a call blocked (for over 99% probability the grade of service is less than 0.01).

The *Erlang formula* assumes that blocked calls hang up and wait before attempting again and that the traffic results from an infinite number of sources. The traffic intensity is measured in erlangs, a dimensionless expression indicating the occupancy of a circuit. One erlang of traffic on one circuit indicates continuous 100% loading of that circuit or 50% loading on two circuits (i.e. one or more circuits carrying an aggregate traffic of 1 call-hour per hour or 1 call-minute per minute).

If T is the number of channels and E is the traffic intensity in erlangs, the probability that P channels are busy with a traffic intensity of E is:

$$P(T, E) = \frac{E^T/T!}{1 + E + (E^2/2!) + (E^3/3!) + \cdots + (E^T/T!)}$$

A multiplexer giving a 0.01 grade of service (1% of calls blocked) with a traffic intensity E of 8 erlangs (8 calls simultaneously) requires 15 channels. Tables for the Erlang B formula show that, at 8 erlangs, 14 channels give a 0.0172 grade of service and 15 channels give a 0.0091 grade of service.

The Erlang B formula is appropriate for use in systems in which blocked calls are cleared by waiting before making another attempt or are passed onto another port by a rotary selector. The Poisson formula is appropriate for use in systems where calls are held until a channel or port is available. The Poisson formula generally requires more channels than Erlang at low traffic intensities and the Erlang formula generally requires more channels than Poisson at higher traffic intensities.

12.3 System integration

12.3.1 Integration problems

It is rarely the case that a network is only required to support computers and terminals from one manufacturer or that no interfaces are required to external networks. There are two common approaches to the computer incompatibility problem:

1) A converter is provided to make one type of computer emulate the communications protocol or to make it appear as a remote cluster controller on the other type of computer.
2) An intermediate protocol, such as the OSI standards, may be used to interface to all types of computer.

When two or more networks wish to intercommunicate, a means of internetworking is required. The common forms of internetworking use:

a) A bridge (see Figure 12.5)
b) A gateway (see Figure 12.6)
c) Wrapping (see Figure 12.7)
d) Mapping (see Figure 12.8).

A *bridge* provides a communication link between two networks using a common transport mechanism which is different to that in either network and supports only common higher-level protocols. (Another use of the term bridge is for a device which provides a communication link between homogeneous networks.) A *gateway*

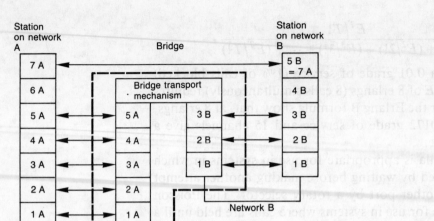

Fig. 12.5 Internetworking through a bridge

Station on network A

7 A
6 A
5 A
4 A
3 A
2 A
1 A

Bridge

Bridge transport mechanism

5 A
4 A
3 A
2 A
1 A

3 B
2 B
1 B

Station on network B

5 B = 7 A
4 B
3 B
2 B
1 B

Network A

Network B

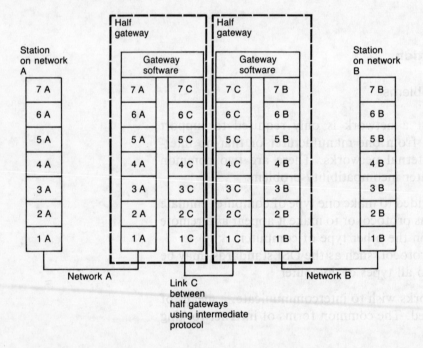

Fig. 12.6 Internetworking through two half gateways

Half gateway

Gateway software

Half gateway

Gateway software

Station on network A

7 A
6 A
5 A
4 A
3 A
2 A
1 A

7 A   7 C
6 A   6 C
5 A   5 C
4 A   4 C
3 A   3 C
2 A   2 C
1 A   1 C

7 C   7 B
6 C   6 B
5 C   5 B
4 C   4 B
3 C   3 B
2 C   2 B
1 C   1 B

Station on network B

7 B
6 B
5 B
4 B
3 B
2 B
1 B

Network A

Link C between half gateways using intermediate protocol

Network B

provides a communication link between heterogeneous computers or networks and has the ability to convert from one protocol to another. A full gateway node is a member of both networks. Half gateways, each owned by one network, may be linked via a communications line where the networks are separated.

Wrapping uses a network with a different protocol to connect similar systems. Data is wrapped by the network protocol for transmission and is unwrapped at the destination. *Mapping* is used to interconnect two computers or networks which have similar

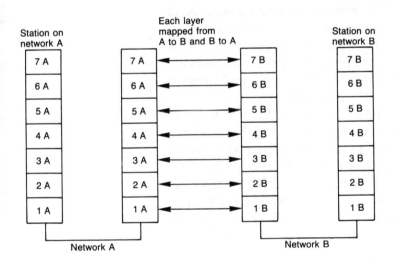

Fig. 12.7 Internetworking by wrapping

Network with type A protocol

| Protocol A header | Data |

WRAPPING

| Protocol B header | Protocol A header | Data |

Transmission by network type B between type A networks

| Protocol B header | Protocol A header | Data |

UNWRAPPING

| Protocol A header | Data |

Network with type A protocol

Fig. 12.8 Internetworking by mapping

Station on network A

| 7 A |
| 6 A |
| 5 A |
| 4 A |
| 3 A |
| 2 A |
| 1 A |

Network A

Each layer mapped from A to B and B to A

7 A	↔	7 B
6 A	↔	6 B
5 A	↔	5 B
4 A	↔	4 B
3 A	↔	3 B
2 A	↔	2 B
1 A	↔	1 B

Station on network B

| 7 B |
| 6 B |
| 5 B |
| 4 B |
| 3 B |
| 2 B |
| 1 B |

Network B

protocols with common functions at each layer. Most interconnections use wrapping and mapping.

The ideal solution is for all computer and network manufacturers to adopt the ISO OSI standards but there are currently a variety of different protocols in use and the usual solution is to employ a gateway. When a gateway links two networks with different routing, error detection and correction or call establishment procedures, it is difficult to diagnose system faults. The gateway must perform many conversion functions and consequently may be slower than other network components and present a performance bottleneck.

Gateways linking dissimilar computers generally do not provide a peer-to-peer relationship between host computers; one machine must emulate a remote cluster controller on the other machine. In many cases the gateway only permits users on one system to access the other system through the gateway but users on the second system may not be granted access to the other system.

12.3.2   X.25 internetworking

Early forms of interconnection between X.25 packet switched networks relied on gateway computers which were not part of either network. The gateway performed address changing, transparent forwarding of packets and signalling. A user on either network had to address the gateway to initiate packet transfer to the other network.

When the CCITT X.75 recommendation, 'Terminal and transit call control procedures and data transfer system on international circuits between packet switched data networks', was introduced, true internetworking between X.25 networks became possible. X.75 is a symmetrical version of X.25 to permit communication via signalling terminal exchanges (STEs) which are the gateways linking X.25 networks (see Figure 12.9). Multiple physical connections are provided between STEs to facilitate load sharing and support graceful recovery from internetwork trunk circuit failures.

Level 1 of X.75 supports V.35 internetwork trunks at 56 kbit/s or G.703 at 64 kbit/s. Level 2 is based on X.25 LAP-B but supports extended frame numbering for use on multiple internetwork trunks including satellite circuits. Level 3 is based on X.25 packet level protocols and is used to establish virtual circuits, exchange information, and clear circuits set up between X.25 packet data networks. Call set-up packets include an additional field which supports transit network identification, call identification, and flow control parameter selection.

12.3.3   OSI internetworking

The problem of interconnecting networks to form a homogeneous overall network is being addressed by the International Standardisation Organisation as part of its OSI development work. Both connection-oriented and connectionless services are being supported. (Connection-oriented services establish an end-to-end connection for the duration of a call but, in the connectionless mode, individual blocks of data, or datagrams, are routed independently through the network.)

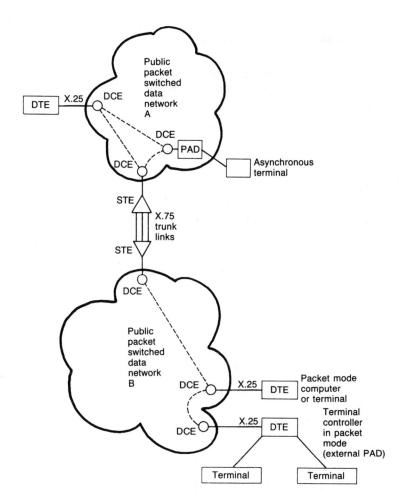

Fig. 12.9 X.75 communication trunks between signalling terminal exchanges (STEs) on separate packet switched data networks

Standards for connection-oriented and connectionless internetworking have been proposed by the ISO subcommittee 6, working group 2, and in IEEE 802.1. These standards make use of the X.25 packet level protocol (PLP) for connection-oriented internetworking and the connectionless network protocol (CLNP) for the network layer in LAN stations and internetworking units (IWUs). The PLP connection-oriented network service is specified in ISO 8348 and supports integrated services digital networks.

ISO 8348 includes a universal addressing scheme which supports many earlier addressing schemes, including:

a) CCITT X.121 for public data networks (14 decimal digits).
b) CCITT F.69 for telex networks (8 decimal digits).
c) CCITT E.163 for public switched telephone networks, including international prefixes (12 decimal digits).
d) CCITT E.164 for ISDN (15 decimal digits).

e) ISO DCC for geographic-defined addressing (4-digit data for the country code).

f) ISO 6523 ICD for binary or digital data-device addressing (4-digit international code designator prefix to identify the specific international network).

g) ISO OSI addressing (binary device address with 48 or 56 bit local network address and network service access point address).

As shown in Figure 12.10, the ISO 8348/DAD 2 universal addressing plan starts the address with a 2 decimal digit authority and format identifier (AFI) which identifies the format of the address. The addressing format is fitted into either an 18-octet field for binary encoded data or a 38-character field for decimal coded digits. Two special AFI codes determine whether the address uses the ISO 646 character codes or some other alternative.

Fig. 12.10 ISO 8348/DAD 2 universal addressing plan

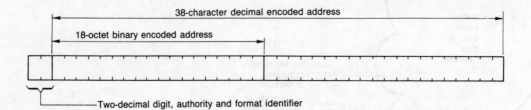

By using the X.25 PLP at the network layer, LAN stations may communicate with local or remote X.25 hosts via the IWU, and with local or remote LAN stations where LANs are interconnected by packet switched data networks. LAN stations may also act as packet assembler/disassemblers for attached asynchronous terminals, the network being used for connecting them to an X.25 packet mode host computer.

The use of X.25 PLP for connection-oriented intra and internetworking of LAN stations and IWUs is specified in ISO 8881; this enables X.25 LAN gateways to intercommunicate and to communicate with packet switched networks and X.25 DTEs on the LAN. Connectionless internetworking is specified in the ISO 8473 CLNP which is incorporated in MAP and TOP. An addendum to ISO 8473 relates to its use on LANs and packet switched networks; this extends the OSI transport layer to include a connectionless network service as specified in ISO 8348 addendum 1.

The IEEE 802.1 committee has specified several standards, one for LAN interconnection using bridges which operate at the medium access control (MAC) sublayer, and also a common MAC sublayer service and standards for network layer routers for communication between a LAN and any subnetwork. Three reference configurations (LAN-to-LAN, LAN-to-X.25 WAN, and LAN-to-X.25 WAN-to-LAN) are used in the definition of network layer routers. The router standard calls up OSI layers 1 to 3 and ISO protocols for internetworking units and OSI layers 1 to 4 for LAN stations.

The IEEE 802.1 committee have also developed a framework of functional requirements for internetworking; this addresses several functions:

a) Addressing
b) Buffering
c) Error handling
d) Flow control
e) Routing
f) Protocol conversion
g) Congestion control
h) Segmentation and reassembly.

12.4 Network protection and reconfiguration

12.4.1 Improving survivability

Data communications networks are subjected to many environmental effects and equipment failures. Power supplies may experience voltage transients, electrical noise, brownouts and blackouts.

Lines may be struck by electrical discharges (lightning) or in the event of nuclear war they will be subjected to nuclear electromagnetic pulses (NEMP). Many military systems must include NEMP protection but all systems with overhead lines should be provided with protection against lightning and transients.

Any piece of equipment or line in the network may fail and it is necessary to consider the probability of these failures in the availability analysis. Some equipment or lines may require duplication, in which case the redundant facilities may be permanently connected and rerouting may take place automatically; alternatively it may be necessary to switch in the standby facilities using data switches.

The configuration of lines and provision of back-up links should take survivability into account. A multipoint circuit, for example, may be configured in three basic ways:

1) Using a passive 4-wire bridge at the central processor with star wired circuits to the terminals (see Figure 12.11). This configuration prevents a fault in one circuit affecting the others but the line cost is high because the total length is great.

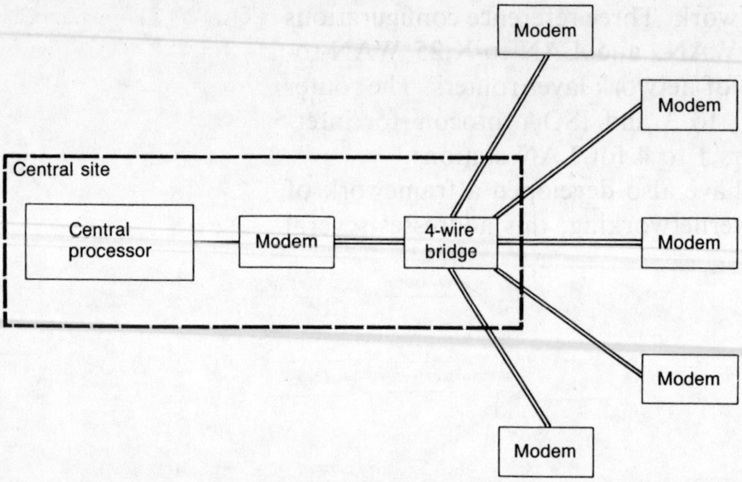

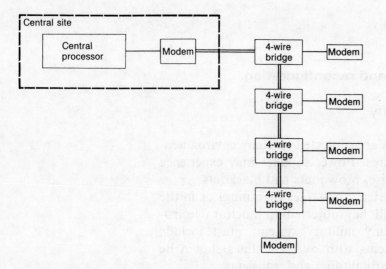

Fig. 12.11 A central star-wired multipoint configuration

Fig. 12.12 A cascade-wired multipoint configuration

2) Circuits may be cascaded through multiple bridges as shown in Figure 12.12. This may minimise the line cost but the loss of a specific circuit or bridge may result in communication with several terminals being lost. Troubleshooting is difficult, making any loss of service lengthy.

3) A bridge may be installed at a site which is remote from the central processor and terminals in its vicinity may be directly wired in a star configuration using relatively short lines. A trunk line links the remote bridge to the central processor as shown in Figure 12.13. This configuration has a lower line cost than (1) but is susceptible to loss of the trunk line, resulting in all communication being lost.

Alternatives (2) and (3) may be made more resilient by adding dial-up links which take over if the main link fails. Devices such as the

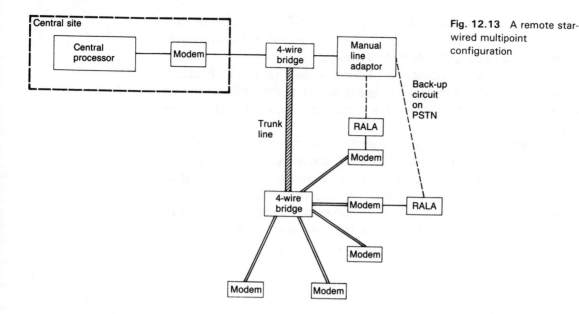

Fig. 12.13 A remote star-wired multipoint configuration

Racal-Milgo Registered Automatic Line Adapter (RALA) permit remote or locally controlled switching between a failed 4-wire leased line and a 2-wire back-up circuit on the public switched telephone network.

12.4.2 Data switches

Data switches may be employed to switch in spare lines or equipment, to switch test equipment on line, to select ports, or to configure the data paths in a network. In the 1960s network fault diagnosis and repair was a purely manual business which involved tracing the faulty equipment and replacing it by removing its connectors. In the early 1970s network control centres began to use manual patch panels by which an operator could insert test equipment onto analog and digital lines and bypass faulty lines or equipment.

In the late 1970s more sophisticated test and measurement equipment such as data line monitors became available and manual or relay operated A/B switches were used for local and remote network reconfiguration. An A/B switch can switch a single line (4-wire analog or 25-wire RS-232) between one or two other lines or devices. Remote operation of an A/B switch is possible with a remote activation unit but operation is cumbersome and limited to small numbers of alternative paths.

In the early 1980s matrix switches were introduced; they provide many alternative switching paths and take up much less space than multiple banks of A/B switches. Matrix switches are electronically controlled, often using microprocessors to permit local or remote control with commands entered on a display terminal. Other modern forms of data switch include data PABXs (which route data channels as required by the user) and intelligent statistical multiplexers (which often have user-selected channel switching and automatic alternative routing capabilities).

A/B switches may be used to substitute a spare modem, as shown in Figure 12.14. The 25-wire RS-232 interface and the two- or four-wire line interface may be rerouted by ganged switches. A more efficient modem standby arrangement where one spare modem can replace two or more modems is shown in Figure 12.15. In this configuration, only one switch may select position B at a time.

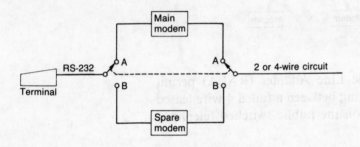

Fig. 12.14 Modem substitution using A/B switches

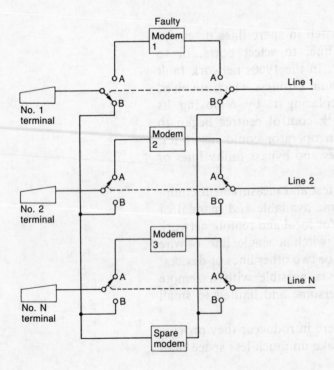

Fig. 12.15 A modem substitution system in which one spare may be substituted for two or more modems

388

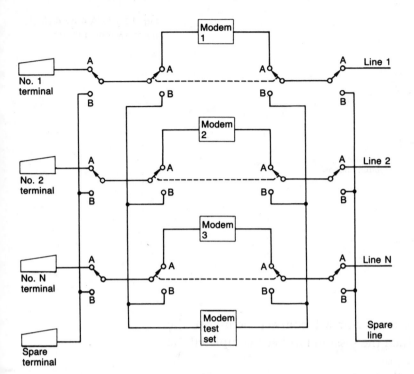

Fig. 12.16 A switching configuration in which one spare terminal may be substituted for one of many operational terminals; a modem test set may replace any modem and a spare line may replace any faulty line

As shown in Figure 12.16, A/B switches may be used to switch a single spare terminal to replace one of many online terminals, to switch a modem test set onto any line in place of any modem, and to replace any faulty line by a back-up link. This switching configuration may be remotely controlled from the network control centre if a command channel and decoder are provided. Error-detection facilities are necessary on the command link and switch position status information should be returned to the network control centre.

Figure 12.17 shows one way in which a 4-by-4 single point switching matrix may be configured. In practice this matrix may be repeated up to 25 times, once for each wire in an RS-232 interface. Each intersection of the matrix with a closed switch links that input channel to an output channel but prevents more than one output being connected to each input channel. Typical matrices may switch up to 16 input and 16 output channels using mechanical or electronic crosspoints under the control of an electronic command decoder.

Port selectors or data PABXs are similar to matrix switches but are used when many terminals are contending for connection to a limited number of ports on one or more processors. This is therefore equivalent to the telephone rotary. The user typically selects the switching path through a port selector by transmitting a control message. After giving a control signal on channel and providing channel identity, the user requests a destination. After confirming

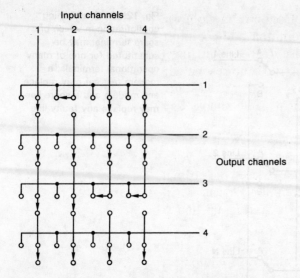

Fig. 12.17 A 4-by-4 single-
point switching matrix

Input channels

Output channels

the user's access rights, the port selector will connect the user to the
requested port if it is free. When the session has been completed the
user will disconnect from the port.

Matrix switches are generally used for monitoring or switching
of non-session-based data communications. The most common
applications are for network fault diagnosis and recovery. Typical
applications include:

a) Interface signal monitoring.
b) Real-time data monitoring.
c) Connecting line test equipment for analog measurements.
d) Patching spare modems, terminals or lines into a network.
e) Group switching of all lines or terminals from one computer
to another.

12.4.3 Power supply protection

Computers and all forms of data communication equipment depend
on mains electricity supplies and their operation may be seriously
impaired by voltage transients, electrical noise and brownouts
(temporary reductions in voltage of 5 to 15%). Total loss of the
electrical supply in part of a network, particularly the control centre,
may create chaos unless the equipment is designed to operate
through the power loss [either by provision of standby generators
for essential equipment or by provision of uninterruptible power
supplies (UPSs)].

Power line noise accounts for around 90% of all power disturbances. The most common form is high-voltage high-frequency

interference conducted down the power line. Common mode noise (between the line and ground) is the most common and the most difficult to eliminate. Transverse mode noise (across the lines) is more easily dealt with. Sources of electrical noise include radio, television and microwave transmissions, radar, arc welding, fluorescent lighting, air conditioning equipment, and almost any electronic or electromagnetic equipment on the same circuit.

Voltage transients induced on power lines include sags, surges and spikes and it is not uncommon to experience 10 000 per year. Lightning is a common cause of spikes which may exceed the normal voltage by more than 1000%. Voltage sags commonly occur when motor-driven equipment on the same circuit is started up and a voltage surge may be caused on shutdown.

Brownouts commonly occur when the electrical supply system cannot meet the instantaneous demand. Most electronic equipment can tolerate up to 10% voltage variations but at the extremes of this range they are more susceptible to voltage transients. Table 12.1 shows the typical incidence of power line disturbances in the USA.

To decide on the need for power supply protection at various parts of a network it is desirable to collect statistics on power line disturbances over a period of time. Power supply monitors which log the time and nature of disturbances are available for this purpose. Because many disturbances have local sources it is desirable to make measurements at the precise point on the circuit where the equipment will be connected.

Table 12.1 Typical incidence of power line disturbances

Disturbance	Average number per month
Power loss	0.6
Voltage transients (over 10% deviation)	14
Voltage spikes (over 25% deviation)	50
Oscillatory transient noise (over 15% deviation)	63

There are many power supply protection methods and each is more effective against certain forms of disturbance as shown in Table 12.2. When the most common forms of disturbance at a site are known, the most appropriate protection method may be selected.

The least-expensive protection devices are passive filters (which reduce noise) and surge suppressors (which clip transients); these devices may be built into some equipment. The ultra-isolation transformer is a relatively inexpensive transformer which has improved insulation and electrostatic shielding between the primary and

Table 12.2 Disturbances handled by various forms of protection device

Protection device	Transients	Sags and surges	Common mode noise	Transverse mode noise	Power loss
		Disturbance Protected Against			
Ultra-isolation transformer			YES		
Constant-voltage transformer	YES	YES (limited)	YES (limited)	YES (limited)	
Surge suppressor	YES				
Passive filter			YES	YES	
Uninterruptible power source	YES	YES	YES	YES	YES
Standby power source			YES	YES	YES

secondary windings. Ultra-isolation transformers help to prevent common mode noise entering or leaving the equipment. Some protection may be provided against voltage spikes and transverse mode noise.

The constant-voltage transformer (CVT) may be relatively expensive if high power is required but it provides tight voltage regulation and clips transients while limiting sags, surges, common mode noise and transverse mode noise. A CVT performs instant regulation without voltage sensing circuitry and its internal capacitors may maintain the output voltage through brownouts up to about 3 ms.

An uninterruptible power supply (UPS) provides protection against complete power supply loss, typically using an inverter to generate AC from a battery supply. The UPS provides a no-break supply but a standby power source which may be a diesel generator or a battery-supported inverter causes a short power loss before it is switched online.

A UPS is an expensive alternative, particularly for systems with high power requirements, but it protects against all forms of disturbance. As shown in Figure 12.18, in normal operation the mains supply is rectified to charge the batteries and power is converted back to AC to drive the equipment; thus the equipment is protected from mains disturbances. When the mains supply fails, the batteries continue to supply output power without a break. If the UPS is overloaded, the direct mains supply is connected to the equipment through a bypass.

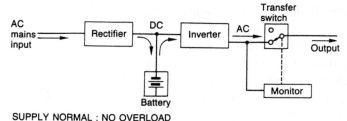

SUPPLY NORMAL : NO OVERLOAD

Fig. 12.18 Modes of operation in an uninterruptible power supply

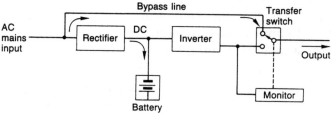

SUPPLY NORMAL : OVERLOAD ON UPS

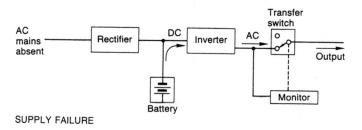

SUPPLY FAILURE

12.4.4 Line protection

Communications lines (apart from fibre optic ones) are susceptible to lightning strikes, particularly if they are suspended overhead in the open. Modern communications equipment based on semiconductor technology is extremely vulnerable to overvoltages on unprotected inputs and outputs, particularly equipment which has subscriber line interface circuits (SLICs) without line isolating transformers. These overvoltages may be caused by lightning, nuclear electromagnetic pulse (NEMP) or switching transients induced by inductive fields from nearby power lines.

Damage to communications equipment caused by overvoltages may be prevented by diverting the energy to earth via lightning protection units (LPUs) or data line protectors (DLPs). A common form of LPU employs a three-electrode gas-discharge tube, followed by zener diodes and fuses. The discharge tubes strike when the line voltage exceeds about 250 V. The zener diodes limit the voltage at the equipment to about 30 V.

More common overvoltages below 200 V present a problem because the discharge tubes do not strike and the zener diodes may be destroyed unless the current is limited by resistors or replaceable fuses. The use of fuses creates a problem because it is necessary to replace the fuses in all equipment affected by the overvoltage. One solution to this problem is to use an LPU with a self-resetting reed relay in place of a fuse.

An LPU diverts surge currents up too 20 000 A to earth when lightning strikes the line. The earth connection of the equipment must be joined directly to the LPU earth and both must be connected to a low-impedance earth (below 0.1Ω) by a short high-current direct conductor.

Fig. 12.19 Data line protectors on an RS-423 link

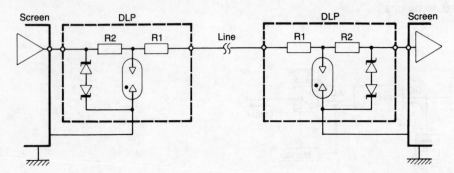

Data line protectors provide protection for low-current data lines such as RS-232 or RS-423. Figure 12.19 shows DLPs connected close to the inputs and outputs of an RS-423 data link. Clamp voltages may be selected from ± 6 V to ± 200 V and each line can absorb 50 joules of energy. The peak input voltage of a typical DLP may be derived from the relationship:

$$V_{peak} = 10^3 \sqrt{[50 \times \text{Series resistance/Pulse width in microseconds}]}$$

Other forms of overvoltage protection devices include voltage-dependent resistors (VDRs), GDTs, transzorbs and TISP devices. Transzorbs are improved zener diodes but, as with VDRs, they produce large voltage increases with high surge currents as shown in Figure 12.20. GDTs and TISPs rapidly crowbar into a low-voltage state as the current increases. When the current falls below the holding current value, the crowbar action ends and the devices return to their high-impedance state where a negligible load is placed on the line.

NEMP is a byproduct of a nuclear explosion. A high altitude burst

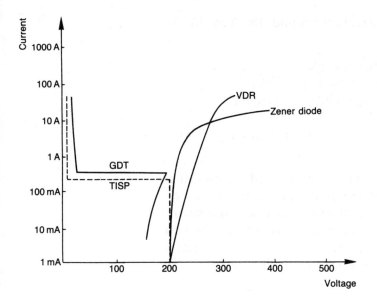

Fig. 12.20 Voltage/current relationships for overvoltage protection devices

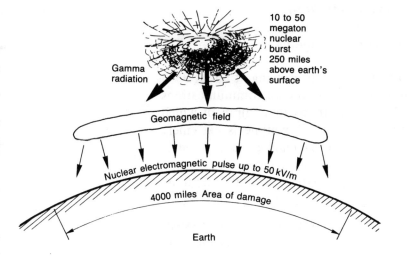

Fig. 12.21 An exo-atmospheric nuclear explosion producing NEMP

could produce an electromagnetic field of 50 000 volts/metre with a pulse rise time of 3 to 5 nanoseconds and a duration of about 1 microsecond. As shown in Figure 12.21, a burst of 10 to 50 megatons, 250 miles above the earth's surface, could damage all unprotected electronic equipment in a radius of about 2000 miles, particularly equipment connected to long cables. Some communications systems must be designed to survive the NEMP effects at expected field strengths of up to 50 000 volts/metre which may generate currents up to 12 000 A in long cables parallel to the source.

Lightning protection devices are unlikely to be effective against NEMP because lightning has a much slower rise time, up to 2 microseconds with a duration of around 100 microseconds. Lightning generally induces a peak current of around 300 A at 15 kV. NEMP protection measures include:

a) Use of fibre optic nonconductive cables.
b) Complete shielding of the equipment and cables.
c) Use of spark gap and discharge tube surge arrestors.
d) Use of passive RC pi filters.
e) Use of VDRs (varistors), high-speed zener diodes or other overvoltage protection devices.

The use of fibre optic cables and completely shielded equipment is the ideal solution because nonconductive cables are unaffected by NEMP and a grounded shield will protect the enclosed equipment. Where conductive cables are used, combined protection circuits with gas discharge tubes, lower-voltage protection devices and pi filters may be attached to each input or output line, including the mains cable.

12.5 Network management and testing

12.5.1 Communications network management

The number of communications networks is growing at about 35% per year and it is not unusual for the cost of a data communications network to exceed the cost of the data processing equipment which it supports. In this environment, network downtime is extremely expensive so a good communications network management system is necessary to ensure the efficient operation of the network.

Network management systems may perform several functions, including:

a) Detection of failures and the restoration of full system performance. Short-term problems may be detected by system test facilities which raise alarms, and fallback switching may be used to restore the functions. When repairs have been carried out, test facilities must confirm satisfactory operation. Long-term performance degradation may be identified by using a database of faults, MTTR and MTBF measurements.
b) Performance monitoring by recording response times, utilisation, availability, etc. and adjustment of parameters to improve performance. The statistics collected may be used to predict future expansion requirements.
c) Configuration monitoring and control to help reconfigure the network when faults occur and to assist in planning changes in topology.

d) Security monitoring by logging calls and controlling access.
e) Billing and other administrative functions.

Network architecture suppliers such as IBM and DEC provide host computer based network management tools which stimulate the use of their networks but often commit the user to the supplier's equipment which has facilities built in to support the network management system. Communications equipment and test equipment manufacturers offer various forms of communications test equipment for multivendor networks and other suppliers offer standalone integrated network management systems.

Some equipment is designed to monitor the physical aspects of the network, such as modems and multiplexers, while other equipment is designed to monitor the performance of the network. Equipment which monitors the physical aspects of the network includes:

a) Handheld test sets or break-out boxes.
b) Analog test sets for signal-noise ratio, bandwidth, crosstalk and transients.
c) Digital test sets such as data line monitors, time domain reflectometers, bit error rate testers and protocol analysers.

Some products use secondary channels to perform monitoring; this avoids interfering with the traffic but may only work with network equipment from the same vendor.

Network performance monitoring systems often display line status on a terminal and some combine the monitoring of physical and performance aspects of networks. Technical control systems provide network test and monitoring at an integrated control site. Patching facilities are provided for lines and modems; some facilities are manual while remote network reconfiguration may be achieved using intelligent matrix switches.

Technical control systems are suitable for small and medium sized networks but larger networks may require a network management system which includes the facilities provided by a technical control system plus high-level network monitoring functions. These facilities may include:

a) Alarm processing.
b) Recording of configuration data, fault and usage statistics and component status.
c) Preparation of reports on network problems and network traffic.
d) Security monitoring and access control.

Host-based network management systems consist of software which is run on the host computers in the network. These programs can communicate with network equipment, such as modems and diagnostic facilities, using the main data channels; this is known as the mainstream method of control. Standalone network management systems do not generally have access to the main data channels so they use the sidestream method of control; this uses a separate frequency division multiplexed supervisory channel to communicate with special monitors which are 'wrapped around' the network equipment.

Sidestream control and monitoring has the advantage that it does not fail when the mainframe computer fails and fault information may be collected more rapidly because the monitoring equipment does not have to wait to be polled before it can give notice of a fault. The main data channels of the network are not loaded with network management data and there is no possibility, as with the mainstream method, of the channel capacity degrading to the point where it is not possible for the network management system to locate the problem.

Network management systems may be implemented as a single centralised system, distributed in all subsystems or a combination of both. Centralised systems tend to create large amounts of additional network traffic and are vulnerable to failure at the central point. Distributed management is more flexible, is less vulnerable, and imposes less additional network traffic, but is less effective at constructing a full picture of network behaviour.

12.5.2 Network test equipment

Independent network test equipment is necessary to locate some forms of fault which network management systems are unable to track down and to monitor the system performance in ways which are not possible for network management systems.

To illustrate the use of network test equipment without a network management system, consider a data transmission fault reported by a terminal user in the simple configuration shown in Figure 12.22. If a spare terminal is available, this may be substituted to rule out the terminal as a possible cause of the trouble. The next likely place to look is the RS-232 interface between the terminal and its modem. A simple interface tester or 'break-out box' may be used to monitor the data and control lines and to cross-patch interface lines.

Fig. 12.22 Configuration used to illustrate diagnosis and location of a network fault using network test equipment

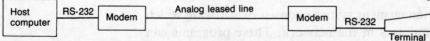

If no data is present on the modem-terminal interface, the fault may lie in the host computer, either of the modems, the leased analog line, or the cables within the computer centre or the terminal site. A check should next be made at the computer-to-modem interface using an interface tester and if data is being transmitted satisfactorily the modems and communications line should be investigated.

A data tester at the computer centre may be used to diagnose the cause and location of the fault by using the loopback facility on the modems to return a test signal down the line. Data testers may check the timing of control signals, bit or block error rates, polling in multipoint circuits and transmission line distortion as well as confirming the presence and correctness of data.

The bit error rate test (BERT) and block error rate test (BLERT) give a good indication of data link performance. The measurement of the percentage of error-free seconds (% EFS) on the link may help to diagnose link faults. Random errors caused by noise are likely to give high BER and BLER figures but a low % EFS. If the BLER is low but the BER and % EFS are high, the problem is likely to be caused by line switching, poor synchronisation or excessive impulse noise.

Protocol analysers may be used to help optimise network performance, particularly when new equipment with complex protocols is installed. Protocol analysers may be used in two modes, data analysis (or monitoring) and simulation. Both modes do not change normal network operation. In the analysis mode, received data is stored and displayed at predetermined events; events may be timed or counted and protocol incompatibilities may be investigated.

In simulation mode, the protocol analyser produces the signals and responses normally provided by part of the network. It may simulate the network when testing a piece of equipment offline or it can simulate a piece of equipment connected to a network in order to uncover network problems. Protocol analysers are available for all the common protocols including X.25 and the IEEE 802 LAN standards. Facilities may be provided, in some cases, for checking the internal operation of X.25 packet assembler/disassemblers.

Analog line testing may be carried out using a transmission impairment measuring set (TIMS) which requires the line to be taken out of service and looped back while a range of test tones within the passband are transmitted. Measurements include noise, delay, frequency shift, attenuation distortion, phase and amplitude jitter.

In-service transmission impairment measuring sets (ITIMS) permit tests to be made on an analog line while data is being transmitted. Apart from avoiding loss of service, this ability makes it possible to measure the effect of line impairments on real data, rather than test tones, and measurements may be made at any point in the circuit. An

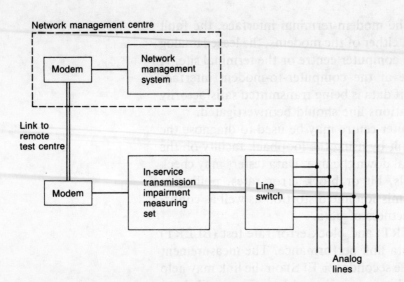

ITIMS may be permanently connected to monitor line changes or automatically switched to regularly check various points in a network as shown in Figure 12.23.

Time division multiplexed channels present a problem in rapidly identifying the cause of a fault which affects only one channel without degrading the service on the other channels in the link. An analysis of faults on the synchronisation or signalling channel usually interacts with all channels in the group. TDM channel access test sets are available; these allow test equipment to examine one channel at a time without interrupting traffic using adjacent time slots. These test sets are portable which permits tests to be made at various points along a link in order to identify the location of the fault.

The installation and maintenance of local area networks requires specialised test equipment. Many LAN faults are caused by poor installation so after installation the cable should be tested for conformance with DC electrical characteristics, sheath earthing requirements, and parameters such as attenuation and impedance at the working frequency.

Propagation delay may be measured and cable faults traced using a time domain reflectometer (TDR) which displays and times signals reflected from shorts and open circuits in the network cable. After installation, a network should be approved by transmitting test messages between pairs of taps and by soak testing, which uses a test set to generate high volumes of data and to log errors over an extended period of time.

Locating some problems in large LANs is like looking for a needle in a haystack so specialised test equipment is necessary. Two types of test equipment are available for IEEE 802.3:

a) Physical testers which are less expensive than protocol analysers and are used to perform tests at the physical and media access control layers. Typically they are used to test cables, transceivers and connections but some include echo test facilities and packet generators capable of producing known network loads. To perform an echo test, one tester is attached as a master station to one transceiver and a second tester is connected as a slave station to another transceiver on the network. The slave station echoes all received data back to the master where errors are logged. Echo testing is useful in tracing intermittent faults.

b) Protocol analysers which may perform tests at the lower OSI layers but also include the ability to conduct tests at the higher OSI layers. Some general-purpose analysis systems may be fitted with a test probe for each particular LAN type. An inexpensive protocol analyser may be constructed by loading a LAN analyser software package on an IBM PC fitted with a LAN interface. Protocol analysers may be used to generate messages, capture and analyse data, or measure system loading and timing parameters. Some protocol analysers may be used to activate loopback tests installed in the software of each OSI layer in network stations and to time stamp each returned frame which is stored for later analysis. Message filtering may be provided to log statistics on the use of particular message types or the use of particular links between stations (which may be useful in identifying security violations).

Appendix
Data communications
standards

EIA STANDARDS

RS-232-C (August 1969)
RS-232-D (1987)

Interface between Data Terminal Equipment and Data Communication Equipment employing Serial Binary Data Interchange.

RS-422 (April 1975)

Electrical Characteristics of Balanced Voltage Digital Interface Circuits.

RS-423 (April 1975)

Electrical Characteristics of Unbalanced Voltage Digital Interface Circuits.

RS-449 (November 1977)

General-purpose 37-position and 9-position Interface for Data Terminal Equipment and Data Circuit-terminating Equipment employing Serial Binary Data Interchange.

ANSI/IEEE STANDARDS

IEEE Std. 488-1978

Standard Digital Interface for Programmable Instrumentation.

ANSI/IEEE Std. 802.3-1985

Carrier Sense Multiple Access with Collision Detection (CSMA/CD): Access method and Physical Layer Specifications.

ANSI/IEEE Std. 802.4-1985

Token Bus Access Method and Physical Layer Specifications.

ANSI/IEEE Std. 802.5-1985

Token Ring Access Method and Physical Layer Specifications.

ANSI X3T9.5

Fiber Distributed Data Interface (FDDI).

ISO OSI STANDARDS

(DP = Draft Proposal. DIS = Draft International Standard.
IS = International Standard)

1 Physical Layer

ISO/DIS/8802/3	Carrier sense multiple access with collision detection (CSMA/CD) = IEEE 802.4.
ISO/DIS/8802/4	Broadband token bus = IEEE 802.4.
ISO/DP/8802/5	Baseband token ring = IEEE 802.5.

2 Data Link Layer

ISO/DIS/8802/2	Logical link control = IEEE 802.2.

3 Network Layer

ISO/DP/8208	X.25 packet-level protocol for data terminal equipment.
ISO/DIS/8348	Network service definition.
ISO/DIS/8348/DAD1 (SC6/N3152)	Addendum to the network service definition covering connectionless-mode transmission.
ISO/DIS/8348/DAD2 (SC6/N3599)	Addendum to the network service definition covering network layer addressing.
ISO/DIS/8472	Connectionless-mode network service definition.
ISO/DIS/8473	Connectionless-mode network protocol specification.
ISO/DP/8473/DAD1 (SC6/N3601)	Addendum to ISO 8473 covering provision of the connectionless-mode, subnetwork service.
ISO/DP/8648 (SC6/N3457)	Internal organisation of the network layer.

4 Transport Layer

ISO/DIS/8072 Rev	Transport service definition.
ISO/DIS/8072/DAD1 (SC6/N3709)	Addendum to the transport service definition covering connectionless-mode transmission.

ISO/DIS/8073 Rev	Connection-oriented transport protocol specification.
ISO/DIS/8073/DAD 1 (SC6/N20)	Addendum to ISO 8073 to include a network connection management sub-protocol.
ISO/DIS/8073 (SCN6/N29)	Amendment to ISO 8073 to enable Class 4 operation over the connectionless-mode network service.
ISO/DIS/8602 (SC6/N3223)	Protocol for providing the connectionless-mode transport service using the connectionless-mode network service or the connection-oriented network service.

5 Session Layer

ISO/IS/8326, 1985	Connection-mode session service definition.
ISO/DP/8326/DAD1 (SCN2/N135 Rev)	Addendum to ISO 8326 covering session symmetric synchronisation for the session service.
ISO/IS/8327, 1985	Connection-mode session protocol specification.
ISO/DP/8327/DAD1 (SC21/N136 Rev)	Addendum to ISO 8327 covering session synchronisation for the session protocol.

6 Presentation Layer

ISO/DP/8822 (SC21/N522)	Connection-oriented presentation service definition.
ISO/DP/8823 (SC21/N523)	Connection-oriented presentation protocol specification.

7 Application Layer

ISO/DIS/8211	Specification for a data descriptive file for information exchange.
ISO/DP/8571	File transfer, access and management (FTAM).
ISO/TC97/SC21/N516	Part I: general description.
ISO/TC97/SC21/N517	Part II: virtual file store.

ISO/TC97/SC21/N518	Part III: file service definition.
ISO/TC97/SC21/N519	Part IV: file protocol specification.
ISO/DP/8649/1 (SC21/N52)	Definition of common application service elements (CASE)—Part I: introduction.
ISO/DP/8649/2 (SC21/N54)	Definition of CASE—Part II: basic kernel subset.
ISO/DIS/8649/3	Definition of CASE—Part III: commitment, concurrency and recovery (CCR).
ISO/DP/8650/1 (SC21/N54)	Specification of protocols for CASE—Part I: introduction.
ISO/DP/8560/2 (SC21/N525)	Specification of protocols for CASE—Part II: basic kernel subset.
ISO/DIS/8650/3	Specification of protocols for CASE—Part III: commitment, concurrency and recovery.
ISO/DP/8831 (SC21/N520)	Job transfer and manipulation (JTAM) concepts and services.
ISO/DP/8832 (SC21/N521)	Specification of the basic class protocol for job transfer and manipulation.
ISO/TC97/SC21/N514	Virtual terminal service—basic class, Part I: initial facility set.
ISO/TC97/SC21/N515	Virtual terminal protocol—basic class, Part I: initial facility set

General

ISO/IS/7498, 1984	OSI reference model.
ISO/TC97/SC21/N391	OSI basic management framework.
ISO/DIS/7498/DAD1 (SC21/N142)	Addendum to the reference model covering connectionless data transmission.
ISO/DIS/8824	Specification for abstract syntax notation 1 (ASN.1).
ISO/DIS/8825	Basic encoding rules for abstract syntax notation 1.

OTHER ISO STANDARDS

ISO/IS 1745-1975	Information processing—Basic mode control procedure for data communications systems.
ISO/DIS 2110-1972	Data communication—Data terminal and data communication equipment —Interchange circuits— Assignment of connector pin numbers.
ISO/DIS 3309-1976	Data communication—High-level data link control procedures—Elements of procedures (Independent numbering).
ISO/DIS 4902	37-pin and 9-pin DTE/DCE interface connectors and pin assignments.
ISO/DIS 4903	15-pin DTE/DCE interface connector and pin assignments.
ISO/DIS 6159	High-level data link control procedures—Unbalanced classes of procedures.
ISO/DIS 6256	High-level data link control procedures—Balanced class of procedures.

CCITT V SERIES RECOMMENDATIONS FOR DATA TRANSMISSION OVER ANALOG NETWORKS

V.1   Equivalence between binary notation symbols and the significant conditions of a two-condition code.

V.2   Power levels for data transmission over telephone lines.

V.3   International alphabet number 5 for transmission of data and messages.

V.4   General structure of signals of the 7-unit code for data and message transmission.

V.10   Electrical characteristics for unbalanced double-current interchange circuits for general use with integrated circuit equipment in the field of data communications. (Equivalent to X.26.)

V.11	Electrical characteristics for balanced double-current interchange circuits for general use with integrated circuit equipment in the field of data communications. (Equivalent to X.27.)
V.13	Answer-back unit simulators.
V.15	Use of acoustic couplers for data transmission.
V.20	Parallel data transmission modems standardised for universal use in the general switched telephone network.
V.21	300 bit/s modem standardised for use in the general switched telephone network.
V.22	Standardisation of modulation rates and data-signalling rates for synchronous data transmission in the general switched telephone network.
V.23	600/1200-baud modem standardised for use in the general switched telephone networks.
V.24	List of definitions for interchange circuits between DTE and DCE.
V.25	Automatic calling and/or answering on the general switched telephone network.
V.26	2400 bit/s modem standardised for use on four-wire leased point-to-point circuits.
V.26 bis	2400/1200 bit/s modem standardised for use on the general switched telephone network.
V.27	Modem for data signalling rates up to 4800 bit/s over leased circuits.
V.27 bis	4800 bit/s modems with automatic equaliser standardised for use on leased telephone-type circuits.
V.27 ter	4800/2400 bit/s modems standardised for use in the general switched telephone network.
V.28	Electrical characteristics for unbalanced double-current interchange circuits.
V.29	9600 bit/s modem standardised for use on point-to-point four-wire leased telephone circuits.
V.30	Parallel data transmission systems for universal use on the general switched telephone network.
V.31	Electrical characteristics for contact closure type interface circuits.

V.35	Transmission of 48 kbit/s data using 60 to 108 kHz group band circuits.
V.36	Modems for synchronous data transmission using 60–108 kHz group band circuits.
V.40	Error indication with electromechanical equipment.
V.41	Code-independent error control system.
V.50	Standard limits for transmission quality of data transmission.
V.51	Organisation of the maintenance of international telephone-type circuits used for data transmission.
V.52	Characteristics of distortion and error rate measuring apparatus for data transmission.
V.53	Limits for the maintenance of telephone-type circuits used for data transmission.
V.54	Loop test devices for modems.
V.56	Comprehensive tests for modems which use their own interface circuits.
V.57	Comprehensive data test for high data signalling rates.

CCITT X SERIES RECOMMENDATIONS FOR DATA TRANSMISSION OVER PUBLIC DATA NETWORKS

X.1	International user classes of service in public data networks.
X.2	International user facilities in public data networks.
X.3	Packet assembly/disassembly facility (PAD) in a public data network.
X.4	General structure of signals of International Alphabet No. 5 code for data transmission over public data networks.
X.20	Interface between data terminal equipment and data circuit-terminating equipment for start-stop transmission services on public networks.
X.20 bis	Use on public data networks of data terminal equipments which are designed for interfacing to asynchronous duplex V-series modems.

X.40 Standardisation of frequency shift modulated transmission systems for the provision of telegraph and data channels by frequency division of a primary group.

X.50 Fundamental parameters of a multiplexing scheme for the international interface between synchronous data networks.

X.50 bis Fundamental parameters of a 48 kbit/s user data signalling rate transmission scheme for the international interface between synchronous data networks.

X.51 Fundamental parameters of a multiplexing scheme for the international interface between synchronous data networks using 10-bit envelope structure.

X.51 bis Fundamental parameters of a 48 kbit/s user data signalling rate transmission scheme for the international interface between synchronous data networks using 10-bit envelope structure.

X.52 Method of encoding anisochronous signals into a synchronous user bearer.

X.53 Number of channels on international multiplex links at 64 kbit/s.

X.60 Common channel signalling for circuit switched data applications.

X.70 Terminal and transit control signalling system for start-stop services on international circuits between asynchronous data networks.

X.71 Decentralised terminal and transit control signalling system on international circuits between synchronous data networks.

X.75 Terminal and transit call control procedure and data transfer system between packet switched public data networks.

X.80 Interworking of interexchange signalling systems for circuit switched data services.

X.87 Principles and procedures for realisation of international user facilities in public data networks.

X.92 Hypothetical reference connections for public synchronous data networks.

X.95 Network parameters in public data networks.

411

X.96	Call progress signals in public data networks.
X.110	Routing principles for international public data services through switched public data networks of the same type.
X.121	International numbering plan for public data networks.
X.130	Call set-up and clear-down times in circuit switched public data networks.
X.132	Grade of service in international data communications over circuit switched public data networks.
X.150	DTE and DCE test loops for public data networks.
X.180	Administrative arrangements for international closed user groups.

CCITT SERIES OF RECOMMENDATIONS X.400 to X.430 FOR DATA COMMUNICATION NETWORKS—MESSAGE HANDLING SYSTEMS (*Fascicle* V111.7)

X.400	Message handling systems: system model-service elements.
X.401	Message handling systems: basic service elements and optional user facilities.
X.408	Message handling systems: encoded information type conversion rules.
X.409	Message handling systems: presentation transfer syntax and notation.
X.410	Message handling systems: remote operations and reliable transfer server.
X.411	Message handling systems: message transfer layer.
X.420	Message handling systems: interpersonal messaging user agent layer.
X.430	Message handling systems: access protocol for Teletex terminals.

CCITT I-SERIES RECOMMENDATIONS FOR INTEGRATED SERVICES DIGITAL NETWORKS (ISDN) (*Fascicle* III.5)

PART I—GENERAL

Section 1: Frame of the I-series recommendations—terminology

I.110	General structure of I-series recommendations.

412

I.412　　　　　　　　ISDN user-network interfaces—Interface structures and access capabilities.

Section 2: Application of I-series recommendations to ISDN user-network interfaces
I.420　　　　　　　　Basic user-network interface.

I.421　　　　　　　　Primary rate user-network interface.

Section 3: ISDN user-network interfaces: Layer 1 recommendations
I.430　　　　　　　　Basic user-network interface—Layer 1 specification.

I.431　　　　　　　　Primary rate user-network interface—Layer 1 specification.

Section 4: ISDN user-network interfaces: Layer 2 recommendations
I.440 (Q.920)　　　ISDN user-network interface data link layer— General aspects.

I.441 (Q.921)　　　ISDN user-network interface data link layer specification.

Section 5: ISDN user-network interfaces: Layer 3 recommendations
I.450 (Q.930)　　　ISDN user-network interface layer 3—General aspects.

I.451 (Q.931)　　　ISDN user-network interface layer 3 specification.

Section 6: Multiplexing, rate adaptation and support of existing interfaces
I.460　　　　　　　　Multiplexing, rate adaptation and support of existing interfaces.

I.461 (X.30)　　　Support of X.21 and X.21 bis based data terminal equipments (DTEs) by an integrated services digital network (ISDN).

I.462 (X.31)　　　Support of packet mode terminal equipment by an ISDN.

I.463　　　　　　　　Support of data terminal equipments (DTEs) with V-series type interfaces by an integrated services digital network (ISDN).

I.464　　　　　　　　Multiplexing, rate adaptation and support of existing interfaces for restricted 64 kbit/s transfer capability.

I.472　　　　　　　　Internetworking services and protocols.

CCITT RECOMMENDATIONS FOR TELETEX SERVICES

F.200	Teletex service.
S.60	Functional characteristics of teletex terminals.
S.61	International character set.
S.62	Control procedures for teletex service.
S.70	Network-independent basic transport service for teletex.
S.71	Data link protocol (extended LAP-B).
T.60	Terminal equipment for use in the teletex service.
T.61	International repertoires and coded character sets for the international teletex service.
T.72	Terminal capabilities for mixed mode operation.
T.73	Document interchange protocol for telematic services.
T.90	Teletex requirements for internetworking with telex services.
T.91	Teletex requirements for real-time internetworking with the telex service in a packet switching environment.

CCITT VIDEOTEX RECOMMENDATION

F.300	Videotex service.

References

2.1   *HF Communications: a Systems Approach*, Maslin (Pitman/Plenum).
2.2   *Fibre Optics: Devices and Systems*, Cheo (Prentice Hall).
4.1   *Introduction to Digital Communications Switching*, Ronayne (Pitman/Howard W. Sams).
4.2   *The Integrated Services Digital Network: from concept to application*, Ronayne (Pitman/Wiley).
5.1   *Computer Network Architectures*, Meijer and Peeters (Pitman).
5.2   *Digital Networks: an Architecture with a Future*, EB 26013-42, DEC.
5.3   *Systems Network Architecture; a tutorial*, Meijer (Pitman/Wiley).
7.1   *Broadband Data Communications and Local Area Networks*, Wilson and Squibb (Collins).
8.1   *General Information: Binary Synchronous Communications*, IBM Systems Reference Library File No. TP-09, GA 27-3004-2.
9.1   *Simulation of Computer-Communication Systems*, Sauer and MacNair (Prentice Hall).
9.2   Performance evaluation of multipoint polled teleprocessing networks, Chou, Nilsson and King, *IEE Computer Society Technical Committee on Computer Communications*, pp. 1–16, Dec. 1979.
9.3   A unified algorithm for designing multidrop teleprocessing networks, Kershenbaum and Chou, *IEE Transactions on Communications*, Vol. Com-22, No. 11, Nov. 1974, pp. 1762–1772.
9.4   Ethernet: Distributed Packet Switching for Local Networks, Metcalf and Boggs (Xerox Palo Alto Research Center), *Communications of the ACM*, Vol. 19, No. 7, July 1976, pp. 395–404.
9.5   Calculating the maximum mean data rate in local area networks, Struck (Bell Laboratories), *Computer*, May 1983, pp. 72–76.
9.6   *Systems Design with Advanced Microprocessors*, Freer (Pitman).
10.1 *Distributed Databases: Principles and Systems*, Ceri and Pelagatti (McGraw-Hill).
11.1 *Security in Computer and Communications Systems*, Shore (Pitman).
11.2 Department of Defense Trusted Computer System Evaluation Criteria, DoD 5200.28-STD.
11.3 Trusted Network Interpretation of the Trusted Computer System Evaluation Criteria, NCSC-TG-005.

Glossary

ACK (Acknowledgement) A positive acknowledgement from a receiving station to a transmitting station indicating that the previous transmission(s) have been received correctly.

Acoustic Coupler A device which permits data transmission through a telephone handset over the public switched telephone network by modulating audible tones.

ADCCP Advanced Data Communication Control Procedure. A bit-oriented synchronous data link control protocol standardised by ANSI. Functionally equivalent to HDLC.

Address A sequence of bits or characters which identify the station to which a message or packet of data must be routed.

Amplitude Modulation (AM) A form of transmission in which the level of a constant-frequency carrier is changed to determine the encoded information.

Analog Transmission A transmission method by which the signal varies continuously in sympathy with the information. Most commonly used to transmit electrical voltages representing variations in sound levels.

Application Layer The upper (7th) layer of the OSI model; also the end user interface layer of IBM SNA.

ARQ Automatic request for retransmission method of control which permits the receiver to request a retransmission of erroneous data.

ASCII American National Standard Code for Information Interchange. The most popular seven-bit character code for data transmission.

Asynchronous (Start/Stop Transmission) A transmission method by which transmitting and receiving equipment are not permanently synchronised and variable idle time exists between succeeding characters. The beginning and end of each character are indicated by start and stop bits.

Bandwidth The data-carrying capacity of a medium expressed as the difference between the highest and the lowest frequencies which may be transmitted.

Baseband The frequency band occupied by the aggregate of the transmitted signals when first used to modulate the carrier. Also used to describe transmissions which are not modulated on a carrier.

Baud The signalling speed of a data transmission; equal to the maximum number of symbols per second. The number of symbols/second may differ from the number of bits/second because one symbol may represent several bits.

BCC Block Check Character which is added to blocks in character-oriented protocols to contain error-checking codes.

Bisync (BSC) Binary synchronous communications, a character-oriented protocol developed by IBM for half-duplex links.

Bit Error Rate (BER) The number of bits received with errors relative to the total number of bits received, e.g. 1 in 10^5 indicating that 1 in 100 000 have errors.

Bit/s Bits per second transmitted down a serial link: 1 kbit/s = 10^3 bit/s and 1 Mbit/s = 10^6 bit/s.

Bit Stuffing A method of ensuring data transparency in bit-oriented protocols.

Block A collection of transmitted information regarded as a discrete entity, often identified by starting and ending delimiters.

Bridge A communication link between homogeneous networks, or a link which uses a transport protocol which differs from those in the two networks but uses common high-level protocols.

Broadband A network which can support a wide range of frequencies, typically employing frequency division multiplexing on a coaxial cable.

Broadcast A transmission addressed to two or more stations at the same time.

Buffer A memory for temporary data storage.

Bus A transmission path with several stations directly attached, each receiving the same data at the same time (apart from propagation delay).

Carrier A continuous frequency which is modulated to transmit information.

CCITT Comité Consultatif International Telegraphique et Telephonique. An international consultative committee which produces standardisation recommendations.

Cellular Radio A low-power radio transmission system with a cellular network of base stations which may be used by stationary or mobile users for voice or data communication linking into the public switched telephone network.

Channel A path for the transmission of information which may be physical or logical.

Character A standard bit representation for a single unit of meaningful data, e.g. a letter in the alphabet.

Circuit A transmission medium linking two or more electronic devices.

Circuit Switching A technique which makes a temporary connection between two or more stations or telephone users on demand giving the callers exclusive use of the circuit until the connection is released.

Closed User Group A sub-group of users on a network who can communicate only with other members of the sub-group.

Clock A regularly occurring signal which provides a timing reference for a transmission and is used to synchronise reception of the data stream.

Cluster Controller A device which provides a remote communications capability to several terminals located in a cluster, e.g. IBM 3274.

Coaxial Cable A transmission medium consisting of a central conducting wire surrounded by an insulator and encased in a conductive tubular sheath.

Compression Application of techniques which reduce the number of bits required to transmit or store information.

Concentrator A communications device which shares a number of transmission channels between a large number of data sources.

Conditioning The provision of filters on leased analog telephone lines to permit higher-speed data transmission.

Connectionless A network system in which virtual circuits or physical circuits are not set up prior to transmission of a packet. Each datagram transmitted contains all the required routing information.

Connector A physical interface which permits connection of an electronic device, usually consisting of a male and female plug and socket.

Contention A condition in which multiple users compete for access to a shared channel or computer port.

CRC Cyclic Redundancy Check. A method used to detect errors in transmitted data whereby a polynomial algorithm is used to generate a CRC code which is transmitted with the data block and the code is compared with a code which is calculated at the receiver.

Crosstalk Unwanted coupling of electrical signals from one transmission medium to another adjacent medium.

CSMA/CD Carrier Sense Multiple Access with Collision Detection. A method of access control used to resolve contention between stations wishing to transmit on a network, e.g. Ethernet (IEEE 802.3).

Data A digital representation of information.

Data Encryption Standard (DES) A cryptographic algorithm standardised by the US National Bureau of Standards using a 64-bit key.

Data Link Layer The second layer in the OSI model; responsible for establishing, maintaining and releasing data link connections between adjacent network stations.

Data PABX A private exchange switch which allows data users to establish connections to host computers or other data users.

Data Transfer Rate The number of bits, characters or blocks of data transferred from a data source to a data sink in a unit time interval.

dB Decibel; a nonlinear unit of measurement used to express the ratio of two values. 10 log of the ratio of power levels or 20 log of the ratio of voltage levels. dB_m references the relative power levels of a signal in decibels to 1 mW, e.g. a signal of 0 dB_m delivers 1 mW to a load and a $-30\,dB_m$ signal delivers 0.001 mW to a load.

DCE Data Circuit-terminating Equipment. In an RS-232-C interface the modem or line interface device is usually regarded as the DCE while the computer or terminal is the data terminal equipment (DTE). A network access and packet switching node is regarded as the DCE in an X.25 system.

DDCMP Digital Data Communications Message Protocol. A DEC data link layer protocol using character count.

Dedicated Circuit A nonswitched dedicated line reserved for only one user. Also called a private line or leased line.

Demodulation The extraction of information from a modulated carrier signal.

Dial-up A circuit switching technique used to establish a temporary connection through a public switched telephone network.

Digital A communications procedure in which information is encoded as either a discrete binary 1 or a binary 0, as opposed to a continuous analog representation.

Distortion Corruption of a signal by modifying the waveform.

Distributed Database One logical database which has been divided among several physical locations.

Distributed Data Processing (DDP) A technique for dispersing the data processing function between several physically separated data processing nodes which are interconnected by a communications network.

DMA Direct Memory Access. A method of transferring data directly into a computer memory without processor intervention.

DNA Digital Network Architecture. The DEC communications network architecture.

DTE Data Terminal Equipment. An end user device such as a terminal or computer connected to a DCE in an RS-232-C or other serial communications interface.

DTMF Dual Tone Multi-Frequency. The touch-tone signalling method employed in telephony throughout the USA. Each key depression generates two audible tones which are transmitted to the exchange.

EBCDIC Extended Binary Coded Decimal Interchange. An eight-bit character code set developed and used by IBM.

Echo Cancellation A technique which isolates and filters out unwanted signals resulting from echoes of the main transmitted signal. Also a technique which permits full-duplex transmission over two wires.

EIA Electronic Industries Association. A US standardisation body.

Emulation The imitation of certain aspects of a computer, terminal, network or communication equipment by another to make the imitating device perform the same functions.

Equalisation A function performed by high-speed modems which compensates for the differences in attenuation at different frequencies in a telephone line.

Erlang The standard dimensionless unit for measuring telecommunications traffic and circuit occupancy. One erlang of traffic on one circuit indicates continuous 100% loading of that circuit or 50% loading of two circuits (one or more circuits carrying an aggregate traffic of 1 call-hour per hour or 1 call-minute per minute).

Ethernet A 10 Mbit/s baseband local area network standard using CSMA/CD access control. Later becoming the IEEE 802.3 standard.

Facsimile (fax) A communication method for transmitting graphic or text documents. CCITT standards define facsimile representations. Group 1 defines analog transmission taking 4 or 6 minutes per page, Group 2 defines analog transmission in 2 or 3 minutes per page, and Group 3 defines digital transmission taking less than 1 minute per page.

FDM Frequency Division Multiplexing. A multiplexing technique in which the available transmission frequency spectrum is divided into bands which are used for separate channels.

Fibre Optic A transmission method which uses modulated light transmitted down glass or plastic optical fibres.

File Server A station which is dedicated to mass data storage services with a file structure for other stations on a network.

Filter An electronic or optical device which removes energy of unwanted frequencies from a transmission system.

Flag A unique bit pattern used in bit-oriented protocols to identify the beginning and end of a frame.

Flow Control A function which can start and stop data flow between peer entities. Usually implemented using a control signal on a physical interface or by using special characters, X-on and X-off.

FM Frequency Modulation. A method for encoding a carrier by changing the frequency according to the data being transmitted.

Forward Error Correction (FEC) An error-correction technique which appends extra bits in the transmission. This permits errors to be detected and corrected without any retransmission of data.

Frame A sequence of contiguous bits, bracketed by opening and closing flags, which are sent serially over a communications channel. Each frame generally contains its own addressing and error-checking information and is sent between data link layer entities.

Frame Check Sequence (FCS) A 16-bit field containing error-checking information which is added to a frame in bit-oriented protocols.

Frequency The number of repetitions per unit time of a periodic waveform. The number of cycles per second for an electromagnetic waveform is expressed in Hertz (Hz, kHz, MHz or GHz).

FSK Frequency-Shift Keying. A modulation technique by which two different tones are used to represent the 0 and 1 states of binary data.

Full-Duplex (FDX) A mode of operation on a data link in which simultaneous transmission is possible in both directions between devices at both ends of the link.

Gateway A communication link between two heterogeneous computers or networks with the ability to convert from one protocol set to another.

Geosynchronous Orbit The position about 23 300

miles above the earth's surface where communications satellites remain stationary in orbit above the same point on the equator. Such satellites may be called geostationary.

Ground An electrical connection or common conductor which is connected to the earth at some point. Alternatively known as the earth wire.

Groundstation An installation on the earth where the communications and control equipment required for a satellite relay is located. Also known as an earth station.

Half-Duplex (HDX) A mode of operation on a data link in which transmission can take place in both directions but not simultaneously. Transmission direction is alternately switched to permit two-way operation.

Handshaking A predefined exchange of signals or control information between two devices to set up the necessary conditions for data transfer.

HDLC High-level Data Link Control. A bit-oriented data-link control protocol specified by ISO. Functionally equivalent to ADCCP.

Head End A component in a broadband network which translates the transmit frequency band to the receive frequency band, thus making it possible for stations to transmit and receive on a single-cable network.

Header Control information which is appended to the front of a data block, frame or packet.

High Frequency (HF) The part of the electromagnetic spectrum between about 3 and 30 MHz used primarily for long-distance communication. Otherwise known as short wave.

IEEE Institute of Electrical and Electronics Engineers. A US professional institute and standardisation body.

Infra-red The part of the electromagnetic spectrum between the submillimetre wave region and the optical region with wavelengths between about 0.7 and 100 μm. Extensively used for fibre optic communication.

Interface A common physical boundary between two systems or devices. A specification for the signals, connectors, timing, handshake, procedures, codes and protocols which enable communication between two dissimilar entities.

ISDN Integrated Services Digital Network. A network which incorporates a number of digital transmission services including speech, data and facsimile. CCITT standards have been recommended for interfaces and operating procedures.

ISO International Standards Organisation.

Isochronous A data transmission technique similar to asynchronous transmission in which the time between two characters is an integral number of bit times.

Jitter Small changes in time or phase of a transmitted signal which can cause errors or loss of synchronisation.

LAN Local Area Network. A short-distance data communications network using dedicated cables serving users within a building or group of buildings up to about 5 km in diameter.

LAP (LAP-B) Link Access Procedure. The data link protocol specified in the CCITT X.25 packet switched interface standard. LAP-B is the balanced version.

Laser Light amplification by stimulated emission of radiation. A device which produces coherent single-wavelength light; used as a light source in high-performance fibre optic systems.

Layering That aspect of a network architecture, such as the OSI reference model, which separates functions into distinct functional levels which communicate individually with equivalent levels at remote stations.

LED Light-emitting diode. A component which converts electrical energy into light. Commonly employed as the light source in multimode fibre optic systems.

Line of Sight An open-air transmission system in which the path between the transmitter and receiver must be unobstructed. Includes microwave, millimetre wavelength, optical and infra-red transmission systems.

Line Turnaround Time The delay in a communications link between the end of transmission for one block of data and the beginning of transmission of the next block. This parameter is particularly significant in half-duplex links, and for RS-232-C interfaces it is measured as the delay between request-to-send and clear-to-send signals being asserted.

Logical Link Control (LLC) A protocol specified in IEEE 802.2 for data link level transmission control. It forms the upper half of the OSI layer 2, the data link layer.

Loopback A diagnostic procedure in which the transmitted data stream is returned, or looped back, to its source for comparison with the transmitted data.

MAC Media Access Control. A protocol for access control to a specific communications medium forming the lower half of the OSI layer 2. Variations in the MAC protocol are found in the IEEE 802 local area network standards.

Manchester Encoding A self-clocking digital encoding technique in which each bit period contains two signalling elements. A negative-to-positive voltage transition in the middle of the bit period designates a binary 0 and a positive-to-negative voltage transition in the middle of the bit period designates a binary 1.

Message Switching A transmission method by which messages are sent to an intermediate switching centre where they are stored temporarily until a suitable outgoing channel is available; then the message is transmitted to its final destination.

Modem Modulator/demodulator. A device which converts (by modulation of a carrier) digital signals into analog form for transmission over analog transmission facilities. At the destination the carrier is demodulated to convert the analog signal into digital form.

Modulation The systematic alteration of amplitude, frequency or phase of an analog carrier to encode information for transmission.

Modulo-N The number of messages (N) or frames which may be counted before the counter resets to zero; alternatively the number of messages (N − 1) which may be transmitted before an acknowledgement is required.

MTBF Mean Time Between Failures. The average time for which an equipment operates before a failure occurs. There is a 36.8% probability that the equipment will not fail during a period equal to the MTBF.

MTTR Mean Time To Repair. The average time required to diagnose a fault and perform a repair to a failed equipment.

Multidrop A network configuration in which a master station communicates successively with multiple end points by polling (inviting to transmit) each end point in turn.

Multimode An optical fibre with a core which is capable of propagating light signals of more than one wavelength.

Multiplexer (MUX) A device which combines several signals to share a common physical transmission medium. Multiplexed signals are demultiplexed to separate the signals at the other end of the link. Common forms of multiplexing are time division multiplexing (TDM), frequency division multiplexing (FDM), wavelength division multiplexing (WDM), and code division multiplexing (CDM).

Multipoint A network configuration in which one communications channel is connected to more than two stations. Multidrop operation is used to ensure that only one station transmits at a time.

NAK Negative Acknowledgement from a receiving station to a transmitting station indicating that previous transmission(s) have not been received correctly.

Network An interconnected group of points, nodes or stations linked by communications channels or the assembly of equipment through which connections are made between data stations.

Network Architecture A specification which defines how a network is to be organised, defining functional modularity, protocols, data formats, procedures and interfaces to enable communication between the elements.

Network Layer The third layer of the OSI model; responsible for the switching and routing of messages and the ordering of packets.

Network Topology A description of the physical and logical relationship between the elements (nodes) in a network. Common topologies include a star, bus, ring or tree.

Node A point in a network where one or more communications lines terminate or a point where one or more functional units are connected to communications lines.

Noise Unwanted signals which interfere with a communications channel.

NRZ Non-Return to Zero. A binary encoding technique in which binary 1 and 0 symbols are represented by high and low voltages with no return to the 0 reference voltage between bits.

NRZI Non-Return to Zero Inverted. A binary encoding technique by which a signal is inverted for a binary 1 and not inverted for a binary 0; thus a voltage change defines a 1 and no change at the bit boundary defines a 0. Also called transition coding.

Null Characters Control characters which do not affect the meaning of the sequence of characters. Often used to pad fields to a required length or to fill in gaps between data blocks.

Offline The state in which a terminal is not connected to a computer or is not active in a network. The alternative state to 'online'.

OSI Open Systems Interconnection. A reference model or logical structure around which an open system architecture may be built. The ISO 7498 reference model specifies a 7-layer network architecture used for the definition of network protocol standards which enable any OSI-compatible device to communicate fully with any other OSI-compatible device.

Overhead All transmitted information in addition to the data originated by the user. Overheads may include control and status information, routing information, error-detection or EDC information, and any repeated data.

PABX (or PBX) Private Automatic Branch Exchange. A switching telephone exchange located on a customer's premises to establish circuits between local users and possibly the public switched telephone network.

Packet Switching A data transmission technique by which information is broken into packets which are routed through the network. Many users may share the communications channels, each using the channels only for the time required to transmit their own packets.

PAD Packet Assembler/Disassembler. An interface to an X.25 packet switched network which allows several asynchronous serial devices to make use of the network. The connected devices are not required to support the X.25 protocol. PAD functions are defined in CCITT standards X.3, X.28 and X.29.

Parallel Transmission Simultaneous data transfer through several parallel conductors or channels, each transmitting different bits of a character or data block.

Parity A technique which is used to detect data transmission errors by adding a redundant parity bit to each character. The parity bit is set to make the number of 1 bits in the monitored data even (for even parity) or odd (for odd parity). Even multiples of bit errors are not detected.

PCM Pulse Code Modulation. A technique for transmitting analog data over a digital channel by sampling the analog data at regular intervals and encoding the sampled values into binary codes for transmission using a digital link (commonly in a time division multiplexed frame).

Phase-Shift Keying (PSK) A phase modulation technique used to transmit digital information by changing the phase angle of a carrier wave to represent different bit values (or symbols representing several bit values).

Physical Layer The lowest layer of the OSI model; responsible for the transmission and reception of data bits, mechanical, electrical and functional compatibility of the interface between the device, and the transmission medium.

PIN Positive Intrinsic Negative. A type of light detector used in fibre optic data links. Also: personal identification number.

Point-to-Point A circuit which connects only two nodes directly, without intermediate nodes.

Port A physical or electrical interface at which a communications channel enters a computer, network or communication equipment.

Presentation Layer The sixth layer of the OSI model; responsible for format translation, codes, languages and encryption.

Propagation Delay The time delay required for a signal to travel from one point to another down a transmission channel. Most electrical cables have a propagation velocity between 0.5 and 0.8 of the velocity of light in free space.

Protocol A formal set of rules governing data format, timing, sequencing, access control and error control required to initiate and maintain communication. The sender and receiver must use the same protocol either at an interface or end-to-end across a network.

PSTN Public Switched Telephone Network. Otherwise known as the dial-up telephone network.

PTT Postal, Telegraph and Telephone. A national authority which operates the public telecommunications network and sets national standards and policy on telecommunications issues.

QAM Quadrature Amplitude Modulation. A form of transmission which combines amplitude modulation and phase modulation. Commonly employed in high-speed modems and transmits symbols which represent several bits.

Queue An accumulation of data items or commands waiting for service which results in temporary delays until the required facilities become available.

Real-time A form of processing which is concurrent with a physical process and in which the results are used to influence the process while it is occurring.

Redundancy The part of the information content which may be eliminated without losing essential information. Alternatively the provision of duplicate hardware within a system which takes over when a similar component fails.

Repeater Equipment which receives a signal and amplifies, reconstructs or retimes it before retransmitting it to permit transmission over greater distances.

RF Radio Frequency. Frequencies above about 300 Hz at which coherent electromagnetic energy is radiated through free space. Voice frequency (VF) is in the range of about 300 Hz to 3.4 kHz.

Ring A network topology in which each node is connected to two adjacent nodes and the chain of nodes is joined at the ends to form a circle.

Rotary An option offered by telephone companies which allows a block of dial-up telephone lines to be accessed by dialling a single number.

Routing The selection of a suitable path through a network.

RS-232-C A common physical interface standard specified by the EIA for interconnection of a DTE and a DCE.

RS-422 A balanced digital interface standard specified by the EIA.

RS-423 An unbalanced digital interface standard specified by the EIA.

RS-449 A physical interface standard specified by the

EIA for interconnection of a DTE and a DCE using RS-422/RS-423 signals.

RS-485 An enhanced version of RS-422 which permits up to 32 stations to be attached to a common bus.

SDLC Synchronous Data Link Control. A synchronous bit-oriented data link control protocol developed and used by IBM. Similar to HDLC.

Serial Transmission The consecutive sequential transfer of data which constitutes a character or word over a single transmission circuit.

Session A co-operative relationship between two application entities which allows them to communicate. Alternatively, the time in which a user is online to an interactive computer.

Session Layer The fifth layer of the OSI model; responsible for end-to-end dialogue between processes and the establishment of logical links between users.

Shield (Screen) A grounded protective enclosure constructed from conductive material surrounding a transmission medium such as the central conductor in a coaxial cable; intended to minimise electromagnetic radiation and susceptibility to electromagnetic noise.

Signal Element The part of a signal which is the smallest unit of the signalling code.

Signal-to-Noise Ratio (SNR) The ratio between the magnitude of the transmitted signal and the noise on a communications channel. Commonly measured in dB.

Simplex Transmission in one direction with no capability for transmission in the reverse direction.

Single-Sideband Transmission (SSB) A transmission in which one modulation sideband of the carrier is transmitted while the carrier frequency and the other sideband are suppressed to minimise the bandwidth required.

SNA Systems Network Architecture. A proprietary architecture used by IBM. Initially based upon the SDLC protocol.

Start-Stop Transmission An alternative name for asynchronous transmission. The data elements of each character are preceded by a start bit and followed by a stop bit (or bits).

Station Any DTE on a data link or network. May be a primary station, a secondary station or a combined station on networks using bit-oriented protocols.

Stepped Index A type of optical fibre which has a core of a different refractive index to the cladding and a rapid change in refractive index at the boundary between the two. Commonly used for single mode optical transmission at high speed over long distances.

Store and Forward A data transmission network in which messages or data frames are temporarily stored at intermediate nodes before being forwarded to their final destination.

STX Start of Text. A control character which designates the end of the header and the start of the text.

Symbol A discrete waveform produced by a modulator which may be uniquely identified by the demodulator. A symbol may represent several bits and therefore the symbol rate (or baud rate) may be different to the bit rate for a transmission.

Synchronous A transmission technique by which uninterrupted data blocks are sent at a fixed rate with the transmitting and receiving devices in synchronisation. Each block is preceded by sync characters but no start and stop bits are required on each character as with asynchronous transmission.

TDM Time-Division Multiplexing. A technique for interleaving data from several users onto one channel by transmitting each user's data in series, each in its own time slot.

TDMA Time-Division Multiple Access. A technique for time division multiplexing a satellite communication channel by giving several earth stations, in sequence, control of (and access to) the channel for a defined period of time.

Telegraphy An early data transmission technique which used teleprinters to send data at speeds up to 50 bit/s using bipolar DC current signalling.

Telephony Voice communication.

Teleprocessing The use of data communications to provide remote access to data processing resources.

Teletex A worldwide switched message exchange service operating at a higher speed than Telex. Intended to replace Telex.

Terminal A device connected to a computer or network at which data may be entered or presented to the user. Equivalent to a DTE.

Text Transmitted characters conveying information in a message. Intended for human comprehension as opposed to data which is intended for computer comprehension.

Timeout The use of a timer to limit the time available before some action must occur, e.g. maximum response times.

Token Bus A local area network access mechanism and topology. A token, or special control frame, must be received by a station before it may transmit on the bus. After transmission of any waiting messages the token is passed to the next station as an invitation to transmit. Employed in IEEE 802.4.

Token Ring A local area network access mechanism and topology. A token is passed from one station to the next around the ring. Stations may only send data when in possession of the token. Data is relayed by each station to the next station until it returns to the originator.

Transceiver A device capable of transmission and reception.

Transients Intermittent short-duration perturbations of signals or power supplies.

Transparency A mode of transmission by which input signals are not modified by the system in any way. The output signal is identical to the input but may be delayed.

Transport Layer The fourth layer of the OSI model; responsible for the reliable end-to-end message transport including message sequencing, flow control and multiplexing.

Tree A network topology popular for broadband networks in which only one route exists between any two stations. Resembles branches of a tree converging at a trunk where a head end is situated.

Trunk A high-capacity communications circuit conveying many channels between two switching centres or concentrators.

Turnaround Time The time required to reverse the direction of transmission in a half-duplex channel.

Twin-Axial Cable A shielded coaxial cable with two conductors within the outer shield.

Two-Wire Circuit A telephone circuit consisting of two electrical conductors, commonly a twisted-pair connecting a telephone subscriber to the local exchange. Most dedicated lines for high-speed transmission are four-wire circuits which make full-duplex operation more practical.

UHF Ultra High Frequency. The part of the electromagnetic spectrum between about 300 MHz and 3 GHz, commonly used for television transmission and voice communication.

Unix A popular computer operating system developed by Bell Telephone Laboratories.

Uplink The data link conveying information from the earth station to a geosynchronous communications satellite. The reverse direction link is called the downlink.

USART Universal Synchronous/Asynchronous Receiver-Transmitter. A large-scale integrated circuit commonly employed to convert parallel data within a processor to serial form for synchronous or asynchronous transmission.

VAN Value Added Network. A network which offers users a service in addition to data transmission, e.g. an electronic mailbox service.

VHF Very High Frequency. The part of the electromagnetic spectrum between about 30 MHz and 300 MHz, commonly used for television, FM radio broadcasting and voice communication.

Videotex (Viewdata) An interactive data communication technique which uses television sets or low-cost terminals to gain access to a remote database which provides pages of textual or graphics information suitable for direct display by the user's terminal.

Virtual Circuit A path through a network which gives the appearance to the user of an end-to-end circuit but is not in fact a physical circuit. Instead it is a dynamically variable network connection.

Voice Frequency (VF) Analog signals within the frequency range commonly employed to transmit speech (typically 300 Hz to 3.4 kHz).

V.24/V.28 CCITT recommendations which define the interchange circuits and physical interface between a DTE and a DCE. The two standards combined are equivalent to RS-232-C.

Wideband A communications channel with a bandwidth greater than a voice grade channel (300 Hz to 3.4 kHz).

Window A data communications flow control mechanism which determines the number of frames or packets which may be transmitted before an acknowledgement is required from the receiver.

X.3, X.28, X.29 The three CCITT recommendations which specify the functions, interfaces and control procedures for a packet assembler/disassembler (PAD) which gives start-stop-mode terminals access to a packet switched public data network.

X.21 A CCITT recommendation which specifies an interface between a DTE and a DCE used for synchronous operation on public data networks. Used as the primary physical interface in the X.25 recommendation.

X.25 A CCITT recommendation which specifies the interface between a user's DTE and a packet switching data circuit terminating equipment (DCE).

X.75 A CCITT recommendation which specifies the control procedures and data transfer system used on international links between packet switched data networks.

X-on/X-off The flow control procedure commonly used by terminals and computers attached to a DCE. An X-on character initiates data flow and an X-off character suspends data flow.

Index